MILLENNIAL
FEVER

AND THE END OF THE WORLD

D1713570

I remain as ever
looking for the
Lord Jesus Christ
unto eternal life.
    Wm Miller.

MILLENNIAL
FEVER
AND THE END OF THE WORLD

A study of Millerite Adventism

GEORGE R. KNIGHT

Pacific Press Publishing Association
Boise, Idaho
Oshawa, Ontario, Canada

Edited by Bonnie Tyson-Flyn
Designed by Tim Larson
Typeset in 11/13 Janson Text

Library of Congress Cataloging-in-Publication Data:

Knight, George R.
  Millennial fever and the end of the world: a study of Millerite
Adventism / George R. Knight.
      p.   cm.
   Includes bibliographical references (pp. 343-374) and index.
   ISBN 0-8163-1178-1. — ISBN 0-8163-1176-5 (pbk.)
   1. Millerite movement—United States—History. 2. Adventists—United
States—History. I. Title.
   BX6115.K55 1993
   286.7'09—dc20   93-25531
                                                       CIP

94 95 96 97 • 5 4 3

Dedicated to

KENNETH A. STRAND

on the year of his retirement.

Thank you, Ken, for
being my teacher,
mentor, colleague in
church history,
co-editor of *Seminary Studies*,
departmental chairman,
and friend.

Contents

A Word to the Reader

William Miller has been called "the most famous millenarian in American history."[1] Between 1840 and 1844, his message that Christ would come "about 1843" swept across the United States. Seen as a harmless aberration at first, by 1843 Miller's teaching polarized individuals and churches as they faced the year of the end of the world.

After the passing of the year of the end, several Adventist denominations arose out of the ranks of the disappointed Millerites. The most significant of those denominations were the Advent Christians and the Seventh-day Adventists.

Millennial Fever and the End of the World provides a historical overview of Millerism. Part 1 deals with the personalities and ideas that shaped Millerite Adventism as it approached the year of the end. Part 2 examines the events and tensions of the climactic year of the end. And Part 3 treats the development of Adventism after the passing of the expected time for Christ to come.

Thus a first purpose of *Millennial Fever* is to set forth a comprehensive overview of Millerism. While several books have been written on the topic, none thus far have sought to be comprehensive. *Millennial Fever* seeks to fill that gap.

A second purpose of this volume is to explore possible reasons for Millerism's surprising success. Beyond the usual sociological explanations that highlight external factors for that success, the present work argues that the vital internal dynamic that thrust the Millerites into the flow of history was a *deep certainty*, based upon concentrated study of the apocalyptic prophecies of Daniel and the Revelation, that Christ was coming soon and an impelling conviction of *personal responsibility* to warn the world of that good yet fearful news. *In short, the Millerites were mission driven because they saw themselves as a prophetic people with a message that the world desperately needed to hear.* That perception appears to be the internal mainspring that led the Millerites to dedicate their all to their task.

Such a deeply held conviction seems to be a precondition to success in all types of millennial movements. Without that prophetic certainty and its accompanying sense of urgent responsibility, millennial movements begin to atrophy; with their mainspring absent, they lose their dynamic for vitality and growth.

Serious study of Millerism has been generally neglected until recently. For decades that study was largely frozen between the poles of Clara Endicott Sears' *Days of Delusion* (1924)[2] and Francis D. Nichol's *The Midnight Cry* (1944).[3] While the first of those books was anecdotal and critical, the second was scholarly but admittedly apologetic. In spite of its defensive flavor, Nichol's work did much to correct misconceptions about Millerism in scholarly works touching upon the topic.

The 1980s witnessed a flurry of book-length studies in this neglected area of American religious history. That decade saw the publication of five significant studies on the history of Millerism: Clyde E. Hewitt's *Midnight and Morning* (1983)[4]; David L. Rowe's *Thunder and Trumpets: Millerites and Dissenting Religion in Upstate New York, 1800-1850* (1985)[5]; Michael Barkun's *Crucible of the Millennium: The Burned-over District of New York in the 1840s* (1986)[6]; Ruth Alden Doan's *The Miller Heresy, Millennialism, and American Culture* (1987)[7]; and the volume edited by Ronald L. Numbers and Jonathan M. Butler entitled *The Disappointed: Millerism and Millenarianism in the Nineteenth Century* (1987).[8]

As an author, I am indebted not only to the work of those scholars listed above, but also to the unpublished work of many other students. Of special value has been the unpublished research of David Arthur[9] and Everett Dick.[10] Two other informative studies have been P. Gerard Damsteegt's *Foundations of the Seventh-day Adventist Message and Mission*[11] and the fourth volume of LeRoy E. Froom's *Prophetic Faith of Our Fathers*.[12] While those last two works focus more on Miller's system of prophetic interpretation than on the history of Millerism, they provide students of Millerite history with an abundance of insight unavailable in other secondary works.

Needless to say, the volumes and research listed above have greatly increased our knowledge of both Millerism and the world in which it developed. The present volume not only builds upon previous published and unpublished research into Millerism, but it endeavors to extend and enrich that research. My many other scholarly debts are indicated in the notes at the back of this volume.

I would also like to express my appreciation to the many libraries and archives that have provided me with documents over the past fifteen years. Foremost among those libraries and archives have been those at Andrews University, Aurora University, Oberlin College, Cornell University, the Massachusetts Historical Society, and the American Antiquarian Society. In particular, I would like to express my gratitude to Sandra White of the interlibrary loan department of Andrews University, to Louise Dederen and Jim Ford of the Adventist Heritage Center at Andrews University, and to Susan L. Craig of Aurora University and her staff in the Jenks Memorial Collection of Advental Materials. For copies of the photographs used in this volume, I am indebted to David Arthur of Aurora University, Jim Nix of the Ellen G. White Estate, and Janice Little of Loma Linda University.

Additional appreciation goes to Bonnie Beres, who typed the manuscript; to Heidi Bergan, who spent countless hours searching out and copying documents; to Joseph Karanja, who also assisted in document collection; to Donald Dayton, Ronald Knott, Gary Land, Alberto Timm, and Richard Schwarz for reading the manuscript; to Bonnie Tyson-Flyn, who guided the book through the editorial process; to Tim Larson for his expertise in designing the volume; and to the administration of Andrews University for providing financial support and time for research and writing.

George R. Knight
Berrien Springs, Michigan

Part I

MOVING TOWARD THE YEAR OF THE END

Chapter 1

MILLENNIAL FEVER

In 1818 a recent convert to Christianity came to the shocking conclusion that Jesus Christ would personally and visibly return to earth to set up His eternal kingdom in about twenty-five years—1843. That conclusion filled William Miller with both joy and uneasiness. The joy stemmed from his belief that the sorrows of earth would soon be over; the uneasiness, from both the realization that he had a responsibility to warn the world if his conclusions were true and the nagging fear that his calculations could be wrong.[1]

Revival of the Study of Prophecy

Miller was not alone in his hope for a soon-coming millennial kingdom. "America in the early nineteenth century," claims Ernest Sandeen, "was drunk on the millennium."[2] Christians of all stripes believed they were on the very edge of the kingdom of God.

The frightfully destructive Lisbon earthquake of 1755 had directed the minds of many to the topic of the end of the world, but the most important stimulus found rootage in the events of the French Revolution in the 1790s. The social and political upheavals then taking place reminded people of biblical descriptions of the end of the world. Eyes were turned to the biblical prophecies of Daniel and the Revelation by the violence and magnitude of the French catastrophe.[3]

15

In particular, many Bible students soon developed an interest in the time prophecies and the year 1798. In February of that year, Napoleon's general Berthier had marched into Rome and dethroned Pope Pius VI. Thus 1798, for many Bible scholars, became the anchor point for correlating secular history with biblical prophecy. Using the principle that in prophecy a day equals a year, they saw the capture of the pope as the "deadly wound" of Revelation 13:3 and the fulfillment of the 1260-year/day prophecy of Daniel 7:25 and Revelation 12:6, 14 and 13:5.[4]

Bible scholars, notes Sandeen, believed they now had "a fixed point in the prophetic chronology of Revelation and Daniel. Some of them felt certain that they could now mark their own location in the unfolding prophetic chronology."[5]

At last, many suggested, the prophecy of Daniel 12:4 was being fulfilled. Six hundred years before the birth of Christ, Daniel had written: "But thou, O Daniel, shut up the words, and seal the book, even to the time of the end: many shall run to and fro, and knowledge shall be increased" (cf. v. 9). Because of world events, many came under conviction that they had arrived at the "time of the end." As never before, the eyes of Bible students literally "ran to and fro" over Daniel's prophecies as they sought to get a clearer understanding of end-time events. The late eighteenth and early nineteenth centuries witnessed an unprecedented number of books being published on the Bible's apocalyptic prophecies.

A belief in the fulfillment of Daniel 12:4 and the unlocking of the 1260-year/day prophecy of Daniel 7:25 encouraged students of prophecy to continue their exciting explorations. They soon came across the 2300-day prophecy of Daniel 8:14: "Unto two thousand and three hundred days; then shall the sanctuary be cleansed." LeRoy Froom has documented the fact that more than sixty-five expositors on four continents between 1800 and 1844 predicted that the 2300-year/day prophecy would be fulfilled sometime between 1843 and 1847. While there was a general consensus on the time of the prophecy's fulfillment, however, there were widely differing opinions over the event to transpire at its conclusion.[6]

Thus there was a sense in which Miller was in good company. After all, he also had come to his conclusion through studying the 2300 days of Daniel 8:14.[7] Miller, however, radically differed with nearly all of his contemporaries on the concluding event of the prophecy.

Beyond the 2300 days, the key symbols of Daniel 8:14 were the sanctuary and its cleansing. Through systematic study, Miller concluded that the only things the sanctuary could represent in the 1840s were the earth and the church. He also had come to believe that the cleansing would be by fire. After all, didn't Peter write: "But the heavens and the earth, which are now, by the same word are kept in store, reserved unto fire against the day of judgment and perdition of ungodly men" (2 Peter 3:7)?

Miller's ultimate conclusion was that the cleansing of the earth by fire at the end of the 2300 days represented the coming of Christ in judgment.[8] Therefore, the second advent would take place about 1843, *before* the one thousand years, or millennium, of Revelation 20. At that time

> the dead saints or bodies will arise, those children of God who are alive then, will be changed, and caught up to meet the Lord in the air, where they will be married to him. The World and all the wicked will be burnt up (not anihilated [sic]) and then Christ will descend and reign personally with his Saints; and at the end of the 1000 Years the wicked will be raised, judged and sent to everlasting punishment.[9]

Millennial Conflict

The conclusion that Christ would come about 1843, *before* the millennium, was the point at which Miller differed from nearly all of his contemporaries. The conventional wisdom of the day was that Christ would come at the *close* of the one thousand years.

As a result, George Bush, professor of Hebrew and Oriental literature at New York City University, could write to Miller:

> While I have no question that well-informed students of prophecy will admit that your calculation of the *Times* . . . is not materially erroneous, they will still, I believe, maintain that you have entirely mistaken *the nature of the events* which are to occur when those periods have expired. . . . The expiration of these periods is to introduce, by *gradual steps*, a new order of things, intellectual, political and moral. . . .
>
> The great event before the world is not its *physical conflagration*, but its *moral regeneration*.[10]

Charles Finney, the greatest American evangelist of the second quarter of the nineteenth century, also set forth the prevailing view when he penned in 1835 that "if the church will do her duty, the millenium [sic] may come in this country in three years." A few years later, Finney wrote: "I have examined Mr. Miller's theory, and am persuaded, that what he expects to come after the judgement, will come before it [i.e., the millennium]."[11]

The *Oberlin Evangelist*, in combating Millerism, noted in 1843 that "the world is not growing worse but better" because of the efforts at reform being carried out by the churches and other reformers. Henry Cowles could write in like manner that "the golden age of our race is yet to come; . . . numerous indications of Providence seem to show that it may not be very distant." But, he hastened to add, "the event cannot take place . . . without appropriate human instrumentality. . . . The Church therefore might have the Millenium [sic] speedily if she would."[12]

In summary, Bush, Finney, Cowles, and others were not out of harmony with Miller on the nearness of the millennium but on its meaning and the events needed to bring it about. For them the soon-coming millennium would be a thousand years of earthly peace and plenty brought about through social reform, national progress, and personal perfection. It was that vision that fueled the multiplicity of social and personal reforms characterizing much of the nineteenth century. One of the century's most powerful ideas was that the millennial kingdom could be brought about by human effort.

That idea not only stood at the center of religious reform, but it also energized Americans in the political realm. From as early as the 1630s, the founders of the Puritan commonwealth had seen New England as a religious/political experiment that would be as a "city upon a hill" to enlighten the old world.

That perspective was greatly heightened by the American Revolution and its resulting democratic "experiment." Even secular Americans came to have a sense of millennial destiny in the nineteenth century as they came to see themselves as "God's New Israel" and a "Redeemer Nation." Thus Ernest Tuveson can speak of a "secular millennialism."[13] Undergirding such perspectives were the extremely positive evaluations of human nature and a concept of the infinite perfectibility of humanity that the nineteenth century inherited from the previous century's Enlightenment.

In other words, social and religious leaders believed that, in spite of a rather brutish past, recent political and technological breakthroughs had begun to provide the machinery for the creation of heaven on earth, with the United States leading the way. Based upon such thoughts, the Anglo-Saxon world of the early nineteenth century was filled with hundreds of social and personal reform movements for the betterment of human society.

Reform societies arose in the early nineteenth century in almost every conceivable area of human interest. It was in these decades that campaigns for the abolition of slavery, war, and the use of alcohol became major factors in American culture. In addition, there were societies established for the promotion of public education; better treatment of the deaf, blind, mentally incapacitated, and prisoners; the equality of the sexes and races; and so on. Beyond the social realm, one finds organizations sponsoring personal betterment in such areas as moral reform and health— including the American Vegetarian Society.[14]

Religionists and secularists generally pooled their energies and resources in the hope of perfecting society through social and personal reform. But religionists went beyond their contemporaries through the establishment of such entities as Bible societies, home and foreign mission societies, Sunday-school unions, and associations for the promotion of Sunday sacredness.

The first half of the nineteenth century was awash in formal societies aimed at individual and social perfection. Such associations were not at the edges of American society, but at its very heart. While the roots of the reform efforts are found in the late eighteenth century, such efforts came to a climax between the 1820s and the 1840s.

Thus Millerism was born into a world rife with millennial expectation: a world affected by millennial fever to such an extent that it is almost impossible for citizens of the late twentieth century, who have witnessed two world wars and innumerable holocausts in the political, economic, and social realms, to grasp its power. Modern people have come to see that new inventions do not necessarily mean social and moral progress. They know that too often the technological and communicative advances of the last two centuries have been put to less than constructive uses.

As a result, the optimism of the early nineteenth century has evaporated. On the other hand, that optimism was quite real to people 150 years ago. In fact, it was the mainspring that fueled their many efforts to bring about the millennium. If people worked harder at reform, the belief ran, they could have a part in ushering in the thousand years of increasing peace and plenty that would climax with the second coming of Christ at the *end* of the millennium.

It was that positive millennial vision and hope that Millerism challenged. It was a challenge to the core belief of mainline America that the golden age could be brought about through human effort. Thus what Ruth Alden Doan has called the "Miller Heresy" was not in Adventism's doctrines but in its "radical supernaturalism."[15]

At Millerism's very foundation was a pessimism that human society would not achieve its grandiose schemes. Instead, the solution to the human problem would come through God's breaking into history at the second advent. That alternative solution set forth in God's Word would have at least two effects:

(1) It would make the Adventist solution immensely popular with those sectors of the population that were also becoming disillusioned with human programs in the late 1830s and early 1840s, and (2) it would eventually lead to a showdown in the churches between the optimistic believers in human effort and the pessimistic Adventists as the "year of the end" approached.

Millerism and the Second Great Awakening

Meanwhile, the rise of Adventism took place during America's greatest religious revival. That revival, known as the Second Great Awakening, did more than anything else in the history of the young nation to transform the United States into a Christian nation.

The early decades of the nineteenth century saw (1) a turning away from Deism (a skeptical belief that rejects Christianity with its miracles and supernatural revelation), which many had come to associate with the atrocities of the French Revolution, and (2) a turning toward evangelical Christianity. A large portion of a generation of Americans (including William Miller, as we shall see in chapter 2) were affected by that change. Between 1800 and 1850, the percentage of church members in the nation increased from about 5 or 10 percent to about 25 percent.[16] Beyond membership figures, Christianity saw a new birth in the life of the nation. One effect of that new birth was the millennial drive inherent in many of the reform movements noted above.

Millerism was born into a world excited with religion and religious themes. Religion was a dynamic, growing enterprise in the United States in the 1830s and 1840s, and Millerism was well adapted to capitalize on that dynamic expansion.

Recent scholarship has repeatedly pointed out the essentially orthodox nature of Millerite Adventism. As Whitney Cross put it, aside from Millerism's advocacy of the personal coming of Christ in the 1840s,

> Miller achieved no startling novelty. His doctrine in every other respect virtually epitomized orthodoxy. His chronol-

ogy merely elaborated and refined the kind of calculations his contemporaries had long been making but became more dramatic because it was more exact, and because the predicted event was more startling.[17]

Again, David Rowe notes, "Millerites are not fascinating because they were so different from everyone else but because they were so like their neighbors." Unlike the Mormons and Shakers and other radical groups of the period, the Millerites were both traditional and orthodox in their theology and lifestyle. "In this fact," Rowe points out, "lies the secret of their success."[18] It was easy for most Americans to accept Millerism once they accepted the premillennial return of Christ, since they did not need to adjust other aspects of their belief structure.

By the late 1830s, the revivalistic enthusiasm of the period between 1825 and 1835 was beginning to wane. Even the Billy Graham of the day—Charles Finney—had settled into a professorship at Oberlin College in Ohio, from which he still made annual evangelistic forays. But evangelism was no longer his full-time business.[19]

Beyond the waning of evangelistic excitement, the severe Panic (or economic depression) of 1837 and its continuing effects into the early 1840s had dampened the optimism of many Americans regarding the efficacy of human effort to bring about the millennium. It should be noted that "prices fell farther between 1839 and 1843 than between 1929 and 1933—42 percent as against 31 percent." Such brutal statistics (coupled with several natural disasters of the period) made many wonder what had happened to human progress.[20]

Thus Miller's message spoke to the times. It is probably no accident that enthusiasm for his message took a giant step forward in 1838 and 1839. In addition, we should keep in mind the fact that agricultural prices, after falling sharply between 1841 and 1843, finally reached their lowest point in March 1843, at the very time that Millerism was moving into its climactic phase.[21]

In the troubled world of the late 1830s, Millerism began to

make sense to more people. People were looking for answers in both their personal and social worlds.

Miller had a message that seemed to many to provide those answers. As a result, throughout the 1830s and early 1840s, he (and later his ministerial colleagues) received an unending stream of invitations to hold revivals in the churches of the evangelical denominations. Pastors found in Miller a man who could revive the sagging evangelistic thrust of the Second Great Awakening.

Millerism, therefore, has been viewed by several scholars as the final segment of the Awakening. Everett Dick has demonstrated that the "maximum point in gains [of church members in several denominations] came at the exact time that Miller expected Christ's advent." And Richard Carwardine notes that "in strictly statistical terms the peak of the Awakening came in this adventist phase of 1843-44."[22]

The Millerite crusade, therefore, should not be seen as a separate movement from the Second Great Awakening, but as an extension of it. As such, Dick is probably correct in his assessment that "William Miller may justifiably be considered the greatest evangelistic influence in the northeastern United States between 1840 and 1844."[23]

Unfortunately for Miller and his cause, most converts made by Adventist preachers between the 1830s and mid-1842 were probably converts to general Christianity rather than to Adventism's peculiar premillennial doctrine. But that would change as Millerism approached the year of the end of the world.

Students of American history have put forth several reasons for what Cross calls "the amazingly rapid growth" of Millerism.[24] Part of that growth can be explained by such sociological forces as economic depression and disillusionment with reform. But the phenomenon extends beyond those explanations.

The present book argues that the vital conviction that thrust the Millerites into the flow of history was a deep certainty, based upon concentrated study of the apocalyptic prophecies of Daniel and Revelation, that Christ was coming soon and that they had a personal responsibility to warn the world of that good yet fearful news. In short, they saw themselves as a prophetic people with a mission to present a message that the world desperately needed to hear.

Just as the postmillennial churches were thrust into social reform in the belief that they needed to do their part to bring about the millennial kingdom, so the Millerite Adventists were catapulted into a "preaching frenzy" by their conviction in the nearness of the second coming. Their mathematical demonstrations of that nearness greatly intensified that burden as they sought to warn a world of the rapidly approaching climactic event of the ages.

Chapter 2

THE MAKING OF A MILLENNIALIST: WILLIAM MILLER'S EARLY YEARS

An unlikely candidate to become a preacher. That would have been the obvious evaluation of those who knew Miller in his twenties.

In fact, William Miller at that time was more interested in making fun of preachers than in emulating them. In particular, he found those preachers in his own family to be especially good targets for that brand of fun. Those "favored" by such activity were his grandfather Phelps (a Baptist minister) and his uncle Elihu Miller, of the Low Hampton Baptist Church.

Miller's mimicking of his grandfather's and uncle's devotional peculiarities afforded high entertainment for his skeptical associates. He imitated, with "ludicrous gravity," his relatives' "words, tones of voice, gestures, fervency, and even the grief they might manifest for such as himself."[1]

Beyond entertainment for his friends, such exhibitions also functioned as a statement of who young Miller was. Like other young people in times of rapid cultural transition, Miller had gone through his own identity crisis. Part of his rebellion against his family had undoubtedly been an aspect of the perennial struggle of adolescents to discover who they are in contradistinction to their parents.[2]

That struggle, unfortunately, is equally hard on both parents and adolescents. Such was the case of William's deeply religious mother, who knew of his entertaining antics but found them anything but funny. To her, the actions of her eldest son were "the bitterness of death."[3] Interestingly, William had not always been a religious rebel.

Not Always a Rebel

Far from being a congenital religious rebel, William in his earliest years had been intensely and painfully devout. In fact, the first page of his diary (which he began to keep in his teens) contains the statement: "I was early educated and taught to pray the Lord." Being the only descriptive statement about himself in the diary's introduction, it must have seemed important to him as a distinguishing characteristic.[4]

Earlier, between ages seven and ten, William reports that he was often concerned with the welfare of his soul, especially in regard to future destiny. "I spent," he later wrote,

> much time in trying to invent some plan, whereby I might please God, when brought into his immediate presence. Two ways suggested themselves to me, which I tried. One was, to be very good, to do nothing wrong, tell no lies, and obey my parents. But I found my resolutions weak, and soon broken. The other was to sacrifice; by giving up the most cherished objects I possessed. But this also failed me; so that I was never settled and happy in mind, until I came to Jesus.[5]

That coming to Jesus, however, was at that time still a decade and a half away. This self-portrait of a fearful-of-judgment preadolescent goes a long way to explain his adolescent rejection of religion. It also helps explain why he developed a vengeance toward his uncle Elihu, who, as pastor of William's local church, undoubtedly exacerbated his anxiety through preaching the hell-fire sermons that were standard Baptist pulpit fare of the times. Such pressure on a tender conscience probably also explains his indecorous caricature of his grandfather Phelps.

His grandfather, however, while perhaps not as sensitive as he could have been in his evangelism, later showed keen insight toward the struggle taking place in the rebellious heart of his post-adolescent grandson. Phelps sought to console William's mother regarding the mimicking by saying, "Don't afflict your-self too deeply about William. There is something for him to do yet, in the cause of God."[6] Unfortunately for her, it would take time for that prophecy to reach fulfillment.

In the meantime, young William developed along other fronts. Of special import was his love of books and learning, an aspect of his character that would have much to do with both his departure from and his reconciliation to Christianity.[7]

Being born into a frontier farmer's home that would eventually include sixteen children meant that, due to financial stringency, William's education was not enriched with a large parental library. The Bible, the psalter, and the prayer book were his parents' only books. Despite the lack, his mother taught him to read. Beyond that, between his ninth and fourteenth years, he attended the rather primitive local school for three months each winter after the farm work was completed for the year. Unfortunately, the caliber of teachers employed then by rural schools left much to be desired, and William soon transcended their limited abilities. As a result, he was largely self-taught through reading.[8]

Reading, of course, implied that he had access to both books and time to spend with them. Young Miller's ingenuity in obtain-ing both commodities says a lot about him as a person.

The stringent economy of the Miller family meant that William would have to borrow books if he were to have anything to read. But even borrowing books did not solve the problem, since he had to work long hours on the family farm if his parents were to make ends meet. Because his father feared that night reading might interfere with the efficiency of William's daily work, he insisted that William go to bed at the same time as the rest of the family.

William, however, had his own plans. When he believed the other members of the family to be asleep, he would read by the light of hoarded pitch wood, which he secreted each day during his wood-chopping duties. That plan worked well until the night his father awoke to the light of the unexpected fire and thought the house was burning. Sylvester Bliss reports that the father "hurried from his bed, and when he saw his son's . . . employment, he seized the whip, and pursuing his flying son, cried out, in a manner which made it effectual for some time, 'Bill, if you don't go to bed, I'll horsewhip you!' "[9]

By William's fourteenth year, his father had mellowed to the extent that he agreed to a plan whereby the son could purchase a book now and then if he earned the money by extra wood chopping during his leisure hours. The first two books attained under that program were the *History of Crusoe* and a novel entitled *The Adventures of Robert Boyle*.[10]

Meanwhile, the better-positioned gentlemen in William's locale, seeing his potential, continued to loan him books. Thus in late adolescence he became a student of ancient and modern history, providing a background that would eventually help him in his study of the Bible. "By the kindness of these gentlemen," Joshua Himes wrote in 1842, "he was enabled to store his mind with a vast collection of historical facts, which have since been of so much service to him in the illustration of the prophecies." During that same time, young Miller was beginning to flex his writing skills, becoming the local "scribbler-general" for young people who needed "verses made."[11]

The Deistic Years and the War of 1812

Miller reached a major turning point in 1803, when he married Lucy Smith of Poultney, Vermont. He not only married a woman from Poultney, but moved there himself. That move would be consequential for him because it put him in contact with both the amply supplied public library of Poultney and the village's deistic intelligentsia. "They put into my hands," penned Miller, "the works of Voltaire, Hume, Paine, Ethan Allen and other deistical writers." Miller also continued to read widely in history. Fortunately for him, his new wife was much more favorable to his scholarly bent than his father had been, making "it her pleasure and business to relieve him as much as possible from all the family cares which might call him away from his books."[12]

Of special importance to Miller's intellectual development was Matthew Lyon, an anti-Federalist whose political activities while a member of Congress had led to his imprisonment under the Sedition Act of 1798. Lyon held to the Deism of Ethan Allen, under whom he had served in the Revolutionary War. The ex-Congressman had amassed a large personal library that served as the "reference center" for his neighbors, including Miller. Both Lyon's books and his companionship aided Miller's drift toward Deism.[13]

Miller's doubts about the Bible, however, did not begin with the move to Poultney. He later admitted that he had always been perplexed by what he deemed to be "inconsistencies and contradictions in the Bible" that he had been unable to harmonize, for he reasoned that if the Bible were what it purported to be, one must be able to harmonize the seeming discrepancies.

Before his doubts about the Bible became serious, Miller had been "exceedingly anxious to reconcile all its various parts, and, unsuccessfully, resorted to all means" within his reach to do so. "I was," he wrote, "particularly anxious to have them harmonized by the preachers of the word; and accordingly embraced every opportunity, to present for their removal, the difficulties under which I labored. But I obtained from them no satisfaction." They usually referred him to the opinions of biblical commentators, which, Miller noted, were as contradictory as the preachers themselves.[14]

It was in that state of mind that Miller moved to Poultney, where his new deistic contacts discussed the difficulties that had perplexed him "in so plausible a manner" that he concluded that "the Bible was only the work of designing men; and," he penned, "I discarded it accordingly." He now viewed the Bible as "a system of *craft*, rather than of *truth*." Its main function seemed to be to "enslave the mind of man." On the other hand, after the manner of Deism, he still believed in a Supreme Being as reflected in the world of nature and in a hereafter in which happiness would be correlated with one's moral virtue in the earthly state.[15]

Miller remained a Deist for twelve years. During that period he became a member of the Masons (advancing to the highest rank available), became a locally active Jeffersonian Democrat, and filled the offices of constable, sheriff, and justice of the peace. Beyond those accomplishments, he owned a relatively prosperous farm. All in all, by 1812 William Miller had become one of the foremost citizens of his community.[16]

Given Miller's leadership role in his community's civil affairs, it is not surprising to find him in a similar position in the military conflict with Great Britain during the War of 1812. With intimation of conflict on the horizon, he had been elected as a lieutenant of the Vermont militia in 1810. Early in the war he was promoted to militia captain, and by the end of the conflict in 1815, he was a captain in the regular army. Much of his tour of duty was spent in being an "evangelist" (recruiter) for the army, another talent as a leader and inspirer of people that he would later put to a vastly different use.[17]

The war with Britain provided another turning point in Miller's life. Before the war, he had begun to harbor doubts about the adequacy of Deism along at least two lines. First, he had begun to suspect that Deism "tended toward a belief of annihilation, which," he wrote, "was always very abhorrent to my feelings." Thus he had begun to find an incongruity in the deistic structure of belief. While Deists claimed to believe in afterlife, in actual fact their presuppositions logically led to nothingness after death.

Miller became convinced of that unsettling reality upon questioning one of his learned Poultney friends, who compared life to a candle that burns to nothing. "I was then satisfied," Miller noted, "that Deism was inseparably connected with, and did tend to, the denial of a future existence." Miller found even the heaven and hell of the Bible preferable to that view but had as yet no basis for regarding the Bible as inspired.[18]

The second flaw that Miller began to perceive in the deistic gospel came from his wide reading in history. Deism, in contradiction to traditional Christianity, posed that human nature at its best was basically good and upright. But Miller could not find that view in history. "The more I read," he wrote, "the more dreadfully corrupt did the character of man appear. I could discern no bright spot in the history of the past. Those conquerors of the world, and heros of history, were apparently but demons in human form. . . . I began to feel very distrustful of all men."[19]

Miller's war years would bring his Deism to crisis in both areas of his discontent. For one thing, the conflict brought him face to face with the reality of death. On the civilian front, December 1812 saw one of his sisters and his father die within three days of each other.[20]

Beyond family deaths, the war years made Miller face up to death in a way he had never had to before. The brutal fact of death forced him to contemplate his own mortality and its meaning. He wrote to his wife along that line on October 28, 1814.

> But a short time, and, like Spencer [an army friend], I shall be no more. It is a solemn thought. Yet, could I be sure of one other life, there would be nothing terrific; but to go out like an extinguished taper, is insupportable—the thought is doleful. No! rather let me cling to that hope which warrants a never-ending existence; a future spring, where troubles shall cease, and tears find no conveyance; where never-ending spring shall flourish, and love, pure as the driven snow, rest[s] in every breast.[21]

The hard facts of life were pushing Captain Miller toward the faith he had once so vigorously rejected.

Not only did the war bring Miller's Deism to crisis in the area of death and annihilationism, but it also brought his doubts about human nature to a climax. While his historical reading had led him to the conclusion that human nature was not as good as Deism claimed, he "fondly cherished the idea" that he would "find one bright spot at least in the human character, as a star of hope: *a love of country*—PATRIOTISM."[22]

"But," he penned, "two years in the service was enough to convince me that I was in an error in this thing also. When I left the service I had become completely disgusted with man's public character."[23]

Thus, on the negative side, the War of 1812 brought two of Deism's cardinal principles (hope of an afterlife and human goodness) into question. Meanwhile, the Battle of Plattsburg in September 1814 led Miller to question a third deistic doctrinal pillar—the nonintervention of God in human affairs. In that battle an American "apology for an army" made up of fifteen hundred regulars and four thousand volunteers met and defeated fifteen thousand crack British regulars, some recently having been victorious over Napoleon.[24]

"At the commencement of the Battle," penned Miller, "we looked upon our own defeat as almost certain, and yet we were victorious. *So surprising a result against such odds, did seem to me like the work of a mightier power than man.*" Comparing the United States to the children of Israel and God's vanquishing of their foes, Miller later noted that it appeared that "the Supreme Being must have watched over the interests of this country in an especial manner, and delivered us from the hands of our enemies."[25]

It was shortly after Plattsburg that Miller began to write letters home about death (noted above) that held indications of a richer and more personal faith. The timing was far from accidental; the war had redirected Miller's religious thinking.

Back to Christianity

At the close of the war, Miller turned away from his deistic friends and toward his Christian heritage. These turnings were symbolized by moving his family from Poultney back to his parental home in Low Hampton, New York, and by his again attending the Baptist church that had once been the pulpit of his uncle Elihu.[26]

Miller's return home with its church attendance did not mean that he had become a Christian. To the contrary, for many months he lived in the confused no man's land between Deism and Christianity. True, he went to church and had begun seriously to doubt Deism with part of his mind, but with the other he still clung to the positive aspects of Deism and wrestled with the problematic portions of biblical belief.

The next turning point in Miller's life came in May 1816, when he discovered himself "in the act of taking the name of God in vain." He had acquired the practice in the army but had come under conviction—probably through the influence of the Low Hampton Baptists—that such a practice was sinful.[27]

The act of May 1816 may seem small to most people, but Miller's mind had been agitated on the subject of religion for some time. As a result, that "small act" precipitated an important crisis in his life. "In the month of May, 1816," he later wrote, "I was brought under conviction; and O, what horror filled my soul! I forgot to eat. The heavens appeared like brass, and the earth like iron. Thus I continued till October, when God opened my eyes."[28]

Two things happened in September 1816 that prepared Miller for the resolution of his crisis in October. The first event was the celebration of the Battle of Plattsburg on September 11. Miller and his friends were making preparations for a festal ball in "high glee," when they stopped their work to attend a sermon the evening before the big party. They returned from the sermon deeply thoughtful. The glee was gone. Mirth and thoughts of the dance had been replaced by prayer and praise as the veterans recalled the circumstances and significance of the bitter battle and their "surprising" victory.[29]

The second event leading toward the resolution of Miller's spiritual crisis took place the following Sunday, September 15. Months before that date, Miller's mother had discovered that he absented himself from church whenever the pastor was out of town. On such occasions the reading of a message from *Proudfoot's Practical Sermons* was delegated to one of the deacons. Upon inquiry, she discovered that Miller did not find the level of the deacon's reading ability to be edifying. Miller intimated that if he could do the reading, he would always be present. After that, the still-deistic Miller was regularly invited to read the preselected sermon.[30]

That was the situation on September 15, 1816, when the deacons chose a sermon on the "importance of Parental Duties." Miller choked up soon after beginning the reading. Before long the moved congregation witnessed the emotionally overwrought reader sit down in the midst of the message. Miller had reached his spiritual crisis point.[31]

A few weeks later, as Miller put it, "God opened my eyes; and O, my soul, what a Savior I discovered Jesus to be!" Yet that discovery was not immediate.[32]

Miller wrestled with himself for some time after September 15. "How," he thought, "can it be proved that such a Being does exist?" After all, "to believe in such a Savior without evidence, would be visionary in the extreme." But Miller was forced to concede the fact that the Bible brought to view just the kind of Saviour he needed to rescue him from his agony. On the other hand, he was "perplexed to find how an uninspired book should develope [sic] principles so perfectly adapted to the wants of a fallen world." He was finally forced to admit to himself that the "Scriptures must be a revelation from God." His point of personal breakthrough had been reached. Subsequently he could rejoice that *the Scriptures "became my delight, and in Jesus I found a friend."*[33]

Again, Miller wrote:

Jesus Christ became to me the chiefest among ten thousand, and the Scriptures, which before were dark and contradictory, now became the lamp to my feet and light to my path. My mind became settled and satisfied. I found the Lord God to be a Rock in the midst of the ocean of life. The Bible now became my chief study, and I can truly say I searched it with great delight. . . . I wondered why I had not seen its beauty and glory before, and marvelled that I could ever have rejected it. I found everything revealed that my heart could desire, and a remedy for every disease of the soul. I lost all taste for other reading, and applied my heart to get wisdom from God.[34]

Thus in 1816 Miller had gone through a conversion experience quite like many of the former Deists of his generation as the Second Great Awakening increasingly eroded the ranks of the skeptics.[35] But some of Miller's acquaintances had not forgotten the strength of his former convictions and the forcefulness of his arguments against the Bible and Christianity.

Shortly after his conversion, one of those friends asked Miller point blank how he knew there was a Saviour and how he knew the Bible was true. He then challenged Miller with his own arguments regarding the Bible's inconsistencies, contradictions, and mysticism.

Miller replied that if the Bible was God's Word, everything it contained could not only be understood but harmonized. Then, Miller later recalled, "I said to him that if he would give me time, I would harmonize all these apparent contradictions, to my own satisfaction, or I would be a Deist still."[36]

Miller's response to his deistic friend drove the new convert into an intense study of the Bible that would not only affect him personally but would also make a mark on the course of Christian history.

An Enthusiastic Bible Student

William Miller was not one to do something halfway. His approach to Bible study can be characterized as energetic, thorough, and methodical. He commenced with Genesis and read each verse, "proceeding no faster than the meaning of the several passages should be so unfolded, as to leave" him "free from embarrassment respecting any mysticism or contradictions."[37]

"Whenever," he explained,

I found any thing obscure, my practice was to compare it with all collateral passages; and by the help of CRUDEN['s concordance], I examined all the texts of Scripture in which were found any of the prominent words contained in any obscure portion. Then by letting every word have its proper bearing on the subject of the text, if my view of it harmonized with every collateral passage in the Bible, it ceased to be a difficulty.[38]

Miller pursued his Bible study in that manner for two years, becoming fully persuaded that the Bible was its own interpreter. During that study he became quite convinced that the chronological portions of the Bible deserved serious consideration. Thus he did not skip over the time prophecies of Daniel and Revelation.[39]

It was through the study of such passages as those referring to the 2300- and 1335-year/day prophecies that in 1818 Miller came to the conclusion that Christ would come about the year 1843. He had not been looking for that information and at first "could not believe it." But after wrestling with his shocking conclusion, Miller finally made up his mind that "whatever the Bible teaches I willhold [sic] on to it."[40] That decision would eventually bring him to the center of national controversy.

Before mentioning his views to anyone else, however, Miller decided to put his conclusions to the test of further Bible study. As a result, between 1818 and 1823 he studied every objection that came to his mind regarding the soon coming of the Lord. "During that time," he wrote in 1845, "more objections arose in my mind than have been advanced by my opponents since; and I know of no objection that has been since advanced, which did not then occur to me." However, each objection disappeared under careful investigation; "the car of truth rolled over them, unimpeded in its progress."[41]

By September 1822, Miller felt comfortable enough with his conclusions to formally set down a twenty-point statement of his beliefs. All of them fit into the orthodoxy of the day except article 15, which stated: "I believe that the second coming of Jesus Christ is near, even at the door, even within twenty-one years,— on or before 1843."[42] Even though by 1822 Miller was secure enough in his beliefs to put his conclusions in writing, he still had a long way to go before he would feel free to publicly preach them.

Before moving to Miller's preaching, however, we should ask

how it was that a layperson like Miller could be so audacious as to develop theological ideas that flew in the face of the doctrines of the highly educated clergy of his day. Beyond that, we should briefly examine the thought world of the early nineteenth century so that we can better understand both Miller and the eventual popularity of his movement.

The first thing to note is that individualism had always been strong in North America. That individualism and its accompanying self-reliance were on the verge of taking giant steps forward as the 1810s turned into the 1820s. The subsequent period in American history would come to be known to historians as the age of the common man or the Jacksonian era.

In the mind-set of the times, a person did not need to be an expert to run for public office, practice medicine, or do theology. Every person could exercise his or her God-given talents. Thus in Miller's rules for Bible interpretation, he could state that individuals could arrive at truth through their own prayerful study of the Bible, even "though they may not understand Hebrew or Greek." In 1841 Miller was challenged in regard to his capabilities to teach his views, since he did not know the biblical languages. He promptly replied to his detractor: " 'If I am not acquainted *with the* HEBREW *and* GREEK, I know enough to quote the *English* texts of the Scriptures rightly.' " On another occasion, he noted that the Bible contains a system of revealed truths, "so clearly and simply given that the 'wayfaring man though a fool need not err therein.' "[43]

Closely related to the Jacksonian view of the potential of ordinary people was the "common-sense" philosophy that had become central to American Christianity. Common-sense philosophy avoided complicated rational explanations and focused on the facts (including biblical facts) as they appeared to the person on the street.[44]

Thus Josiah Litch could rejoice that Millerism had given the world "a simple, plain, common-sense system of interpretation of the sacred canon, so that every man, who will take the trouble of reading the Bible, and collating the different portions of it, may understand the word of God without the aid of learned commentaries."[45]

The Millerite approach had been to make the Bible into a "self-interpreting book" so that all could understand it. That approach to Scripture, coupled with relatively new ways of looking at the Bible as a historical book and at numbers as the unlockers of universal secrets, provided Miller and his followers a powerful avenue for reaching out to the American population through collating the Bible with history and mathematical certainty. Such a composite methodology greatly appealed to a population only then becoming a "calculating people" in the 1820s and 1830s. Given the recent developments in mathematical literacy, almost anyone could perform the necessary computations, once provided the historical starting dates, to arrive at Miller's conclusions.[46]

Another important element in American Christianity in the early nineteenth century that greatly influenced and aided Millerism was restorationism. Christian restorationism at its heart is the drive to get back to and to restore the ideals of the Bible.

Undergirding restorationism is the belief that the New Testament church is the ideal model for God's people in all ages. That model had been lost in the medieval period. Recovery of New Testament Christianity had begun in the Reformation, but the post-Reformation churches had not completed their task of getting altogether back to the forms and doctrines of first-century Christianity.

That task, many evangelical believers in the new nation held, was part of their millennial mission. Such a view of Christian mission drove people back to the Bible in their attempt to recover what had been lost. Thus the Bible in the early nineteenth century became a potent force in the development of new forms of Christianity in a way that it had not been for most of Christian history. Restorationism provided a religious perspective that tended to bypass such modes of authority as the church, tradition, philosophical speculation, and all human theories.[47]

Millerism found itself in the mind-set of the restorationist drive as it both directed people back to the Bible and sought to restore the "true" (or New Testament) doctrine of the second coming. As a result, restorationism provided Millerism with both a theological method and a dynamic force that propelled it across the nation. Along that line, historian Whitney Cross has noted that "no other enthusiasts of the half century . . . stuck so closely and exclusively to the Bible as did the Millerites."[48]

Two final points that we should note about the thought world of the times of William Miller are that it put a premium on rationalism and literalism. The rationalistic element was the heritage of the eighteenth-century Enlightenment and its religious expression, Deism. Miller and his generation lived in a world highly appreciative of rational approaches to everything, including religion. Thus Miller could refer to his experience with Scripture as a "feast of reason."[49] Following that lead, Miller's evangelistic method, as we shall see, definitely aimed at his hearers' heads rather than their hearts or emotions.

Literalism also stood close to the spirit of Miller's time. Most people believed that literalistic interpretations of the Bible spelled faithfulness, while allegorical or metaphorical interpretations implied that the Bible was not being taken seriously.[50]

Miller was in tune with that mentality when he wrote in his rules of Bible interpretation that if a Bible passage "makes good sense as it stands, . . . then it must be understood literally." Beyond that, once he had discovered the biblical passages that unlocked their symbolism, Miller even gave literal, historical meanings to figurative passages of Scripture, such as the parables and prophetic imagery. Such a straightforward approach made Miller's exegesis appealing and perhaps, notes Ernest Sandeen, gave the Millerites "their most effective recruiting argument."[51]

So far we have seen that both William Miller's theological views and his methods were in harmony with his times. That inevitably raises the question as to whether he really got his interpretation of prophecy from independent Bible study or whether he imbibed it from others.

The answer to that query is probably much more complex than is generally granted. On the one hand, Miller had been an avid reader for most of his life. In a world in which much of the published literature was theological and biblical, it seems to be quite reasonable to assume that he had examined various religious and biblical works before he began his intense study of the Bible in 1816. It was only at that time that he said: "I laid by all commentaries, former views and prepossessions, and determined to read and try to understand for myself."[52]

It is also reasonable to believe that a man with Miller's breadth of interest in reading along historical and religious lines could not have been completely ignorant of the interpretations of his day. After all, he did have, he claims, some views to lay aside. In addition, even in his deistic days, he was aware that the views of biblical commentaries were as diverse as those of preachers. That statement shows at least a minimal acquaintance with such works. Along that same line, one of his daughters remarked in 1843 that two authors on the prophecies that he distinctly remembered having read prior to 1816 were Newton and Faber. Beyond those facts, there appears to be some validity to Michael Barkun's assessment that "the congruence between his Biblical interpretations and older readings of millenarian symbols strongly implies access to an oral if not a written exegetical tradition."[53]

On the other side of the issue, there is every indication that in formulating his prophetic position he stuck to his intention of studying the Bible alone through the aid of *Cruden's Concordance*. Even before his deistic years he had developed a distaste for commentaries. Again, one of his most fundamental beliefs relating to Bible interpretation was that

> scripture must be its own expositor, since it is a rule of itself. If I depend on a teacher to expound it to me, and he should guess at its meaning, or desire to have it so on account of his sectarian creed, or to be thought wise, then his *guessing, desire, creed, or wisdom*, is my rule, not the Bible.[54]

Such a belief not only ruled out commentaries, but it fit in perfectly with the restorationist imperative to get back to the New

Testament by bypassing human interpretations. It also linked up with the Jacksonian faith in the ability of the common man to understand the Bible without the aid of experts.

From all the evidence that we have, Miller appears to have lived by his own rules and deep-felt convictions. One contemporary anecdote shedding light on his practice was published by one of Miller's associates in 1843.

A minister, the story goes, stopped by Miller's home in his absence. Being disappointed at not being able to meet with Miller, the clergyman requested the privilege of examining his library. "His daughter conducted the visiter [sic] into the northeast room, where he has sat so many hours at his . . . desk." Only two books—the Bible and Cruden's—" lay upon the table. 'That is his library,' said she. The clergyman was amazed."[55]

In spite of the above facts, Miller understood by the early 1840s that his findings were in harmony with those of other prophetic interpreters. Thus he could write that he believed that "all commentaries agree that these *days* are to be understood *years*." There are several such statements by Miller and his colleagues. By the early forties, either Miller himself or his associates had done some comparative study between his prophetic system and that of other expositors.[56]

Sandeen notes that "few non-Adventist scholars would contest the general position of Adventist historians that Miller formulated his positions on the return of Christ in 1843 quite independently." And Barkun attributes Miller's similarities to others to "independent invention rather than diffusion."[57] On the other hand, nothing essential is lost if Miller's nondependence is not as complete as some would have it. For the Millerites it was the biblical faithfulness of his conclusions, not their origin, that was the essential element.

The core of those conclusions was Miller's conviction that Christ would come about the year 1843 to rescue His people and to cleanse the earth (sanctuary of Daniel 8:14) with fire. That conviction, he penned, filled his heart with "joy," but it also laid on his conscience a duty to warn the world of coming judgment.[58]

To Preach or Not to Preach

It was "immediately" after he discovered the nearness of the advent that Miller began to feel a pressing burden for souls. From the beginning he had believed that multitudes of Christians would rejoice in the good news he had discovered. He had no intimations of rejection by either the churches or their ministers, even though he did suppose "that it would call forth the opposition of the ungodly."[59]

Yet he hesitated to present his message to anyone as yet. After all, he could be in error. That thought, as we noted above, drove him into another five years (1818-1823) of study as he sought to raise and answer every possible biblical objection to his theory.[60]

Thus for five years he was able to shield his sensitive conscience from painful thoughts of his responsibility. But by 1823, upon satisfying himself on the correctness of his original conclusions, his protection was gone. "The duty," he wrote, "of presenting the evidence of the nearness of the advent to others . . . again came home to me with great force."[61]

In an attempt to allay his conscience, Miller began in 1823 to privately explain his views more clearly to some of his neighbors and even to some ministers. Their response certainly did not embolden the reluctant prophet with confidence. Most thought it an "idle tale," and few listened with any interest. Miller's greatest disappointment came in not being able to find a preacher to take his burden from him.[62]

Thereafter, Miller continued to find refuge from responsibility in Bible study. That ploy, however, was counterproductive, since that very book fueled his anxiety. Thus he became "more and more convinced" that he had a "personal duty to perform respecting this matter." "When I was about my business," he penned,

it was continually ringing in my ears, "Go and tell the world of their danger." This text was constantly occurring to me, "When I say unto the wicked, O wicked man, thou shalt surely die; if thou dost not speak to warn the wicked from his way, that wicked man shall die in his iniquity; but his blood will I require at thy hand. Nevertheless, if thou warn the wicked of his way to turn from it; if he do not turn from his way, he shall die in his iniquity; but thou hast delivered thy soul."—Ezek. xxxiii.8, 9.[63]

Even that oft-repeated impression failed to move Miller to action. Apparently his fear of rejection by people outweighed his fear of God. For another eight years (1823-1831) the reluctant prophet continued to resist what he believed to be the unction of the Holy Spirit, even though he claimed to have had a dream on November 4, 1826, in which God had indicated that He would bless him if he would be faithful in warning the world.[64]

On January 14, 1829, however, Miller gave some indication of his future direction, even though he was moving infinitesimally slowly when one considers that he believed Christ would come in a mere fourteen years. On that January date, he made his first entry in a small book in which he noted important remarks on Sunday sermons. At times he provided lengthy outlines of those sermons. Whether he realized it or not, he had begun a practical course in sermon preparation.[65]

In the meantime, Miller took three approaches to avoiding the increasing tempo of the pressure on his conscience. First, he continued his search to find a preacher to take his burden. It may have been with that hope in mind that he penned "A Few Evidences of the Time of the 2nd Coming of Christ to Elder Andrus" on February 15, 1831. Undoubtedly, his interviews with Elder Truman Hendryx and other ministers in the summer of 1831 had a similar end in view.[66]

Second, being unsuccessful in finding a substitute, he fell back on the "Moses ploy." "I told the Lord," he wrote, "that I was not used to public speaking, that I had not the necessary qualifications to gain the attention of an audience, . . . that they would 'not believe me nor hearken to my voice,' that I was 'slow of speech, and of a slow tongue.' " But he got no relief.[67]

Third, the fifty-year-old Miller harbored the hope that he could escape the responsibility for publicly presenting his beliefs to live audiences if he put them in print. With that in mind, he prepared a series of articles over the signature W. M. The articles were sent to the *Vermont Telegraph*, a Baptist paper, but the editor refused to publish them unless he knew the author's identity. Miller, supposing the editor wanted the information for his private use, disclosed his full name. The articles appeared in sixteen numbers of the paper beginning on May 15, 1832.[68]

To Miller's chagrin, it soon became known that he was the author of the articles. He was thereafter, as he put it, "flooded with letters of inquiry respecting my views; and visitors flocked to converse with me on the subject."[69] The printed page had given him more publicity than preaching could have.

Unfortunately for Miller, he could find no relief from his burden to warn the world. The urgency of his millennial vision was driving him into mission. "I could not," he penned, "escape the impression, 'Go and tell it to the world, their blood will I require at thy hand.' "[70]

Chapter 3

MILLER'S MISSION TO THE WORLD

William Miller was "tricked" into presenting his first public sermon before his *Vermont Telegraph* articles had even come off the press. The occasion was a Saturday morning in the summer of 1831. He had been hit with the usual impression to "go and tell it to the world," but this time it came with such force that he was compelled to sit down. After telling the Lord that he couldn't go, the words "Why not?" came to his mind. He gave all his well-worn excuses but was so distressed that, as he put it, "I entered into a solemn covenant with God, that if he would open the way, I would go and perform my duty to the world."[1]

" 'What do you mean by opening the way?' " his mind queried. "Why, said I, if I should have an invitation to speak publicly in any place, I will go and tell them what I find in the Bible about the Lord's coming." With that commitment made, Miller's thirteen-year burden was gone at last. After all, he had little expectation of being called to preach on the advent, since he had never had even one invitation to do so up to that point. He could relax at last, but not for long.[2]

In about a half-hour, he had his first-ever invitation to present his beliefs regarding the second coming. "I was," he wrote,

> immediately angry with myself for having made the covenant...; I rebelled at once against the Lord, and determined not to go. I left the boy [who had come with the request]

45

without giving him any answer, and retired in great distress to a grove near by. There I struggled with the Lord for about an hour, endeavoring to release myself from the covenant I had made with him; but I could get no relief. It was impressed upon my conscience, "Will you make a covenant with God, and break it so soon?" and the exceeding sinfulness of thus doing overwhelmed me. I finally submitted, and promised the Lord that if he would sustain me, I would go, trusting in him to give me grace and ability to perform all he should require of me.[3]

The following day Miller preached his first sermon on the second advent at Dresden—sixteen miles from his home. In spite of initial uneasiness, he noted that "as soon as I commenced speaking, all my diffidence and embarrassment were gone, and I felt impressed only with the greatness of the subject, which, by the providence of God, I was enabled to present."[4]

His first sermon was a resounding success, so much so that the Dresden congregation requested that he remain to lecture the following week. He did so, with several converts resulting from his expositions. Upon returning home he found an invitation from the Poultney congregation asking for a similar series of lectures. Those invitations were the beginning of an unbroken stream of requests that would continue for the rest of his active life.[5]

A Profile of Miller the Man

Miller was not impressive to look at. That fact is illustrated by the experience of Timothy Cole, pastor of the Christian Connexion congregation in Lowell, Massachusetts. Having heard (in the late 1830s) of Miller's outstanding success as a revivalist, Cole invited him to hold a series of meetings in his church.

Cole went to meet the successful evangelist at the train depot, expecting a fashionably dressed gentleman whose demeanor matched his reputation. Cole watched closely as the passengers debarked the train but saw no one who corresponded with his expectations. Eventually an unimpressive old man, shaking with palsy, alighted from the car. To Cole's dismay, the "old man" turned out to be Miller. At that point he deeply regretted having invited him to speak at his church. Someone of Miller's appearance, he concluded, could not know much about the Bible.

More than a little embarrassed, Cole led Miller through the back door of his church and, after showing him the pulpit, took a seat among the congregation. Miller felt a bit ill-used at being left on the platform alone but proceeded with the service.

But if Cole was unimpressed with Miller's appearance, the opposite held true for Cole's reaction to his preaching. After listening fifteen minutes, he arose from his chair among the congregation and went up and sat behind Miller on the platform. Miller lectured daily for a week and came back the next month for a second series of meetings. A successful revival followed in which Cole baptized forty. He eventually had sixty join his church. Cole himself became a convert to Miller's views on the nearness of the second advent.[6]

At this juncture we want to look at Miller as a man. How did others perceive him, and how did he perceive himself? We will discover that Cole's experience was quite typical.

Reports concerning Miller are consistent in implying that there was nothing extraordinary in his physical appearance. For example, the *Maine Wesleyan Journal* referred to him as a "plain farmer." According to the New York *Herald*, Miller was "about five feet seven inches in height, very thick set, [with] broad shoulders; lightish brown hair, a little bald, a benevolent countenance, full of wrinkles, and his head shakes as though he was slightly afflicted with the palsy." Certainly there was nothing in Miller's physical appearance that was outstanding.

On the other hand, the *Herald* points out, "his manners are very much in his favor." Even though "he is not a very well-educated man; . . . he has read and studied history and prophecy very closely; has much common sense, and is evidently sincere in his belief."[7]

Miller's utter and transparent sincerity was frequently commented upon, even by his detractors. For example, the editor of the Lynn *Record* gives us the following report of his visit to a lecture by Miller.

> We took a prejudice against this good man, when he first came among us, on account of what we supposed a glaring error in interpreting the Scripture prophecies so that the world would come to an end in 1843. We are still inclined to believe this an error or miscalculation. At the same time we have overcome our prejudices against him by attending his lectures, and learning more of the excellent character of the man, and of the great good he has done and is doing. Mr. Miller is a plain farmer, and pretends to nothing except that he made the Scripture prophecies an intense study for many years. . . . *No one can hear him five minutes without being convinced of his sincerity*, and instructed by his reasoning and information. All acknowledge his lectures to be replete with useful and interesting matter. His knowledge of Scripture is very extensive and minute; that of the prophecies, especially, surprisingly familiar. . . . We have reason to believe that the preaching or lecturing of Mr. Miller has been productive of great and extensive good. Revivals have followed in his train.[8]

Many other newspapers commented on Miller's sincerity. For example, the Sandy Hill *Herald* (published in his home county) declared: "We are not prepared to say how far the old man may be from correct, but one thing, *we doubt not that he is sincere*." Again, the Cincinnati *Commercial* states that "whatever people may think of his belief, which is peculiar, one thing is conceded by all, that he is a Christian at heart."[9]

Miller's sincerity must have been a major factor in his success as a preacher. After all, from all reports, his preaching style was not any more spectacular than his physical appearance. The Cincinnati *Commercial* noted that "he is quite an old-fashioned man in his speech." Again, Pastor L. D. Fleming, of the Casco Street Christian Church of Portland, Maine, wrote of Miller: "The interest awakened by his lectures is of the most deliberate and dispassionate kind." "There has been nothing like passionate excitement. If there has been excitement it has been out of doors among such as did not attend Br. M's lectures." On the other hand, Fleming reported that Miller preached in a manner that placed an "almost universal solemnity on the minds of all the people."[10]

Such evaluations of Miller's attitudes toward preaching are also evidenced by his own remarks. "I have," he observed, "often obtained more evidence of inward piety from a *kindling eye*, a *wet cheek*, and a *choked utterance*, than from all the *noise* in christendom." Again, in 1832 when the Low Hampton church was looking for a pastor, Miller wrote: "Some of our people want a quick gab. But I [would] . . . rather [see] a quick understanding."[11]

Yet this rather bland-looking farmer with his colorless style, according to the *Maine Wesleyan Journal*, "succeeds in chaining the attention of his auditory for an hour and a half to two hours." The editor of *The Fountain*, a temperance paper, attended several of Miller's lectures in the New Haven, Connecticut, Methodist Church. While being "utterly disappointed" in not witnessing the expected fanaticism, he noted that Miller was "one of the most interesting lecturers we have any recollection of ever having heard." "Almost breathless silence . . . reigned throughout the immense throng for two or three hours at a time" as Miller presented his messages.[12]

What, we must ask, was the secret of Miller's appeal, of his preaching power? We have already noted hints of the answer in his sincerity of belief and the solemnity that accompanied his judgment-hour messages. However, at least two more factors should be added to round out the picture.

The first is his use of the Bible in a manner that not only linked prophecy and history but also spoke to the felt needs of his audience. L. D. Fleming, after wondering in print as to the source of Miller's ability to reach especially the male community with such life-changing force, went on to provide an answer. Brother Miller, Fleming penned, "simply takes the sword of the spirit, unsheathed and naked, and lays its sharp edge on the naked heart, and it cuts! that is all. Before the edge of this mighty

weapon[,] Infidelity falls, and Universalism withers. False foundations vanish, and Babel's merchants wonder."[13]

Another aspect of Miller's preaching style that had universal
power and appeal was his logical, rational approach. That point is
highlighted in *The Fountain*. "We have," the editors noted,

> not the least doubt that he [Miller] is fully convinced of the
> truth of the doctrine he labors so diligently to inculcate, and
> he certainly evinces great candor and fairness in . . . proving
> his points. And he proves them, too, to the satisfaction of
> every hearer;—that is, allowing his premises to be correct,
> there is no getting away from his conclusions.[14]

Miller's evaluations of himself largely matched those of both
his friendly and not-so-friendly contemporaries. He was particularly open in his remarks to Truman Hendryx, his closest friend in
the 1830s. When the Low Hampton Baptist Church early in 1833
first talked of giving the fifty-year-old Miller a license to preach,
he wrote to Hendryx for advice on whether he should accept.
After all, Miller mused, he was "too old, too wicked, and too
proud" for the honor. Two months later he was still filling the
Low Hampton pulpit. Again he wrote to Hendryx: "We have no
preacher as yet—except the old *man* with his *concordance*. And he
is so shunned by his cold, dull & lifeless performance, that I have
strong doubts whether he will attempt again—but hush not a
word of what I tell you. Send us a minister if you can."[15]

A year later he penned: "You laugh Bro. Hendryx: to think old
Bro. Miller is preaching. But laugh on, you are not the only one
that laughs, and it is all right, I deserve it." Then Miller goes on
to suggest that he was beginning to take his old-age call to the
ministry ever more seriously. "If I could preach the truth," he
continued to Hendryx, "it is all I could ask. Can you tell me how
old Noah was when he began to preach? And Lot, Moses, etc?"
Earlier he had written, in the context of his weaknesses, that
"God . . . is able to take *worms* and thrash *mountains*."[16]

The thought that God could use him undergirded the positive

side of Miller's self-perception. "I know my own weakness," he wrote to his son, "and I do know that I have neither power of body or mind to do what the Lord is doing by me as an instrument." To Hendryx he wrote in response to his success in the midthirties:

> It astonishes me, and I can only account for it by supposing that God is supporting the *old man*, weak, wicked, imperfect and ignorant as he is, to confound the wise and mighty, and bring to nought things that are. . . . Infidels, Deists, Universalists, Sectarians: All, all are chained to their seats, in perfect silence, for hours, yes days, to hear the *Old Stammering Man*. . . . Oh, my Br., it makes me feel like a worm, a poor feeble creature. For it is God only that could produce such an effect on such audiences. Yet it gives me confidence.[17]

Coupled with his progressively unshakable conviction that God was with him was Miller's growing sense of urgency to warn the world. His burden for those "sleeping over the volcano of God's wrath" pushed him to the limit of his endurance. In a similar vein, he wrote to Joshua Himes that the souls that he had been speaking to "are continually before me, sleeping or waking; I can see them perishing by thousands."[18]

Such thoughts undoubtedly provided Miller with the solemnity that others perceived in his preaching. Beyond solemnity, Miller's sincerity was informed by the certainty of his interpretation of the prophecies and the conviction that God was behind his mission to the world.

But solemnity was not the only element in Miller's approach to his work. There are many examples of his good humor, even in the face of personal criticism. Miller told one such example in the form of a dialogue in which he compares his proclaiming the soon coming of Christ to Noah's warning his neighbors of a flood. The dialogue not only provides a message on the second coming, but it answers some of the criticisms leveled at Miller through the use of a Bible parallel. Miller imagines a conversation between one of Noah's neighbors and a guest who had just arrived at his home.

Guest. What great building is that in yonder field, on that eminence?

Host. That is called "Noah's Ark."

Guest. But what use is he going to put it to? It seems to be built for sailing. Surely the old man does not expect to sail on dry land.

Host. Yes; you are right. The old man says the world is coming to an end (Gen. 6:13), and he has prepared an ark to save himself and family; for all flesh will be destroyed by water, as he says.

Guest. But how does he know this?

Host. He says God told him.

Guest. What kind of a man is he? He must be a great fanatic, I am thinking.

Host. Why, yes; we think he is crazy a little; but you cannot discover it in anything else but his building that great ark, and neglecting his farm and other worldly matters. But what he has lost I have gained.

Guest. A farmer, say you?—a farmer! Why did not God tell some of our "mighty men, which are men of renown"? (Gen. 6:4.) A farmer, too! There is no truth in it. But do any believe him?

Host. Believe him! No. We have other things to attend to, and cannot spend time to hear the old farmer. But we were all very much startled, no longer ago than yesterday; for the old man has been telling some that he had prepared rooms for the beasts of the field, and for the fowls of the air, and every creeping thing; and yesterday they came, two and two of every sort, and entered the ark, apparently of their own accord. (Gen. 7:8, 9.) This, you may be sure, startled us some; but the banquets and feasts of last night have dissipated the fears of all, and to-day things are as they should be.

Guest. It is rather strange; yet it cannot be true. God will not destroy the world in the midst of this hilarity and glee, and in the height of all these improvements at the present day. Much, much of the earth remains yet to be cultivated and inhabited. Our western wilderness is yet to be explored and settled. Then the world is yet in its infancy—not two thousand years old yet; and you know we have a tradition that the earth is to wax old like a garment. It cannot be true, what the old man tells you. I will warrant you the earth will stand many thousand years yet.

Host. Look! look! there goes the old fool and his family now, I dare say, into the ark. I remember me now, the old man told us, four days ago, that, in seven days (Gen. 7:4-10), God would cause it to rain sufficient to destroy every living thing from the face of the earth. I shall have a chance to laugh at the old man four days hence. I told him to his face that, after his seven days were ended, he would be ashamed to preach any more, and we should have some quiet then.[19]

On another occasion, when Miller was under criticism for his beliefs, he told his audience: "They have reported that I was insane, and had been in a mad-house seven years; if they had said a mad world for fifty-seven years, I must have plead guilty to the charge."[20]

Of course, Miller, like other human beings, was capable of emotions other than humor. From time to time he felt himself pushed too far or too hard by his critics and would lash out. Thus he could refer to the clergy as "dumb dogs," "ravening wolves," "Wise-heads," and "wiseacres" who loved the word "reverend" attached to their names. God, he held, would ultimately deal with such "priestly dandies," who had their "consciences cased in corsetts of steel."[21]

Again, Miller in his exasperation once claimed that

our learned critics are worse on the waters of truth than a school of sharks on the fishing-banks of the north, and they have made more infidels in our world than all the heathen mythology in existence. What word in revelation has not been turned, twisted, racked, wrested, distorted, demolished, and annihilated by these voracious harpies in human shape.[22]

Miller felt as he got older that his temper was becoming shorter. Late in 1842 he admitted to Himes: "I find that, as I grow old, I grow more peevish, and cannot bear so much contradiction. Therefore I am uncharitable and severe." Miller wasn't the only one to note the problem. Ten days later an anonymous correspondent counseled him that calling the clergy liars was "not the best way" and that it turned some people from his teaching.[23]

Fortunately, the down side of Miller was not the most prominent. He had a largely positive message that made a significant impact on the Christians of his day.

A Profile of Miller's Message

That message, as we have repeatedly noted above, was that Jesus would return about the year 1843. Contrary to the majority view of his day, Miller preached that Jesus would come *before* the beginning of the millennium. That was the *one* doctrinal distinctive of his movement. He believed that that truth was so important that his followers should not cloud the clarity of their message by emphasizing other doctrinal points. To do so would be to risk creating division in the Adventist ranks. Time was too short for doctrinal divisiveness, for soon Christ would come. That was his message. All other controverted points were sidelines to that one great truth; after all, doctrinal controversy would end with the second advent. It was that *one, all-important* truth that must be preached.

Miller, of course, had developed an extensive scriptural rationale for his belief in the soon coming of Jesus. That rationale was particularly strong in its interpretation of Bible prophecy. Perhaps the best record of his argumentation has been preserved in his *Evidence From Scripture and History of the Second Coming of Christ About the Year 1843*. That book is a transcript of what had by the early 1840s become his standard nineteen prophetic lectures. The purpose of this section is not to explore those prophetic interpretations,[24] but briefly to look at a few aspects of the approach Miller used to get his message across.

The most obvious feature of Miller's preaching and writing was its focus on the Bible. From the time of his conversion until the end of his life, Miller was a Bible student. His emphasis comes through in his advice to Hendryx. "You must," he penned, "preach *Bible*; you must prove all things by *Bible*; you must talk *Bible*; you must exhort *Bible*; you must pray *Bible*, and love *Bible*; and do all in your power to make others love *Bible*, too."[25]

On another occasion he wished Hendryx were with him so they could "sit down and have a good dish of *Bible* together." Miller's entire approach to life and ministry centered upon the transcendent world in which God was truly King. And it was the Bible that contained the transcendent King's revelation to humanity. "If the *Bible* is not true," Miller queried Hendryx, "then who can tell us what is truth?"[26]

Miller not only believed the Bible to be the ultimate authority, but he also held for its assertive use in preaching. Rather than relying upon "anxious seats" or other evangelistic props, Miller utilized the "naked word" in spiritual combat. "Depend, in doing battle for God," he counseled Hendryx,

> wholly on the power of the Spirit. Keep your sword the right side up, the edge to the heart, and your arm well nerved, bring home the blow with an intent to kill, be not afraid of hurting your hearers, wind no silk handkerchiefs around your blade, nor withhold one moiety [part] of power when you make a thrust. Some are in the habit of hiding a part of the sword, for fear the enemy will dodge the blow; but this will never do. The moment your enemy discovers your cowardice or fear, they will despise you. They rouse to action with redouble[d] vigor.[27]

Beyond constant use of the Bible in preaching, Miller hoped to drive other people to a study of the Word. He did not want them to look at him for authority, but to the Word of God. Thus he could write near the end of his career: "I do not ask you to embrace an opinion of mine; but I ask you to weigh well the evidence contained in the Bible." Miller's method was calculated to push people to the Word of God. "If this doctrine," he wrote, "does not make men search the Scriptures . . . , I cannot conceive what would." One of the criteria for his own success was that "thousands have been brought to read their Bibles with more pleasure."[28]

Going hand in hand with Miller's use of the Bible in preaching was his use of history. It seemed obvious to Miller, notes David Dean, that secular history would develop according to the Bible prophecies and that "exact parallels between prediction and fulfillment would be present."[29]

Litch set forth his and Miller's approach to the topic when he wrote: "All we profess to do is to state certain texts of Scripture, 'INFALLIBLE TRUTHS,' and collate with them certain historical facts; and tell the world the impression that collation makes on our minds." Of course, Miller expected people to come to the proper conclusion after viewing the evidence. Those who did not would soon face their Master.[30]

A third central feature of Miller's preaching was the Jesus who was soon to return to gather His people. Jesus was not only the solution to the world's problems but the answer to those of individuals as well. Thus Miller could advise his readers to "go to Christ . . . ; lay hold on the promise of God, trust in his grace, and he will cleanse you by his blood."[31]

That evangelical teaching, however, was shared by most other Christians of the day. As a result, Miller's teachings on salvation were not controversial. Thus these teachings did not receive as much emphasis in either the Millerite or non-Millerite press as his "peculiar doctrine" of the soon return of Christ.

A fourth ever-present characteristic of Miller's preaching was his burden for souls. The souls of those he had preached to, he noted, "are continually before me, sleeping or waking; I can see them perishing by thousands." That constant vision led him to be fervent in both preaching and in appealing to people to accept Jesus as their soon-coming Saviour.[32]

The poignancy of Miller's burden comes through clearly in one of his sermon appeals as he pictured the second coming. "And then, my dear hearer," he urged, if you have had your heart broken off from sin; if you have by faith been united in spirit to the Lamb of God; . . . then you will live and reign with him on the earth. . . . You will rise up in that general assembly, and, clapping your hands with joy, cry, "Holy, holy, holy is the Lord God Almighty, which was, and is, and is *now come*. . . .

But you, O impenitent man or woman! where will you be then? . . . *In hell!* O think! *In* hell!—a dreadful word! Once more think! *In* hell! lifting up your eyes, being in torment. Stop, sinner; think! *In* hell! where shall be weeping, wailing, and gnashing of teeth. Stop, sinner, stop; consider on your latter end.[33]

But it was victory rather than defeat that most often filled Miller's mind as he preached and wrote. We will therefore look at victory as a final element that pervaded his message to the world. That victorious strain is nicely caught in the conclusion to one of his letters as he describes the apocalyptic destruction just preceding Christ's return. "At this dread moment," he penned, "look! look!—Oh! look and see. [W]hat means that ray of light? The clouds have burst asunder, the heavens appear, the great white throne is in sight. Amazement fills the universe with awe. [h]e comes—[h]e comes [B]ehold, the Saviour comes. [L]ift up your heads ye saints, he comes!—he comes!!—he comes!!!"[34]

In spite of Miller's hopes and fears, his sincerity and his convictions, his preaching was greeted with widely varying responses. It is to those responses that we now turn.

A Profile of Miller's Results

A person with a message like that of William Miller had at least two major groups to reach—ministers and lay members. With both groups he had mixed results, but even the majority of those who responded to his preaching positively did so for different reasons in the 1830s than the majority would in the early 1840s.

As we noted earlier, Miller's public work got off to a rather slow start, with his first sermon on the second advent being given in

1831 and his first published statement on the topic appearing in 1832. Both modes of expression brought immediate attention to Miller and inquiry regarding his message.

Outside of an increasing number of preaching appointments and people visiting and writing to him to find out more about his views, the first public recognition for Miller's work came on September 14, 1833, when he was issued a license to preach by his own and a neighboring congregation. Not only, read the certificate, had he been "improving his gifts . . . in expounding the words of Divine Truth . . . in public," but his work had edified the church.[35]

"My brethren," he wrote his sister two days later, "have given me a *license*—unworthy, and old, and disobedient as I am. 'Oh to grace how great a debtor.' " He seemed to be genuinely awed and humbled by the recognition. Unlike his early days when he caricatured the things of God, he now had a reverence for everything connected to Him. Thus Miller refused to use the title of Reverend for himself, although he used it for others if they so desired. He raised the point after Hendryx had addressed his new ministerial colleague as "Rev. William Miller" in a letter early in 1834. "I wish," Miller replied to his friend, "you would look into your Bible and see if you can find the word Rev. applied to a sinful mortal as myself. . . . Let us be determined to live, and die, on the Bible."[36]

The proud "must be brought low" in the face of coming judgment. "What care I for what the world calls great or honorable[?] Give me *Jesus*, and a knowledge of his <u>word</u>," and faith, grace, love, and His righteousness. "Yes, let me have J[esus] C[hrist], and then vanish all earthly toys." Such comments in a private letter indicate that Miller's conversion was no charade; it had led to complete dedication. He had given his life to God and the burden he believed God had laid upon him.[37]

Miller had decided to devote his full time to preaching by the end of 1834. He could no longer fill the number of calls that were coming for his services on a part-time basis.

Working full time at his new vocation was a genuine sacrifice, since he received no wages for his work. In fact, before 1836 he did not even receive any money for traveling expenses. In that year he received $1.00 on a trip to Canada. The next funds he claims to have received came in 1837 to cover stage fare for one of his many preaching appointments. Other than for travel from time to time, Miller received no reimbursement. And even at that, he penned in 1845, "I have never received enough to pay my travelling expenses." It should also be noted that he received no profit from the sale of his books.[38]

If that is so, we might ask, how did he support himself and his family? Miller had two sources of income. The first was from his farm, which he put into the hands of his sons. That arrangement provided for the sustenance of his large family and provided him with an agreed-upon $100 a year to clothe himself, meet his incidental expenses, and pay for his travel. Only after his journeys became too long and numerous for him to cover out of the $100 annuity did he permit the churches he labored for to share in his travel expenses.[39]

Miller's second source of support came from his modest savings. Those also were relied upon to cover his expenses. By early 1843 he claims to have expended $2,000 of his own money in his mission to the world. It should be recognized that $2,000 was no small amount in an age when a laboring man might receive fifty cents or a dollar for a ten-to-fourteen hour day. His sacrificial ministry leaves no doubt that he had given up "earthly toys" for his friendship with Jesus.[40]

The year 1836 saw a major step forward in Miller's ministry with the publication of a greatly enlarged edition of *Evidence From Scripture and History of the Second Coming of Christ.* Then, in June, thirty-eight ministers, all apparently Baptists, signed a certificate vouching that they had heard his lectures. Twenty-one of that number claimed that they could not "avoid the conclusion that the coming of Christ will be as soon as 1843." Another seventeen, while not convinced regarding Miller's teachings, could still recommend his ministry to the churches.[41]

About that same time Miller claimed in a letter to Hendryx

that eight Baptist ministers were "now preaching" his views, while "many others believe but dare not preach it." He gave the name of each, and concluded that his best friend "Hendryx belong[s] to this [latter] camp."[42]

One of the great frustrations of Miller's life was that his dear friend Hendryx could not bring himself to come out in the open and preach what he claimed to believe about the second coming. After wondering out loud in a letter to Hendryx as to why ministers and laypeople did not wake up and trim their lamps, Miller chided his colleague.

> Yes, my br[other,] almost two years since you heard the news, *"Behold the bridegroom cometh."* And yet you cry, A little more sleep, a little more slumber. [B]lame not your people if they go to sleep under your preaching. You have done the same. . . . Are you waiting for all the world to wake up before you dare get up[?] "Where has your courage fled[?]" Awake! awake! O sluggard. . . . You must not, you cannot, you shall not, be a neuter. Awake! Awake!![43]

Miller discovered that "ministers generally are the hardest to be convinced" of his interpretation of the second coming. On the other hand, he noted that "they say 'they can bring no argument but what the *old* man will remove.' " Miller certainly had plenty of exposure to the clergy. Early in 1835 he wrote that "I now have four or five ministers to hear me in every place I lecture."[44]

Those ministers who did confront Miller found a formidable opponent. For example, D. I. Robinson, pastor of the Portsmouth, New Hampshire, Methodist Church, attended a series of Miller's meetings thinking he "could stop his wheels and confound him." But not wanting to publicly embarrass Miller, Robinson visited him in his room with a list of objections. "To my surprise," Robinson recalled, "scarcely any of them were new to him, and he could answer them as fast as I could present them. And then he presented objections and questions which confounded *me*, and the commentaries on which I had relied." Robinson returned home "used up, convicted, humbled, and resolved to examine the question" of the second advent. He eventually became a preacher of the advent near.[45]

Perhaps Miller's first solid ministerial convert was Henry Jones, a Congregationalist Harvard graduate who served as an agent for several journals related to temperance and other reforms. Jones had been stimulated during a conversation on the millennium with another minister in New York in June 1832. The minister had referred Jones to Miller's *Vermont Telegraph* articles that had begun to be published that May. Jones later secured the first eight articles and wrote to Miller that he desired to have an interview with him, even though "most of our Bible men would consider you very visionary or fanatical" if they knew his views. Jones granted that, for all he knew, Miller might be fanatical and "running wild." But he desired an interview anyway.[46]

Through continuing correspondence, Jones came largely into line with Miller's views of prophecy and the second coming, but he never could accept Miller's idea about knowing the approximate date of the advent. Jones would eventually serve as the secretary for the first general conference of Millerites in October 1840. He also authored several books on prophecy and the second coming.[47]

The first minister to fully accept Miller's views, including the 1843 date, was an Elder Fuller. Fuller had also been the first minister to invite Miller to lecture in his church. Beyond that, Fuller was the *only* ministerial convert to all of Miller's prophetic scheme (including the 1843 date) before 1838 to remain faithful to his convictions. All the others, notes Miller, "relapsed and abandoned its advocacy." "The current of public opinion," Litch pointed out in 1844, "was too strong for them to stem it successfully."[48] Miller's ministerial converts after 1838 found more permanence in his belief system. Undoubtedly the increasing crisis rooted in the economic depression that began in 1837 provided believers with external credibility and thus led to stability.

Not all ministers reacted favorably to Miller and his theories. Some, in fact, became downright ugly. One such was the Reverend

T. F. Norris, who penned in the *Olive Branch*: "We hope ministers or churches will not encourage such a madman or deceiver as Miller is. He is probably mad, and ought to be put under the care of Dr. Woodward, at the State Lunatic Hospital. If not a lunatic he is a dangerous man, and his attacks on Christianity are of the most insidious character."[49]

The Boston Universalist's *Trumpet* was equally harsh with Miller, asserting that he "is a weak-minded, vain, and self-confident old man, who has learned some passages of Scripture by heart; but who in our judgment, either dishonestly perverts the sacred writings, or is almost totally ignorant of their true sense."[50]

Alexander Campbell, the leader of one of the fastest growing Christian groups in nineteenth-century America, thought that "the year 1843 will pass along with dreams of felicity." But even though he disagreed with Miller's teachings, Campbell disagreed even more with the way Miller was treated. He suggested that even if Noah, Daniel, or Job had reappeared as Miller and preached the Word of God, "they would have been derided, slandered, misrepresented, and denounced as disturbers of the peace" just as Miller had been by the "troublers of modern Israel in her one hundred and one factions" of modern orthodoxy. After all, the immediate return of the Lord, Campbell held, should be the Christian's greatest anticipatory delight.[51]

The clergy were not Miller's only detractors. Many laypeople were also deeply upset by his work. In 1834, for example, Miller reported that after his first lecture in one town he had received a letter "from some bullies and black guards, 'that if I did not clear out of the state they would put me where the dogs could never find me.' " The letter had ten signatures affixed to it. Miller disregarded the warning and, as he put it, began a work under God's Spirit "which gainsayers could not resist."[52]

Others, dispensing with physical threats, merely ridiculed Miller. The Lowell *Courier*, for example, published the following statement:

Mr. Miller has been holding forth on his narrow-minded

humbug at Trenton to large audiences. . . . This Miller does not appear to be a knave, but simply a fool, or more properly a monomaniac. If the Almighty intended to give due notice of the world's destruction, He would not do it by sending a fat, illiterate old fellow to preach bad grammar and worse sense, down in Jersey![53]

And what was Miller's response to such treatment? "I have heard lions *roar*, and jackasses *bray*, and I am yet alive."[54]

In spite of opposition, the success of William Miller as a preacher was as outstanding as it was surprising to him and others. From his very first sermon, his hearers had experienced conversions. Beyond that, he faced a continuously increasing stream of speaking opportunities in the churches of all the evangelical denominations. By 1835 he could write that "the Lord opens doors faster than I can fill them."[55] The tempo would take a sharp upturn in 1838 as the Panic of 1837 began to erode the confidence of many people in humanistic solutions to the world's problems. Miller reported the meetinghouses crowded to overflowing.

In late 1838 Miller wrote to his son of a meeting he had held in which there was "a great breaking down . . . and much weeping."[56] Such reactions to his preaching seem to be the rule rather than the exception. By the late 1830s, Miller had become an effective revivalist.

Just as important as the fact that Miller brought revivals to communities was the fact that the revivals *continued* after he left. Thus it was in Portland, Maine. Sometime after Miller's departure, the pastor of the church in which Miller held services wrote:

At some of our meetings since Br. Miller left, as many as 250, it has been estimated, have expressed a desire for religion, by coming forward for prayers; and probably between *one* and *two hundred* have professed conversion at our meeting; and now the fire is being kindled through this whole city, and all the adjacent country. A number of rum-sellers have turned their shops into meeting-rooms, and those places that were once devoted to intemperance and revelry, are now devoted to prayer and praise. Others have abandoned the traffic entirely, and are become converted to God. One or two gambling establishments, I am informed, are entirely broken up. *Infidels, Deists, Universalists*, and the most abandoned *profligates*, have been converted; some who had not been to the house of worship for years. Prayer-meetings have been established in every part of the city by the different denominations, or by individuals, and at almost every hour. Being down in the business part of our city, I was conducted into a room over one of the banks, where I found about thirty or forty men, of different denominations, engaged with one accord in prayer, at about eleven o'clock in the daytime! In short, it would be almost impossible to give an adequate idea of the interest now felt in this city. There is nothing like extravagant excitement, but an almost universal solemnity on the minds of all the people. One of the principal booksellers informed me that he had sold more Bibles in *one month*, since Br. Miller came here, than he had in any four months previous.

According to J. V. Himes, similar accounts to the Portland revival "might be given from most of the places where he has given a *full course of lectures*" and where the minister and church were behind him.[57]

The question naturally arises, What were people being converted to? If one examines the remarks above, it will be discovered that for many it was "to God" and to a "desire for religion." It seems reasonable to conclude with most students of Millerism that the bulk of Miller's conversions before 1840 were to Christianity rather than to his peculiar doctrine.

Many pastors who invited him to their churches were undoubtedly more concerned with his evangelistic appeal and success than they were with his millennialism. They invited him because he was effective as a revivalist, could draw a crowd, and added numbers to their churches.[58]

Of course, Miller's millennial emphasis did have its utility. After all, the thought that Christ was coming in the near future undoubtedly forced many a sinner toward repentance. Then again, millennialism itself had a drawing power in that period of American history. It seems that Ruth Doan is correct in suggesting that most Christians in the 1830s were probably more interested in millennialism itself than with any particular form of premillennial or postmillennial thought.[59] That nonchalant attitude toward millennialism would change in the early 1840s as the year-of-the-end crisis approached and the sides hardened their positions.

But meanwhile, the 1830s continued to witness Miller being invited because he could draw a crowd. Thus the Universalist *Trumpet*, which was aggressive toward both mainline evangelicalism and Millerism, was undoubtedly correct when it charged that "certain Societies and clergyman [sic] in different parts of New England have seen fit to make a tool of the old man, for the purpose of getting up excitements, and gaining converts for their churches."[60]

Miller was well aware of the fact that some pastors were using him, and he resented it. "They like to have me preach," he told J. V. Himes in December 1839, "and build up their churches; and there it ends, with most of the ministers, as yet."[61]

Meanwhile, Miller, as perhaps the most successful revivalist of the last phase of the Second Great Awakening, continued to hold forth in the small towns and villages of northern New England. That would radically change with the entrance of Joshua Himes into his life in December 1839.

Chapter 4

ENTER JOSHUA V. HIMES: MISSION ORGANIZER

"The politicians of this age have spent *millions of silver and gold* to elevate a *man*, to the Presidency of these United States! Shall we not pour out our treasures, to give the slumbering church and world, the news of the approach and reign of our Eternal King?"[1]

Such were the words of the man who would transform Millerism from a one-man crusade into a major religious movement. His name was Joshua V. Himes, a man who, inspired by the urgency of Miller's prophetic message, would develop into one of the public-relations geniuses of the first half of the nineteenth century.

Meet J. V. Himes

Joshua Vaughan Himes[2] was born in Wickford, Rhode Island, on May 14, 1805, to the family of a prosperous West India merchant. His father's goal for his eldest child was that he should be educated at Brown University with an aim to entering the ministry of the Episcopal Church. Those plans, however, came to an abrupt halt when dishonest associates brought the family business to ruin.

As a result, Joshua's formal education ended when he was eight. He was later bound as an apprentice to a cabinetmaker, his father having concluded that he would have to be a tradesman. Joshua remained in his New Bedford, Massachusetts, apprenticeship until age twenty-one.

During his stay in New Bedford, he began attending the First Christian Church, a church belonging to a restorationist movement known as the Christian Connexion. It was the aim of the Connexionists to avoid human creeds and to get back to the Bible. The Bible, they held, was their only creed. "When the Bible speaks, we respond; when the Bible is silent, we are silent."

The Connexionists, like other restorationist groups, were in earnest in their desire to get back to the New Testament church. Beyond their emphasis on the Bible, the movement emphasized Christian freedom by avoiding all church organization above the congregational level. In addition, they uplifted Christian character as the only test of fellowship. Their desire was to put the doctrinal controversies of church history behind them as they moved toward the ideal of practical Christianity.[3] It was among the Connexionists that young Himes claimed he "found the open Bible and liberty of thought, and made good use of both."[4]

Himes became a member of New Bedford's First Christian Church in 1823. He soon felt impressed that it was his duty to preach the gospel. As a result, he began holding religious meetings. Revivals followed his labors. Then in 1827 he gave up his secular calling to enter the full-time ministry. Between 1827 and 1830 he raised up churches and served as a revivalist in several areas of Massachusetts. In 1830 he became the pastor of the First Christian Church in Boston, where he remained until 1837.[5]

While at Boston's First Church, Himes gained prominence in the Connexionist movement. In 1833 he served as secretary at their general conference (not an organizational level, but the annual meeting of Connexionist leaders).[6]

Also developing during Himes' years at the First Church were his interests in social reform. In 1835, for example, he initiated the establishment of a manual-labor training school where boys could receive a book education and learn a trade at the same time. Meanwhile, their work would pay the costs involved.[7]

Boston during the 1830s was becoming the reform center for nearly every radical movement in the United States as men and women strove to end injustice and to bring in the millennium. Himes was progressively drawn into the realm of the radical reformers in the 1830s. Not only was he involved in the educational, temperance, women's rights, world peace, and health reform movements, but he was one of the founders of the New England Non-Resistance Society and a member of its executive committee.[8]

But central to Himes' radicalism in the 1830s was his participation in the abolitionist movement during the period when abolitionism was feared and despised even in the northern states. For the radical abolitionists surrounding William Lloyd Garrison, the end of slavery was the central element in bringing about the millennium. "Their logic," suggests Lewis Perry, "unfolded categorically: to end slavery was to end all coercion; to end all coercion was to release the millennial power of God; to end coercion, again, was to secure peace and order on earth; to secure peace was, of course, to realize the millennium."[9]

Not only did Himes participate in the founding of the Massachusetts Anti-Slavery Society, but he had also figured prominently in Garrison's earlier New England Anti-Slavery Society. Beyond that, his wife was a member of the Boston Female Anti-Slavery Society and served as one of its directors.[10]

A perpetual activist, Himes did not sit on the sidelines in the struggles of the day. As one writer put it regarding the opposition to the anti-slavery movement, Himes "made speeches upon every occasion, facing mobs, defying them to do their worst and pouring hot shot into their ranks in his peculiar and emphatic style of denunciation of the nation's disgrace and burning shame."[11]

Garrison himself remarked of Himes:

At a very early period, he avowed himself an abolitionist, and has been a faithful supporter of the anti-slavery movement, never ashamed to show his colors, never faltering in the darkest hour of its history. He is a remarkably active and zealous man in whatever he undertakes, doing with all his might whatsoever his hands find to do.[12]

Himes' heavy involvement in radical reform eventually led to reactions among the membership of Boston's First Christian Church, with the more conservative members desiring his resignation. In the words of Garrison, "Our friend Himes is to leave his people, and go elsewhere, owing to his abolition sentiments." But "he is determined to cling to the truth, and to preach it. . . . He is a lovely man, and has a mind of his own, and a soul to feel and act. We shall feel his loss in this city."[13]

But Himes didn't leave Boston. The unrest eventuated in the progressive members withdrawing to form the Second Christian Church in 1837. They requested Himes to be their pastor.[14]

The next year, Himes' new congregation built the Chardon Street Chapel. Under Himes' leadership, the chapel would become the site of some of the nation's most radical reform conventions. As Whitney Cross put it, Himes "made his congregation the virtual center in New England of every variety of enthusiastic reform."[15]

Himes' participation in the reform movements had been an important part of his education. He had both seen and participated in methods for spreading knowledge and promoting action. Beyond that education, his natural abilities set him up for a leadership role in what he came to view as the ultimate cause.

Himes Meets Miller

The publication of the expanded version of Miller's lectures in 1836 opened what Josiah Litch has referred to as a "new era" in the history of the advent cause. From that time on, the lectures could preach their silent message where their author had never been. Before 1838 Millerism had not attracted much attention in Massachusetts. But copies of Miller's *Evidence From Scripture and History* gradually spread abroad, eventually coming to the attention of the editor of the *Boston Times* in early 1838.[16]

On March 13 an editorial announced that the *Times* intended to reprint extended excerpts from Miller's book. The book, penned the editor,

> is destined . . . to create a tremendous excitement in the Christian world. Indeed, this excitement is already beginning to be felt. We have just read the principal part of the work; and although we are not prepared to sanction it as containing incontrovertible truth either in its facts or inferences, yet we must say that it shows a depth of research into the prophetic portion of the Scriptures, and a boldness of conception, which we have not met with in any other work on the prophecies.

The editorial went on to give a brief synopsis of Miller's views, including the conclusion that Christ would come "only *five years from the present!*" "We know of nothing at the present time calculated to excite more deep and universal interest."[17] The next two weeks saw nine extracts appearing under the heading "END OF THE WORLD!"

Within the following year, Miller began to receive his first invitations to preach in Massachusetts. Between April 21 and June 10, 1839, he lectured at Stoughton, East Randolph, Lowell, Groton, and Lynn.[18]

One of the pastors Miller lectured for was Timothy Cole, who was so embarrassed (as we saw in chapter 3) by Miller's unimpressive appearance that he at first refused to sit on the platform with the evangelist. By the end of the ten-day revival, however, Cole had concluded that "if I have ever seen a man, that I believe is a true servant of God sent by the Holy Spirit to proclaim the Gospel of Christ, I consider William Miller the man."[19]

The Lowell meetings in Cole's church were crucial in the history of the advent movement for at least two reasons. First, it was there that Miller met Methodist pastor Josiah Litch, who had already accepted his views. (Litch, as we will see in chapter 5, would become one of the foremost Millerite leaders.) Second, and even more important, Cole introduced Miller to many of the pastors and churches of the Christian Connexion.[20]

Those introductions brought Miller back to Exeter, Massachusetts, in November 1839 for another series of meetings—this time with almost twenty Connexionist ministers present. One of those ministers, Joshua V. Himes, would change the nature of Miller's career.[21]

Himes, who had extended an invitation to Miller in October, took the opportunity at Exeter to renew his offer. As a result, Miller agreed to lecture for the first time in Boston. That was quite a challenge for the aging revivalist, who had spent his entire preaching career up to then in the small towns and villages of northern New England. Miller commenced his first course of lectures in Boston's Chardon Street Chapel on December 8.[22]

During the meetings, Himes and Miller had several long conversations. "When Mr. Miller had closed his lectures," Himes noted, "I found myself in a new position." He could no longer preach as he had previously. He then asked Miller, " 'Do you really believe this doctrine?' "

> He replied, "Certainly I do, or I would not preach it."
>
> "What are you doing to spread or diffuse it through the world?"
>
> "I have done, and am still doing, all I can."
>
> "Well, the whole thing is kept in a corner yet. There is but little knowledge on the subject, after all you have done. If Christ is to come in a few years, as you believe, no time should be lost in giving the church and world warning, in thunder-tones, to arouse them to prepare."
>
> "I know it, I know it, Bro. Himes," said he; "but what can an old farmer do? I was never used to public speaking: I stand quite alone; and, though I have labored much, and seen many converted to God and the truth, yet *no one*, as yet, seems to enter into the *object* and *spirit of my mission*, so as to render me much aid. They like to have me preach, and build up their churches; and there it ends, with most of the ministers, as yet. I have been looking for help,—I want help."

It was at this time that I laid myself, family, society, reputation, all upon the altar of God, to help him, to the extent of my power, to the end. I then inquired of him what parts of the country he had visited, and whether he had visited any of our principal cities.

He informed me of his labors. . . .

"But why," I said, "have you not been into the large cities?"

He replied that his rule was to visit those places where invited, and that he had not been invited into any of the large cities.

"Well," said I, "will you go with me where doors are opened?"

"Yes, I am ready to go anywhere, and labor to the extent of my ability to the end."

I then told him he might prepare for the campaign; for doors should be opened in every city in the Union, and the warning should go to the ends of the earth! Here I began to "help" Father Miller.[23]

Millerism would never be the same after that conversation.

In spite of Himes' affirmation of Miller, he was still not completely behind him. Part of the problem was that he was "not fully satisfied respecting the time" of the advent, even though he was convinced as to its nearness. Miller returned to the Chardon Street Chapel for a second course of lectures between December 28 and January 5.[24]

Mid-January 1840 still found Himes in a state of quandary over throwing his influence fully behind the older man. On the seventeenth he wrote to Miller: "I shall speak again soon—but mean to know what I say and know whereof I affirm. *I am coming on—and when I come—look out—all my soul will be in it.*"[25] And Himes did come on strong for Miller, even though he apparently never accepted the 1843 time until the summer of 1842.[26]

The main way that Himes began to " 'help' Father Miller" was through publications. The first of the multitude of advent publications initiated by Himes originated in conversations between

Miller and Himes during Miller's third Boston series, held at the Marlboro Chapel—another center of reform radicalism—from February 8 to 29, 1840.[27]

For a long time, Miller had desired a periodical to set forth his views, since the existing papers had been filled with "abusive stories" respecting his labors but had refused to publish his defenses. The problem with the idea, noted Miller, was that he had not been able to find a man willing "to run the risk of his reputation and the pecuniary expense, in such a publication."[28]

Himes saw the need, responded to it, and, in Miller's words, "without a subscriber or any promise of assistance" began to issue the *Signs of the Times* in March 1840. Even though the first issue is dated March 20, internal indicators suggest that it was being circulated in late February or early in the first week of March. Thus when Miller claims that Himes had the first issue out one week after agreeing to the idea, he is probably correct. When Himes got behind a project, he certainly did put all his soul into it.[29]

Himes' biographer notes that his motto became "*what we do must be done quickly.*" That phrase is found over and over in his writings and informed the actions of a man quite convinced that the end of the world would be upon its unsuspecting inhabitants in a few short years.[30]

In Millerism, Himes found the ultimate cause, the cause that made all other reforms appear insignificant in comparison. After all, when Christ returned to set up His kingdom, all earthly evil would come to an end. In that sense, Adventism was the reform of reforms. The second coming of Christ would be the complete and final solution to all earthly problems.

On the other hand, after accepting Adventism, Himes did not immediately give up his activity in what had become lesser causes for him. Between 1840 and 1842 the Chardon Street Chapel would continue to be a leading reform center, and Himes continued to participate in many reform activities, even though ever more of his energies were channeled into promoting his belief in the nearness of the second advent. He had given up hope that the reforms would cure all of society's ills. But the impossibility of full victory, Himes held, should not be used as an excuse for inaction. He was driven on in reform by Christ's words to His followers—"Occupy till I come."[31]

After mid-1842, however, when Himes had accepted 1843 as the year of the end of the world, his reform activity dropped off almost to nothing. After all, he had only a few short months left to spread the message of the coming Christ. That cessation of activity on Himes' part did not mean that he had lost sympathy with reforms. Even as late as January 1844, he still opened his "Miller Tabernacle" for Garrison's antislavery meetings.[32]

Garrison, meanwhile, became a bit discouraged with his friend's apostasy to Millerism. "I am sorry that he has become the victim of an absurd theory," Garrison penned, "but I still regard him as a sincere and worthy man."[33]

Himes would certainly prove his worthiness in the years to come. He and Miller formed what can best be thought of as a symbiotic team, with each complementing the other's weaknesses with his own strengths. Miller was a convincing preacher but a poor promoter. Himes, on the other hand, was an excellent promoter, but, from what we know of him, only average in the pulpit. Himes was a man of action, while Miller was more of a thinker and theologian. Thus Himes generally deferred to Miller in matters relating to the message to be preached, and Miller to Himes on evangelistic and promotional strategy.

Himes was just what Miller needed to organize and promote his ideas. Thus Himes became the commander of the cause, even to the extent of manipulating Father Miller from time to time—for the "good of the cause," of course. In short, Himes provided the necessary organization and structure to transform Millerism from a one-man show into a genuine social movement; he transformed a doctrine into a cause. Without Himes, Miller might well have remained simply another obscure preacher predicting the end of the world in the byways of northern New England.[34]

Along that line, it should be remembered that in 1840, when Miller began preaching in the nation's large cities, he was fifty-eight years old, afflicted by palsy, and would suffer from various and prolonged illnesses till the end of his life. He needed the energy, industry, know-how, and endless perseverance of Himes, who was not quite thirty-five when he "began to 'help' Father Miller." The helper became the dominating figure in the day-to-day operations of Millerism in early 1840.

With Himes, Millerism no longer passively waited for doors to open. Rather, Himes aggressively pushed them open for the sake of the message. Lecture tours were arranged, and avant-garde public-relations techniques spread the influence of Miller far beyond the bounds of even his most optimistic dreams.

Miller's work also changed its tone under Himes' efforts. David Arthur has pointed out that "Miller was no longer simply a pleasant but moderately effective revivalist, saving sinners and building up churches. He and his movement became independent forces" that were progressively more "capable of disrupting and dividing the churches. With Himes leading the way, Millerism became increasingly self-conscious—a major religious movement with which the churches would have to reckon."[35]

By the summer of 1840, Himes' leadership was being felt. He had already seen to it that Miller had given a lecture series in New York City in May. Beyond that, Himes' public-relations skills were in the process of highlighting and sharpening Miller's millennial concepts in a manner that would not only give them visibility but would also cause their spread to accelerate with ever-increasing speed up through the time of the expected end of the world. It was the progressive clarity of that millennial vision that would push the Millerite message to the far corners of the republic and around the world. Himes, Miller, and their colleagues were increasingly driven to warn the world as their sense of prophetic mission and its urgency became clearer to them. Without that sense of mission and urgency, Millerism would have gradually withered away.

"The Napoleon of the Press"

Himes developed into one of the public-relations geniuses of the 1840s, earning from one of his detractors the title "Napoleon of the press." Nathan Hatch, a leading historian of American religion, has described Himes' publishing efforts as "an unprecedented media blitz" and "an unprecedented communications crusade."[36]

The young preacher was at the cutting edge of communications technology. Mass publication and distribution of reading material were just coming into their own in the 1830s and 1840s. It was not until 1822 that the first steam-power cylinder press had gone into operation in the United States, and the great New York daily newspapers did not arise until the 1830s. As of 1833 the largest newspaper print run in the country was the New York *Courier and Enquirer's* forty-five hundred. Advances in printing technology, however, soon made the penny daily a success.[37]

As the 1830s turned into the 1840s, there was a massive increase in the number of newspapers, the magnitude of their circulation, and the size of the reading public. The reformers and religious leaders of the day adopted the new technologies for their own purposes. One ecstatic clergyman noted in 1839 that "a well conducted religious periodical is like a thousand preachers, flying in almost as many directions, by means of horses, mailstages, steam boats, rail road cars, ships, etc., etc., offering life and salvation to the sons of men in almost every clime."[38]

Himes was well placed to ride the crest of the publication explosion. He had learned the basic techniques of journalism through his work in the great reforms of the day and through the use of the religious press in the Second Great Awakening.

Himes' first significant task in establishing an Adventist periodical literature, as we noted above, was the creation of the *Signs of the Times* in February and March 1840. For the first two years, the *Signs* was issued twice per month, but in April 1842 it became a weekly.[39]

During the first year, the *Signs* published articles both for and against the Millerite position. Thus it provided a sort of open forum on the topic. But as time went on, the paper exhibited less and less anti-Millerite theology, except to refute it.

By early 1842 Himes viewed the *Signs* as an instrument for developing Adventist self-consciousness and community. It was his desire to make the "paper a Second Advent Family Newspaper, that shall not be behind the best religious periodicals of the day." The sense of community and cooperation he hoped to achieve through the *Signs* was essential to the success of the Millerite mission.[40]

Himes was not backward in spreading the *Signs*. Following the lead of the reform associations and other religious groups, he used agents to extend his subscription list. These agents generally represented several organizations and publications simultaneously. They traveled from place to place selling subscriptions. During its first year, agents handling the *Signs* received a commission of from seventeen to forty cents per subscription. In 1841 readers were invited to become agents, and a 20 percent commission was offered.[41]

Himes' aggressive subscription policy paid off. The list of subscribers grew from none in March 1840, to eight hundred by July 15, to one thousand by October 1, and to fifteen hundred by the end of the year. By January 15, 1842, he claimed five thousand subscribers and fifty thousand readers.[42]

The increased publicity was beginning to create a stir. Thus the *Princeton Review* for January 1841 could report that the second advent was attracting increasing attention in the American churches, with "probably ten times as many students of the prophecies concerning this event, as there were ten years ago." Meanwhile, the publicity was bringing Miller an increasing number of invitations to lecture. Miller wrote to Himes in the late summer of 1840, indicating that he had "more business on hand than two men like me could perform."[43]

It was soon discovered that Miller's message took hold better in rural areas than it did in the cities. The problem was not a dearth of interest in the cities but rather the lack of a network of support institutions to keep the interest alive after the lectures were over. City dwellers faced a richness of options and distractions seldom available in rural areas. And since converts to Millerism from 1840 through 1842 generally remained in their original churches, they often lacked a support group of like-minded Adventists. As a result, it was hard to keep their advent faith alive. Another problem in the cities was the issue of publicizing the meetings in a decentralized community.

To overcome both of those problems, Himes initiated the practice of founding temporary periodicals in connection with selected Millerite revivals. Many of these papers were published for a few weeks or months and then discontinued. Such a program allowed the Adventist periodicals to add local color. After ceasing publication, efforts were made to merge the temporary subscription list with that of more permanently established periodicals, thereby linking the new believers to the larger movement.

The first and most successful of these "temporary" papers was established in New York City to support the effort in that city and to present the main Millerite arguments to the public in "a cheap and popular form." It was called *The Midnight Cry* and was edited by Himes, with Nathanial Southard as his associate. The first issue is dated November 17, 1842. The original intention was to publish only twenty-four issues on a daily basis. Ten thousand copies of each number were distributed, most of them gratuitously. Thus in a little over four weeks, some 240,000 copies of the *Cry* were released. Part of the publicity campaign was to send copies to every minister in the state.[44]

The expenses of this innovative program were great, but Himes believed the sacrifice to be worth the cost. After all, he penned in the first issue,

> OUR WORK - is one of unutterable magnitude. It is a mission and an enterprise, unlike, in some respects, anything that has ever awakened the energies of man. . . . It is an *alarm*, and a CRY, uttered by those who, from among all Protestant sects, as Watchmen standing upon the walls of the moral world, believe the WORLD'S CRISIS IS COME.[45]

The success of the *Midnight Cry* was so great that it was decided to extend its life as a weekly after the first volume of twenty-four issues had been distributed. The first five months of publication saw over half a million copies circulated. The *Cry* would come to rank with the *Signs* as one of the two most important Millerite papers.

After the success of the New York paper, Himes and his colleagues made it a practice to run a local paper for a few weeks in selected vantage points where the paper could extend a revival's benefits into the surrounding countryside. While many of these papers ceased publication after a short time, some became major voices for Adventism in their regions. Falling into the latter category were Josiah Litch's *Trumpet of Alarm* in Philadelphia, Charles Fitch's *Second Advent of Christ* in Cleveland, R. Hutchinson's *Voice of Elijah* in Montreal, and George Storrs and Enoch Jacobs' *Western Midnight Cry* in Cincinnati. Himes' influence and often his money stood behind these periodicals. Through these and other publications, thousands accepted the Millerite message who never heard a living preacher.

In addition to its standard periodicals in North America, the Millerite movement also spawned a paper geared especially for women, *The Advent Message to the Daughters of Zion*, and a scholarly quarterly, the *Advent Shield*. The first was edited by Clorinda S. Minor and Emily C. Clemons and the second by Himes, Sylvester Bliss, and Apollos Hale. Great Britain also saw its own *Midnight Cry* and a journal entitled the *Second Advent Harbinger*. All in all, the Millerite movement spawned over forty periodicals before October 1844.

But periodicals were only a part of the Himes-inspired publication blitz. Another element in Himes' crusade was the Second Advent Library, which eventually included nearly fifty volumes, running from a few pages to over two hundred each. This series, published by Himes, covered the full gambit of Millerite teaching on the second advent and prophetic interpretation.

Another brainchild of the ever-active Himes was the Words of Warning series. Each of these inexpensive tracts consisted of a single 5 x 8 inch sheet printed on both sides. The series contained thirty-six titles.

The aim of the series as a whole was to expound upon the Adventist understanding of prophecy and to bring sinners to repentance. Some of the titles with the latter goal are "How Awful to Meet Our Angry God" and "That Day Will Be a Day of Separation." These little sheets, the least-expensive Millerite literature, were circulated by the hundreds of thousands.[46]

Of course, the major Millerite publications were supplemented by independently published books and tracts. Nor was English the only language of concern. Some works were translated into French and German.[47]

Himes also compiled and published an Adventist songbook in 1842 entitled *Millennial Harp, or Second Advent Hymns: Designed for Meetings on the Second Coming of Christ.* Now the Millerites had their own hymnals from which to sing such verses as

> How long, O Lord our Savior,
> Wilt thou remain away?
> Our hearts are growing weary
> Of thy so long delay.[48]

Wanting to use every possible avenue of outreach, the Millerites, under Himes' creative guidance, even went so far as to develop seals for fastening letters. The seals were sold in sheets like stamps and were used to seal letters shut. Each bore a Scripture passage related to the nearness of Christ's return.[49]

Beyond their own productions, the Adventists used the daily newspapers to present their message through the publication of announcements, sermons, and news items. Some of the newspaper space was free, but some of it had to be purchased.

It should be pointed out that Himes' public-relations tactics did not originate with him. Rather, they were standard techniques of the various reform movements of the day. Himes was a man of his times. The main difference between him and his contemporaries was not in kind but in intensity. What Himes did, he did with more enthusiasm and perseverance than most. After all, as he saw it, he was rapidly approaching the end of a time line. The end of the world was coming, and he needed to get the message out.

Himes' intensity in publication was matched by his exuberance in the distribution of those publications. Beyond the timeworn circulation methods, he and his colleagues used several others that had been developed by the contemporary reform movements.

One was the establishment of Second Advent Libraries in every town or village. These lending libraries were "free for all who will take, read, and return the books." Such a library could be set up at a cost of five or ten dollars for the literature. The plan was to make Adventist literature available so that none "need be in darkness on the doctrine" of the soon coming of Christ. By 1844 these lending libraries dotted the northern states.[50]

Another method of distribution was to bundle up Adventist literature and send it to postmasters all over the country. Each bundle contained instructions for the postmaster to distribute the literature to those calling for their mail.[51]

The postmaster from Canton, Ohio, was delighted with this approach. He wrote to Himes on May 12, 1843, describing the impact the literature made.

> The papers which you forwarded, viz., "The Midnight Cry" and "The Trumpet of Alarm," came to hand last evening. In half an hour from the time of their arrival at this office, they were distributed in every part of this town. A general rush was made to the office to obtain the papers. Many country people, who were in town, as soon as they learned that papers could be had, came and received. I was forced to discontinue giving to the town's people any more of the papers, having reserved half a dozen copies to send into the country. Some came to the office and begged for a copy only to read, if I would not let them have it by paying postage. I could not, of course, refuse, and by this means I gave out all I had, except a few copies, as before stated. Can you not send me another such roll of papers? You have no idea of

the good which is accomplished by these papers. Many persons that would not receive the glad tidings of the near approach of our Saviour by other means are thus put in possession of the facts.[52]

Closely related to sending bundles of literature to postmasters in the United States was the sending of literature on ships leaving for various world destinations. The ships' officers were requested to drop bundles off at their ports of call. Protestant missionary outposts were especially targeted.[53]

Josiah Litch, in expounding on the implications of Matthew 24:14 ("This gospel of the kingdom shall be preached in all the world for a witness to all nations; and then shall the end come"), noted that

> within the last few years, there has been a continuous effort by the believers in the speedy coming of the Lord, to send light on this subject to the whole world. And so far as the opportunity has offered, publications have been sent to every English and American Mission in the world. These publications have gone to the various parts of the four quarters of the earth and various islands of the sea.[54]

On another occasion, Litch claimed that "Advent publications have been sent by the hundred thousand broadcast all over the world." As a result, "the sailors who come into port testify that the coming of Christ is a subject of conversation all over the world."[55]

As "the Napoleon of the press," Himes had done all in his power to spread the prophetic message that Christ was soon to come in the clouds of heaven. By November 1843 Litch could claim that more than four million pieces of Adventist literature had been issued. By May 1844 that estimate had jumped to five million—nearly one for every four men, women, and children in the United States. That production did not end with the October disappointment of 1844. Isaac Wellcome estimates that by 1854

Himes had been responsible for distributing over ten million pieces of literature from the Boston office alone.[56]

Truly Himes had lived up to his Napoleonic image. Miller, in evaluating Himes in 1845, claimed that he "has been more instrumental in the spread of these views than any other ten men who have embarked in the cause."[57]

Organizational Strategist

Beyond publications, a second major contribution of Himes to the spread and stability of Millerite Adventism was the holding of regular general conference meetings. On August 15, 1840, he announced in the *Signs* that several friends had suggested the advisability of holding a general conference of believers in the second advent for the edification of the believers and for the "full and free discussion" of topics related to the second advent. The next month a call was issued for a general conference to be held in Himes' Chardon Street Chapel in mid-October.[58]

The concept of general conferences was undoubtedly inspired by the growing influence of Himes and other Christian Connexionists in the Millerite movement. The Connexion had been holding such meetings since 1816 to provide some structure and unity to their essentially congregationalist movement.[59] The Connexionist general conferences should not be confused with a permanent denominational structure. Rather, they were periodic meetings of like-minded believers and had no denominational authority outside of passing resolutions for the consideration of the believers.

Thus periodicals and general meetings were the only organizational structure that the Connexionists had to hold them together. Under Himes' leadership those same two elements would form the only structure of Millerite Adventism. Of course, unlike the Christian Connexion, Millerite believers remained in the denomination they belonged to before coming to believe in the advent near. That is, they had no intention of forming a new denomination.

It is difficult to overestimate the importance of the general conferences to the spread of Millerism. The conferences put leaders in contact with one another, provided forums for developing strategies and coordinating the efforts of the rapidly growing number of believers and preachers, and gave opportunity for mutual inspiration and encouragement. Between October 1840 and June 1842 the general conferences stood at the center of the Adventist work.

The first "General Conference of Christians Expecting the Advent of the Lord Jesus Christ" took place in Boston on October 14 and 15, 1840. The conference organizers went out of their way to reassure both participants and onlookers that they were not attempting to organize a new religious body.

At ten o'clock on the first morning of the meeting, Himes read the opening remarks. "The object of the conference," he pointed out,

> will not be to form a new organization in the faith of Christ; nor to assail others of our brethren who differ from us in regard to the period and manner of the advent; but to discuss the whole subject faithfully and fairly, in the exercise of that spirit of Christ in which it will be safe immediately to meet him at the judgment seat.

By so doing, he went on, they could accomplish much for the rapid "spread of 'the everlasting gospel of the kingdom at hand,' that the way of the Lord may be speedily prepared, *whatever may be the precise period of his coming*."[60]

It is important to note that the very wording of the conference's call to order indicates that the common belief holding the Adventists together at this point in their development was that the advent was near, rather than any consensus on 1843, 1844, or any other date. In fact, neither Dr. Henry Dana Ward (a prominent Episcopal clergyman) nor Henry Jones (a Congregational pastor) —chair-person and secretary, respectively, of the first general conference—accepted Miller's conclusion on the time of the advent. In other words, they did not accept 1843 or any other date.

Like many others, they were drawn to Adventism because of their belief in the nearness of Christ's premillennial return.

But while the conference organizers did not expect unanimity of opinion, they did feel that a large degree of harmony was necessary if anything of value was to be achieved. The organizers, therefore, set forth rules for "active" participants. None could take part in the discussions "except he confess his faith in the near approach of our Lord in his kingdom." Also, no one could enter the discussion "until he has been introduced to the committee of arrangements and has made known to them the part or point which he is prepared to discuss." Long experience with such conferences in other movements had taught the organizers that social control was a crucial element in the success of such meetings. Without that control, enemies of the cause could easily usurp the agenda. As Himes put it, "We do not want a fanatical rabble and an ignorant set of persons to take up the time of debate . . . ; and hence something must be done to prevent it—for all these elements will be there."[61]

Chairman Ward delivered the conference's first major address. He pointed out that their view on "the near coming of our Lord in his kingdom" was not a new doctrine. Rather, "sound Christians in every age have cherished it; it was the universal faith of the primitive church; it is the plain doctrine of the New Testament." It only seemed new to most people because of the almost-universal falling away from biblical faith during the great apostasy. The object of the conference, Ward held, in line with the restorationist emphasis of the times, was "to revive and restore this ancient faith, to renew the ancient landmarks."[62]

Other major speakers at the first general conference were Henry Jones and Josiah Litch. Miller had been scheduled to speak but was prevented from gratifying that desire by a "severe attack of typhoid fever." His absence was a disappointment to the nearly two hundred conferees and to Miller himself. For the first time in nearly a decade of preaching, he would have had an opportunity to meet with the leaders of his growing movement.[63]

Miller dictated a few lines to the attendees on October 15 in which he at one point questioned God's providence. "Am I never to have *my will?*" he queried. "No, never, until my will shall harmonize with thine, O Father!" He then went on to count his blessings and affirm his faith. "I have a hope," he declared, "—yes, yes, 'a blessed hope,'—founded on that Word that never fails. My hope is in Him who will soon come, and will not tarry. I love the thought; it makes my bed in sickness; I hope it will in death. I wait for [H]im." Miller's presentations on the "Chronology of Prophecy" and the "Judgment" were read to the conference by Himes.[64]

Besides devotional exercises, lectures, and discussions, the first general conference sponsored business sessions. Some of the most important actions were the endorsement of the *Signs of the Times*, the recommending of the paper to all believers, the appointment of a committee of correspondence charged with corresponding with believers both in North America and abroad, and the designation of a committee to oversee the movement's publications. Himes, of course, was selected as chair of the latter committee.[65]

Of special importance was an action to call "another General Conference, as soon, and at such place" as deemed expedient. It was also voted to have Himes publish the nearly two-hundred-page report of the conference, which was later widely circulated to clergymen, theological seminaries, prominent laypeople, and even foreign missionaries. Three thousand copies of the document had been published by November 1, and ten thousand copies of the entire document were distributed "in a short time," besides innumerable bits and pieces of the report that were printed and circulated separately.[66]

The first general conference, while disclaiming any desire to create a separate religious body, was a giant step forward in the development of the Adventists into an identifiable group on the frontier of American religion. That distinct identity would become more focused during the next four years.

The second general conference would take the Millerite Adventists another step toward separate identity. Held in Lowell,

Massachusetts, from June 15 through 17, 1841, it had an explicitly missiological thrust. "The same untiring love" that activated Christ's earthly ministry, the conference circular read, "will fire our bosoms, and prompt us to put forth all our energies to snatch perishing men as brands out of the burning." After all, "what truth [is] more powerful to awaken the slumbering, dying sinner, than that we must all *soon* stand before the judgment seat of Christ?"[67]

The second conference established a nine-point program of aggressive evangelism as Millerite Adventism moved toward the year of the end of the world. The points included: (1) "personal consecration to God," (2) "personal conversation with others on religion, and especially on the near coming of our Lord," (3) "the formation of Bible classes for the mutual study of this great question," (4) the establishment of "social meetings for prayer and exhortation" for like-minded believers, (5) "the practice of questioning your ministers on the subject" of the advent, (6) the circulation of books on the topic, (7) advice to remain with their former congregations whenever possible to do so, (8) advice to be patient in the face of scorn and opposition, and (9) "the establishment of Second Advent Libraries" in as many communities as possible.[68]

As we read these nine points, three ideas regarding Millerism begin to form. First, that the Millerites were self-consciously becoming more aggressive in both their communities and their congregations. Second, that such activity was meeting resistance to the point where many were tempted to withdraw from their denominational fellowship. Third, that the conference was even encouraging some separatism by its call for social meetings of advent believers "for prayer and exhortation." In spite of itself, Millerite Adventism was slowly but progressively taking on the shape of a distinct religious movement.

The chairperson of the second general conference was D. I. Robinson. One of his assistants was an ex–sea captain by the name of Joseph Bates.[69] Once again Miller was too ill to attend. He would, to his dismay, be confined to his home all summer.

Soon after the second conference, Josiah Litch was hired as a full-time general agent to sponsor the circulation of Millerite literature and to lecture on the topic. That was another step in giving substance and stability to the movement.[70]

The third general conference was held in October 1841 in Portland, Maine. From that time forward, the conferences were held with greater frequency. Miller was not able to attend until the fifth general conference. In order to ensure his attendance, the leaders held the fifth conference in his home community of Low Hampton in November 1841.

All told, more than a dozen general conferences were held. Of special import was the one convened in Boston in May 1842. That conference, under the chairmanship of Joseph Bates, took three advance steps that would change the very nature of Millerite Adventism. The first was to come out solidly for 1843 as the year of the end of the world. The conference leaders believed it was imperative to take a strong stand on the date "because of the stupidity of the Church on the subject and the shortness of the time we have to work."

Second, the conference decided to hold camp meetings in various localities, since other religious groups had used them successfully. The delegates believed they would be "criminally negligent" not to utilize camp meetings for spreading the midnight cry that the bridegroom was coming in 1843. The third major event of the May 1842 meeting was the presentation by Charles Fitch and Apollos Hale of an 1843 prophetic chart, which graphically portrayed the prophecies of Daniel and Revelation and provided several ways of calculating the year of the end as 1843. (A copy of the chart can be found in the photograph section of this book.) All three of the major decisions taken at the May 1842 conference will be more fully treated in chapters 5 and 6.[71]

In addition to the general conferences, the Millerite Adventists sponsored some 120 local conferences. The local conferences appear to have been less business oriented and more evangelistic than the general conferences, but most students of the topic sense a blurring between the two. Himes' biographer concluded that "the final designation" between the two "usually rested with Himes and the *Signs of the Times*, and it is not entirely facetious to suggest that he often judged this designation by his own presence or lack of it!"[72]

That last remark points to the suggestion that Himes tended to see himself as being at the center of the Millerite universe. While that disease is well-nigh universal among human beings, in people of great talent, such as Himes, it is often magnified. Because of his choleric personality, Himes found it all too easy to try to control everything around him—including Miller. Beyond that, he could be severe to his opponents, and, as his biographer points out, he enjoyed both his extensive power and influence and desired to have neither diminished. Even though the unsavory parts of his character seem to be greatly outweighed by the good, Himes still came in for his share of criticism—much of it unjust.[73]

Himes Under Criticism

Some of the criticism surrounding Himes centered on his having made "a tool of the old man" for his own good. "Joshua," accused the Universalist's *Trumpet*, "is very much in need of converts; and he is in hopes to get a good batch out of Miller's oven. We are afraid some of them will not be more than half baked."[74]

Of course, it is to be expected that those who saw no light in Miller's interpretation of the Bible prophecies would not be able to credit his foremost publicist with either much common sense or integrity. Thus the Methodist *Olive Branch* could claim that "Elder Himes is a man with a mind in a nut shell, extremely weak in every point of light. . . . To a sane man he must be an object of pity. He is fat as an Alderman and lives like a Prince."[75]

That last sentence brings us to the most frequent of the allegations made against Himes and his colleagues in leadership—that of milking their Millerite followers financially. Or, as the *Olive Branch* put it, of playing the role of "vampyres" in sucking the "life-blood" out of "those whom they dupe."[76]

Himes' leadership in the Millerite publishing empire left him especially vulnerable to the charge of enriching himself at the expense of the people. That point is nicely illustrated by a broadside (or poster) of about two by three feet entitled "GRAND ASCENSION OF THE MILLER TABERNACLE" (see the photograph section).

The upper half of the cartoon pictures Himes' Boston Tabernacle ascending to heaven. Miller is shown on the roof, seated on a prophetic chart. Numerous Millerites are hanging on, while others are falling off.

The bottom half pictures the Boston masses looking upward in amazement and anger. Meanwhile, Himes is left behind, standing on the foundation of the tabernacle, on which are inscribed the names of the leading Millerite papers. He is surrounded by moneybags, and his coat tail is being pulled by a fork-tailed devil who is saying, "Joshua V. you must stay with me."[77]

Himes, as might be expected, received his share of death threats. One in 1842 read: "Mr. Himes, your life may be taken away in a sudden and unexpected manner, I would advise you therefore, if you value your own interests, and those of your family[,] to immediately leave this city."[78]

How, we might ask, did Himes respond to these charges? Generally he kept about his work and did not waste too much energy defending himself. At other times he published the accusations against himself, Miller, or other Adventists. Thus in September 1842 he initiated the "Liar's Department" in the *Signs*. In introducing the new department, he wrote that

> the spirit of lying is so prevalent, especially among many of the conductors of the public press, that we shall hereafter devote a portion of our sheet to chronicle the deeds of our opponents who have no arguments to urge against the truth but *lying and scoffing*. We shall publish their shame in their own words, in general, without note or comment.[79]

There were occasions, of course, when Himes did mount a defense against unjust accusations. Prior to the inauguration of the Liar's Department, the *Signs* sometimes had a section titled

"Refuge of Scoffers." Such scoffers were seen as a sign of the last days.[80]

There appears to be no evidence that Himes profited financially from his publication or leadership ventures. The most serious valid charge against him before 1845 is that he tended to be overbearing at times.

That overbearingness, however, was probably an essential ingredient in his successful promotion of Millerite Adventism. It took a forceful personality to push an unpopular doctrine into the consciousness of a world that didn't want it.

But Himes was the man for the task. He had caught a vision of the end of the world, he had a firm conviction of his place in prophetic history, and that understanding energized him to put his considerable talents behind Miller and his cause. Under Himes' leadership, Millerism was transformed from a one-man operation into a national, and even international, religious movement.

Himes, of course, did not work alone. We now turn to some of his associates.

Chapter 5

MORE MILLENNIAL MISSIONARIES

The printed word has a life of its own. So it was after the 1836 edition of Miller's lectures. Not only did a copy fall into the hands of the editor of the *Boston Times* (as noted in the previous chapter) in early 1838, but one was passed on to a twenty-eight-year-old Methodist minister about the same time. The book's owner requested that the minister, Josiah Litch, both read the book and provide the lender with an evaluation of its merits.

Josiah Litch Joins the Adventist Mission

Litch greeted the request with a large measure of skepticism. After all, the idea of attempting to pinpoint the time of Christ's second coming "was to him so strange, that he could scarcely make up his mind to give the book a perusal." He had no doubt that "he could entirely overthrow the whole system in five minutes."[1]

Thus, to gratify a friend and to satisfy his curiosity as to what arguments could possibly be used to support such a novel doctrine, Litch read the book. But, to his surprise, prejudice began to melt away as he read. "The great argument against the coming of the Lord, which had appeared so strong and invulnerable, soon vanished." Before concluding the volume, Litch penned, "I became fully satisfied that the arguments were so clear, so simple, and withal so scriptural, that it was impossible to disprove the position which Mr. Miller had endeavored to establish."

At that point, Litch confronted the same crisis that Miller had in the face of what he considered to be incontrovertible evidence that Christ would come in a few short years. " 'If this doctrine is true,' " his conscience queried, " 'ought you not, as a minister of the gospel, to . . . proclaim it!' "

"If it is true that the Lord is coming so soon," Litch concluded, "the world should know it. . . . It is my duty to make it known to the extent of my power." He then resolved that no matter what the cost to his reputation, he would present the truth on the second coming.

As soon as Litch had committed himself to Millerism, he began to act on his decision through preaching and writing. His first published contribution was a forty-eight-page synopsis of Miller's views entitled *The MIDNIGHT CRY, or a Review of Mr. Miller's Lectures on the Second Coming of Christ, about A.D. 1843.* The pamphlet received wide circulation and "awakened a permanent interest in many minds." At that time (early 1838), Litch claims, "there was not another minister known in New England, who had advocated the views, except BROTHER CHARLES FITCH."[2] It should be noted that Litch's conversion to Millerism probably took place before the publication of Miller's *Evidence From Scripture and History* in the *Boston Times* and before the conversion of Cole and Himes.

In April 1838, Litch began writing a book on Millerism. Unlike his earlier pamphlet, however, this book presented his own views rather than summarizing Miller's. June saw the publication of *The Probability of the Second Coming of Christ About A.D. 1843,* a book of 204 pages. Thus when Miller and Litch first met at Timothy Cole's Lowell church in 1839, Litch had already been more public in his views than any other of Miller's converts up to that point.[3]

Unlike many of Miller's early converts, Litch agreed with Miller on the 1843 date from the beginning. Thus he could write in early 1838 that "although the views of Mr. M. may not be correct on every point, yet, so far as his calculation of time is concerned, the writer can but consider his plan irrefutable."[4]

Even before reading Miller's book for the first time, Litch had had an interest in the time prophecies of Daniel and John. In fact, it was on the basis of another interpretation of the 1260-year/day prophecy that he believed he could prove Miller wrong.[5]

That interest in the time prophecies is evident throughout Litch's *Probability of the Second Coming of Christ.* In that early volume Litch first set forth his interpretation of Revelation's sixth trumpet as being the collapse of Ottoman supremacy in August 1840, a date that was later refined to August 11. What Litch and other leading Millerites interpreted as early as February 1841 as an exact fulfillment of prophecy on August 11, 1840, greatly encouraged them in their preaching of the advent near.[6]

In spite of Litch's precise prediction of the fulfillment of the August 11 time prophecy, he presented a soft edge to his interpretations in case they were not fulfilled just as he and others expected. In replying to a query as to whether his faith in the Bible would be destroyed "if the event does not come out as you believe," he replied that enough of the prophetic framework of Scripture had already been fulfilled that he could not "doubt that the prophecies have a meaning, and that they were written by the unerring Spirit of the Holy One, and will, in due time, be fulfilled."[7] That tentativeness and modesty in claims related to the exact fulfillment of dates was shared by many of the early Millerite leaders up through the summer of 1844, and it helped cushion them from disillusionment between March 1843 and April 1844.

Litch not only had a deep burden for the salvation of souls as the end of the world approached, but he also continued to write, providing "one of the most active pens of the movement." He did much to define and extend Miller's interpretive framework. One student has called Litch the "leading theologian" of the Millerite movement. Litch should certainly be viewed as Millerism's third most important personality, following only Miller and Himes.[8]

In May 1840 Litch penned "An Address to the Clergy," in which he appealed to his fellow ministers to examine the evidence for the premillennial coming of Christ between "the fall of the Ottoman empire, which will probably take place this year, and the termination of 1843."[9]

His aggressive preaching and writing were bound eventually to bring him into conflict with the Methodist hierarchy. The crisis point came in the spring and summer of 1841. During the spring Litch began to question whether he could hold on to his belief in the second advent and still retain his ecclesiastical relation to the Methodist Church. On the side of continuing his Methodist ministry were the welfare of his "beloved family" and the strong collegial ties he had with the Methodist ministry. These "were presented to his mind, as an insuperable barrier in the way of being exclusively devoted to the work of proclaiming the Lord's coming."

On the other hand were his "firm persuasion that the doctrine was true, and a conviction that it was high time the church and the world were aroused to their danger." These considerations, Litch claimed, "pressed upon him until they overcame, and he concluded to throw himself upon the providence of God, and go forth."

One major problem, however, was that no Millerite ministers made their living from preaching the advent near. As Litch put it, "It was an unbeaten way;—not one minister of the gospel was then devoted exclusively to the cause, excepting Mr. Miller." And Miller, as we saw earlier, was not dependent upon his preaching to earn a livelihood.[10]

The issue came to a head on June 9, 1841, at the meeting of the Providence, Rhode Island, Conference of the Methodist Episcopal Church, the regional conference that employed Litch. Having made his decision to preach his beliefs, Litch took the offensive during the meetings by giving several sermons on the advent in the nearby Christian Connexion chapel. Several of the ministers from the conference were present at each lecture, and Litch discerned an increasing interest among them.

His aggressive action led to his being publicly examined for thirty-five to forty minutes by his bishop concerning his preaching of Miller's doctrine. The bishop frankly asked Litch if he felt his beliefs were "Methodism." "I do," replied Litch. "At least it is not contrary to the articles of religion of the Methodist Episcopal Church."

The conference concluded that Litch believed nothing contrary to Methodism, although he went "in some points beyond it." At that juncture Litch requested to be released from his responsibilities so that he could devote his "whole time to the dissemination of this important subject."[11]

Less than a week after giving up his Methodist ministry—on June 15 through 17—Litch attended the second general conference of those expecting the advent. That meeting, we noted in chapter 4, adopted a nine-point strategy to spread the advent message. A large part of that strategy had to do with the distribution of literature.[12]

Then, on July 15, the newly appointed Committee on Publication formally appointed Litch as "general agent" of the movement. In an attempt to reassure Litch in his concerns for the welfare of his family, the announcement of his appointment noted that "the Committee will depend upon the friends of the cause to supply the wants of their Agent, wherever he may work. 'The laborer is worthy of his hire.' " Thus Litch became the first full-time paid Millerite minister. His job would be to lecture and improve the circulation of Adventist literature.[13]

The week after the second Millerite general conference, Litch was on the road in his new function. The week of June 23 found him laboring for the ministers of the New Hampshire Conference of the Methodist Church at their yearly meeting at Dover. Through "the kindness of . . . friends," Litch secured the use of the Dover Freewill Baptist meetinghouse for three evenings and that of the Calvinist Baptists for two others. He was able to lure quite a few of the Methodists from their meetings to his. Shortly afterward he extended his ministry to the Methodist clergy by holding meetings in Worcester, Massachusetts, during the yearly meetings of Methodism's New England Conference. Litch distributed literature to the clergy and created a fair interest in the second advent at both the New Hampshire and the New England meetings.[14]

It was at the Maine Conference in July, however, that Litch made the largest impact upon and created the greatest agitation among the Methodist clergy. In Maine his friends were audacious enough to apply to the conference's appointment committee to get Litch time in the official pulpit for the yearly meeting. The committee declined the request, but that did not stop the attempt to get the Millerite an officially approved hearing. Litch's friends took their request to the floor of the session, where a lengthy and warm discussion ensued. "The effect," penned Litch, "was like a firebrand in a magazine of powder." Both friends and foes of his cause came publicly to the fore, and the dissension "probably excited more interest than could have been raised by a half dozen lectures." The petition was finally voted down in a vote of thirty-one to thirty.

At that point the local Baptist minister readily granted Litch the use of his pulpit. In the meantime, the heated discussion "had awakened an interest in the preachers to hear for themselves on the great question." Litch estimated that two-thirds of the conference preachers attended his lectures and that many were swayed toward his doctrine. In fact, he believed that there was more interest among the Maine Methodist clergy than in any other portion of the New England states.[15] In that estimation he was correct. In future chapters we will again run across the problems that attraction to Millerism brought upon the Maine Methodist Conference.

In the light of Litch's aggressive work for the Methodist clergy, Himes' previous judgment that he was "a strong man in Israel" seems to be justified. Litch would continue to carry a special burden for Methodist members and clergy.[16]

By late 1842 and early 1843, Litch had centered his work in Philadelphia in "the first effort to introduce the message south of New York." Under his leadership, a company of believers was raised up, a book depository was opened for the circulation of Millerite literature, and a small paper—the *Philadelphia Alarm*—was begun with Litch as editor. He remained in Philadelphia as the regional leader of the movement in that area.[17]

The Millerite Camp Meetings

One Millerite institution in which Litch played a major role was the camp meeting. Such meetings had been used by the Methodists and other groups during the previous four decades with outstanding success.[18] The initiatives for the first Millerite camp meetings took place at the Boston general conference in May 1842.

By that date the year 1843 was looking perilously close, with most of the world yet to be warned. L. C. Collins expressed the faith of many when he wrote:

> My faith is *strong* in the coming of Christ in '43. I make no calculations for any thing beyond, but glory. . . . But with so short a time to awake the slumbering virgins, and save souls, we must *work*; *work* night and day. God has thrust us out in haste, to give the *last* invitation, and we must labor in earnest, and *compel* them to come in, that his house may be filled. . . . Strong men in Israel are rallying to our help. The midnight cry must yet be made to ring, and ring through every valley and over every hill-top and plain. An awful trembling must yet seize upon sinners in Zion. A crisis *must come*, before the door of mercy is everlastingly shut against them. They must be made to feel that it is *now or never*.[19]

Such a sense of crisis and responsibility was resting heavily upon the Millerites by mid-1842. The day after Collins penned his letter, the momentous Boston general conference opened, with Joseph Bates at the helm. That conference not only voted to hold camp meetings, it also appointed a committee to superintend them. The "principal object" of the meetings was "to awake sinners and purify Christians by giving the Midnight Cry, viz. to hold up the immediate coming of Christ."[20]

Some Millerites felt that the very attempt to hold such meetings was a bit presumptive. After all, a camp meeting is a great undertaking. "What," suggested some, "a little handful of Adventists hold a camp-meeting! Why, they are hardly able to hold a house meeting, much less a camp-meeting! However," Litch notes, "there was sufficient faith and zeal in the [Boston] meeting, to say 'TRY.' "[21]

The first camp meeting planned by the official committee was to be held in East Kingston, New Hampshire, from June 28 to July 5.[22] Meanwhile, Litch had begun a series of meetings in Stanstead in eastern Canada in early June. That revival series caught on in unexpected ways and led in unanticipated directions.

Litch reported that "the country, for thirty or forty miles around, was awake to the subject of the Lord's coming," and "immense concourses assembled." As a result, he determined then and there to hold a camp meeting in Canada that would build upon his meetings and those being held across the border in Vermont.[23]

Thus, from June 21 through June 28, the first advent camp meeting was held, not in East Kingston as planned, but in Canada. Litch's excitement shines through in his description of the meetings. "Waves on waves of people have flowed in upon us, day after day, until our arena within the circle of the tents has been almost crowded with a living mass of beings, eagerly enquiring, 'Watchman, what of the night?' To which we say, 'the morning cometh and also the night.' " The closing three hours were spent in a testimony meeting. The final act in the meeting was the singing of "When thou my righteous Judge shall come."[24]

Hearing of the success of the camp meeting, the people of Bolton (also in Canada) requested one. Thus, in the week following his first endeavor, Litch held a second camp meeting. It ended on July 3. "During that month's labor," he recalled, "as near as could be estimated, five or six hundred souls were converted to God."[25] The Canadian camp meetings had been a success.

In the meantime, the East Kingston camp meeting had begun on June 29. The Boston *Post* reported that from seven to ten thousand people attended and that the meetings were orderly. There were twelve to fifteen preachers presenting lectures, with Miller giving a regular course of lectures. Some of the people, the *Post* suggested, attended out of curiosity, but the major portion of them, as evidenced by "their solemn looks and close attention to the subject, were evidently actuated by higher and more important motives."[26]

The one criticism of the meetings leveled by the *Post* was that some were discouraged that no time was given for opponents of Millerism to present their views. That restriction, however, had been a foundational element in planning the event. The camp-meeting committee, in announcing the convocation, plainly stated that controversy was not their purpose. Thus they forewarned that "none will take part in public speaking except those who are believers in the second coming of Christ, near, even at the door." The Millerites had no doubt of the purpose of their camp meetings. They were evangelistic crusades rather than debating societies.[27]

The *Signs* version of the East Kingston meetings was essentially the same as that of the *Post*, except that the *Signs* estimated attendance at from ten to fifteen thousand. In addition, it pointed out that the attendees represented nearly all sects and creeds and that they came from all the New England states as well as Canada and "Old England."

The *Signs* also reported several resolutions passed at the camp meeting. They centered on the nearness of the end and the responsibility of the believers to warn the world with all possible haste. One resolution called for more camp meetings, since the East Kingston experience had convinced them that such convocations were "a most efficient means for spreading the truth on this subject and for preparing those who embrace it for the coming of the Lord."[28]

Two other results of the East Kingston camp meeting should be noted. First, at least two of its converts to Millerism would play central roles in subsequent developments in the movement. S. S. Snow, who would later spearhead the acceptance of the October 22, 1844, date for the second coming of Christ, consecrated himself to the full-time occupation of spreading the Millerite message at that camp meeting. In addition, Robert Winter, who would later do much to spread Millerism in Great Britain, was converted at the East Kingston meeting.[29]

A second important result was the proposal for the construction of the "big tent" and the successful fund raising to pay for it. With a seating capacity of four thousand, it was reportedly the largest tent in America up to that time. Originally, its center pole stood at fifty-five feet, and it had a diameter of 120 feet. A streamer bearing the words "Thy Kingdom Come" flew from its masthead. It took a full-time tent company of four men to move, set up, and care for the big tent.[30]

The tent had several values. First, it provided a ready-made auditorium in localities where suitable meeting places were not available or where the Millerites were shut out of existing buildings due to increasing tension as the year of the end approached. Second, the tent extended the season for mass meetings, since it could be pitched in weather that prohibited outdoor meetings. Third, it was an attention getter; many people who attended meetings merely to see the tent stayed to hear the preaching of the message. Himes, who directed construction of the tent, did not miss its public-relations value. Because massive crowds were drawn to the big tent, it was soon enlarged to seat approximately six thousand people.[31]

The growing urgency of spreading the Millerite message as the year of the end approached is evidenced by the speed with which the big tent was moved from place to place. In spite of poor transportation facilities, it was transported eight times between July 27 and November 3, 1842.

Though the early Millerite camp meetings had their "groans," shouts of "glory," and other spiritual exercises, they were quite well ordered by the standards of the day. In fact, the relatively good order was one of the most noted aspects of the East Kingston meeting. Of course, it is not surprising that the *Signs* claimed that "for good order this meeting stands without a parallel." It is more significant, however, that the Boston *Post* could declare that "the meeting was conducted with great regularity and good order from beginning to end." Similar sentiments were expressed by the *Daily Mail* and the *Christian Herald*.[32]

In a similar vein, the New York *Herald* could say of the Newark,

New Jersey, meetings in November 1842 that "those who think that one of these Millerite meetings resembles a Methodist camp meeting are greatly mistaken; there is much more order, decorum, and argument in these Miller meetings."[33]

The key to understanding the comparative order and decorum in Millerite meetings is hinted at in the *Herald*'s remark that the Millerite meetings were characterized by "argument." As noted earlier, Miller's approach to religion was one aimed at the intellect rather than at the emotions. Coming out of a Deist background, Miller placed rationalism at the center of his personal approach to religion, and it was similarly important for those who were convinced by his biblical reasoning.

That rationalism was Miller's preferred style does not mean that overemotionalism and fanaticism never found a place in Millerite camp meetings. The case of John Starkweather and the ascendence of others on the emotional end of the spectrum certainly affected Millerite camp meetings in 1843 and the summer of 1844. That topic will be treated more fully in chapter 9.

Meanwhile, the Millerite Adventists took strenuous steps toward keeping their camps orderly. One of those steps was the publication of a list of regulations stipulating the daily routine for both the camp and individuals.[34]

Another means of maintaining order in the camps was the hiring of security guards. The most interesting of those guards was Hiram Munger, a powerful man who stood at six feet six inches. Munger, a Methodist, had been working on the camp-meeting circuit for his own denomination when Himes offered him $25 to allow his equipment and services to be used for a Millerite meeting. Having not previously been impressed when he heard Miller, Munger "felt crusty and objected" to Himes' offer. But he eventually decided to accept, since he could act the part of " 'the dog in the manger' and keep off the Millerites."[35]

He later regretted offering even minimal cooperation. But when the big tent arrived, he was so astonished by its size that his reluctance disappeared for a while.

"The meeting," he penned, "was so different from the other

that I took but little interest in it—excepting for the $25, and I hoped that they would not make out much." When Himes made an altar call, Munger thought he would have few results, since the Methodists had just completed a very successful meeting on the same campground. But, to Munger's shock, "there was such a rush to the altar for prayers as I had never seen. This gave me the 'lock-jaw' for a while, for I was so astonished to see those [go] forward who had stood through our meeting, that I did not speak for some time. Truly, I thought, God was in the place and I knew it not."[36]

Though Munger did not convert at the Chickopee camp meeting, he soon worked at a second Adventist meeting. At this meeting, he penned,

> I had more time . . . to examine their doctrine, and I was astonished, when I read the Bible for myself without a Papal comment upon it. I was convinced that they had got the truth on the *nature of the events*, saying nothing of the *time*, and many things I learned that I never knew were in the Bible before. It was a new book indeed, and had some promises that I never had thought belonged to us.[37]

After his conversion to Millerism, Munger regularly worked on the movement's camp-meeting circuit. Many were his experiences as head security guard. When, for example, two "Cainites" (as he called the rowdies) tried to disrupt a meeting, Munger informed them, playing on a Millerite emphasis, that "this was a 'time meeting,' and it was *time* for them to be going, and I would give them one minute to start."

On another occasion, three rowdies showed up at camp meeting "on purpose to fight with me." Munger challenged one of them to a wrestling match. Going into the woods, he recalled, "I made up my mind to use him rather hard." After he cried " 'fairly done,' a number of times," Munger continued, "I kept him moving until he was satisfied he was much better off than he would have been to have fought, as he first proposed." Pitying the man, Munger took him to his tent for a night of rest. The next morning the man told him "that he had not a well bone in him."[38]

On a third occasion, some seventeen Cainites arrived and commenced tearing down tents and singing obscene songs. Munger had arranged for an ambush. After their wagon was stopped in an abortive getaway, Munger climbed into it and "commenced pitching them out over the sides on the ground" while the other Adventist guards secured them with rope. One of the rowdies pulled a knife on Munger, who, upon being warned, took "him by the collar and the seat of the pants" and sent him "overboard so quick that he only had time to say 'O dear,' before he, dirk and all, after an aerial journey of some twenty feet, landed on the ground."

After keeping his prisoners bound for some hours, Munger told them he would let them go if they would give their names and confess their folly. Unbinding them, he then led them in a season of prayer. Most confessed, and the man who drew the knife "begged us not to prosecute him." After further discussion, Munger reports, they "left us docile as lambs. . . . We had no more disturbance from that source."[39]

The combination of rational (rather than emotional) preaching, stringent rules, and "dedicated toughs" like Munger helped the Millerites maintain order in their camp meetings. All in all, the Adventists held at least 125 camp meetings between June 1842 and October 1844, with an estimated combined attendance of no fewer than half a million people.[40]

Thus as Millerism moved toward 1843, it had discovered the camp meeting to be one of its most powerful engines for evangelism as time itself brought ever-increasing pressure to warn the world.

The Zealous Charles Fitch

Charles Fitch was the fourth most influential and well known Millerite preacher. In 1838, about the same time that Litch and the Boston *Post* first obtained copies of Miller's published lectures, a copy fell into Fitch's hands.

"I have *studied* it," he penned to Miller on March 5, "with an overwhelming interest, such as I never felt in any other book except the Bible. I have compared it with scripture and history, and I find nothing on which to rest a single doubt respecting the correctness of your views."[41]

Fitch, true to his zealous and sincere character, wasn't satisfied with merely one reading. He was so carried away that he read Miller's book *six times*, noting that his "mind was greatly overwhelmed with the subject." Impelled by Miller's message, the new convert to the cause immediately "wrote and preached to the people of Boston" concerning his newfound faith.[42]

Preaching his first two sermons on Miller's views on March 4, he exuberantly wrote to Miller the next day, noting that he desired to be "a watchman on the walls," and wanted "to *'give the trumpet a certain sound.' "* As a major step in faithfully acting the part of the watchman, Fitch announced to Miller that there was to be a meeting of his ministerial associates the next day (March 6), "and, as I am appointed to read an essay, I design to bring up this whole subject for discussion, and trust that I may thereby do something to spread the truth."[43]

That bold step proved to be premature for the impetuous young minister. After all, he had hardly had time to examine the doctrine himself. He was both shocked and intimidated by the response he received. To his ministerial colleagues it was "moonshine." "There was much laughter over the subject," Fitch recalled, "and I could not help feeling that I was regarded as a simpleton." He left the meeting "much pained, and . . . not a little mortified." After that, he gave up preaching the advent near. As he later saw it, "the fear of man brought me into a snare."[44]

On the other hand, the experience and his later change of heart must have taught him a lesson in standing firm for his convictions. For the rest of his life, as we will see, Fitch would sponsor unpopular causes without backing down in the face of opposition from those he respected.

It was Josiah Litch who would lead Fitch back to Millerism. Fitch, sensing something lacking in his spiritual experience, had "fasted," "prayed," "groaned," and "wept before the Lord." While he was in that condition, Litch (a stranger to him) visited him in mid-1841 and urged him to restudy the Bible on the topic of the second advent. Fitch later wrote to Litch that he could not feel "anything like cordiality in seeing you," but upon reading the literature Litch left with him, Fitch's second-advent beliefs revived.[45]

The *Signs* of December 15, 1841, reported that Fitch had "come into the full faith of the Second Advent."[46] The zealous Fitch would preach his new faith until the end of his life in October 1844. In fact, his faithfulness in spreading that advent message brought about his death (see chapter 11).

In the meantime, Fitch's Adventist ministry was fruitful from the very start. Even his letter to Litch announcing his conversion wrought Millerite fruit. For example, a druggist from western New York, after being led to Millerism through Fitch's published letter, ordered 160 copies for distribution. "Scarcely a day passes," he wrote, "but some [of the pamphlets] are issuing from the Drug Store of which I am proprietor, medicine and truth going out together."[47]

Prior to 1838 and his first contact with Millerism, Fitch had been a broad-based reformer and a prominent abolitionist. His 1837 publication of *Slaveholding Weighed in the Balance of Truth* provided a forceful attack on the issue. "Up, my friends," Fitch urged in the pamphlet's conclusion, "and do your duty, to deliver the spoiled out of the hand of the oppressor, lest the fire of God's fury kindle ere long upon you."[48]

William Lloyd Garrison, the great anti-slavery agitator, considered Fitch to be a "brave and eloquent" speaker and activist for the abolitionist movement. Fitch had not only been eloquent, but he was also noted for his forthright "hard" language in attacking slavery. Some felt he was "out-Garrisoning Garrison" in the vigor of his rhetoric.[49]

Unfortunately for Garrison, in August 1837 Fitch would become a formidable opponent of Garrison's anti-slavery organization. In that month Fitch became one of the two principal authors of an "Appeal of Clerical Abolitionists on Anti-Slavery Measures."[50]

Fitch was not so much out of harmony with Garrison's anti-slavery principles as he was with Garrison's teachings against the clergy and his downplaying of the Sunday-Sabbath as a holy day (Garrison taught all days were holy), the visible church, and the Christian ordinances. Fitch and his colleagues had decided to split off from the Garrisonians and create a society of "Evangelical Abolitionists." Henry Stanton and others believed most clerical abolitionists had sided with Fitch, while Fitch claimed a majority of nine-tenths. Garrison, for his part, saw Fitch as a "deserter" and a traitor.[51]

Garrison went out of his way to attack Fitch on the occasion of the dedication of Fitch's Marlboro Chapel. "The flaming aboli-tionist," asserted Garrison, ". . . cares as little for the cause he once so furiously espoused, as he is ignorant of true righteousness." Instead of speaking on the great cause for which the chapel was founded, "he gave a hum-drum discourse about the Sabbath, infant sprinkling, and the sacrament!" Garrison's evaluation hit directly on the fault line that separated him from Fitch. Though Fitch was a zealous abolitionist, he was even more resolutely an orthodox Christian as he then defined the term.[52]

The cleavage between Fitch and Garrison remained until January 1840. On January 9, however, Fitch wrote to Garrison, expressing regret that he had participated in the "Appeal" and had condemned Garrison. Fitch had been led to his apology by thoughts of "JESUS CHRIST in the clouds of heaven, coming to judge the world, and to establish His reign of holiness and right-eousness and blessedness over the pure of heart."[53]

Fitch's confession gives the impression that even at that early date he was concerned with the advent near, a position he would not fully accept for another eighteen months. But the confession also expresses a new doctrine that Fitch had espoused after his rejection of Millerism in 1838. His emphasis on wanting to be "pure of heart" to meet his Lord reflects his new belief in Chris-tian perfection or "full sanctification." It is also an emphasis that helps us see into the personality of this utterly sincere minister.[54]

By 1839 Fitch had become a convert to "Oberlin perfection," a view that "holiness consists primarily of the perfection of the will and is available to every Christian after conversion." Although not officially connected with Oberlin College (in Ohio), Fitch linked up with their theology and thus became a colleague in the cause with such Oberlin theological professors as Asa Mahan, Henry Cowles, and Charles Finney.[55]

All four men published books on the topic of perfection. Fitch's *Views of Sanctification* came out in 1839, the same year as Mahan's *Scripture Doctrine of Christian Perfection* and a year before the publication of Finney's *Views of Sanctification*. The strong advocacy by these four Calvinist ministers of what had traditionally been a Methodist doctrine raised a furor in the Calvinist community. Leonard Woods, professor of theology at Andover Seminary and a leading defender of orthodox Calvinism throughout the first half of the century, published a book critiquing Mahan's and Fitch's works. Beyond that, Fitch's neighboring pastor in Newark, New Jersey, published a booklet challenging his view of full sanctification.[56]

The greatest challenge to Fitch, however, came from his employing organization. The Newark Presbytery of the Presbyterian Church accused him of heresy and put him on trial. Fitch, in replying to the presbytery's charges, wrote:

> With my name you must do what you think right before God, and in view of an approaching judgment. I have no further defence to make [than his letter of explanation to them]. If you cannot own me as one of your number while I tell the church of Christ . . . that He was manifested to take away their sins, and that they may and ought so to abide in Him that they sin not . . . , then just blot me out of your book, and let the transaction be recorded, as it will be, in the book of God, to be reviewed before the universe in the final day.[57]

From thenceforth, Fitch considered himself to be "an ecclesiastical outcast." In 1842, while seeking to convince his good friend Phoebe Palmer (the leader of the revival of the teaching of perfection among the Methodists in the late 1830s and early 1840s) of the nearness of the advent, he noted that in accepting his view of complete sanctification he had "sacrificed all my friends on earth for the truth's sake." After resigning from the Presbyterian ministry because of his new belief, he became a full-time evangelist "for the promotion of holiness" in April 1841.[58]

Since his abortive experience with Millerism in 1838, Fitch had become a staunch defender of what he believed in spite of the position of those opposing him. The development of that trait had prepared him well for the battles he would have to fight as a leading Millerite. One of those battles would be with his old colleagues in perfection (Mahan, Cowles, and Finney) as Fitch twice invaded the campus of Oberlin College for the only prolonged dialogue between a Millerite and a major theological faculty.

Fitch, of course, was no stranger to Finney and his Oberlin colleagues. Not only had he been their theological ally and a frequently featured writer in their periodical, but he had also been the dedicatory speaker for Finney's new Broadway Tabernacle congregation in New York City in 1835.[59]

The Oberlin community had been mightily stirred by the message of William Miller. That stirring, however, had been one of reaction rather than of agreement. After all, Oberlin—being the first collegiate institution in the United States to allow blacks and females into its academic program on a par with white males—considered itself to be the vanguard of the movement for setting up God's millennial kingdom on earth through reform.[60]

Oberlin's consternation with Miller's doctrine is indicated by the fact that between February 17, 1841, and December 22, 1841, the *Oberlin Evangelist* published a series of twenty-three articles on "The Millenium [sic]." That series was succeeded by a second one of seventeen articles entitled "No Millenium [sic]" that extended from January 19 through August 31, 1842. Both series were aimed at Miller, but the second more openly specified the problem as Miller's "doctrine that the world is never to be converted to God." The *Evangelist* deplored the fact that many of the "best ministers" were "renouncing the doctrine of the temporal

Millenium [sic]." The February 16, 1842, issue noted "with grief" that their beloved Fitch had accepted Miller's theory.[61]

Fitch's conversion to the advent near brought him into dialogue with the Oberlin theologians, first through a series of letters published in the *Evangelist* and then through public presentations at Oberlin. His first public meetings at Oberlin took place in September 1842. The *Evangelist* noted that while its editors had "great respect for Bro. Fitch, we cannot but say we think he is mistaken on this subject." Fitch, for his part, was "utterly astonished" that such men as Cowles and Mahan "could make such a use of the Bible" in rejecting the advent near. But not everyone in the Oberlin community responded negatively. Even one of the professors converted to Fitch's perspective.[62]

Fitch returned to Oberlin for a second series in September 1843. This time, however, the Oberlin theologians forced him into a public debate on the topic, even though "Mr. Fitch would rather have gone on and preached merely—giving his own views without any discussion." But partway through the debate, Fitch refused to "contend" any longer. After that, his sermons and the Oberlin replies occupied alternate evenings.[63]

At the conclusion of Fitch's second Oberlin series, the *Evangelist* once again stated that his presentations had "not resulted . . . in any change in the public mind" in favor of his beliefs. But there are indications in the Oberlin records that Fitch's presentations at Oberlin and in the *Evangelist* were more disruptive than the Oberlinites wanted to admit. One preacher influenced by Fitch's interaction with the Oberlin community was John Starkweather— a man we shall hear more about in chapter 9.[64]

By and large, however, Oberlin continued in its previously accepted postmillennial path in spite of Millerism in general and Fitch in particular. An early Oberlin graduate summed up the position nicely when he penned:

Millerites, when they knew how eager we were to renovate the world, thought we would readily unite with them in burning it up by 1843. But Henry Cowles—blessed his memory and blessed be his commentaries!—went into such a thorough study of prophesy [sic] as to detect the shallow imposture, and such an exposition of prophesy [sic] as to confound, not Millerism only, but all other Judaistic inter-pretations of the old prophets that look to a literal rather than a spiritual kingdom of God.[65]

By 1843 Fitch had located in Cleveland, Ohio. From there he not only made forays into neighboring Oberlin, but he also issued a paper entitled the *Second Advent of Christ*. Fitch became the foremost Adventist leader in the trans-Appalachian region.

An important contribution of Fitch to the Millerite movement was the "1843 Chart." In May 1842, Fitch and Apollos Hale pre-sented their chart to the general conference session meeting in Boston. The chart graphically portrayed the major prophetic symbols of Daniel and Revelation and indicated several ways that the prophetic numbers added up to the year 1843 as the time of the second advent (see a reproduction of the "1843 Chart" in the photograph section).

The chart, as it was later replicated, measured roughly three by five feet and could be hung up as a visual aid for preaching in a lecture hall or any other place an audience could be gathered. In fact, the hanging of an "1843 Chart" on the deck of a canal boat or in some other public place was often a means used to draw a curious crowd for a preaching service.

The conference believed that Fitch and Hale's chart "had ful-filled a prophecy given by Hab. 2[,]468 years before, where it says, 'And the Lord answered me and said, *write the vision and make it plain upon tables, that he may run that readeth it.*' " It was therefore "voted to have three hundred of these charts lithographed . . . that those who felt the message may read and run with it." Millerite preachers now had an important addition to their standard equip-ment—the latest development in visual technology.[66]

Another important contribution of Fitch to the Millerite movement was his call in July 1843 for the advent believers to "come out of Babylon." (That contribution will be more fully explained in chapter 7.) In 1844 Fitch also accepted such biblical teachings as baptism by immersion and death as a sleep until the resurrection.

Evaluations of Fitch were mixed. The *Christian Reflector* noted that he had a "sensitive heart" and "a mind very much undisciplined." As a result, "he was easily led astray by the wild, the powerful influences which . . . operated upon it."[67]

Garrison claimed in early 1843 that "no one who knows him [Fitch] can doubt his honesty or ability; but his mind appears to be impulsive." Garrison went on to note that it perhaps was fortunate for Fitch that "with the expiration of the present year," all necessity for him "to tax his concentrativeness on the subject of 'the Second Advent near' " would close.[68]

From a more positive point of view, it can be claimed that Fitch was as sincere as he was zealous and impulsive. He was a man who had come to the place where he would do *whatever* he believed God willed for him, no matter what the consequences. As a result, after his conversion on the advent near, Fitch put his whole soul into the Millerite millennial mission.

From another perspective, given Fitch's impulsiveness and sensitivity, he should be seen as a bridge between the more stable and rationalistic Millerite leaders (such as Miller, Himes, and Litch) and those of a more charismatic bent (such as S. S. Snow and George Storrs), who came to dominate the movement in the late summer and early fall of 1844. Fitch exhibited a delicate balance between rationalism and an impulsive openness to innovative ideas. As a result, he played a unique role in the Millerite drama. In Fitch we glimpse a foreshadowing of the tension that would split Millerism asunder after the disappointment of October 22, 1844.

Additional Millerite Leaders

No one knows the number of ministers preaching the Millerite message, but Himes estimated it at three to four hundred in January 1842, while the *Christian Herald* six months later suggested at least seven hundred. At the height of the movement in the spring of 1844, the *Midnight Cry* reported that "something like *fifteen hundred* or TWO THOUSAND lecturers are in the field proclaiming '*The Kingdom of Heaven is at hand.*' " At any rate, the evidence is clear that a large number of clergy and dedicated laypeople took up the message of the advent near. Some of them preached it full time, while others sounded the warning part time in connection with earning a livelihood.[69]

The lecturers came from all denominations. Everett Dick has made the only study of the denominational affiliations of Millerite lecturers. Of the 174 whom he was able to identify denominationally, 44 percent were Methodist, 27 percent Baptist, 9 percent Congregational, 8 percent Christian Connexion, and 7 percent Presbyterian. Several other denominations were represented by one or two lecturers each. According to Litch, the lecturers held certain commonalities, including zeal for God and the salvation of humanity. Beyond that, they were Bible students who sought to make the Bible a self-interpreting book.[70]

Aside from the soon coming of Christ, there was no doctrinal uniformity among the lecturers. Millerism was essentially a one-doctrine movement. Miller, Himes, and others believed that to broaden their doctrinal platform would necessitate much discussion and thus use up precious time. After Christ came again in the near future, they could work out their doctrinal differences. Meanwhile, the world needed to be warned of impending doom.

Like the Methodist circuit riders, Millerite lecturers often risked their lives and existed in discomfort to get their message out. Along that line, the report of Joel Spaulding is of interest. "I have traveled in forty days," he penned,

> two hundred and seventy-five miles, had my beast fall twice, while on horseback, in sloughs; and once in the midst of Kinnebec river [sic] while fording, where the current was considerably rapid. . . . As I was cast into the river, the horse fell on me; but I escaped unhurt, with the exception of a lame ankle, on which I was unable to bear my weight for some

days. But none of these things moved me. I could hobble with the assistance of a staff into the desk, happy in having the privilege still of arousing a slumbering church to a sense of the immediate "appearing of the great God, and our Savior, Jesus Christ["]; of warning the sinner of the impending storm which awaits him; and in showing them the hiding place from the same.[71]

Other leaders of special note in the 1842-through-early-1844 phase of Millerism were Joseph Marsh, Elon Galusha, and Nathaniel Southard. Marsh accepted Millerism in 1842. For twelve years prior to that time, he had been editor of *The Christian Palladium* (an organ of the Christian Connexion) in upstate New York. In April 1842 he began to call for "a candid and careful *investigation*" of the Adventist doctrine in the *Palladium*. Beyond that, he printed things in favor of the doctrine. That course of action "raised *much* opposition." By November 23 he was able to write: "I am fully convinced as to the time, and mean to proclaim it fearlessly from the pulpit and the press. My course is fixed—let the consequences follow. I fear not the result. God will defend his cause."[72]

Marsh's faith did not save his job. During late 1842 and early 1843, he found himself under increasing opposition. By November 1, 1843, he had been completely forced out of his editorial position with the *Palladium*.[73] He was then free to put his full strength into Millerism. As a result, on January 1, 1844, he began publication of the *Voice of Truth*.

Another leader of Millerism in western New York was Elon Galusha. The son of the Vermont governor who had signed Miller's military commission, Galusha had become one of the most powerful New York Baptists of his day. Beyond that, he was a foremost agitator in New York for the ending of slavery, fully believing that slavery "must cease before the millennium can come." In 1840 he went as a delegate to the world antislavery convention in Scotland. Having served in a number of influential pastorates, Galusha, according to Whitney Cross, was "one of the most influential individuals ever to join the Adventist movement."[74]

Galusha began to convert to Millerism in 1843. By early 1844 he had tendered his resignation to his church so that he might be wholly free to preach his convictions. Miller wrote of him: "Bro. Galusha came out in full in the faith of '43. He is a happy man, and a strong man in the faith. . . . With him I am well pleased." And pleased he had a right to be. Galusha reportedly brought eight hundred souls to Christ in one session in March 1844. He became the foremost leader of Millerism in western New York state.[75]

Southard was another who brought editorial skills into Millerism. An active anti-slavery man, Southard at one time had been acting editor of the *Emancipator*. In late 1842 he would take over the editorship of the Millerite *Midnight Cry*.[76]

Two commonalities should be noted about the Millerite leaders who came into the movement as the year of the end approached. First, these, as well as those of lesser status, tended to lose their denominational positions because of Millerism. That was unlike the general experience of the earliest leaders, but it did indicate that the split taking place between the Millerites and the churches was accelerating in 1843 and 1844.

Second, like the earlier Millerite leaders, the latter ones tended to be heavily involved in the reform movements of the day, especially the freeing of the slaves. Garrison was frustrated beyond measure when talented leaders converted to Millerism. "Multitudes," he penned, "who were formerly engaged in the various moral enterprises of the age, have lost all interest in works of practical righteousness, and think and talk of nothing else but the burning up of the world." Again, he penned, "a considerable number of worthy abolitionists have been carried away by it [Millerism], and, for the time being, are rendered completely useless to our cause. But the delusion has not long to run, and let us rejoice."[77]

On one point, Garrison's critique is in error. Millerites had not lost "all interest in works of practical righteousness." Rather, they had lost faith in human ability to achieve a sufficient solution.

Whereas Garrison taught that the best way to prepare for the millennium was to work for it in the present, and whereas Oberlin's Henry Cowles believed that it was a "dreadful mistake" to think that "God will bring in the Millenium [sic] by a sort of miracle . . . without human agency," the Millerites held the second coming to be an immediate solution to slavery and all other problems.[78]

Thus by 1843 Millerism was at loggerheads with the reform movements, as well as with the churches, in terms of strategy for bringing in the kingdom. It had not always been so. In 1840 Garrison's *Liberator* had even advertised Miller's lectures, suggesting that since Miller was "a thorough abolitionist, non-resistant, temperance man, and etc," his lectures would "be of a salutary character—aside from his computation of the end of the world."[79]

The fact that Miller's sentiments regarding the evils of slavery did not change across time is evident from the fact that two weeks after the October 1844 disappointment, he was earmarked as a trusted participant on the "underground railroad" that unlawfully moved slaves from the American South to Canada, where they would be beyond the legal reach of their masters.[80]

Miller and his followers were not against reform. Rather, they believed in more radical agencies and a more extensive solution than other reformers. The second coming would be the reform of all reforms. It was the ultimate cause. On that basis Millerism had a magnetic drawing power for those reformers who were struggling with the failure of human action.

Black and Female Lecturers

There are traces of Millerite work among the black population,[81] but it is not highlighted in Adventist publications. That situation resulted partly from the fact that it was a white, male-dominated movement (as were nearly all causes of the day) and partly from the fact that Millerism was largely a northern movement at a time when the great bulk of the black population still lived in the South.

Yet there are consistent evidences that blacks attended Millerite meetings and that the Adventist leaders had a burden to give them the warning message. At first the contact between the largely white advent movement and the black minority was probably informal in the sense that blacks just began attending Millerite meetings in the usual manner of the times by sitting in the back rows or balconies of churches or standing around the edges. In a similar manner, they attended camp meetings but had their own tents. Thus in 1842 Hiram Munger became incensed when the " 'Cainites' tore down the tent of the colored people." Sojourner Truth, a black woman who became a formidable orator in the struggle against slavery, attended one of Miller's lectures and at least two Adventist camp meetings but concluded that they were "laboring under a delusion."[82]

By mid-1843 the need to work aggressively among the black population was becoming more obvious to the Millerite leaders. As a result, Fitch made a successful motion at a major meeting in May "to take up a collection for a laborer to go among our colored brethren."

The next day a collection of more than twenty dollars was received to enable John W. Lewis, "a highly esteemed colored preacher," to work full time "among that much neglected class of our brethren, with whom he is most closely connected."[83]

By February 1844, Himes was able to report that "many of the colored people have received the doctrine" in Philadelphia. "One of their most efficient ministers has embraced the doctrine in full, and will devote himself wholly to the proclamation of it. The people of color, therefore, will have a congregation where the advent doctrine will be fully proclaimed."[84]

While it is impossible to determine the extent of Millerism's spread among the black population (a situation that is equally mystifying for white Millerism), we do have record of at least two[85] blacks lecturing on the advent near. The first was Lewis.

A second black lecturer who preached the Millerite message was William E. Foy, who claimed to have had several visions beginning on January 18, 1842. Those visions led him to a belief in the soon coming of Jesus, even though, as he put it, "I was opposed to the doctrine of Jesus' near approach" until he received the visions.[86]

Beyond a belief in the soon coming of Christ, Foy wrote that "the duty to declare the things which had thus been shown me, to my fellow creatures, and warn them to flee from the wrath to come, rested with great weight upon my mind." Despite his convictions, Foy resisted them for some time, partly, he noted, because their message was "so different" from what people expected and partly because of "the prejudice among the people against thos [sic] of my color." That last statement suggests that Foy (and probably other black lecturers) preached to audiences composed of both blacks and whites. Such a situation is not out of harmony with what we know of black preaching in the first half of the nineteenth century.

In the midst of a prayer of deep distress, Foy received a definite impression that God would be with him if he shared his message. As a result, he began preaching his new faith in various localities.[87]

Female lecturers appear to have had a more prominent role than blacks in Millerism. Not only was the women's-rights movement getting a major boost from female participation in abolitionism, but restorationism and the Second Great Awakening were also giving them new opportunities. The Christian Connexion, in particular, had a strong tradition of women preachers. And during the 1830s female participation in public religion received encouragement from the revivalism of Charles Finney, while the ministry of Phoebe Palmer was renewing the acceptability of women leading out in public worship in the Methodist tradition.[88]

The new beginnings for women in ministry, however, did not always mean that female Millerite lecturers had an easy time of it. Take the case of Lucy Maria Hersey, for example. Converted in her youth, at eighteen she felt the Lord had called her to publicly proclaim the gospel.

In 1842 she accepted Miller's doctrine. Soon after, she accompanied her father on a trip to Schenectady, New York, where a believer asked her nonclergyman father to address a non-Adventist group on the evidence for his faith. The people were "so opposed to *female speaking*" that the host thought it best if the father made the presentation. But he found himself speechless. As a result, after a long silence, the host remarked: "Bro. Hersey has a daughter here who talks some in conference meetings when at home in N.E., and if there is no objection raised by any one present, we would like to hear from *her*."

Since no objections were made, she presented her message with forceful effect. The meetings were soon shifted to the courthouse, where she spoke to a full audience. That was the beginning of a fruitful ministry that included the conversion of several men who took up the preaching of the advent message.[89]

Olive Maria Rice appears to have met with both more opposition and more success than Hersey. Converted to Millerism in 1842, Rice had wanted to be a missionary from her childhood. After becoming "convinced that the Lord had something more for me to do than to assist in prayer meetings," she entered a public evangelistic ministry that had led to the conversion of hundreds by March 1843. She wrote to Himes that "there are constantly four or five places calling for my labors at the same time."[90]

Rice's ministry, of course, regularly faced male prejudice. One young New Yorker complained to his brother that he had recently had "to take another dose of Millerism . . . [,] and that too from a woman who to all appearance would better be discharging her duty and more becoming the dignity of her sex in the private walks of life in the domesticated circle.

"Some," he continued, "said the woman was an *angel*[;] others said if she once was an angel she had fallen from her first estate." He went on to note that there were "a goodmany [sic] 'fellers' after her" and claimed that two of them had "flipped a cent to see which should go home with her the last *night*."[91]

Rice recognized the opposition to her preaching but declared that she "dare not stop for the only reason that I am a sister." "Though men may censure and condemn, I feel justified before God, and expect with joy to render my account for thus warning my fellow beings."[92]

Elvira Fassett was another who had to break through both her own and her husband's prejudices against women preachers. "She," like most women of her day, "had been taught to believe it immodest and unbecoming a woman to speak in public; and considered it forbidden by Paul." But, being pressed upon by others, she finally gave in, only to find that the Lord blessed her labors.

Her husband's prejudice was eventually overcome by the fruits of her preaching and by the prophecy of Joel 2 and Acts 2: " 'On my servants and on my handmaidens I will pour out in those days of my spirit; and they shall prophecy[sic].' " "This," he penned, "kept me from ever hindering, or placing the least thing in the way of her duty, fearing I might grieve the Holy Spirit, by which she was divinely aided in reaching the hearts of her hearers with the words of life as they fell from her devoted lips. I soon felt I had an 'help-meet' indeed." Subsequently the Fassetts preached the advent message as a team.[93]

Other women preaching the advent near were Sarah J. Paine, Emily C. Clemons, and Clorinda S. Minor. The latter two also edited a periodical aimed especially at women. The first issue of *The Advent Message to the Daughters of Zion* came off the press in May 1844.

The conviction that impelled the host of advent preachers— black and white, female and male—was nicely stated by Olive Maria Rice. After her conversion, she wrote,

> I could not conscientiously return to my studies in North Wilbraham, Ms., to prepare for future usefulness, when *a few months at the longest must close not only my labors in this world, but those of all mankind. I was compelled by a solemn sense of duty, by the influences of the Spirit, and the power of truth, to go and warn my fellow men, to the extent of my ability, to prepare for Christ's second coming, and the solemn scenes of judgment.*[94]

It was that deep-seated sense of prophetic urgency and destiny that *drove* the Millerite messengers day and night to preach their message wherever they could get a hearing. That urgency increased as they approached the year of the end of the world.

Part II

THE YEAR OF
THE END

Chapter 6

ENTERING THE YEAR OF THE END

"This year . . . is the last year that satan [sic] will reign in our earth. Jesus Christ will come. . . . The kingdoms of the earth will be dashed to pieces. . . . The shout of victory will be heard in heaven. . . . Time shall be no more." Thus wrote William Miller in his "New Year's Address to Second Advent Believers" on January 1, 1843. At long last the year of the end of the world had arrived.

Despite his hope in the promise of the "glorious year," Miller was his level-headed, rational self. He recognized that Satan would still be alive and well during the year of the end of the world. Miller also realized that scoffers would continue to scoff and liars to lie regarding the Adventist message and its messengers. But believers must not let that hinder them from putting forth their "best energies in this cause."

Beyond that, the world would be watching for the "halting and falling away of many" if Adventist hopes were not fulfilled according to their own specifications. Miller spoke with more prophetic accuracy than he realized when he wrote: "This year will try our faith, we must be tried, purified and made white, and if there should be any among us, which do not in heart believe, they will go out from us."

Miller feared one other element as time ticked toward its final hour—fanaticism. "I beseech you my dear brethren," he penned in his New Year's address, "be careful that Satan get no advantage over you, by scattering coals of wild fire among you; for if he cannot drive you into unbelief and doubt, he will then try his wild fire of fanaticism, and speculation, to get us off from the word of God. Be watchful and sober, and hope to the end."[1]

Miller's insightful address indicates that he was as perceptive in his study of human nature as he was in his examination of Scripture. The year 1843 would indeed be one of mixed blessings and reactions.

Progressively Focusing on the Time

January 1, 1843, also witnessed Miller define, for the first time, the year of the end. Urged by his followers to be more specific, he wrote: "I believe the time can be known by all who desire to understand and to be ready for his coming. And I am fully convinced that some time between March 21st, 1843, and March 21st, 1844, according to the Jewish mode of computation of time, Christ will come." He then provided fifteen proofs from prophetic chronology for his conclusion regarding his dates.[2]

It should be noted that Miller set no specific date. He only indicated that Christ would come between March 21, 1843, and March 21, 1844. That holds true for other main Millerite leaders as well. When George Storrs was falsely reported as having set the exact day as April 3, 1843, the *Signs* noted that such brethren as Miller, Himes, Litch, Hale, and Fitch had "most decidedly" protested "against . . . *fixing* the day or hour of the event." Thus, claimed the *Signs*, even though they had pinpointed 1843 as the year of the end, they had "*fixed NO TIME in the year* for the event." Neither Miller nor his established leaders ever set an exact day for the second coming. That development, as we shall see in chapter 10, awaited the rise of a new group of leaders in the late summer of 1844.[3]

Miller had not even wanted to set a year for the return of Christ. He was quite happy with the phrase "about the year 1843." As he put it, "the day and hour is not revealed, but the *times* are." Even regarding the year, Miller tended to qualify his interpretation by adding "*if* there were no mistake in my calculation." But in 1845 he wrote, "Some of my brethren preached with great positiveness the exact year, and censured me for putting in an IF." Beyond that, the public press had been stating that he had set an exact day. In response to these pressures, and because he could see no error in his calculations, in December 1842 Miller decided to put forth his March 21 through March 21 span of time for the second coming.[4]

That dating scheme, however, was apparently not new to Miller. As early as 1831 he had firmed up the 1843 date. And both Josiah Litch and Isaac Wellcome claimed that Miller had personally told them in 1839 that Christ would come between the spring of 1843 and March 21, 1844. Miller, they noted, held for a late-in-the-year fulfillment, since he "thought our faith would be tried."[5]

Not only did Miller become more open on the time element as the year of the end approached, but the entire movement progressively shifted its emphasis. In essence, the time element of the Adventist movement was not central in 1840 or 1841. The focal point of agreement was the *fact* of the approaching premillennial second coming of Christ, *not the date* of that event. Thus the circular announcing the proceedings of the first Adventist general conference in October 1840 could state:

> Though in some of the less important views of this momentous subject we are not ourselves agreed, particularly in regard to fixing the year of Christ's second advent, yet we are unanimously agreed and established in this all-absorbing point, that the coming of the Lord to judge the world is now specially "nigh at hand."[6]

Again, the second general conference resolved to solicit the cooperation of all who accepted the advent near, "whatever may be their views of prophetic numbers on which some of us found our argument that the advent will take place about the year A.D. 1843."[7]

It is of interest to note that many of the central leaders early in the movement flatly rejected the time element. Thus Henry Dana Ward and Henry Jones (chairman and secretary of the first general conference) both rejected the 1843 (or any other) time. To Jones, who had first written to Miller in 1833 and had begun preaching the advent near in 1834, the 1843 date was "founded on human presumption, and profane history." To him, the "prophetic *times and seasons* were *indefinitely foretold*."[8]

Ward, Jones, and certain others never did accept the 1843 date. Other individuals, such as Himes, failed to accept the date at first but changed later. Himes freely admitted in 1840 that "IT IS *possible* THAT WE MAY BE MISTAKEN IN THE CHRONOLOGY. It may vary a few years, but we are persuaded that the end cannot be far distant."[9]

But the time element progressively came into more prominence as the 1840s advanced. That was partly because those who had accepted the 1843 date had more zeal. Thus in June 1841 Himes could write Miller that those who had accepted the 1843 date were "*more confirmed* as the time *draws* near."[10]

The turning point on the time issue took place at the Boston general conference in May 1842. That conference, wrote Joseph Bates and J. V. Himes (chairman and secretary, respectively), took "higher ground on the subject of the time of Christ's coming than ever before . . . because of the stupidity of the Church on the subject and the shortness of the time we have to work."[11]

Part of that "higher ground" was a coming out for "not only the manner, but also the time of Christ's Second Advent." The conference's most lengthy resolution strongly favored the 1843 date. The official resolution argued that "no other termination can be found for them [the prophecies of Daniel] than 1843" and that the opponents of that date "do not pretend to give any other solution to these portions of prophecy." It was "therefore *resolved, that in the opinion of this Conference, there are most serious and important reasons for believing that God has revealed the time of the end of the world and that that time is 1843.*" Then, given the shortness of the remaining period before the advent, the conference called for massive literature distribution and the holding of camp meetings. As David Arthur put it, "The time for discussion had ended, the time for unquestioning propagation had begun."[12]

From the May 1842 conference through April 1844 (and again in the autumn of 1844), the time element was at the focal point of Millerite concern. Some, such as Ward and Jones, gradually slipped out of the movement. Jones, who always held to the nearness of the advent, had begun to feel distinctly uncomfortable with the time issue as early as the third general conference in October 1841. But after the "set time . . . was made a standard of union," he later penned, "I was seemingly no longer one of the union."[13]

Other Millerite leaders came out firmly for 1843 after the May 1842 conference. One of those was Himes, who for the first time openly declared his advocacy of the date on July 25, 1842. Probably, as a result of questions regarding his loyalty to the movement, he penned, "I will here say once for all, that I am *confirmed in the doctrine of Christ's personal descent to this earth, to destroy the wicked, and glorify the righteous, some time in the year 1843.*"[14]

That declaration, however, did not mean that Himes had thrown all caution to the wind. Like Miller, he always allowed for the possibility of human error, as in this statement: "If we are mistaken in the *time*, and the world still goes on after 1843, we shall have the satisfaction of having done our duty."[15]

That soft edge on time tended to be held by the central leaders on the 1843 date. As a result, the Boston general conference of May 1843 could declare that "a mere *point* of time . . . is not an essential part of our belief." The essence of their belief, the conference's "Declaration of Principles" held, was the fulfillment of prophecy and the soon return of the Saviour. That soft edge on the time issue would serve as a buffer to disappointment as the Millerites approached and finally passed March 21, 1844.[16]

Meanwhile, the less stable elements among the Millerites began to set specific dates in 1843. Some were apparently looking toward April 3 on the basis that Christ was crucified on that day. Others set their hope on February 10, the forty-fifth anniversary of the French victory over Rome in 1798. Still others hoped for February 15 (the anniversary of the abolition of the papal government),

April 14 (the Passover), the Day of Pentecost in May, the autumnal equinox in September, and so on.[17]

Litch tells us that as each date approached, the "expectation with many was on tip-toe." But, he noted, "those periods came and passed with no unusual occurrence. As soon as they had gone by, a flood of scoffing, reviling and persecution burst forth, not from the infidel world, so much, but from the professed friends of the Savior." That scoffing will be covered in our next chapter. One illustration will be enough at this point. The New York Sunday *Mercury*, the *Signs* reported, "proves the truth of Parson Miller's End-of-the-world-in-1843-doctrine, by multiplying the wrinkles upon the horns of a five-year-old ram by the twelve signs of the zodiac, and that product by the number of seeds in a winter squash."[18]

Back in November 1842, the editors of the *Signs* had sought to protect their followers from such abuse by disclaiming any specific day within the year of the end. "The editors of this paper," we read,

> . . . *solemnly* PROTEST against the setting [of] the hour, day, or month, of the end of the world. There are various events, the anniversaries of which, within the year, may be the end of all things, but we have never fixed on any particular day. . . . Neither does [sic] Mr. Miller or the principal lecturers look to any particular time in 1843. That, we are willing to leave in the hands of God, and will endeavor to be ready whenever he may come.[19]

It is unfortunate that such counsel went unheeded by so many within the movement.

A Year of Expectancy and Evangelism

The year of 1843 opened with an air of expectancy among the Millerites. The *Midnight Cry* adopted a three-month subscription policy, and appointments were often qualified with such phrases as "if time should last."

The building excitement increased in February, when a comet

appeared at the proper psychological moment. The fact that the February comet had special brilliance and was totally unexpected by astronomers led many to view it as a supernatural sign of the Lord's appearing. Himes penned, "I could not but think of *'the Sign of the Son of Man in heaven.'* "[20]

While such "signs" must have been impressive to many both within and without the Millerite ranks, it is important to note that the movement's leadership never emphasized the comet nor any of the other astronomical signs of the era. They were much more comfortable with the great panoramic prophecies of Daniel and Revelation and the correlation of those prophecies with history. Their rationalism continued to guide the movement.

Meanwhile, the intensity continued to build as more and more people gave ear to Miller's message. In February, Miller preached a series that put Adventism on solid footing in Philadelphia. According to Litch, "The city was convulsed throughout with the influence of the lectures. Saints rejoiced, the wicked trembled, backsliders quaked, and the word of the Lord ran and was glorified." In his farewell to the Philadelphia believers, Miller noted that they "sould see his face no more in this life, but that in a few months he expected to see all the children of God in the everlasting kingdom of the Saviour."[21]

By early 1843 the very name of Miller could draw a crowd. In late January handbills were put up all over Washington, D.C., stating that he would speak from the steps of the patent office the following Sunday. Over five thousand people "of all sexes, ages, and colors" amassed for the presentation, with a special section being roped off for congressmen, their wives, and other dignitaries. Unfortunately, Miller was not in town. When that fact was discovered, there was a great cry of "hoax" followed by some disorder. The event was probably engineered by some "printers' *devils*" who had produced the handbills and distributed them.[22]

Unfortunately for Miller, during much of 1843, illness prevented him from capitalizing on the peak of his popularity. He was sixty-one years of age, tremulous with palsy, and given to serious and prolonged illnesses. His health had no doubt been jeopardized by the years he had preached to the limit of his endurance to get out the warning of coming judgment. In late July 1842 he wrote to Himes of his endless toil, noting that he had not "enjoyed one day's repose since the first of March."[23]

On March 27, 1843, Miller became ill, remaining so for the next crucial five months, often approaching the point of death. "My health," he penned on May 3,

> is on the gain, as my folks would say. I have now only twenty-two biles [carbuncle boils], from the bigness of a grape to a walnut, on my shoulder, side, back and arms, I am truly afflicted like Job. And [I have] about as many comforters— only they do not come to see me as did Job's, and their arguments are not near so rational.

Two weeks later Miller was again feeble. He would not be preaching again until the fall.[24]

On the other hand, early 1843 found Miller with many things to rejoice in. One was that his wife and eight children were "all the children of God, and believers in the same doctrine with myself." That was a far cry from 1838, when he prayed for his children and the people of Low Hampton who "are sleeping over the volcano of God's wrath." "Do my father," he had prayed in a letter to his son, "convert my children!"[25]

In spite of Miller's personal inability to preach, 1843 was a banner year in the spread of the message. Those Adventists holding to the 1843 date pushed ahead with great vigor, while those not holding to 1843 fell into obscurity as Millerism moved into high gear.

Up through late 1842, Millerism was largely a northeastern phenomenon. Thus in September 1842 the editors of the *Oberlin Evangelist* felt obliged to apologize to their western readers for their extensive treatment of millennialism. They went on to point out that the many articles had been included for their readers in the East, "where the subject is undergoing a discussion."[26]

The neglect of the West would change radically in 1843. In

May of that year, it was decided to push the work in both the West and the South.[27] In the next few months, such cities as Rochester, New York, and Cincinnati, Ohio, would become centers for the spread of the message, and Cleveland would be strengthened as a center.

Beyond new areas, new workers would come into prominence to help share the increasing burden of the work. Nathaniel Whiting, J. B. Cook, F. G. Brown, George Storrs, Joseph Marsh, and Elon Galusha joined the ranks of influential Millerite leaders. Some of these, along with others, would do much to push the Adventist work forward from central New York to Iowa and Wisconsin. Cincinnati's *Western Midnight Cry* (under Storrs) and Rochester's *Voice of Truth* (under Marsh) soon joined Cleveland's *Second Advent of Christ* (under Fitch) as regional Millerite periodicals in the West.

Not only were new leaders sent to the West and new periodicals started there, but there were also plans to blanket the area with Second Advent Libraries so that "they shall be left without excuse." "We hope and expect," penned the editors of the *Signs*, "to see one mighty gatheri[n]g in the west."[28] From the summer of 1843 on, we also find Miller and Himes putting more of their personal time into the West as the urgency of the burden of their message pressed them on with ever greater force.

By December 1843 the message had been carried to St. Louis. From there the Adventist preachers reached out to the frontier.[29]

The year of the end also saw attempts to plant the message more firmly in the American South. But whereas, as Litch put it, "the whole West seemed ripe and ready for harvest," the South was a much more difficult field of Millerite labor.[30]

Perhaps the major reason that Millerism won few adherents in the South was its largely abolitionist leadership. Not only was the region pro-slavery, but the other major reforms of the day had not made the same impact in the South as in the rest of the nation. By and large, southerners sought to preserve the status quo. Such an attitude provided a soil relatively unreceptive to the seeds of radical millennialism.

But to say that Millerism had a difficult time in the South is not to say that it made no impact at all. As early as 1841, J. M. Thomas, a southern minister, was preaching the "midnight cry" successfully in South Carolina. Thomas appealed for the help of northern ministers to come to his aid. However, Thomas seems to have been a voice crying in the dark, and there were apparently no lasting results from his work.[31]

The turning point in Millerite attention to the South came in 1843. In February of that year, two advent preachers began a "southern tour" but made it only as far as Richmond, Virginia, before deciding to return home. After a second unsuccessful foray into Virginia, Litch concluded that "it seemed as though some fatal spell had fastened on the south, that it could not be approached." Early 1843, however, did see some success in the Washington, D.C., area.[32]

It was reported to the New York general conference in May 1843 that there had been "urgent and repeated" requests from the South for lecturers to be sent, but, reported the *Signs*, "the existing prejudices and jealousies of the South on the subject of slavery, renders it difficult and next to impossible" to fill those requests.[33]

Past experience seemed to bear out that statement. After all, George Storrs (an ardent abolitionist) had been mobbed that very month in Norfolk. The experience of Joseph Bates also illustrates the problems of preaching in even the border states, where the hold of slavery was weakest. Bates had been warned of Storrs' experience and was told, he writes, "that if I went South the slave-holders would kill me for being an abolitionist." He saw the danger but was convicted of his responsibility to give the warning anyway.[34]

After experiencing some modest success in Maryland, he was challenged and denounced by a Methodist lay leader. The man began "to talk," noted Bates,

> about *riding us* [H. S. Gurney was with Bates] *on a rail*. I said, "We are all ready for that, sir. If you will put a saddle

on it, we would rather ride than walk." This caused such a sensation in the meeting that the man seemed to be at a loss to know which way to look for his friends.

I then said to him, "You must not think that we have come six hundred miles through the ice and snow, at our own expense, to give you the Midnight Cry, without first sitting down and counting the cost. And now, if the Lord has no more for us to do, we had as lief [gladly] lie at the bottom of the Chesapeake Bay as anywhere else until the Lord comes. But if he has any more work for us to do, you can't touch us!"[35]

On another occasion on that same Maryland tour, Bates was accosted by a southern judge who said that he understood that Bates was an abolitionist who had come "to get away our slaves." Bates replied:

Yes, Judge, I am an abolitionist, and have come to get your slaves, and *you too*! As to getting your slaves *from* you, we have no such intention; for if you should give us all you have (and I was informed he owned quite a number), we should not know what to do with them. We teach that Christ is coming, and we want you all saved.[36]

Bates' experiences not only illustrate some of the problems northern Millerites faced in even the border states, but they also demonstrate the faith and courage that drove them forward as the "end of time" approached.

The rest of 1843 saw several additional attempts at evangelizing the South, but, with the exception of Maryland and Kentucky, the Millerites had little success. By the end of the year, however, a few Millerite preachers were seeing some results in Virginia and the two Carolinas. By early 1844, Miller, Himes, and Litch were receiving calls to work in such cities as Charleston, South Carolina; Savannah, Georgia; and Mobile, Alabama.[37]

The message had reached the deep South not so much by the

living preacher as by the printed word, but reach it it did. Robert W. Olson, the only scholar to extensively study Millerism in the South, claims that the Millerite message was "very well known" in the region and that southern religious papers periodically printed articles on the topic.[38]

While Millerite literature by mid-1843 had made converts in such faraway places as the Sandwich Islands and Norway, it was in Great Britain that Millerism made its largest overseas impact. The premillennial second coming had been preached there for decades by such men as Edward Irving, Henry Drummond, and John Nelson Darby. As a result, a strong body of premillennialists had developed.[39]

In 1840 the Millerites in America had attempted to link up with the "literalistic" Adventists in Britain, but hopeful expectations were snagged on irreconcilable theological differences centering on the return of the Jews to Palestine and whether nonbelievers would be kept alive during the millennium and could be converted after the second coming of Christ. As a result, Millerism and traditional British premillennialism failed to find enough common ground to enable them to work together. The same can be said for the largely Presbyterian, Congregational, and Episcopalian "literalistic" premillennialists in the United States. The British and American "literalists" would later develop into the dispensational premillennialism that is so popular among fundamentalists and Pentecostals in the twentieth century.[40]

Because of the incompatibilities with premillennial literalism, Millerism had to cut its own path in Great Britain. That task, however, did not take long to get underway, since Millerite literature soon found its way across the Atlantic. In fact, writes Louis Billington, "there is some evidence that William Miller's exegesis was being studied in Great Britain before he had achieved more than a local reputation in the United States."[41]

Millerite preachers began to appear in Britain as early as 1841, but the event that gave the most impetus to British Millerism was the conversion of Robert Winter at Millerism's first camp meeting in June 1842. After his conversion, Winter returned to

England, where he headed up a publishing work that not only re-printed much of the American literature but also generated its own periodicals.[42]

By the spring of 1843, Winter could report that he had printed fifteen thousand copies of selected Millerite books. "Many preachers," he penned, "have received the truth by reading these works." Those preachers also were beginning to sound the message. Winter himself preached in the streets with his "chart hoisted up on a pole." The British believers planned to hold a camp meeting that summer, "if time continues; but if the Lord comes, we will hold it in the new earth." Winter invited help from America. If they could send preachers, he assured the editors of the *Midnight Cry*, they would find the English people more responsive than the Americans.[43]

That May the general conference held in Boston responded to Winter's call by proposing to send a missionary to England. Litch volunteered for the assignment, and a committee was formed to raise money for the project.[44] In spite of the best intentions, however, no leading Millerites were scheduled for the British mission until the late summer of 1844. On the other hand, there is evidence that substantial funds were sent from the United States to aid the work in England.

By late 1843, Winter could write that "the Advent doctrine is chiefly the talk in this country. . . . Thousands are now looking for the coming of the Lord, and believe it is at the door—and preachers of all denominations are now giving the midnight cry." In some parts of the country, "nearly whole villages have turned to the Lord."[45] While it is impossible accurately to evaluate the impact of Millerism in Great Britain, there is no doubting the fact that it had become a significant movement in that nation.

The years prior to 1843 had seen a great deal of Millerite activity, but the year of the end of the world saw that activity multiplied as a sense of urgency and responsibility gripped the believers as never before. By November, Litch was able to write that Millerite publications had gone "to the various parts of the four quarters of the earth and various islands of the sea."[46]

Non-Millerite Responses to the Arrival of the Year

By late 1842 and early 1843 it was becoming difficult, if not impossible, for non-Millerites to ignore the advent phenomenon. As a result, press coverage of the movement radically increased as the crisis neared. That was particularly true as the very month of the predicted end arrived. Thus the March 1843 issue of *Graham's Magazine* sported a lead article entitled "The End of the World." It is also of significance that this lengthy article ended as the author hears little boys in the street "crying out 'April fool! April fool!' "[47]

The month also saw Horace Greeley's New York *Tribune* devote an entire issue to reporting Millerism on March 2, 1843, only nineteen days before the beginning of the year of the end. Most of the front page was given over to the reproduction of a Millerite chart. The balance of the edition consisted of a "clear and complete refutation of Mr. Miller's interpretation of the Prophecies" penned by the "Rev. Mr. Dowling," a Baptist clergyman. The public press was equally hostile in Boston and many other cities.[48]

Even such American literati as Edgar Allan Poe, Nathaniel Hawthorne, and John Greenleaf Whittier made contemporary references to Millerism. Miller's apocalyptic themes also informed several of their literary productions.[49]

In February 1843 Garrison's *Liberator* began a series on Millerism in Garrison's usual biting style. According to him, the best argument in favor of Millerism was that it had been "assailed by a benighted and corrupt priesthood" and its "rabble" following. Even though the crusty abolitionist believed that "the odium" heaped upon the Adventists was unjustified, he could still rejoice that "the theory of Mr. Miller is soon to be ignominiously exploded." Garrison was quite astonished that "one illiterate, though strong-minded man, like Mr. Miller, should, in this enlightened age and country have succeeded in so short a space of time in enlisting such a multitude of converts." To Garrison the Millerite movement was "an event scarcely paralleled in the history of popular excitements." On March 1 he penned, "The delusion has not long to run, . . . let us rejoice."[50]

The approaching year of the end also created a great stir among the foremost religious leaders of the day, especially those who (like Miller) had recently founded new movements. Thus Alexander Campbell, a friend of Himes and the leader of the Disciples of Christ ("the fastest growing religious movement in nineteenth-century America"), could claim that while the second advent of Christ should be "hailed with . . . overwhelming joy," Millerism was built upon biblical "ignorance" and was not based upon the " 'sure word of prophecy.' " "Methinks," wrote Campbell in July 1843, ". . . the year 1843 will pass along with dreams of felicity and sweet antepasts of blessedness whose remembrance will in years to come be as the delightful oasis in a parched desert."[51]

Even the great evangelist Charles Finney had personally reached out to Miller in an attempt to correct his "errors." In 1842 Finney, who had already dealt extensively with Millerism through his friend Fitch's work at Oberlin College, attended some of Miller's lectures in Boston. Afterward, Finney invited Miller to his room "and tried to convince him that he was in error." Finney finally concluded that it "was vain to reason with him and his followers at that time." Miller, in turn, sent Finney an autographed copy of *Miller's Works*. But Miller apparently had no more success with the great evangelist than Finney had had with him.[52]

Those more to the sectarian edge of American religion than Finney also had to reckon with Miller as the year of the end passed. Joseph Smith, prophet of the rising premillennial Mormons, expressed surprise when some of his followers were drawn to Miller's views. That dynamic may have been the reason that among the last of Smith's published revelations was God's assurance to him that "the Lord will not come to reign over the righteous in this world in 1843."[53]

In a similar manner, the erratic communitarian perfectionist John Humphrey Noyes noted that the wind of Millerism was sweeping over the country and "has found some weathercocks among our nominal brethren." Some had converted to Millerism, while others, who were "honest, but weak-minded," had also been "shaken by the popular tempest."[54]

Millerism, as might be expected, showed up in the advertising copy of the day. One advertisement pictured an angel flying in the clouds of heaven holding a scroll featuring the motto "THE TIME HAS COME." Below the picture were the words: "When consumption may be classed with the curable diseases. Wistar's Balsam of Wild Cherry." Another advertisement, headed "the second advent," advertised cigars, which the readers were recommended to purchase in order to enjoy "the tip end of felicity" while the world lasted.[55]

While many of the comments on Millerism were humorous and some even friendly, others came packed with a conscious barb. One such was written by Moses Stuart, one of America's foremost biblical scholars of the 1840s. When the New York *Herald* erroneously announced that Miller had set April 3, 1843, as the day of the advent, Stuart wrote:

> I would respectfully suggest, that in some way or other they [Miller and his followers] have in all probability made a small mistake as to the exact day of the month when the grand catastrophe takes place, the FIRST *of April* being evidently much more appropriate to their arrangements than any other day of the year.[56]

In tenor, that remark did not stand alone. The sharpness of rhetoric on both sides of the line separating Millerism from the rest of Christianity increased as the year of the end of the world progressed. One result would be an unplanned Millerite separatism.

Chapter 7

COMING OUT OF BABYLON

The year 1843 became a crisis year for Millerism in more ways than one. Not only did the Adventists believe that Christ would come that year, but as they became more fixed on the date and as the time came closer, they redoubled their missionary assertiveness. That assertion in the face of entrenched ideologies and established churches would bring increasing rejection and Millerite separationism as 1843 progressed.

Those results had not been expected by Miller. At first, in his sincere but naive enthusiasm, he believed that both clergy and church members would gladly accept his findings once they saw the Bible evidence. That initial enthusiasm, although dampened considerably by his early contact with ministers, seemed to some extent to find validity throughout the 1830s as increasing numbers of churches from most Protestant denominations opened their doors to his preaching. Little did Miller realize, however, that the great majority of them were not so much interested in his "peculiar" teaching on the second coming as they were in his ability to bring in converts to fill their churches. Only gradually did it dawn on Miller that he was being used. The very nature of his message, however, made that realization inevitable.[1]

It was one thing to preach Miller's 1843 message when it was some years off. It was quite another thing when the time was near at hand. A message that seemed harmless enough in the late 1830s threatened to disrupt both churches and society by 1843.

By the arrival of the year of the end, the success of Millerism had created what Ruth Alden Doan has called a "boundary crisis."[2]

"Boundary Crisis"

Because of their total rejection of American progress and avenues of hope outside the radical supernaturalism of the second advent of Christ, Millerites gradually but progressively found themselves in opposition to both the churches and society. Therefore, as the predicted time came close, neutrality became impossible: one either had to accept Millerism or reject it. It was not date setting that caused the showdown crisis. After all, John Wesley had once set a date for the end in 1836. And several Baptists had set dates between 1830 and 1847. Rather, it was the assertiveness, popular success, and closeness of the time, as preached by the Millerites, that made it difficult for many people to ignore Millerism, especially in light of the increasing burden of the Adventists to warn the world. Millerism and its culture were on a collision course that could only intensify with time.[3]

As the predicted end approached, each side became increasingly severe with the other. For example, the *Signs* editors saw it to be their duty "to expose the *fabulous* and soul-destroying doctrine of what is termed the *temporal millenium* [sic]. . . . We brand this doctrine as a fable—a deception." Such hard words did not exactly endear the Millerites to those who taught alternative views of the millennium. Nor did it help matters when a significant number in a congregation began to see their pastor as the perpetrator of such "deception." The more certain the Millerites became of their interpretation of the Bible, the more aggressive they became with others.[4]

The opposition to the Millerites was neither genteel nor insignificant. From every side the Adventists faced caricature and abuse. In a six-month period, for example, the Hartford-based *Universalist* referred to the Millerites as "simple," "deluded," "ignorant," "ridiculous," "notorious," "illiterate," "excited," "coarse," "ill-bred," "blind," "fanatical," "evil," "weak-minded," "imposters," and "humbugs."[5]

The Millerite leaders especially came under fire. Much of the criticism against them clustered around two points. First, they were accused of stirring up religious excitement to line their own pockets and "gorging and fattening on what they extort from the fears, or pious contributions, of those whom they dupe." Again, charged the *Olive Branch*, "The amount of poverty and misery produced by such fellows as Himes, and his tools, can only be known in the last great day."[6]

A second line of criticism aimed at the Millerite leaders accused them of hypocrisy because their lifestyles, according to some onlookers, did not reflect their predictions. Criticisms along this line included such items as the fact that Miller had built a "STONE WALL" on his farm. Then again, said others, Miller could not be sincere, since he refused to sell his farm. To Litch, that was the most "wonderful" of all the accusations. "*How, O! how CAN Christ come*," he parodied, "*when Mr. Miller will not sell his farm???*"[7]

Other caricatures of Millerism centered on the rumor that Miller was dead, that the Millerites were preparing long, flowing ascension robes in which to meet the Lord, and that the leaders had carefully checked their figures and discovered they were off by one thousand years (some versions of this story give one hundred years).[8] Thus the *Journal of Commerce* reported in January 1843:

> It is understood that Miller and his associates have recently carefully reviewed their calculations upon which they found the prophecy of the near approach of the end of the world, when an error was discovered in the footing of the column of a thousand years. This is a very important discovery just now. The "ascension robes" with which many of the Millerites on Long Island have provided themselves, are not likely to be wanted.[9]

Then, of course, there were jokes and cartoons to add richness to the "high humor" surrounding Millerism. One wit has Miller so busy preaching judgment to come that he had forgotten to prepare himself. "Bless my soul," Miller said in surprise, "I had no idea it would be so hot." Another cartoon shows Miller ascending to heaven with his followers hanging onto him. One ascension cartoon has the saints arising to meet their Lord in various postures. The "fat ones" are being drawn up with hooks by angels. To the Millerites, such graphics were sacrilegious and "the dirty work of the devil." Their response was to publish such items in their "scoffers'" column as one more sign of the last days.[10]

With the approach of the year of the end, accusations of Millerite-induced insanity increased. According to the *American Journal of Insanity*, many had become deranged because of Millerism, and "thousands who have not yet become deranged, have had their health impaired to such a degree as to unfit them for the duties of life forever; and especially is this the case with females." The technical name for the Millerite disease was "*epidemic or contagious monomania.*" According to this professional journal, "the prevalence of the yellow fever or of the cholera has never proved so great a calamity to this country" as Miller's doctrine.[11]

Of course, the way some Adventist believers acted, or were reported to have acted, certainly helped supply material for the gristmills of the budding "science" of psychiatry. It was common, for example, to view people as being abnormal if they gave away their earthly possessions as a sign of their belief that Christ was coming and that they would have no more need of them. Likewise, people appeared demented to nonbelievers when they spent their life's savings in the rush to publicize the doctrine of the soon-coming advent.

On another level, those already on the margin of emotional stability could be pushed over the edge by intensive preaching of soon-coming judgment. Falling into this category is the man in New York who attempted to commit suicide by swallowing molten lead. Another, a tailor from Cleveland, was found three miles out of town sitting on a log, Bible in hand, awaiting the second coming.[12]

Then there were the purported stories of Millerites involved in erratic activities while clothed in their so-called ascension robes. Thus the *Niles National Register* could report that April 23, 1843, found the Millerites of Providence, Rhode Island, facing flood rather than fire. "On that day several Millerites in that city walked the streets and fields all day arrayed in their ascension robes, dripping from top to bottom, looking for the Saviour to come in the pouring clouds to receive them and set the world on fire." Again, local tradition in Macedon, New York, recalls one Millerite who "dressed himself in white, and spent the whole day, either on the wood pile, or on the top of the hog-pen" waiting for his Lord.[13]

While the accusations regarding ascension robes and Millerite-induced insanity were denied by the Millerites at the time (and were later proved to be without significant factual basis by such researchers as Francis D. Nichol and Ronald and Janet Numbers), the accusations did much to color contemporary attitudes toward advent believers among certain sectors of the population. Of course, as will be pointed out in chapter 9 and as the Numbers' research indicates, Millerism did attract its share of those afflicted by mental instability. But such acquisitions have been the bane of intense religious revivals down through history. In fact, those in previous eras who lived what the larger society considered to be aberrant lives because of either total dedication to God or emotional imbalance have often been labeled as saints on one end of the spectrum and witches on the other end. But for Millerites the label was insanity.[14]

Some Millerites may have been genuinely crazy. But, on the other hand, the opponents of revivals had been charging for decades that the emotional excitement and pressures of the camp meeting had driven people to distraction. Along that line, Alexis de Tocqueville, in his tour of the United States in the early 1800s, reported that heightened religious enthusiasm was responsible for "religious madness." Similar accusations of religion causing insanity would later be leveled by psychiatrists at the work of Dwight L. Moody in the 1870s. According to some, his "emphasis on 'conviction of sin' and 'a sense of divine wrath' seemed to be upsetting 'the mental equilibrium of many a youth, at least temporarily.' "[15]

Beyond verbal abuse and name calling, the Adventists also experienced such harassment as vandalism, intimidation, and attempts to break up their meetings. Similar tactics have been used against unpopular movements down through history—especially when such movements threatened the status quo. Such persecution, however, has generally functioned in the eyes of participants as a validation of their heaven-directed mission. After all, did not the apostles and prophets of old suffer under similar treatment?

Though Miller and his colleagues met a great deal of abuse in the public press, they also had their defenders against misrepresentation. Thus the *Oberlin Evangelist* could decry the "absurd stories . . . kept in circulation" "by a large portion of the religious press. . . . Bros. Miller and Fitch may be wrong, but they are not knaves, nor dunces. They may err, but they have a right not to be misrepresented."[16]

Again, the editor of the *Gazette and Advertiser* set out to personally investigate Miller, "who has probably been an object of more abuse, ridicule and blackguardism, than any other man now living." To his surprise, the editor found the Adventist leader conversing on religious subjects "with a coolness and soundness of judgment which made us whisper to ourselves, 'If this be madness, then there is method in 't.' "[17]

Millerite preachers, of course, often made their own successful responses to the criticisms leveled at them. When the Rev. William Brownlee went to Newark to preach against Miller during an Adventist camp meeting, Himes recognized the positive value in the publicity this enemy of the cause had stirred up. In retrospect, Himes penned: "Brother Brownlee's coming over here has done us so much good, that I'd cheerfully pay all his expenses if he'd come again. We want the people aroused."[18]

On another occasion Himes received what he believed to be a bogus invitation to speak at Princeton College. Deciding to take advantage of the hoax, he made the trip, spending the day conversing with the college's officers and students. Himes considered the trip to be quite worthwhile, since "the subject has not been agitated here as yet." Beyond his own agitating on the topic, he left behind a Second Advent Library and a prophetic chart for each of the Princeton libraries.[19]

A young Adventist preacher by the name of James White also demonstrated that he could take advantage of hostility. Upon returning to a town where he had previously held meetings, White was met by a critical Congregational preacher. " 'Why, Mr. White,' " said he, " 'are you yet in the land of the living?' 'No, sir,' was the reply, 'I am in the land of the dying, but at the soon coming of the Lord I expect to go to the land of the living.' "[20]

Even though Miller and his fellow believers were often able to come back with similar retorts, the constant accusations did take their toll. In February 1843 Miller wrote to his son, expressing his sensitivity to "the thousand and one falsehoods, which a proud & haughty Priesthood have invented, and an hireling press has circulated." A few months before, Miller had noted that he needed to drive "anger, malice and revenge" from his mind.[21] Perhaps the surprising thing about the man is not that he fell into the pit of anger and revenge from time to time but that he did it so infrequently.

Growing Resistance to Millerism

The "boundary crisis" between Millerism and the larger Christian culture not only existed in the world in general; it also took place on a daily basis in local congregations as Millerites and non-Millerites came face to face with disparate views of reality.

The "boundary crisis" was heightened by the firm Millerite belief that God's demands took precedence over the demands of the church community. Thus the Adventists believed themselves to be duty bound to sound their warning "midnight cry" even in churches that did not want to hear it. If the Adventists would have remained silent, things might have been all right. But such a silence went against their deepest conviction of the need to warn their neighbors about soon-coming judgment. Their ongoing and unrelenting agitation could lead to only one possible result:

growing resistance to Millerism in both congregations and denominations.

That resistance took at least three forms. The first was that an
increasingly larger number of congregations forbade the Millerites to hold services in their buildings as the time of the end
approached. That problem had been sporadic at first. Miller
reports that the first time he was shut out by a congregation was
in December 1839. But by the late summer of 1842, the problem
was becoming a common occurrence. As Himes put it in August
1842, "We are exceedingly blamed, censured, judged and condemned, shut out of most pulpits." Again, we read in March 1844:
"The doors of most of the ch[u]rches in our land have been closed
against this doctrine. Pastors have boasted that their churches
were free from it."[22]

In addition, the article goes on, "sarcasm and ridicule have been
the arguments used to disprove it. Members of churches, in good
and regular standing, have been denied the privilege of exhorting
their fellow servants to prepare for the coming judgment. And they
have been excommunicated without a cause."[23]

That last point brings us to the second form of resistance to
Millerism as the time of the end approached—revoking the church
membership of Adventists because they would not be quiet about
their beliefs. Such a move is certainly understandable from the
perspective of the various denominations; after all, they already
had a doctrinal agenda. In addition, the Millerites not only
preached their peculiar doctrine, but in the preaching of it they
often taught, or at least inferred, that the denominations were in
error. Some even saw their denominations as apostate, especially
in the face of their refusal to accept the Millerite teachings on
the advent and the millennium. The denominations could hardly
be expected to accept such pronouncements with joy.

The results were predictable. Many advent believers were not
permitted to speak of their beliefs in their own churches. That
meant that they were either forced to go against the ruling—a
move that often led to their excommunication—or to stop attending their home churches because of the pressure. Both alternatives

left them without a church home. Not all Millerites faced such harsh alternatives, of course, but tens of thousands did.

The third form of resistance to Millerism in the denominations was the expulsion of preachers who had accepted the advent doctrine. Representative of that dynamic was the resolution adopted by the Congregational ministers of Vermont in 1843 to prohibit all teaching of Christ's immediate coming and the action of the New York Presbytery to reject an " *'entirely satisfactory'* " candidate for ordination on the sole basis that he believed in the soon coming of Christ.[24]

In a similar manner, 1843 witnessed Joseph Marsh lose his editorial post among the Connexionists for his advocacy of Millerism. Likewise, in early 1844, Elon Galusha, due to increasing pressure, "tendered his resignation . . . , and is now free to preach the whole truth, without being desired to conform his preaching to the taste of a Laodicean Church." Such experiences were the lot of many ministers as they struggled with their dual responsibilities of faithfulness both to their denominations and to their Adventist beliefs.[25]

The experience of the Maine Conference of the Methodist Episcopal Church illustrates the crisis nicely from both the perspective of individual preachers and a highly organized denomination. By the summer of 1843, as the *History of Methodism in Maine* puts it, "the second advent excitement had become quite extensive [in the state] . . . ; lecturers had traveled over the country, with charts and hideous diagrams."[26]

The success of the lecturers had brought Maine Methodism to the point of crisis, since about thirty of its ministers were either interested in Millerism or preaching it. As a result, in July the Maine Conference, meeting at Bath, passed a series of resolutions against Millerism. The second resolution claimed that the Millerite beliefs were contrary to Methodism and must be regarded "as among the erroneous and strange doctrines which we are pledged to banish and drive away." The third resolution claimed that the preaching of Millerism was "irreconcilably inconsistent" with the duties of the Methodist ministry and had, ultimately, a "disastrous tendency." The final resolution ordered those preaching Millerite doctrines "to refrain entirely from disseminating them in the future."[27]

The Bath resolutions encouraged many, but not all, of the pastors to mend their ways. A case in point is that of Levi Stockman, who continued to preach his advent beliefs "as a matter of duty to God and the world." As a result, he was brought to trial by a council of preachers in Portland, Maine. Stockman was charged and convicted of heresy on the basis of the Bath resolutions, in spite of the fact that those resolutions had no legal standing in Methodist ecclesiastical law and were contrary to the theology of John Fletcher (one of Methodism's formative theologians).

Stockman left no doubt that the entire proceeding made the Maine Methodist Conference look "enough like the old 'MOTHER OF HARLOTS' to be one of her DAUGHTERS." Accordingly, he wrote in early 1844, "we are very near a crisis—an awful crisis—between ourselves and the churches on this question; it is not a difference of opinion *merely*, but a difference of action and spirit. . . . The line of division is fast being drawn."[28]

But Methodism was not finished with Stockman yet. Even though he was dying of tuberculosis, after the close of the trial, he was entreated to confess and recant, but he refused. Stockman was then approached by his superior, indicating that if he did not recant, he would be turned out of the church, and his widowed wife and three orphaned children would not receive the benefits reserved for such cases after his death. "This dastardly impious threat," reports one of his fellow Maine Methodist ministers who had also accepted Millerism, "did not turn him; but it gave him the opportunity to give the ministers present a Scriptural lesson on Christian charity, which he improved."[29]

Stockman was expelled and died a few months later on June 25, 1844, at the age of thirty-two. One of his Methodist associates wrote Stockman's obituary, "giving him a noble Christian and ministerial career, 'with the exception of this one dark blot upon his character,' referring to his faith in Christ's immediate coming."[30]

The object lesson had its desired effect. The *History of Methodism in Maine* reports that

the brethren who had been led astray by this delusion [Millerism], with a few exceptions, saw their error, and, like honest men, meekly submitted to the censure of the conference. They were restored to the confidence of their brethren, and most of them rendered valuable service to the church, in their subsequent life. The few recalcitrant offenders withdrew from the church, went on from bad to worse, till, like wandering stars, they disappeared in darkness.[31]

Toward Millerite Separatism

Like Martin Luther, John Wesley, and many other church founders, William Miller and his early followers did not set out to form a new church—some sort of Adventist denomination. To the contrary, it was their desire to warn the world of Christ's coming from within the framework of the existing churches.[32]

The first Millerite general conference in October 1840 had made that position explicit. "We are not," reads the conference report, "of those who sow discord among brethren, who withdraw from the fellowship of the churches." Again, "we have no purpose to distract the churches with any new inventions, or to get ourselves a name by starting another sect among the followers of the Lamb." Rather, they merely desired to "revive and restore . . . the ancient landmarks" within their churches.[33]

But in the very action of organizing a conference and starting a paper, the advent believers had already begun an independent existence, even though they remained in their churches. The second session of the general conference, with its aggressive recommendations that believers should agitate the question of the advent in the churches, pressure their ministers on the topic, and form special Bible classes for the study of the advent, was a giant step forward in the crisis that would lead to Adventist separation from the existing denominations. The very agitation of the issues in the face of a rapidly approaching fulfillment of a time prophecy all but guaranteed separation for many Millerites.[34]

If the advent believers would have remained quiet inside their denominations, they could have stayed in them, but such silence was diametrically opposed to the very essence of the Millerite sense of responsibility. They perceived their primary task to be the sounding of the midnight cry that the hour of God's judgment was close at hand.

The next significant step in Millerite separatism came in May 1842. That month saw the organization of the Second Advent Association of New York and vicinity by Henry Jones and others. The Association's charter read: "The undersigned, believers in Christ's second personal coming at hand, are hereby associated for the purpose of strengthening and comforting each other with these truths, and in every practical way to disseminate knowledge in the subject, and to strive by all means, to promote the glory of God."[35]

While not a church, the Association did collect funds and elect officers. They also rented a hall for their Sunday-afternoon meetings and formed a Bible class for the study of the advent truth. The Association was not seen as a replacement for church attendance, but as a supplement, thus the Sunday-afternoon meeting. Believers could attend both their regular church and the Association's meeting.[36]

Soon after the formation of the New York Association, similar groups were established in Philadelphia and other places. While not perceived as churches, many local associations would evolve into churches after Christ did not come in October 1844.

Another move in the direction of Adventist separatism was the building of Millerite tabernacles. The first and most significant of those tabernacles was completed in Boston in May 1843. Built because of overcrowding in the Chardon Street Chapel, it seated over three thousand people and was frugally yet substantially built.[37]

The Boston Tabernacle became the forerunner of many such church buildings where Adventist congregations could meet. Many of those buildings were built in great haste as the year of the end of the world approached its crisis point. In Toronto, for example, the rapidly growing band of believers decided to put up their own building, since "every hall in the city, and every church was against us." Within two hours of setting forth the idea, the "whole amount" for the house of worship had been subscribed. They expected to have it completed in six to eight days. "Our house," penned one of their leaders, "will be a temporary affair, expecting soon, as we do, to exchange it for that which has foundations, whose builder is God."[38]

Between the summer of 1842 and that of 1844, the advent believers had slowly positioned themselves to have all the attributes of a denomination, including the ordaining of ministers.[39] But even then they had no desire to form a new religious body. Why should they? Jesus would be coming shortly. After that event there would be no need for denominations.

Thus in May 1844, Litch could write: "So far as there is anything which may be called an organization, [it] is of the most simple, voluntary and primitive form. . . . We neither expect nor desire any other organization, until we reach the New Jerusalem, and organize under the King of kings. Here, we are pilgrims and strangers, with no abiding place." The only reason they had established separate meetings at all, Litch claimed, was that they were forced to the hard choice between separation or not having meetings at all. That thought brings us to the active call to separate from the churches sounded by *some* Millerite leaders beginning in July 1843.[40]

"Babylon Has Fallen"

Miller had never encouraged his followers to leave their churches. In November 1842 he wrote, "I have advised all men of every sect not to separate from their churches." Significantly, however, that sentence goes on to specify "*if* they could live among them and enjoy christian [sic] privileges."[41] By the summer of 1843, as we have seen, that peaceful coexistence was becoming impossible for many.

On July 26, 1843, Charles Fitch preached what became one of

the most famous Millerite sermons. Based on Revelation 18:1-5 and 14:8, it was titled " 'Come Out of Her, My People.' " In essence, that apocalyptic passage deals with the fall of Babylon and the consequent need of God's people to flee from the corrupt system it represented.

Up through the summer of 1843, the Millerites had generally identified Babylon as the Roman Catholic Church. Fitch would change that perspective. After identifying Babylon with the antichrist, Fitch went on to suggest that "whoever is opposed to the PERSONAL REIGN of Jesus Christ over this world on David's throne, is ANTICHRIST." That, he held, included both Roman Catholics *and* those Protestants who rejected the teaching of the premillennial soon coming of Christ. The Protestant churches had fallen in the sense that they, like their Catholic forerunner, had become oppressive and had succumbed to the temptations of self-aggrandizement and the lust for power.[42]

Fitch then went on to proclaim that "to come out of Babylon is to be converted to the true scriptural doctrine of the personal coming and kingdom of Christ." At that point Fitch was coming perilously close to suggesting that to be a Christian, one must be an Adventist, a point he soon made explicit. He saw no way one could avoid the advent truth and be a Christian. Thus, he appealed, "if you are a Christian, *come out of Babylon!* If you intend to be found a Christian when Christ appears, *come out of Babylon*, and come out Now! . . . Dare to believe the Bible."[43]

Moving toward his conclusion, Fitch noted that the book of Revelation taught that those who remained in Babylon must be destroyed. Thus in his final appeal, he cried for his hearers to "come out of Babylon or perish. . . . Not one that is ever saved can remain in Babylon."[44]

Fitch's sermon made a major impact upon Millerism. It was first published in July in his own *Second Advent of Christ.* Then in September it was reprinted in the *Midnight Cry*, even though the editors felt the need to preface its publication with a note stating that they would "make a different application of the Scriptures relating to the fall of Babylon." It was also published by Himes as a pamphlet, in spite of the fact that Himes was not in agreement with some of the sermon's ideas.[45]

In essence, Fitch had provided his fellow advent believers with a theological rationale for separating from the churches. In one sense, that rationale was a response to the times. After all, large numbers of Millerites were being thrown out of their churches, while others were being shut out from giving the message that was at the center of their being and Christian experience. It was only natural for them to conclude that those who opposed them also opposed Christ. The hostile action of the churches merely confirmed the Adventists' interpretation of them as anti-Christian.

On the other hand, the separation rationale was built into the very fabric of Scripture itself. Nine years before Fitch's sermon, Henry Jones had written to Miller suggesting, given the corruption of the Protestant churches, that Babylon and the call to come out might mean *our* churches." Joseph Marsh had also anticipated the call out of Babylon in 1839.[46]

Beyond the biblical foundation, " 'Come-Outerism,' " in the words of Doan, "formed part of the social and cultural context in which Millerism flourished." "Come-Outerism" had formed the initial stage in the establishment of a large number of religious and secular groups of the age as they quested for greater purity and more room for conscience. The Revelator's words, "Come out of her, my people," generally informed the rhetoric of such groups. Compromise with error was unacceptable.[47]

Thus Fitch's sermon not only hit at the right time, but it was also packaged in a meaningful terminology. As a result, the people responded, especially in upstate New York and the Midwest.

The more conservative leadership in the East, however, balked at Fitch's inflammatory sermon. Miller, in particular, never really accepted the message to come out. In January 1844 he reiterated his basic position that he had not "advised any one to separate from the churches to which they may have belonged, unless their brethren cast them out, or deny them religious privileges."[48]

A couple of months later, Miller expressed his fear "that the enemy has a hand" in the call to come out "to divert our attention from the true issue [of] the midnight cry, '*Behold the Bridegroom cometh.*' " He also had his doubts as to whether Babylon included the Protestant churches. In 1845 Miller would look back at the call to come out of Babylon as "a perversion of Scripture" that harmed the Adventist work by deflecting goodwill. Again in 1846 he bemoaned the trouble brought about by the "unholy crusade" against the Protestant churches. That crusade had "brought in men of blood instead of men of peace." In retrospect, he held that Adventism's troubles had begun with the call to come out of Babylon.[49]

Miller had forgotten that the cry had come about, to a great extent, because of the persecution of Adventists by the Protestant sects. From time to time, however, the situation had looked different to him when he was pressed in the heat of battle. For example, while under the pressures of early 1844, he noted "that if the Roman church was the mother of harlots, then her daughters must be harlots: and therefore that portion of the Protestant churches that imitate and partake of the spirit of the old mother must be the daughters referred to." He went on to teeter on the brink of uttering the message to come out at that time and on one other occasion in early 1844. On the second occasion, he penned that "it would be wicked" to fellowship with those "who have no faith in Christ's personal coming."[50]

Yet such statements were not typical of Miller. With but few exceptions, he stood against both the message to voluntarily leave the churches and the designation of the Protestant churches as Babylon. Miller's position was shared by most other established leaders of the movement. Himes, for example, did not publicly accept the message to come out until September 1844. By that time he had reluctantly concluded that "it is death to remain connected with those bodies that speak lightly of, or oppose, the coming of the Lord." Litch had also held back from advocating the message to come out. It is quite significant that the first history of Millerism, published by Litch in May 1844, contains no mention of Fitch's call to leave the churches.[51]

But while the old-line Millerite leadership largely rejected the cry to come out, a new group of leaders welcomed it with open arms. Among the new leaders was George Storrs. In February 1844 Storrs managed to condemn all Christendom except Adventists when he included "the *old mother* and all her children" in Babylon. Storrs directly challenged Miller's position when he told people not to stay in their churches until they were "*turned out.*" To the contrary, " '*Come out of her my people,*' " Storrs claimed, is a divine command from God to His people.

After they left their churches, Storrs continued, the Adventists should not form a new one, since "no church can be organized by man's invention but what it becomes Babylon *the moment it is organized.*" Fitch wrote to the *Midnight Cry* a few days later, endorsing Storrs' position and announcing to the world that he had given up all ecclesiastical connections. From now on he would be "a member of no sect, and a subscriber to no creed."[52]

Joseph Marsh was another of the new breed of Millerite leaders. In December 1843 he wrote that

> it is evidently as much our duty *now to come out of Babylon*, as it was for Lot to flee from Sodom, on the morning before its overthrow. I am aware that by some this will be called ultraism, come-outism, or some other ism; but what of that? [W]e should not seek to please men, but God. If he has told us to come out of Babylon, I do not know how we can be saved from the doom that awaits her, unless we obey his imperative command.[53]

It would be difficult to overestimate the impact of Fitch's call to leave Babylon on the Adventist movement. By late 1843 and early 1844, it had become one of Millerism's central features. By October 1844 it has been estimated that over fifty thousand had left their churches.[54]

That coming out, however, merely stamped Millerites as sectarians in the eyes of many, thus destroying even more sympathy for them. That lessening sympathy, of course, had the effect of speeding up the exodus from the churches. Thus the Millerites and the larger Christian culture were caught in a vortex as they proceeded through the year of the end of the world. That "year," as we will see in the next chapter, was fraught with more than one Millerite disappointment.

Meanwhile, it is important to recognize that a not-so-subtle power shift had taken place in Millerism in late 1843. Whether they knew it or not, the leadership had begun to shift from Miller, Himes, and Litch to a newer and more radical group that contained such men as Storrs, Marsh, and others yet to rise to prominence. Charles Fitch was the middleman in that shift. In some ways he possessed the characteristics of both camps, even though he tended toward the impetuous and experimental end of the leadership spectrum rather than the conservative. Millerism would never be the same after July 1843.

Chapter 8

THE SPRING DISAPPOINTMENT

"The virgins are truly waking up, in every part of the country. The saints are 'lifting up their heads, and looking up.' The scoffers are raging and 'foaming out their own shame.' But *the Lord is at the door*. '*Come Lord Jesus, come quickly*.' " Such were the enthusiastic words of Joshua Himes in November 1843. The closing date of the year of the end of the world was only four months off, and the Millerites were bursting with anticipation. They had time, as they saw it, for one last surge of evangelism as they sought to warn their doomed world of coming judgment.[1]

A "Final" Evangelistic Thrust

In January 1844, Miller estimated that in the previous twelve years he had delivered some 4,500 lectures to at least five hundred thousand different people. In the process, he noted, he had broken his constitution and lost his health that he "might be the means of saving some." He looked forward with his "whole heart and soul" to the arrival of Christ in the clouds of heaven.[2]

But the work of Miller and his followers was not over yet. The year 1844 would witness their greatest effort thus far. December 1843 found Himes planning to publish one million little tracts in the few short months left. Those would be circulated in addition to the thousands of publications coming off the press weekly. He appealed to the believers to support the publishing work in a hearty way, since "the advent of the Lord is right upon us."

159

"Indifference now," Himes wrote, "is sin."[3]

Beyond publications, the spoken word would continue to go forth with undiminished vigor. While others were spreading the work in the West, the South, and in New England, Himes, Miller, and Litch decided to concentrate their energies in the metropolitan areas of Boston, New York, Philadelphia, and Washington, D.C.

On January 28, Miller began his seventh series of lectures in Boston. The crowds, sensing the magnitude of the issue, were larger than he had ever before faced in that city. Not only were the seats filled, but many stood for hours to hear the message. "Had the Tabernacle been twice its size," we read in the *Midnight Cry*, "it would probably have been densely filled, as multitudes were obliged to go away, unable to obtain admittance."[4]

Miller began his meetings in New York on February 6 and in Philadelphia on February 11. Both series of meetings were heavily attended, with the crowd in Philadelphia being estimated at between four and five thousand.[5]

The climax of the tour began on February 20 in Washington, D.C. Although the capital had been entered by Millerism a year earlier, the movement had not made the desired impression. It was the hope of Miller and his colleagues to bring the message to "C[a]esar's household," even though the dignitaries were even then "engaged in their political squabbles for the next Presidency, as if their little 'brief authority,' were to last forever." "I will show them," penned Miller, "that an important revolution will take place before long, which will supersede the necessity of choosing a President by ballot; for the King of Kings will soon be inaugurated into the Chair of State."[6]

Speaking to large crowds, including "a goodly number of persons belonging to both houses of Congress," Miller noted that "this place is being shaken." During the Washington meetings, a terrible disaster aided the Millerite cause. As Himes saw it, "God was pleased . . . to speak . . . in awful judgment." On February 28 a large gun exploded on a naval ship named *The Princeton* during governmental festivities. The United States secretary of state was killed in the disaster, and several congressmen were injured. "The dreadful catastrophe," claimed Himes, "called all to a most serious consideration of preparation to meet God. The event has had a great influence upon the public mind, and has aided us essentially in our work."[7]

The Washington meetings closed on March 3, with Miller having preached nineteen times and Litch and Himes a combined total of fifteen. In addition, Himes had inaugurated a temporary paper entitled the *Southern Midnight Cry*. Ten thousand copies of the first issue alone were circulated in Washington, Baltimore, and the neighboring towns.[8]

After preaching at several other locations, by March 14 Miller was at his home in Low Hampton to wait for his Lord, whom he expected to return by March 21.

But Christ Did Not Come

There were mixed reactions as March 21, 1844, approached. While thousands of Millerites waited in hope and anticipation, other thousands awaited the day in fearful agony lest Miller be right. Large numbers undoubtedly just ignored both the day and the warnings. But there were also those who took the occasion to be one of mirth as they prodded and teased their Millerite neighbors.

Falling into that latter category was a person who signed his name as William Miller. In an apocryphal letter dated March 17, 1844, the so-called Miller wrote to A. P. Weaver, the only Adventist in Sackets Harbor, New York. The letter announced that "the 'World' has commenced burning in Main [sic] in the North East corner. It does not burn verry [sic] fast, so I had time to write you a few lines before I got ready." The writer then requested that Weaver "spread the news as fast as possible. . . . We shall soon meet in another world I hope where parting shall be no more."[9]

The "real" Mr. Miller waited throughout March 21 with a great deal more seriousness than the Miller of the Weaver letter. But the last day of the year of the end of the world passed by without Christ coming. Four days later the still-expectant Miller wrote to Himes:

I am now seated at my old desk in my east room. Having obtained help of God until the present time, *I am still looking for the Dear Savior. . . . The time, as I have calculated it, is now filled up; and I expect every moment to see the Savior descend from heaven. I have now nothing to look for but this glorious hope. . . .* I hope I have cleansed my garments from the blood of souls. I feel that, as far as it was in my power, I have freed myself from all guilt in their condemnation. . . .

. . . If God has any thing more for me to do in his vineyard, he will give me strength, open the door, and enable me to do whatever may be his will, for his glory and the best good of man.[10]

Himes answered a few days later, noting that Miller's friends had a deep interest in him and that Himes and his colleagues were planning future work, "*if time continues.*"[11]

On April 5 Miller wrote to Elon Galusha that he was "looking every day and hour for Christ to come." He looked forward to being "like him, whom twenty-eight years ago I loved. . . . I thought before this time I should be with him, yet I am here a pilgrim and a stranger, waiting for a change from mortal to immortal."

Miller went on to note that the scoffers must scoff, but, he affirmed, God would take care of him. "Why then," he queried, "should I complain if God should give a few days or even months more as probation time, for some to find salvation, and others to fill up the measure of their cup, before they drink the dregs, and wring them out in bitter anguish. It is my Savior[']s will and I rejoice that he will do things right."[12]

On April 10 and 11, Himes issued a public statement in the *Advent Herald* (the new name for the *Signs of the Times*) and the *Midnight Cry*. "It has been our sincere and solemn conviction, for three years past," he penned,

that the second glorious and blessed Advent of the Savior of the world, would have taken place before the present time. *I still look for this event as being nigh; and cannot avoid the entire conviction . . . that it is the next great event, and must transpire within a very short time.* It is not safe, therefore, for us to defer in our minds the event for an hour, but to *live in constant expectation, and readiness to meet our Judge.* With such views, *we can make no certain arrangements for the future; except in conformity with the views of the shortness and uncertainty of time.*

Himes went on to call for "continued effort" to spread the message "while probation shall last."[13]

Reactions to the nonappearance of Christ on March 21, 1844, were many. While the leadership and most members continued to wait in expectation, Miller pointed out that many of those who had looked forward to the advent "walked no more with us." Yet others, in their relief, made the disappointment an occasion of merriment. Millerites walking abroad heard such comments as "What!—not gone up yet?—We thought you'd gone up! . . . Wife didn't go up and leave you behind to burn, did she?"[14]

Many felt the Millerite movement would collapse if Christ failed to come on March 21. But it went on. That continuity, in a large part, resulted from the fact that the Millerite leaders had been "soft" on the time. That is, they allowed for the possibility of small errors in their calculations and even in some of their historic dates. Thus L. B. Coles could look at the problem of March 21 as "an incidental," rather than a "fundamental . . . error."[15]

Miller's "soft" approach to the exact time is evident in a letter he wrote on February 28, three weeks before the termination of his predicted end of the world. "If Christ comes, as we expect," he penned, "we will sing the song of victory soon; if not, we will watch, and pray, and preach until he comes, for soon our time, and all prophetic days, will have been filled." Again, another Millerite wrote in February that "IF we are mistaken in the time, we feel the fullest confidence that the event we have anticipated is the next great event in the World's History."[16]

That tentativeness on the exact time, as we noted above, saved the Millerite movement from disintegration in March 1844. In fact, as early as June 21, 1843, it had been suggested that their calculations for the spring date should have been based on the reckoning of the Karaite Jews rather than on that of the Rabbinical Jews. As a result, the *Signs* had suggested that April 18/19, 1844, really represented the end of the Jewish year 1844. Himes had adopted that explanation by early April 1844.[17]

But the April date also came and went. In the very next issue of the *Advent Herald*, Himes "frankly" admitted "that all our expected and published time, has passed: the Jewish year, civil and ecclesiastical, in which we expected the Lord, has expired, and the Savior has not been revealed; and we would not disguise the fact at all, that we were *mistaken* in the precise time of the termination of the prophetic periods." But even though Christ had not come during their predicted year of the end of the world, both Himes and Litch held, no one had been able to show where their calculations were incorrect. Litch surmised that they were probably "only in error relative to the event which marked its close."[18]

A week after Himes' admission that all the dates were past, Miller wrote to his fellow believers. On May 2 he noted that if he were to live his life over again, with the same evidence he had had, he would take the same course of action. After all, his opposers had "produced no weighty arguments."

Still, the bewildered Miller continued, "I *confess my error*, and acknowledge *my disappointment*; yet I still believe that the day of the Lord is near, even at the door." He especially warned his friends and fellow believers not to draw away from the Bible and its teachings on "the manner and object of Christ's coming; for the next attack of the adversary will be to induce unbelief respecting these."[19]

During the last week in May, Miller once again publicly confessed his error in regard to the definite time, this time at the major annual conference of the Adventists in the Boston Tabernacle. A reporter from the Boston *Post* noted that even though disappointed, Miller had not lost faith or courage. "I never heard him," wrote the reporter, "when he was more eloquent or animated, or more happy in communicating his feelings and sentiments to others." The audience, apparently including a large number of non-Adventists, was generally satisfied by his remarks on "the 'conclusion of the whole matter.' "[20]

Miller, the *Advent Herald* reported, claimed that, because of his error, he was glad that his followers had not trusted in him. " 'Father Miller,' " Miller said of himself, " 'has proved himself to you all to be only a poor fallible creature, and if you had trusted in him you would have given up your faith, and I don't know what would have become of you; but now you stand on the word of God, and that cannot fail you.' "[21] *True to his initial counsel, Miller ever pointed people to the Bible rather than to any human authority.*

The annual Boston conference, in its official report, reaffirmed belief in "*the time*" of the second advent as indicated in prophetic history. And even though the leaders recognized that calls for their services might be fewer than before March and April 1844, they still pledged themselves "to labor as we may have opportunity, to arouse our fellow men to the work of preparation."[22] In other words, they were still mission driven in the face of their belief in their place in prophetic history.

Thus as of the beginning of June 1844, the Millerites remained firm in their convictions, even though they appear to have been somewhat disillusioned and disoriented. However, back in the last week in April, they had found the biblical key that was even then helping them make sense out of their experience. An April 24 *Advent Herald* editorial provided the explanation when it tied the fact that all the virgins in the parable of the midnight cry of Matthew 25 *tarried*, slumbered, and slept (verse 5) to Habakkuk 2:2, 3, which says: "Write the vision, and make it plain upon tables, that he may run that readeth it. *For the vision is yet for an appointed time, but at the end it shall speak, and not lie: though it tarry, wait for it; because it will surely come.*"[23]

Two years earlier the Millerites had applied the Habakkuk passage to their movement when they linked the prophetic chart of Fitch and Hale to Habakkuk 2:2, where it refers to making a message plain on tables so that "*he may run that readeth it.*"[24] Now as they looked at verse 3, they again saw their movement, this time in relation to the great eschatological parable of the midnight cry—a parable that stood at the very heart of the biblical symbolism they used to describe their movement. One essential connection was that both Matthew's parable and Habakkuk spoke of a tarrying time before the end of the vision.

The Millerites found confirmation for this interpretation in Hebrews 10:36-39:

> For we have need of patience, that, after ye have done the will of God, ye might receive the promise. *For yet a little while, and he that shall come will come, and will not tarry.* Now the just shall live by faith: but if any man draw back, my soul shall have no pleasure in him. But *we are not of them who draw back* unto perdition; but of them that believe to the saving of the soul.[25]

With that biblical justification in place, the Millerites entered into the next phase of their history, *the tarrying time.* All the prophecies had been fulfilled. Christ would soon come at the completion of the tarrying time. Meanwhile, it was their job to continue to sound the midnight cry of the soon-coming bridegroom.

Chapter 9

THE TARRYING TIME

The spring disappointment at the nonappearance of Christ drove the Millerites back to their Bibles to find an explanation for their predicament. They not only discovered the "tarrying time" of Habakkuk, Matthew, and Hebrews, but they also found illustrations of the experience. One such was the case of Sodom, where the fire tarried before the final conflagration. As the *Western Midnight Cry* put it, "the threatened destruction did not fall upon the city as soon as *some* of them expected, or his [Lot's] wife would not have *looked back*." Thus we begin to find the idea expounded that the delay was a time for the testing of the believers and a period of faith building in anticipation of the eschaton.[1]

Another illustration along that line of thought was Noah. Look how Noah and his family must have felt, admonished certain Millerite leaders. After all, they were shut up in the ark for seven days of good weather. Meanwhile, "the vision tarried, and the wicked had their fill of laughter and their height of triumph, while the faith of the man of God, and those around him, was put to the severest test." While Noah and his fellow believers had seen signs at the end of the seven days, another forty days passed "before Noah was out of the reach of the taunts of the ungodly . . . and [their] cries of 'your time has gone by.' " Then, to cinch the argument, some quoted Luke 17:30: " 'Even thus shall it be in the day when the son of man is revealed.' "[2]

Those biblical illustrations seemed to capture not only a bit of hope for the disappointed Millerites, but they also captured the tone of their evangelistic experience. They had, as we noted earlier, pledged themselves to keep preaching their message of warning to the world, but the results were different after March and April 1844. Himes reported hearty responses on the part of believers but went on to report that "there was but little impression made upon the wicked. The word took hold of them, but seemed not to melt or break the heart, as in former times."[3]

Thus the period between June and August reflected a "flatness" in Millerite evangelism. The people heard but with reserved conviction. One can surmise that the Millerite preachers were also suffering from diminished certainty. Such nagging doubt was bound to show through in their preaching.

Persevering in "the Work"

The work of preaching went on because Jesus had commanded His disciples to "occupy till I come" (Luke 19:13). As a result, claimed Himes, "we must therefore continue our efforts in lecturing, Conferences, Tent, and Camp-Meetings, and the distribution of publications. We must work with more zeal, decision, and perseverance, than ever, until the 'Nobleman shall return' and receive the faithful to the everlasting kingdom."[4]

The renewed preaching mission of the Millerites appears to have gotten off to a rather halting start in June 1844, picked up speed in July, and by August was aggressively moving into new territory.[5] Early July found most of the established leadership strengthening the believers in the East. Late July, however, saw a major shift in focus toward the West.

On July 21, Miller, Himes, and Miller's son George began an extended preaching tour of the West. They found receptive audiences wherever they went. The terminus of their expedition was Cincinnati, where Miller preached to "4,000 people, who listened to him with almost breathless attention." They worked there for about a week and hoped to go farther west, but rainstorms prevented them. In the meantime, they had met with the Millerite leadership from Michigan, Wisconsin, and other points west. The calls for laborers were many.[6]

Upon returning from their western tour, Miller and Himes found that their movement had taken a new turn in the East, a turn that would largely take the initiative out of their hands. They returned to find a growing belief throughout Adventist ranks that Jesus would come in October. We will return to the October movement and the new shape of Millerism in our next chapter.

Meanwhile, early August witnessed Himes and Litch planning to go on a mission to England in October, "if time be prolonged." This was not the first time that Himes had planned personally to go to England. For three years he had wrestled with a conviction that he must go, and two times he had made arrangements to do so. But both times his friends had convinced him that his talents could not be spared in the United States. He would not be dissuaded this third time, even though the pressure from his colleagues was stronger than ever.[7]

Himes, in speaking of his overseas plans in the *Herald* of September 25, 1844, recognized that he could not expect the sympathy or support of those who expected Christ to come in October—a position he had not as yet accepted. But, he added, he had to do his duty as he personally saw it to the "Great Judge who now 'standeth at the door.' " Himes claimed that even if Christ came while he was in "mid-ocean," he still had to go. "I have," he penned, "done my duty, thus far, to this country. I have cleaned the skirts of my garments from the blood of all. I feel that I owe a duty to the old world, and if there is time to do it, Providence permitting, I hope to have grace to discharge it."[8]

In his work of bringing "before the groaning population of Europe . . . a hope of deliverance," Himes desired to establish a printing press in London. From that center he aimed to send out literature and lecturers in every direction. Thus, in essence, his European mission would be a recapitulation of his work in America.

Himes hoped to "send the *glad tidings* out in a number of different languages" besides English, "if time be continued a few months." The mission would include both Protestant and Catholic nations. And he certainly did not intend to forget *"Babylon, in Italy."*[9]

The plans to go to England, however, would once again be disrupted, this time by Himes' acceptance of the October 22 date for the end of the world. His English plans would not see fulfillment until 1846.[10]

Meanwhile, during the summer of 1844, tensions continued to increase between the Millerites and the churches. Paralleling that tension was the accelerated expulsion of Millerites from the denominations. Many of the Adventist lecturers, however, opposed the creating of a new religious body in the short time remaining. Some of them even complained about the use of the name *Adventist* to identify themselves. But the stand for separation itself became well-nigh universal among Millerites when Himes capitulated on separationism in August 1844. He noted that "it is death to remain connected with those bodies that speak lightly of, or oppose the coming of the Lord." Sylvester Bliss had said it nicely a few months before, when he wrote that to remain in the churches, supposing that some good can be done, "is very much like an attempt to warm an ice-house with a lamp—which thing cannot be done. Besides, it would chill your oil, and put out your light."[11]

The tarrying time saw the publishing work carried on in a healthy manner, even though some papers, including Fitch's *Second Advent of Christ*, went out of print. On the other hand, at least two new papers found their beginning in the summer of 1844. One was the scholarly *Advent Shield* and the other the *Advent Message to the Daughters of Zion*. The first was remarkable because it was the only scholarly Millerite journal, the second because it was both aimed at and edited by women.

From a historian's perspective, one of the substantial contributions of the tarrying time was Litch's publication of the first history of Millerite Adventism in the May 1844 *Advent Shield*. The early tarrying time was one of reflection as the Millerites contemplated the significance of their experience prior to regrouping for renewed action in the autumn.

The tarrying time also witnessed Miller and many of his colleagues vacillating over the significance of their preaching the "time" message. L. B. Coles had concluded that "a certain limited year, should never have been set." Furthermore, Coles wrote, "to continue to fix the time upon any definite point in [the] future, is the consummation of folly."[12]

Miller himself seemed somewhat confused on the date issue during the summer. A reporter for the *Christian Watchman* presented a firsthand account of Miller on the time issue in the late spring of 1844. "He tried," reported the *Watchman*, "to define his present position, but appeared not himself to know what it was. One minute he would confess that he was mistaken, and the next say that he could discover no possible mistake, and go over his old calculations." Miller eventually confessed "that Christ did not come in 1843—but I can't see where I'm wrong." By July 31, 1844, Miller had finally come to a resolution. "Time," he penned, "has shown my error, as to the exact time of the event," but not its nearness.[13]

Subsequently, Miller never had much interest in providing any dates for the advent. The same, as we shall see in our next chapter, was not true of some of his followers. Only in early October 1844 would Miller again develop any interest in the date of the second coming, and he would come to that October decision with a great deal of reluctance.

While Miller and his top associates managed to maintain their equilibrium during the disorienting spring and summer months of 1844, the same cannot be said for all the advent believers. For those with a less rational orientation toward religion, the excitement of the year of the end of the world pushed them toward fanatical attitudes and actions that have tended to be present in various time-of-the-end movements from biblical times to the present. Millerism was no exception. By the tarrying time in the summer of 1844, such elements in the Millerite camp had become problematic.

Fanaticism in the Ranks

Perhaps a most surprising fact about Millerism is not that it housed some believers belonging to the fanatical edge or even the lunatic fringe, but that it had so few of them. But have them it did. From one point of view, William Lloyd Garrison was right on target when he noted that "it would be strange indeed, if, among their extended ranks, some cannot be found who behave most inconsistently with their profession." In a similar manner, the editors of the *Signs* pointed out that "a hot-bed that will not produce some weeds will not produce any good fruit." Religion, the editors noted, is ever a "hot-bed in which . . . fanaticism germinates."[14]

Ronald and Janet Numbers indicate that due to its very nature, Millerism "attracted some marginally and poorly functioning persons to its fringes, Americans who might have gravitated toward any religious fad." The leaders of the Oneida perfectionists (an aberrant group itself) recognized that truth when they claimed that those who had been "wildest in their speculations" regarding another religious fad a few years earlier had, by late 1842, become "flaming Millerites."[15]

William Miller and his leading associates were aware of their movement's fanatical potential. That awareness led Miller in his 1843 New Year's address to warn his followers that Satan would seek to get advantage over them by "scattering coals of wild fire among you; for if he cannot drive you into unbelief and doubt, he will then try his wild fire of fanaticism." A few months later, one of the main points of warning in the dedication of Himes' Boston Tabernacle was to "avoid all extravagant notions, and everything which may tend to fanaticism."[16]

May 1843 also saw the important annual Boston conference declare: "We have no confidence whatever in any visions, dreams, or private revelations. 'What is the chaff to the wheat? saith the Lord.' We repudiate all fanaticism, and everything which may tend to extravagance, excess, and immorality, that shall cause our good to be evil spoken of."[17]

A similar warning was issued at the 1844 annual Boston conference, but this time it went on to add that those at the fanatical edge, who thought they were being guided by the Holy Spirit, often believed that they possessed "the gift of *intuitive discernment of spirits*, the *power to work miracles*, and to believe in the possibility of obtaining what they call *resurrection bodies* here in this mortal state." Again, in January 1844 Miller flatly stated that he had not "countenanced fanaticism in any form." Nor had he used "dreams or visions except those in the word of God."[18]

The many remonstrances of the leading Millerites were not made in a vacuum. The reality of the problem was pointed out in the *Christian Reflector* of May 1844 by L. B. Coles, who wrote that some Millerites had "imbibed very erroneous, soul-destroying notions on sanctification, and the influences of the Spirit. In some instances, no excesses have been too extravagant to be attributed to the Holy Ghost."[19]

A case in point was Calvin French, a Millerite lecturer who "embraced some of the abominable and licentious doctrines of the Cochran school," which taught "spiritual wifery." French had apparently come to believe in a deceptive view of Christian perfection that held that since perfect people were free from sin, anything they did reflected the promptings of God's Spirit and was therefore right to do. Thus it was not wrong to have sexual relations with persons other than one's spouse. For "perfect" people it was a spiritual experience. The Millerite response was to warn the believers that French was "a very unsuitable person to lecture on the Second Advent . . . or on any other Scriptural doctrine."[20]

Then there was Michael Barton, who wrote Miller in late April 1844 to confirm the Adventist leader's interpretations. The staid Miller must have read Barton's letter in despair as he realized that such people had attached themselves to the movement. "I left my body," wrote Barton, "and found myself flying thru the air. At length I found myself in heaven, and heard a voice saying 'I am Christ.' But the Being who said I am Christ left heaven with us and drawed me after him to the earth, as a nickel would be drawn by a powerful load stone." Subsequently in the vision, Barton witnessed God blessing the Millerites. That, according to Barton, was proof that God was preparing the world for the advent. With such believers about, it is little wonder that the May 1844 Boston annual conference once again warned against fanaticism, "impressions," and "private revelations."[21]

The most troublesome and persistent source of Millerite charismatic fanaticism before 1845 is found in John Starkweather. One of the better-educated Millerite lecturers, Starkweather was a graduate of Andover Theological Seminary. Converted to Millerism in the early autumn of 1842, he became Himes' associate pastor at the Chardon Street Chapel in October. Prior to that time, he had been pastor at Boston's Marlboro Chapel and several other places. Himes' object in hiring Starkweather was to be free to travel more in behalf of the Adventist cause. But Himes' generally good judgment misfired regarding Starkweather, as time would shortly demonstrate.[22]

Although Miller and Himes had a long-established policy of not emphasizing doctrinal distinctives other than the premillennial advent, Starkweather soon began preaching his "peculiar views" respecting personal sanctification and even making them a test of fellowship. "He taught that conversion, however full and thorough, did not fit one for God's favor without a second work [of the Holy Spirit]; and that this second work was usually indicated by some bodily sensation." Thus a loss of strength or certain other bodily manifestations were viewed as the great power of God in sanctification, or the " 'sealing power.' "[23]

While some of Himes' members looked upon such exhibitions with awe, others were suspicious but feared to challenge Starkweather lest they " 'offend against the Holy Ghost.' " The problem had become so disruptive by April 1843 that Himes had to face the problem publicly. His challenge brought a great outcry from Starkweather and his followers. " 'You will drive out the Holy Ghost!' cried one. 'You are throwing on cold water!' said another. 'Throwing on cold water!' said Mr. Himes, 'I would throw on the Atlantic ocean [sic], before I would be identified with such abominations as these, or suffer them in this place unrebuked.' " Needless to say, Starkweather no longer worked as Himes' associate pastor, but he did manage to take a portion of the membership out of Chardon Street Chapel with him.[24]

Starkweather's dismissal was not the end of the matter. He was a man of great personal appeal, and his teaching that the " 'gifts' were to be restored to the church" impressed many. Before long, his followers were seeking to walk on water and hold back locomotives through the power of their wills. Starkweather himself claimed that those with the gift of the Spirit could invariably tell who were and were not Christians, and that such people (including himself) " 'had no need that other Christians should tell them what is, and what is not their duty.' "[25]

Even though Himes, Miller, and others recognized the seriousness of Starkweather's problem, without church organization it was impossible to disfellowship him. Beyond that, he was popular with a significant segment of the believers. Thus even to speak out against Starkweather by name was inadvisable, especially after he pictured himself to his followers as a "holy" but "abused man." The leadership decided that his followers would have to find out for themselves the fruit of Starkweather's work, even though the process would be costly and painful. As a result, the summer of 1843 found Starkweather's influence to be a major factor in at least three Connecticut camp meetings.[26]

The Philadelphia *Public Ledger* reported that while Starkweather preached at the Bridgeport meeting, a man passed through the audience waving a green leaf over his head crying "Hallelujah" and "Glory" as loud as he could. At times he pointed to various individuals, making a muttering sound that his fellows interpreted to mean that such individuals were eternally damned. This discerning-of-spirits exercise was accompanied by other acts of public fanaticism, all of which were reported in the public press.[27]

Litch, who witnessed the event, reported that the papers had not exaggerated. "A more disgraceful scene, under garb of piety," he penned, "I have rarely witnessed." Such a spirit

> *is evil, and only evil, and that continually.* . . . The origin of it, is, the idea that the individuals thus exercised are entirely under the influence of the Spirit of God, are his children, and that he will not deceive them and lead them astray; hence

every impulse which comes upon them is yielded to as coming from God, and following it there is no length of fanaticism to which they will not go. . . .

. . . If Second Advent meetings must be the scenes of such
disgraceful proceedings as I there witnessed, I protest against
more being held. It would be better for the cause never to
have another at such a price.[28]

Unfortunately, the fanatical elements prominent at the Bridgeport meeting were also evident that summer in two other Connecticut camp meetings before Starkweather's influence began to
wither.[29]

In November, Miller made a public protest on the front page
of the *Signs* against the fanaticism that had distracted so many.
In his own travels that summer, he wrote, he had witnessed the
same spirit at work. "My heart," he penned, "was deeply pained
during my tour east, to see in some few of my former friends, a
proneness to the wild and foolish extremes of some vain delusions,
such as working miracles, discerning of spirits, vague and loose
views on sanctification, & c."[30]

The counsel of the established leadership in the face of fanaticism was to recommend a rational reliance upon the Bible. "Cling,
cling to the word of God," admonished the editors of the *Signs*.
"Lay first hold of its promises, and walk in accordance with its
sacred teachings, and all will be well."[31]

Starkweather's last major attempt to gain control of a significant
portion of Adventism took place soon after the spring disappointment of 1844. In April he attempted to unite Adventism's various
disaffected elements. Himes' friends wrote that "such a medley of
discordant elements has not been often assembled. No two were
of one mind," and "each wished to lead off in his own direction."
Starkweather soon lost control of the meeting, and the various
factions accused the others (including Starkweather) of having
the devil and of going off into various "mesmeric ecstacies [sic]."
Some participants concluded "that instead of escaping from
Babylon, they had landed in the wilderness."[32]

After the April meeting, Starkweather had little following among the Millerites. He eventually deserted his family and followed Calvin French's path in letting his perfectionism lead him into "spiritual wifery." The residue of Starkweather's influence, however, did not die. It would find new life in the fanatical movements arising after the failure of Christ to appear on October 22, 1844.[33]

Though fanaticism in pre-October 1844 Adventism was present, it did not involve a major part of the movement. Nor were any of the established teachers involved. Miller, Himes, and Litch in particular had always sought to inculcate a rational, cool-headed religion that was more cognitive than emotional. The discordant elements were nearer the edges of Adventism than the center. But, as should be expected, they were always there. During the tarrying time, the fanatical elements smoldered, but, unfortunately, they would achieve greater prominence in late 1844 and in 1845.

Before moving away from the tarrying time, it is important to examine one more case of fanaticism. That case took place at the Exeter, New Hampshire, camp meeting in August 1844. The trouble began in the Watertown, Massachusetts, tent, where meetings continued "nearly all night, and [were] attended with great excitement, and noise of shouting and clapping of hands, and singular gestures and exercises." Some shouted so loud and long that they were reduced to whispering. Others had "literally blistered their hands" through much clapping.[34]

Unfortunately for its inmates, the believers from Portland, Maine, had pitched their tent quite near the Watertown tent before they realized the problem. James White, a young Millerite preacher from the Portland tent, claims they had to move their abode to the other end of the grounds to obtain peace. But the move, he noted, merely created sympathy for "the fanatics," who cried "persecution, and shouted glory to God over it, as if a new and brilliant victory had been gained."

The problem began to spread in the camp, and the preachers were in a state of gloom. Finally one pastor publicly faced the issue. He claimed that "he had no objections to shouts of praise to God, over victories won in his name. But when persons had shouted 'Glory to God' nine hundred and ninety-nine times, with no evidence of one victory gained, and had blistered their hands in striking them together with violence, he thought it was time for them to stop." If they did not stop, however, he suggested that the rest of the camp should withdraw sympathy from them.[35]

That speech helped the tone of the camp in general, even if it failed to reach "those who were wild with fanaticism." It would take a more electrifying utterance than that to reach their gospel-hardened minds. Such an utterance was soon forthcoming at Exeter, and when it did come, it would prove to be a major turning point in the history of Adventism.

Courtesy of Jim Nix.

William Miller

Courtesy of Jim Nix.

Lucy Miller

The Miller home about 1853.

Joshua V. Himes, public-relations
genius and Miller's chief lieutenant.

Charles Fitch, zealous advocate of the
movement for Millerite separatism.

Josiah Litch, a foremost Millerite
leader with a scholarly bent.

Elon Galusha, Millerite leader in
western New York.

In 1848 Miller donated land for an Adventist chapel to be built near his farmhouse.

The interior of Miller's chapel. The text from Daniel 8:19 was one of Miller's favorites.

Hiram Munger, camp-meeting super-
intendent who struck terror into the
hearts of "Cainites."

Joshua V. Himes in his later years.

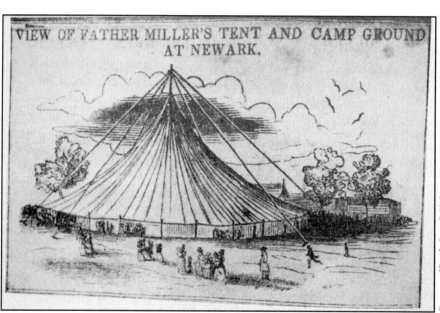

Contemporary drawing of the Millerite big tent.

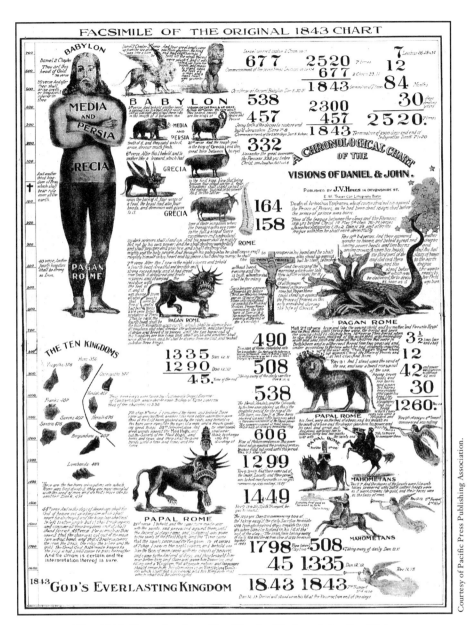

The 1843 Chart developed by Charles Fitch and Apollos Hale.

Anti-Millerite broadside depicting ascension of Boston
Tabernacle. Miller is shown seated on a prophetic chart, and
Himes is standing below, surrounded by bags of money and
being held by a devil.

S. S. Snow, the stimulus behind the
seventh-month movement.

George Storrs, a powerful preacher
who did much to push the seventh-
month movement.

Sylvester Bliss, Millerite editor, Albany leader, and Miller's biographer.

Miles Grant, aggressive Advent Christian editor opposed to J. V. Himes.

Isaac C. Wellcome, Advent Christian preacher and author of the first substantial history of Adventism in 1874.

James White, one of the founders of Sabbatarian Adventism.

Ellen G. White, prophetic voice among the Sabbatarian Adventists.

Joseph Bates, Millerite activist and early Sabbatarian tract writer.

Chapter 10

THE "TRUE MIDNIGHT CRY"

"You are going to have new light here! something that will give new impetus to the work." Such was the repeated premonition of Joseph Bates as he traveled by train to the Exeter, New Hampshire, camp meeting in August 1844.[1] And the Adventists did receive new light at Exeter, a message that proved to be one of the most significant turning points in Millerite history.

A New Message

The Exeter meetings, as we noted in chapter 9, were not an unmixed blessing. Fanaticism had caused confusion among the already somewhat demoralized believers. The definite time of expectation had passed, the tarrying time was dragging, and neither people nor preachers had any assurance of where they were in prophetic history. The preaching may have been good, but it "failed to move the people." An unhealthy listlessness had settled over the believers, in spite of the enthusiastic efforts of the leaders to buoy them up.[2]

Under those circumstances, Bates was doing his best in the pulpit as he preached the well-worn advent message to the people. Suddenly he was interrupted in midsermon by Mrs. John Couch, who stood to her feet and addressed both preacher and audience. " 'It is too late, Bro. [Bates],' " she called out. " 'It is too late to spend our time upon these truths, with which we are familiar, and which have been blessed to us in the past, and have served their purpose and their time.' " She went on to note that a speaker among them had a new message for this time.[3] That speaker was Samuel S. Snow, heretofore a minor player in the Millerite movement.

At Exeter, Snow presented a message that would thrust him into the center of Millerism. His contribution was a new interpretation of Daniel 8:14 on the cleansing of the sanctuary. That interpretation, in turn, led to a new understanding of the bridegroom parable of Matthew 25. Both of those passages had stood as foundation pillars of the advent message.

Snow argued on the basis of scriptural typology that the Millerites had been in error in looking for Christ to come in the spring of 1844. Viewing the Old Testament ceremonial sabbaths as types and the ministry of Christ as antitype, Snow demonstrated from the New Testament that the feasts of Passover, First Fruits, and Pentecost had been fulfilled by Christ at the exact time in the year as in the annual celebration. That was so because "God is an *exact time keeper*." Snow then pointed out that "those types which were to be observed in the 7th month, have never yet had their fulfillment."

He then connected the annual day of atonement with the second coming of Jesus. "The *important point* in this type," Snow penned,

> is the *completion* of the reconciliation at the *coming* of the high priest *out of* the holy place. The high priest was a type of Jesus our High Priest; the most holy place a type of heaven itself; and the coming out of the high priest a type of the coming of Jesus the second time to bless his waiting people. As this was on the tenth day of the 7th month, so on that day Jesus will certainly come, because not a *single point* of the law is to fail. *All must be fulfilled.*

Combining that finding with his conclusion that the 2300-day prophecy of Daniel 8:14 ended in 1844 (rather than 1843), Snow proclaimed that Christ would come on "the *tenth day* of the *seventh month*" of "the *present* year, 1844."[4]

It was determined that the tenth day of the seventh month in 1844, according to the reckoning of the Karaite Jews, would fall on *October 22, 1844*. That date soon became the focal point of Millerite interest.

The new date set the stage for a new interpretation of the parable of the bridegroom in Matthew 25. The new interpretation found expression in the very title Snow chose for the periodical he established to spread his seventh-month message—*The True Midnight Cry*.

That new interpretation found full exposition in George Storrs. According to Storrs, the earlier message was "but the *alarm*. NOW THE REAL ONE IS SOUNDING." He indicated that according to the parable, "all" the virgins slumbered and slept during the tarrying time. He then pointed out that the tarrying time could not be more than six months, since the night of tarrying represented one half of a prophetic day. Thus the tarrying time would end in the autumn. But, according to the parable, the cry of the coming bridegroom is to go forth at midnight, or about halfway through the tarrying time. And thus it was, claimed Storrs, that "the present strong cry of *time* commenced about the middle of July, and has spread with great rapidity and power, and is attended with a demonstration of the Spirit, such as I never witnessed when the cry was '1843.' It is now literally, '*go ye out* to meet him.' " The time had come for "the TRUE *Midnight Cry*."[5]

Snow's seventh-month message took the Exeter camp by storm. As Bates put it, the seventh-month message

> worked like leaven throughout the whole camp. And when that meeting closed, the granite hills of New Hampshire were ringing with the mighty cry, "Behold the bridegroom cometh; go ye out to meet him." As the loaded wagons, stages, and railroad cars, rolled away through the different States, cities and villages of New England, the cry was still resounding, "Behold the bridegroom cometh!" Christ, our blessed Lord, is coming on the tenth day of the seventh month! Get ready! get ready!![6]

From Exeter the new message soon permeated Adventism, providing believers with a renewed "burden of the work" of spreading the message and a solemnity that put much of the earlier fanaticism to rest. According to James White, a "power almost irresistible" attended the preaching that Christ would come in October.[7]

Interestingly, the Exeter camp meeting was not Millerism's first exposure to Snow's seventh-month theory. Around January 1844, Snow recalled in June of that year, "I felt it my imperative duty to impart to the world, and especially to the Advent band, the light which my heavenly Father had given me, concerning the termination of the prophetic periods."[8]

The *Midnight Cry* first published Snow's exposition of the seventh-month argument on February 22, 1844, several weeks *before* the end of Miller's predicted terminal point for the year of the end. The editors, however, added a cautionary note to Snow's article, indicating that while it was "possible" that he might be correct, they did not see it that way. They continued to hold to the spring date. Snow's article was subsequently published in the *Advent Herald* with similar cautionary remarks.[9]

In actuality it was not Snow who first indicated that Christ might come in the autumn rather than the spring, but Miller himself. On May 3, 1843, Miller argued in a letter to Himes that "the ceremonies of the typical law that were observed in the first month, or vernal equinox, had their fulfillment in Christ's first advent and sufferings; but all the feasts and ceremonies in the seventh month or autumnal equinox, can only have their fulfillment at his second advent."

He then went on to point out that in the Jewish calendar, atonement was made on the tenth day of the seventh month and that that atonement "is certainly typical of the atonement Christ is now making for us." He then noted that the high priest blessed the people after he came out of the holy of holies. "So will our great High Priest. . . . This was on the seventh month tenth day." "If this should be true," he concluded, "we shall not see his glorious appearing until after the autumnal equinox."

Publishing Miller's letter in the *Signs* of May 17, 1843, the editors commented that they had seen the forcefulness of his argument and that he just might be correct. Miller's letter, however, seems to have been largely forgotten until September 1844. As we shall see, Snow's reasoning found little acceptance among the Millerite leadership until early October.[10]

In spite of the cold shoulder he received, Snow, who considered himself "the least of all the saints," felt it to be his "indispensible duty" to proclaim the seventh-month message. During the spring and summer of 1844, Snow preached his message in New York, Philadelphia, and other places. But, reported the *Advent Herald* in late October, "while many embraced his views, yet, no particular manifestation of its effects was seen, until about July."[11]

Snow's message began to catch hold on July 21, when he preached it in the Boston Tabernacle.[12] But after the Exeter meeting in August, the seventh-month movement became a virtual whirlwind. The rapid spread of the new message can be attributed to several causes. Not the least of those causes was the convincing logic of Snow's reasoning and the fact that it was based on several supporting lines of evidence.

Coupled with the forcefulness of the cognitive element in Snow's presentation was the fact that the psychological time was right. The disappointed Adventists were tired of "tarrying" and longed with all their hearts for Jesus to come. That longing was inextricably connected with the deeply felt need to warn their neighbors of soon-coming judgment. The upshot of these and other factors was that the seventh-month message spread with a rapidity unparalleled in the Millerite experience.

Beyond Snow, who scattered his message in the *True Midnight Cry* "by the tens and hundreds of thousands," one of the most exuberant and forceful of the Millerite preachers to accept Snow's argument was the irrepressible George Storrs. "I take up my pen," wrote Storrs in the *Bible Examiner* of September 24,

with feelings such as I never before experienced. Beyond a *doubt*, in my mind, the *tenth day* of the *seventh month*, will witness the revelation of our Lord Jesus Christ in the clouds of heaven. We are then within a *few days* of that event. Awful moment to those who are unprepared—but glorious to those who are ready. I feel that I am making the last appeal that I shall ever make through the press. My heart is full.[13]

The *Oberlin Evangelist*, in response to the *Bible Examiner*, noted that "time will . . . soon show whether the writer or Mr. Storrs is correct." In another article in the same issue, the *Evangelist*, after asserting that the second Adventists were "utterly mistaken," pointed out that "when the lapse of time shall show them that all their calculations are wrong, they will not be tempted to reject divine revelation, nor be discouraged from patiently laboring for Christ, and for the salvation of souls."[14]

The seventh-month message had catapulted the Millerites both into revived meaning and into a collision course with an exact date that would put to the test their interpretation of Daniel 8:14 and other passages. Meanwhile, the rise of the seventh-month movement had brought with it a major shift in Adventist leadership from Miller, Himes, Litch, and their colleagues to such new leaders as Snow and Storrs.

New Leaders

Because Snow and Storrs made a large impact on both pre- and post-October 22, 1844, Adventism, we should become acquainted with them at this point. Snow, although raised as a member of the Congregational Church, had become a "hardened Infidel" in early adulthood. As a militant unbeliever, he became an agent of, and an author for, the Boston *Investigator*, an infidel paper.[15]

To Snow, the Bible was filled with "nothing but gross absurdities." To please his friends, he had read several books defending Christianity, but none affected his thinking. Then in 1839 Snow's brother bought a copy of Miller's book from a peddler. "I had often heard of Mr. Miller and his views," reported Snow, "and supposed them to be all moonshine." But he decided to read Miller's work anyway. After reading it through several times, Snow commenced, "at the same time, to search the scriptures diligently, to learn if these things were so." After three months' study, he became not only a professing Christian, but a believer " 'looking for that blessed hope' " of the soon-coming Saviour.[16]

At the East Kingston camp meeting in June 1842, Snow consecrated his life to preaching the Millerite message. He was ordained to the gospel ministry at an Adventist meeting in December 1843. In the meantime, he had "come out" from his church because he was "virtually prohibited from speaking amidst his brethren in the church, concerning the glorious theme which was dear to him." It was soon after his ordination that Snow was impressed with his duty to impart his seventh-month message to the world. That message, as we noted above, changed the very nature of Adventism. We will return to Snow's story in chapter 12.[17]

In many ways George Storrs' contributions to Adventism were just as significant as those of Snow. Storrs not only became a foremost publicist of the seventh-month movement, but he became the major instigator of the view that human beings did not have innate immortality—a doctrine that eventually became central to several Adventist groups in the 1840s and 1850s. Beyond that, in the period surrounding October 1844, Storrs joined Snow in pushing some advent believers toward extreme conclusions and practices.

Storrs, who was raised as a Congregationalist, joined the Methodist Church in his late twenties and became a minister of that denomination in 1825. In the mid-1830s, however, he got crosswise with the Methodist leadership because of his growing advocacy of the abolitionist cause.[18]

While Storrs' activism may not have been favored by the Methodist bishops, he was viewed as a champion by the antislavery forces. He achieved a minor sort of fame in 1835, when he was arrested and dragged from his knees in a church in Northfield, New Hampshire, while in the midst of prayer. The action was taken to prevent him from preaching a sermon against slavery to a congregation whose members had invited him to address them on that topic. In the name of the law, he was accused of being " 'an idler, a vagrant, a brawler.' "[19]

According to William Lloyd Garrison, Storrs was a "power-ful" speaker. Elizur Wright wrote to Theodore Dwight Weld in April 1836 that "Storrs—a host himself—is gone to Cincinnati to thunder in the M[ethodist] E[piscopal] Gen[eral] Con-[ference]."[20]

Storrs, along with Orange Scott and LeRoy Sunderland, led the battle to capture Methodism for the antislavery cause. To further that cause, he and Sunderland founded *Zion's Watchman* in 1836. That year also saw Storrs resign from the traveling ministry of the Methodist Church, largely over the problem of slavery. A man of great individualism and strong convictions, in 1840 he withdrew altogether from the Methodist Church. By that time he was quite convinced that "he could not submit to leave his responsibility [for his actions and beliefs] in the hands of Bishops, nor any body of men, however good they might be."[21]

Storrs' struggle with Methodism's hierarchy over slavery and other issues convinced him once and for all that church organi-zation was an unnecessary evil. In his opinion the bonds of love were all that was needed to hold believers together. Thus Storrs, after accepting Millerism, found Fitch's call to come out of Baby-lon to be quite to his liking. Storrs opposed church organization and doctrinal creeds to the end of his life. In 1844 he wrote that "no church can be organized by man's invention but what it be-comes Babylon *the moment it is organized*." The legacy of Storrs on church organization would live on to frustrate the several Adventist bodies for decades in the post-1844 period.[22]

Storrs was converted to Millerism under the ministry of Charles Fitch in 1842. Before long he became an itinerant Ad-ventist preacher. In that role he evolved into one of the out-standing spokespersons for Adventism. In the autumn of 1843, for example, he teamed up with Himes in Cincinnati to hold one of the most successful meetings ever conducted by the Millerites. More than five hundred were won to the second-advent faith. Storrs remained in Cincinnati to lead out in the work in that region and to edit the *Western Midnight Cry*, a periodical established to aid the Cincinnati meetings.[23]

In the meantime, Storrs had begun to pioneer another doctrine among the Millerites that would be as unpopular with the Adventist leadership as it had earlier been with the Methodists. Back in 1837, Storrs had come across a book by Henry Grew that dealt with the final destiny of the wicked. Grew argued for the "entire extinction of being and not endless preservation in sin and suffering."[24]

Up to that time, Storrs had never doubted that people were born with immortal souls. But Grew's work drove him to a thorough study of the Bible on the topic. As a result, Storrs "became settled that man has no immortality by his creation, or birth; and that 'all the wicked will God destroy'—*utterly exterminate*." He had come to believe in what theologians refer to as conditionalism (i.e., people receive immortality only through the condition of faith in Christ) and annihilationism (the final or eternal destruction of the wicked rather than their preservation alive in the fires of hell throughout the ceaseless ages of eternity). The teaching of those doctrines brought Storrs into conflict with the Methodist establishment and contributed to his eventual departure from the denomination in 1840.[25]

To set forth his views on immortality and the fate of the wicked, Storrs published *An Enquiry: Are the Souls of the Wicked Immortal? In Three Letters* in 1841. The next year saw the publication of an expanded version of his argument as *An Enquiry: Are the Souls of the Wicked Immortal? In Six Sermons*.

A few weeks after the publication of his *Six Sermons*, Storrs came across his first Millerite lecturer. Allowing the lecturer to preach in his nondenominational church, Storrs was partially convinced on the truthfulness of the premillennial second advent. That led Storrs to invite Fitch to present the series that finally led him to become a Millerite preacher in 1842.[26]

At first Storrs did not present his views on immortality in his public Millerite ministry. But he was stimulated to act by an article in the *Signs* that "came out strong" against a minister who believed it his duty to preach both the second advent and the non-immortality of the wicked. After the censure was repeated several times, Storrs came to the conviction that "he was bound not to keep silence and let him suffer alone."[27]

As a result, in January 1843 Storrs issued the first number of the *Bible Examiner*. In that paper Storrs taught both the second advent and his views on immortality. Like so many other Millerites, Storrs was a tireless publicist. The first number of the *Examiner* published Storrs' *Six Sermons*. Within a few weeks he had sent out some fifteen thousand copies and, as he put it, "the seed was sown, and it sprung up in all directions." By 1880 at least 200,000 copies of his *Six Sermons* had been circulated.[28]

Storrs' advocacy of conditionalism eventually brought him into conflict with the Millerite leadership. But preach it he must, since, as he saw it, the theory of consciousness in death was a papal corruption, and the New Testament position needed to be restored to its rightful place in Christian belief.[29]

It should be pointed out that one other prominent Adventist leader published on the subjects of annihilationism and conditionalism about the same time as Storrs. Henry Jones broached the topics in 1843.[30] But Jones did not prove to be much of a threat to the Millerite leaders because his voice was progressively sidelined in the movement as it drifted toward the year of the end of the world. Jones, it will be recalled, never accepted the dating scheme of 1843 or any other year. Storrs, of course, did accept the dates, and his charismatic personality increasingly pushed him toward the very center of Millerism as the autumn of 1844 approached.

Charles Fitch was Storrs' first ministerial convert in the Adventist ranks on the topic of conditionalism. On January 25, 1844, Fitch wrote to Storrs, notifying him of his convictions.

> As you have long been fighting the Lords [sic] battles alone, on the subject of the state of the dead, and of the final doom of the wicked, I write this to say that I am at last[,] after much thought and prayer, and a full conviction of duty to God, prepared to take my stand by your side.

I am thoroughly converted to the Bible truth, that "the dead know not anything."[31]

Not wanting to hide his "light under a bushel," Fitch preached two sermons on the topic to his congregation in late January. "They have produced a great uproar," he penned to Storrs. "Many thought I had a devil before, but now they feel sure of it. But I have no more right my Brother, to be ashamed of God's truth on this subject than on any other."[32]

Despite his sincerity, Fitch could not carry his congregation on the topic. On February 13 the Cleveland *Herald* reported that his members had "Resolved: That in the opinion of this church, the views expressed by our pastor, Rev. Mr. Fitch . . . respecting the final destruction of the wicked, are unscriptural, and consequently erroneous."[33]

The reaction against the new teaching in Cleveland was mirrored by the Millerites. Fitch was the only top leader in the 1843 movement to accept conditionalism and annihilationism in the 1840s. Miller, Himes, and Litch found the topic both distasteful and erroneous.

Miller had expressed his feelings against annihilationism in 1814 at the death of an army friend. That experience was one of several that had pointed him back to Christianity, with its hope of "a never-ending existence." Again, he penned, "I began to suspect [in the 1810s] that Deism tended to a belief of annihilation, which was always very abhorrent to my feelings." Miller may never have been able to disentangle his early identification of annihilationism with infidelity and no life after death. As a result, it is probable that he was not able to read Storrs in a dispassionate or positive manner.[34]

Miller's attitude toward the teaching was undoubtedly not helped by the wide influence Storrs' preaching and writing on the topic were having in the movement in early 1844. I. E. Jones had written to Miller in April that "something ought to be done to separate our influence from Bro. Storrs' view of the end of the wicked; for, as it now is, he virtually wields from our silence, the whole, or almost the whole Advent influence."[35]

That letter helped spur Miller into a public statement on annihilationism a month later. On May 7 he wrote a letter for publication in which he disclaimed "any connection, fellowship, or sympathy with Br. Storrs' views of the intermediate state, and end of the wicked."[36]

Himes was likewise against the doctrines of "soul sleeping" and the "destruction of the wicked." In 1834 he had had to meet those issues head on in his Boston church. To Himes, those teachings "had been the canker-worms that had gnawed the spirit, life, zeal and good works out of not only the Boston 'Christian Church,' but every other where it had been made prominent."[37] Himes had not changed his opinion on that topic in the 1840s. He was dead set against Storrs' position, even though he and his fellow editors gave Storrs room in the Millerite journals to set forth his views.

The most active of the Millerite leaders against Storrs was Litch. In April 1844 he began publishing a thirty-two-page periodical on the topic entitled *The Anti Annihilationist*, since the mainline Millerite papers were seeking to stay clear of the controversy.[38]

But by May public silence was proving to be impossible. In that month an article in the non-Adventist *Christian Reflector* indicated that "the doctrine of annihilation has too extensively obtained [in Millerism] to pass unnoticed. It is a fearful detraction from the motives which the gospel urges upon an ungodly world."[39]

At the annual Boston general conference in May, the leading Millerites finally made an official pronouncement on the topic. Surprisingly, they came down with a relatively soft public hand that seemingly belied their private convictions. They apparently did not want to create any further schism on the topic as they finished their work of warning the world of soon-coming judgment.

The official pronouncement merely stated that the intermediate state of the dead and the final condition of the wicked were "no part of the Advent faith" and did not involve points "essential to salvation." As a result, they were issues of minor importance, and all such theoretical issues would soon be settled with the return of the Lord. Before that time, the pronouncement reads, "we have no expectation that God's people will all see alike."[40]

Such official pronouncements, however, did not mean much to those who were convicted otherwise. They would continue to agitate. Thus Fitch could write to Storrs in May 1844:

> I have received a long letter from Bro. Litch touching the state of the dead, the end of the wicked, &c. It would be exceeding pleasant to me, to be able to please him, and the dear brethren who agree with him, for I love them all, and could rejoice to concede anything but truth, to be able to harmonise [sic] with them in my views. But there is a friend who has bought me with [H]is blood, and I take more pleasure in pleasing Him, than in pleasing all the world besides.[41]

Thus, whether Millerism's foremost leadership liked it or not, the battle had been joined. Storrs and his men would push ahead in spite of Miller's dictum that the premillennial advent should be the "only" doctrinal focal point in the movement.

As a result, we find that by the time Storrs accepted Snow's seventh-month teachings in the late summer of 1844, there was already a great deal of tension between the established Millerite leaders and those relative newcomers who were increasing in influence. That tension would not diminish in the early weeks of the "true midnight cry."

Older Leaders Join the Seventh-Month Movement

The seventh-month movement caught the established Millerite leaders by surprise. At the time it began, Himes and Miller were working in the West, and they did not find out about it until it was well underway. There is no evidence that any of the foremost Millerite preachers accepted this grass-roots development until late September. Most did not accept it until October.

While part of the difficulty may have been tied to personalities and leadership prerogatives, there were also definite theological reasons for hesitancy. Miller, for example, had never recommended any specific date for the second coming, since he believed that no one could know the day or hour of that event. Likewise, the editors of the *Signs* had always protested when individual Adventists had set exact dates in 1843. And now, in the face of that established viewpoint, the new theory put forth the very day for the advent.

The first public recognition of the seventh-month movement in a major Millerite periodical is found in the *Advent Herald* of August 21. The editors reported that "Brother Snow remarked with great energy on the *time*, and displayed much research" in presenting his views. Granting that his conclusions were a possibility, the *Herald* cautioned that "we should hesitate before we should feel authorized to attempt to 'make known' the very *day*." It went on to suggest that all should examine the evidence.[42] On the other hand, the *Herald* did not print his argument at that time. That job would be left to Snow's *True Midnight Cry* on August 22, which would be scattered by the thousands in a short time.

The August 21 *Advent Herald* also saw the first public statement by Litch on the seventh-month excitement. Admitting that the movement was picking up speed, he wrote: "I cannot see, for the life of me, how our dear brethren make it out so much to their own satisfaction, that the 2300 days end in that month." He went on to provide nine arguments against Snow's conclusions. In September, Litch flatly denied any validity to the seventh-month movement and feared "that many will be injured by their confidence in the Lord's coming only at that time."[43]

By mid-September, Apollos Hale, one of the editors of the *Herald*, was much more conciliatory than Litch. By that time he was willing to suggest that the evidence was "highly worthy of consideration." He went on to note that "from a fair consideration of all the facts in the case, we must say, that if we should look to any one day, in preference to others, as the time for the Advent, we should be disposed to look to" the tenth day of the seventh month—or October 22. He then provides a lengthy two-part critical analysis of the evidence that raises some issues that "do not appear to have been properly considered" by the seventh-month advocates.[44]

It seems clear that the Millerite leadership did not quite know what to do with the seventh-month movement. On the one hand, they recognized its influence in the Adventist community and the impossibility of ignoring it. On the other hand, they did not feel comfortable in endorsing it.

In the meantime, as the "true midnight cry" was spreading throughout the ranks, the established leadership seemed intent on going about business as usual in the hope, one supposes, that Christ would hurry up and come and rescue them from their compounding dilemma.

As of September 20, Himes and Litch were still planning to go on the mission to Great Britain. Himes wrote that he "dare not" alter his plans, even though he could not "reasonably expect assistance from the dear brethren who have strong faith in the *seventh month*." And on September 30, Miller still saw the task ahead as he always had, even though he wrote that his western campaign in August had so exhausted his worn-out body that he thought he would "never be able again to labor in the vineyard as heretofore." He also ominously reported that he and his followers had lost control of his church in Low Hampton. Miller seemed to be surrounded by difficulties on every side as September 1844 melded into October. But he would soon be viewing his difficulties as the darkness before dawn.[45]

In the last week of September, viewpoints began to change rapidly among the Millerite leadership as one by one they accepted the seventh-month date. September 25 saw Joseph Marsh's *Voice of Truth* come out in favor of the seventh month, even though less than two months before, the same magazine rejoiced that Millerite time setting appeared to be over. Nathaniel Southard, editor of the *Midnight Cry*, capitulated on September 26 and committed his paper to the October date.[46]

Four days later Himes penned a letter to Miller that indicates a major shift taking place in his own thinking. Himes, the perpetual pragmatist, had been impressed with the results of the seventh-month movement. "This thing," he wrote on September 30, "has gone over the country like lightning. Nearly every lecturer has come into it, and are preaching it with zeal, and great success." Beyond that, and certainly important in the eyes of Himes and Miller, it had

> done away [with] all Fanaticism, and brought those who were given to extravagance into a sober discreet state of mind. 43 never made so great, and good an impression as this has done upon all that have come under its influence. The worldly minded have been quickened and made alive—and all classes have been blessed beyond anything we have seen in time past. With this view of the matter, I dare not oppose it, although I do not yet get the light as to the *month* & *day*.

On the other hand, Himes was quite willing to admit that Christ might come on the tenth day of the seventh month.[47]

With those convictions in his heart, Himes wrote that he had decided to give up his mission to England, which only ten days before he "dare not" surrender. Now it was his "hope to go to the *New world*, instead of the *Old*." He concluded his letter by asking Miller a series of questions on his own article on the seventh month that had been published in May 1843. The questions seem to be engineered to push the ailing Miller toward an acceptance of the October date. After all, Miller was still, in Himes' mind, the leader of the advent movement. His support was important.[48]

What was implicit in Himes' September 30 letter to Miller becomes more explicit in Sylvester Bliss' letter of October 3. Bliss wrote to Miller that he had accepted the seventh month and was "under the most solemn impressions that the Lord will be here in a few days. . . . The Lord our God must be in this matter."

"We want," Bliss appealed to the aging leader, "you to look this question over . . . & give all the light possible. . . . Give us your prayers that we may be guided aright in this important crisis." Thus by early October the pressure was increasing on

Miller to make a decision regarding the October date. His chief lieutenants were moving toward acceptance, and they wanted their leader with them.[49]

October 6 was a high day for the proponents of the October 22 date. On that day, wrote a participant in the service at the Boston Tabernacle,

> Brother Himes came out . . . & expressed his belief that the Lord would come on the tenth of the seventh month. A great sensation was produced. Many who had been hoping that he would not embrace the trying truth & that they in consequence would have an excuse to shelter them in the day of the Lord. These souls Brother Himes very emphatically shook off from his skirts. He then gave a summary of the work of arousing the world to judgment. . . .
>
> Glory be to God! dear brother we shall soon meet in the kingdom—Till then a short farewell![50]

That same day, unbeknown to Himes, Miller also accepted the October 22 date. "Dear Brother Himes," he penned,

> I see a glory in the seventh month which I never saw before. Although the Lord had shown me the typical bearing of the seventh month, one year and a half ago, yet I did not realize the force of the types. Now, blessed be the name of the Lord, I see a beauty, a harmony, and an agreement in the Scriptures, for which I have long prayed, but did not see until to-day.[51]

Apparently Himes' letter of September 30, which had encouraged Miller to reexamine his May 17, 1843, treatment of the seventh month, had had its desired effect. Miller had come to realize that Snow's seventh-month argument was really an extension of his own position.

"Thank the Lord, O my soul," Miller continued in his October 6 letter.

Let Brother Snow, Brother Storrs and others, be blessed for their instrumentality in opening my eyes. *I am almost home. Glory! Glory!! Glory!!!* I see that the time is correct. . . .

. . . My soul is so full I cannot write. I call on you, and all who love his apearing [sic], to thank him for this glorious truth. My doubts, and fears, and darkness, are all gone. I see that we are yet right. God's word is true; and my soul is full of joy; my heart is full of gratitude to God. Oh, how I wish I could shout. But I shall shout when the "King of kings comes."

Methinks I hear you say, "Bro. Miller is now a fanatic." Very well, call me what you please; I care not; Christ will come in the seventh month, and will bless us all. Oh! glorious hope. Then I shall see him, and be like him, and be with him forever.[52]

Himes and Bliss both responded joyfully to Miller's commitment. "Yours of the 6th is just rec[eive]d," wrote Bliss on October 9. "Praise God[,] praise God. May we all be ready to meet in the skies." That same evening Himes read Miller's letter to the crowded Boston Tabernacle.[53]

Within a short time after Miller and Himes accepted the October 22 date, the rest of the established Millerite leaders came over to that view. Litch may have been the last to accept the new date, but as of October 12, he could rejoice that his High Priest would be coming out of the Holy of Holies of the heavenly sanctuary to take His people home. I now, he penned, *"lift up my head in joyful expectation of seeing the King of kings within ten days."*[54]

The excitement was contagious. On October 11, Miller wrote that he had "never seen among our brethren such *faith* as is manifested in the seventh month. 'He will come,' is the common expression. 'He will not tarry the second time,' is their general reply. There is a forsaking of the world, an unconcern for the wants of life, a general searching of heart, confession of sin, and a deep feeling in prayer for Christ to come." Miller appreciated the quiet calmness as the believers prepared to meet their God.[55]

The next day he wrote to Himes that "the seventh month be-gins *tomorrow*." "I do not expect to see you again in this life, but I do hope to see you soon crowned in glory, and robed in the spot-less garment of Christ's righteousness."[56]

The Millerite leadership had been brought over to the seventh-month position because of what they saw as the "irresistable [sic] power attending its proclamation, which prostrated all before it" and "swept over the land with the velocity of a tornado." Its wholesome effect on Christian lives, they concluded, could "be accounted for only on the supposition that God was [in] it."[57]

A continuation of that power was definitely witnessed in the final weeks of spreading the message. Mrs. E. C. Clemons re-ported from Boston that the tabernacle was crowded every night and two power presses were running constantly day and night to produce the last issue of the *Advent Herald* before it ceased publi-cation in anticipation of the second coming.[58]

The editors of the *Midnight Cry*, meanwhile, reported that they had four presses constantly in motion as they made one last effort to spread their message through the free distribution of hundreds of thousands of the final issues of their papers. The same can be said for most of the other Adventist editors as they moved into what they believed would be the last few days of earth's history. Supplies of literature were made available to all who could dis-tribute it. All this was made possible by those who freely gave of their earthly goods, since they would have no more need of them.[59]

Beyond the printed page, October 1844 saw major efforts to reach a world ripe for judgment through private conversation and public meetings. Never had the interest in Millerism been higher.

"Real" and "Perceived" Fanaticism in the Seventh Month

In spite of disclaimers by Miller, Himes, and others, as the seventh-month movement entered the final weeks, there was an increase of both actual extremism on the part of some Millerites and perceived extremism in the minds of many in the onlooking populace. Himes and Miller were undoubtedly correct in a com-parative sense, since there had been a sharp decrease in fanatical activity from what had been experienced in the Starkweather excitement and during the tarrying time earlier in the year. But sharp decrease does not imply total absence of borderline activity.

On the other hand, in light of their faith and in the eyes of the watching world, the advent believers did face a genuine dilemma as October 22 approached. From one perspective, if they continued daily business as usual, they would be accused of not really believing what they preached. But, from another perspective, if they ceased doing business as usual, they would be labeled fanatics. In such a circumstance, it was impossible for them to win in the eyes of those who leaned toward criticism.

Unfortunately, millennial movements by their very nature tend to attract fanatical and extremist types who become carried away by the general excitement and sensationalism that accompany them. Millerism was no exception to that rule, but the cool rationalism of Miller, Himes, Litch, and the majority of the advent leaders appears to have kept the extreme elements down to a minimum. That was especially so up through early 1842. The Millerite message was more apt to affect the head than the emotions.

But Miller and his colleagues recognized the potential for imbalance to distort their movement. As a result, they periodically warned against extremist actions in the face of the imminent return of their Lord. Thus as they neared the beginning of the year of the end of the world, the *Signs* editors cautioned their readers to follow the counsel of Jesus, who had said to His followers, "Occupy till I come." It is necessary, penned the editors, "that all should act conscientiously, and pursue their business just as they would wish to be found employed whenever the Lord may appear." Believers were counseled to neglect "none of the duties of this life." Miller never did depart from that advice.[60]

But Miller was not the entire movement. The counsel of some of the newer leaders would be quite different from that of the movement's founder. In late July 1844, for example, Joseph Marsh, while telling his readers that they did not need to give away "*all*" their property, counseled them to "dispose of *all* you have which you do not actually need for the present wants of your-self and family" and business. Believers should sacrifice to aid the cause of spreading the message. After all, "covetousness is *idolatry*, and no idolator shall inherit the kingdom of God." Those prac-ticing "*covetousness* . . . will doubtless be found wanting in the day of the Lord." In this way, Marsh, in all sincerity, turned up the pressure on the believers.[61]

That pressure did not decrease as the exact day of the advent approached. The enthusiastic Storrs, in an article published re-peatedly in the Millerite papers, took Marsh's counsel a giant step forward. While Marsh had counseled believers to dispose of their surplus, Storrs advised them to "venture *all*" rather than bring upon themselves " 'swift destruction.' " When the true midnight cry gets hold of people, "there is a leaving *all*. . . . When this cry gets hold of the heart, farmers leave their farms, with their crops standing, to go out and sound the alarm—and mechanics their shops."[62]

That type of pressure was well-nigh impossible to resist for those who were certain that the end of all things was a few days off. By mid-October, even the more staid editor of the *Midnight Cry* suggested that the command to "occupy till I come" was be-ing used by many as a justification for being "wholly absorbed in the affairs of the world." "Break loose from the world as much as possible," he suggested. But "if indispensable duty calls you into the world for a moment, go as a man would run to do a piece of work in the rain. Run and hasten through it, and let it be known that you leave it with alacrity for something better. Let your actions preach in the clearest tones: 'The Lord is coming'—'The time is short'—'This world passeth away'—'Prepare to meet thy God.' "[63]

With the multitude of pressures upon them, many advent be-lievers followed the advice of Storrs and others as the excite-ment, conviction, and anticipation of the second coming built up through 1844 to its climax in October. Some of their excitement was quite reasonable, given the circumstances, but some was just plain fanatical.

One of the more reasonable or even quite understandable expressions of what some interpreted to be extremism centered on the cessation of business activities as the time of the end neared. Some believers in New Hampshire, for example, had been so impressed in the spring of 1844 that Jesus would come before another winter that they did not even plant crops. Others, having planted crops, chose not to harvest them in the fall in order "to show their faith by their works, and thus to condemn the world."[64]

Yet other Millerites closed their businesses or otherwise suspended their commercial activity as the end approached. For most of them, such cessation took place only in the last few days. Thus the Cleveland *Herald* reported on October 19 that "many have suspended their usual avocations, and now devote their whole time and substance to the work of proselyting.... Meetings are held day and night."[65]

About that same time, the Philadelphia *Ledger* reported the following wording affixed to the front of a store owned by a Millerite. " 'This shop is closed in honor of the King of kings, who will appear about the 20th of Oct. Get ready, friends, to crown him Lord of all.' " Another Millerite advertised in a similar fashion, noting that " 'the Bridegroom is coming.' "[66]

Yet another report indicates that people were responding to Storrs' call to give up all. "Many," reported the *Midnight Cry* of October 3, "are leaving all, to go out and warn the brethren and the world." After one preaching session by Storrs, thirteen volunteered "to go out and sound the alarm." In both Philadelphia and Norfolk, Virginia, the report continued, "stores are being closed, and they [the closed stores] preach in tones the world understands, though they may not heed it." The children of faithful Millerites, as might be expected, were pulled out of school. After all, schooling implied a future.[67]

Even more radical than those who closed their shops or refused to plant and harvest were those who, taking Storrs at his word, ventured their "*all*" by giving away their property. The New York *Evangelist* noted that in Philadelphia, where Storrs was preaching, some believers "disposed of their furniture, some of them of their houses, and others of their investments in corporate insti-tutions, and brought the money and laid it, as they said, upon the altar."[68]

That mentality was fairly widespread as the day approached. Jane Marsh Parker, daughter of Joseph Marsh, recalled that the chief hatter of Rochester, New York, threw open the doors of his shop on October 21 and invited the crowd to "help themselves to hats, umbrellas, etc., which they naturally did." A nearby baker disposed of his goods in the same way.[69]

Henry Bear also became generous with his goods as a result of his belief in the end of the world. Visiting those indebted to him, he presented their accounts. He took the money if they had it but forgave it if they didn't, since he "believed the Lord would come by such a time which would settle up all accounts between creditor and debtor." Bear also reported that he had some things for sale but chose to give them away to those who wanted them. "When they wanted to pay for them," he recounted, "I would not receive it, telling them that the world was coming to an end by such a time, and I needed no money as it would do me no good. Of course they sometimes stared at me, astonished." The money he did collect from his debts he used to pay for the distribution of advent publications and for assisting "the poor in the advent faith, as they had by this time quit work." By the middle of Sep-tember 1844, Bear had disposed of all his money but eighty dollars and had given away the key to his house.[70]

Bear truly believed that Christ was coming. Onlookers, of course, thought that he and others like him were crazy. As is so often the case with intense religious zeal, what appears to be faith to insiders looks like insanity to outsiders.

Many, of course, would soon regret their rash course of action. On October 29, after Christ hadn't come, Storrs confessed that he had been "led into error, and thereby . . . led others astray, in advising advent believers to leave business entirely and attend meetings only." He counseled all to return to their employment so that they could care for their families.[71]

Others later turned irrevocably against Millerism as a destructive belief. One such case was the "mad disciple" in Vermont who had left his crops to rot in the ground because " 'the end of all things was at hand.' "[72] But it needs to be remembered that at the time, such a course of action seemed quite rational to believers. In fact, in the eyes of those tending toward extremism, it seemed to be demanded by their faith.

Even the scholarly John Dowling, one of Miller's most assertive clerical opponents, could see the logic in the extremist line of reasoning. Back in 1840, Dowling had written,

> Were this doctrine of Mr. Miller established upon evidence satisfactory to my own mind, I would not rest till I had published it in the streets, and proclaimed in the ears of my fellow townsmen, . . . "THE DAY OF THE LORD IS AT HAND!" Build no more houses! plant no more fields and gardens! FORSAKE YOUR SHOPS, AND FARMS, AND ALL SECULAR PURSUITS, and give every moment to preparation for this great event! for in three short years this earth shall be burned up, and Christ shall come in the clouds, awake the sleeping dead, and call all the living before his dread tribunal.[73]

The editors of the *Advent Herald* complained that many condemned the Millerites for doing what the condemners themselves would have done had their convictions lain along different lines. After all, even secularists spent thousands for summer vacations of pleasure, and many were the stirring appeals to drop one's business and religion for the call of politics. Yet "when a man makes a sacrifice for his faith, the world . . . regards him as crazy."[74]

Perhaps it is worth noting at this juncture that the calm and rational William Miller never did sell his farm. That, however, was not seen as sanity or religious wholesomeness in him, but as hypocrisy.[75] It seems that it was difficult, if not impossible, for the Millerites to please their contemporaries. Their real sin appears to have been the holding of a world view that radically differed from that of the larger culture. That was bad enough, but when that world view predicated the immediate end of the world, it brought the Millerites into a position of combat with the rest of their world—both religious and secular.

One result of that confrontation was the frequent jibes that the Millerites had to put up with in their everyday life. As we noted in earlier chapters, many were the public accusations of insanity and fanaticism. While the majority of those accusations had no basis in fact, some were quite true. As in the previous stages of Millerism, the final stage of pre-October 22 Millerism did push some of the more excitable believers over the edge of propriety. A case in point is a Mrs. Baker of Oswego, New York, who had given up eating because the time was so short. As of October 10, she had gone twenty-nine days without eating anything. Yet she claimed good health, while her "neighbors say that her strength has lately been increased."[76] Presumably both Mrs. Baker and her neighbors interpreted the whole affair as a spiritual blessing.

Other pockets of Adventism also experienced charismatic excess in October 1844. Nathaniel Whiting wrote to Miller on October 24 that his Adventist community had experienced "a tempest of real fanaticism. Our poor brothers were deluded into a belief of 'signs & lying wonders'—[the] gift of tongues & modern prophecies."[77]

The most serious case of fanaticism among the Millerites took place in Philadelphia. There an otherwise unknown Millerite by the name of Dr. R. C. Gorgas claimed to have had a vision that Christ would come at three o'clock in the morning of October 22 at the ninth hour of the Jewish day. "I was," penned Gorgas, "led to the Cross on the Clock striking 3, after which I was prostrated to the floor by the Holy Spirit, when the above was represented to me." After six days of guidance by the *Holy Ghost*," Gorgas claimed that the truth of the vision had become clear to him. He then (about October 16) prepared a broadside featuring a graphic chart of his predictions and set about to win converts.[78]

Fortunately for Gorgas, but unfortunately for the reputation of Philadelphia Adventism, he managed to convert the excessive

George Storrs to his prophetic scheme. On October 18, Storrs managed to get the broadside featuring Gorgas' prophecy published in a *Midnight Cry* Extra so that it could be distributed throughout the ranks of Adventism. Since Storrs by then was a leading spokesman for the October 22 date, editor Southard merely assumed that the document was orthodox. As a result, he did not read it until it had been printed and several hundred copies sent out.[79]

By the next morning, however, the *Cry* editors had discovered their mistake, stopped the presses, and burned those copies that had been produced. But it was too late. Some of the copies sent out had fallen into the hands of newspaper editors. As a result, Philadelphia Adventism, and, by extension, Adventism as a whole, was developing a further reputation for fanaticism. This time, however, unlike so many other occasions, the charges were based on fact.[80]

The broadside would have been bad enough, but Gorgas managed to extend the public folly. With the aid of George Grigg and Clorinda S. Minor (a prominent Millerite writer and lecturer), he managed to convince about 150 of the Philadelphia believers to flee the city as Lot fled Sodom and to dwell in tents to await Christ's arrival at three o'clock in the morning on October 22. Litch tried to halt the fiasco, but to no avail.[81]

While the actual fanaticism involved only a few of the several thousand Philadelphia Millerites, it made good newspaper copy. As a result, reports of the Gorgas episode—with a great deal of literary license regarding the extent and shape of the fanaticism— spread across the nation. The Philadelphia fanaticism became the source of many of the developing legends of Millerite fanaticism that extended all the way from the usual ascension robes to babies frozen by the October weather as the believers awaited the Lord in tents.[82]

Moving Toward October 22

As the designated day approached, reactions varied. The non-Adventist press, of course, kept up its generally unfavorable treatment. But beyond that, anti-Millerite violence reached an all-time high in many places. Mobs forced the closure of Millerite meetings in such places as New York City (where the mayor volunteered to take a strong hand against the rowdies if the Adventists desired him to do so), Boston (where the police force had to come into action), Philadelphia (where the sheriff ordered all further Millerite meetings to be cancelled because of mob action on October 14), and many other places. The editors of the *Advent Herald* "could only liken the conduct of the [Boston] mob to that which surrounded the door of Lot, on the evening pending the destruction of Sodom." It appears that extremist actions were not limited to the advent believers as the climactic day approached.[83]

Another non-Adventist response to the Millerite prediction was a haunting fear that the Adventists just might be correct in their interpretation. As Luther Boutelle put it, "some were exceedingly frightened with awful forebodings."[84] Thus uncounted numbers tensely faced October 22. With its passing, many of these also felt free to vent their true feelings. As a result, anti-Millerite mob action did not cease with the believers' October disappointment.

As might be expected, the advent believers looked toward October 22 with unbridled joy. And why shouldn't they? That was the day their Lord would come. Their trials and frustrations would be over; even death and pain would meet their final defeat.

The number awaiting that victory is impossible to calculate with any sense of accuracy. *The Proceedings of the American Antiquarian Society* put the figure at 150,000 to 200,000, but Miller estimated only 50,000 situated in "nearly a thousand . . . Advent congregations." Of course, while it is well-nigh impossible to estimate those separated from their churches into advent congregations, it is totally impossible to estimate the number who had remained in their churches or who had no formal church connections at all. Whitney Cross has estimated that besides regular believers, there may have been "a million or more of their fellows [who] were skeptically expectant." Suffice it to say, there were considerable numbers anticipating the great day.[85]

The same statistical problems frustrating any exact knowledge of the size of the movement also block our way to ascertaining the number of advent preachers. Miller, who is known for his conservatism in such estimates, put the figure at 200 ministers plus 500 public lecturers. Everett Dick suggests that a contemporary estimate by Millerite Lorenzo D. Fleming of 1,500 to 2,000 lecturers "is more realistic."[86]

Whatever their number, the believers awaited October 22 as the climax of world history. In the records left by participants, there is widespread agreement that "the time immediately preceding the 22d of October was one of great calmness of mind" on the part of most of the Adventists. The same impression is gained from a perusal of the Millerite periodicals in October. "During the last ten days," Bliss recalled, "secular business was, for the most part, suspended; and those who looked for the Advent gave themselves to the work of preparation for that event, as they would for death, were they on a bed of sickness, expecting soon to close their eyes on earthly scenes forever."[87]

"With joy," Boutelle reminisced, "all the ready ones anticipated the day." Confessions were made, wrongs righted, and many sinners inquired what they should do to be saved. However, he points out, the last family gatherings were solemn for the believers as they said their goodbyes to loved ones whom they did not expect to meet again.[88]

The Millerite leaders, with the exception of Nathaniel Whiting, had all accepted the October 22 date. But one of the foremost leaders was now missing. The exuberant and impulsive Charles Fitch had died in Buffalo, New York, on October 14 at the age of thirty-nine. Fitch, traveling home to Cleveland from Rochester, had stopped in Buffalo for an appointment in the final days of September. While there, according to his daughter, he baptized a group of believers by immersion in Lake Erie on a cold, windy day. After starting for his lodging in wet clothes, he was twice turned back to baptize more candidates. The extended exposure led to a fever that resulted in his death.[89]

It was while on his bed of serious sickness that one of the be-

lievers read Storrs' September 24 article on the seventh-month
movement to Fitch. On hearing it read, "he shouted glory several
times; said it was true, and [that] he should be raised to proclaim
it."[90]

But such was not to be. The following week a visitor found
Fitch "just alive. His soul, however, was full of hope and glory.
He said that it was indelibly written on his soul, that the Lord
would come on the tenth day of the seventh month, and if he went
to the grave, he would only have to take a short sleep, before he
should be waked in the resurrection morn." He passed away a few
days later.[91]

It is an interesting footnote to Adventist history that it was
Fitch's convert Storrs who led him into the doctrine of both con-
ditional immortality and baptism by immersion. Fitch accepted
both views in early 1844. He was himself baptized on a cold winter day. That March found the intrepid Fitch baptizing twelve
believers in the Ohio Canal in a driving snowstorm.[92] Thus the
later September baptisms in the frigid Erie that led to his death
were not an exception to his usual practice. Fitch comes across as
one of the most faithful of men. After his initial waffling on
Millerism in 1838, he seems to have stood solidly for his beliefs,
once he was convinced of their biblical validity.

At this point it is also of interest to note that Fitch's Cleveland
congregation that had rejected his views on annihilationism had
accepted his position on baptism by immersion. The Cleveland
Herald reports that the local Adventists, following their late pastor's example, had baptized several converts by immersion in mid-
October.[93]

Josiah Litch, who had brought Fitch into Millerism, had a
similar reaction to his new teachings as did the Cleveland congregation. While strongly reacting against Fitch's view of immortality, Litch let Fitch convince him on baptism by immersion. He was baptized by Fitch in early September 1844. Litch,
rising from the water with praises to God, "walked to the shore
and took his wife by the hand and baptized her."[94]

It should be pointed out that both Litch (a Methodist) and

Fitch (a Presbyterian/Congregationalist) came from traditions that had stood for infant baptism by methods other than immersion. While Baptists like Miller already held to immersion, the practice was a major shift for these other leaders. Apparently under the restorationist impulse of the times, they desired to bypass the religious history of their traditions and adopt what they believed to be New Testament teachings.

Thus by the autumn of 1844, several of the leading Adventist preachers were in the process of merging several new doctrines into their premillennial belief system. Baptism by immersion and the non-immortality of the soul were two of those new doctrines. In their restorationism, some of the believers were also arguing for a return to the seventh-day Sabbath. By September, that agitation had become strong enough for the *Midnight Cry* to reply to the seventh-day believers with a lengthy two-part article.[95] These struggles at doctrinal formulations among the advent believers had begun to set the stage for events in the months and years after October 1844.

But before we get to that part of the story, we have to rejoin the Millerites on the eve of October 22 as they wait for Christ to exit the Most Holy Place of the heavenly sanctuary to come and rescue them from their world of darkness. Most Millerites spent the day with fellow believers in their churches or in private homes. The Boston *Post* gives a brief glimpse of the believers in that city. "The Tabernacle," the report reads, "is crowded night and day with Millerites, who express a perfect confidence that the judgment day will be here by the 22d inst.—Hundreds from the neighboring towns sleep in the Tabernacle every night. The excitement is very great."[96]

But the tabernacle's pastor was not with his people on that momentous day. Himes had traveled to Low Hampton to be with his revered Miller when Christ descended with His myriads of angels.

Unfortunately for both of them and their followers, Christ did not come.

Chapter 11

THE OCTOBER DISAPPOINTMENT

"The Millerites . . . kept it up all night before last," noted the Baltimore *Sun*, "and yesterday they went to bed—their public haunts are silent as the grave."[1]

"The world still hangs fire," reported the Cleveland *Plain Dealer*. "The old planet is still on the track, notwithstanding the efforts to 'stop 'er.' The 'believers' in this city, after being up a few nights watching and making noises like serenading tom cats, have now gone to bed and concluded to take a snooze. We hope they will wake up *rational beings!*"[2]

The ultimate crisis of Millerism had taken place. Jesus had not come. The believers were still on earth. The October disappointment was much more devastating to the movement than that of the spring, not only because it was the second one, but also because the Adventists had pinned all their hopes on an *exact* date. In October there was not the softness in dating that there had been in the spring. As a result, there was no cushion in the letdown.

Immediate Reactions

As might be expected, reactions among the believers were anything but cheerful. "I waited all Tuesday [October 22]," penned Henry Emmons,

> and dear Jesus did not come;—I waited all the forenoon of Wednesday, and was well in body as I ever was, but after 12

217

o'clock I began to feel faint, and before dark I needed some one to help me up to my chamber, as my natural strength was leaving me very fast, and I lay prostrate for 2 days without any pain—sick with disappointment.[3]

On October 24, Litch penned a letter to Miller that opened with the words, "It is a cloudy and dark day here—the sheep are scattered—and the Lord has not come yet."[4]

Hiram Edson wrote:

Our fondest hopes and expectations were blasted, and such a spirit of weeping came over us as I never experienced before. It seemed that the loss of all earthly friends could have been no comparison. We wept, and wept, till the day dawn.

I mused in my own heart, saying, My advent experience has been the richest and brightest of all my christian [sic] experience. If this had proved a failure, what was the rest of my christian [sic] experience worth? Has the Bible proved a failure? Is there no God—no heaven—no golden home city—no paradise? Is all this but a cunningly devised fable? Is there no reality to our fondest hopes and expectation of these things? And thus we had something to grieve and weep over, if all our fond hopes were lost. And as I said, we wept till the day dawn.[5]

For young James White, the thought of turning "again to the cares, perplexities, and dangers of life, in full view of the jeers and revilings of unbelievers who now scoffed as never before, was a terrible trial of faith and patience." He recalled that when Himes visited Portland, Maine, soon after October 22, "and stated that the brethren should prepare for another cold winter, my feelings were almost uncontrollable. I left the place of meeting and wept like a child."[6]

It was bad enough that the believers had been disappointed, but the added burden of facing a jeering world complicated the lives of believers in late October. As Miller put it, "it seemed as though all the demons from the bottomless pit were let loose upon us. The same ones and many more who were crying for mercy two days before, were now mixed with the rable [sic] and mocking, scoffing, and threatening in a most blasphemous manner."[7]

After a few days, some of the advent preachers began to move about and meet with hushed groups of believers. One such was Luther Boutelle, who, after comforting several companies of Adventists, finally came across one "that had come together to stay until the Lord came." He found about seventy believers in a large house, all living together and having daily meetings. They had pooled their money in a milk pan and cared for their needs from that common fund.

"We held a meeting with them," Boutelle recalled, "and advised them as best we could to keep the faith and separate, and see to their individual interests, and those of their families, which advice they kindly took, and very soon separated, going each to his and her calling."[8]

In many ways Himes was at his best as an organizer in the post-disappointment period. He not only resumed his publishing endeavors but also traveled to various groups to strengthen the believers. In addition, on October 26 he set forth the idea of forming Adventist committees "in every city and town" to aid the destitute among their numbers.

After all, many had been quite "sincere" in the desire to "glorify God" when they gave away their possessions or chose not to harvest their crops. "And now," claimed Himes, "they must not suffer." His aim was to get the Adventists to pull together in the face of both their internal difficulties and external critics. "We must not permit" the destitute believers "to be dependent upon the world, or that portion of the professed church, who scoff at our hope. . . . Some among us still have this world's goods, and can render present aid to the destitute. I doubt not all will do their duty."[9]

Within a week after October 22, the *Advent Herald* and *Midnight Cry* were back in production, even though the remaining months of the year would see decreasing finances with which to print. In early 1845 the *Midnight Cry* was renamed the *Morning Watch*, symbolizing the new focus of the advent movement. July 1845 would see the *Watch* absorbed into the *Advent Herald*.

One significant difference in the Millerite work after October 22 from before that date is the shift in emphasis from evangelism toward simply holding the movement together. Millerite activity now focused on inreach as the disoriented believers sought to make sense out of their experience and to create wholeness and continuity in their ranks.

The reaction of believers to the October disappointment was one thing; the reaction of the non-Adventist world quite another. Those reactions were both verbal and physical.

On the verbal level, Garrison's *Liberator* noted on November 8, 1844, that Miller and his followers had been led "by a deplorable fantasy of the brain." The *New York Evangelist* had pointed out a day before that "the last day of this world has not yet come, notwithstanding the confident predictions of Miller . . . and his deluded followers. . . . The wheels of nature roll on unchecked. . . . The sun has not forgotten to rise." The sun "will run his ample round for ages yet to come; when the prophets and prophecies of the present day shall have been forgotten." Of course, the misnamed *Olive Branch* had its bit to offer as it called down "thunderbolts red with uncommon wrath" upon Himes and his "fellow authors of the Miller mania."[10]

The "wicked" Mr. Himes was the target of much of the public abuse. Himes had long been accused of duping well-meaning people out of their money for his personal gain. The learned John Dowling had written of the Adventist leadership that he could "conceive of no conduct more dishonorable and mean than that of prevailing upon weak-minded and ignorant, but in many instances well-disposed and pious persons, to part with their little savings, their worldly all," under "false pretense" by the Millerite "pretenders." Dowling spoke of the "vast sums" placed in the hands of "these men" by "multitudes of simple-hearted people."[11]

The issue came to a head when the Boston *Post* published an article soon after the October disappointment, accusing Himes

and his colleagues of being " 'unprincipled men; perfectly conscious of the absurdity of the opinions they inculcate, and entirely
reckless of the injury they inflict, if they can only turn the evil to
their pecuniary benefit.' "

Himes was fed up. On November 1 he made a statement to the
public that he had been grossly and unfairly assailed by the press.
"I have been represented," he penned,

> as dishonest, speculating out of the fears of the community,
> a disturber of the peace, as duping the unsuspecting, and ob-
> taining money under false pretenses,—soliciting it for public
> purposes, and appropriating it to private uses. I have been
> reported as having absconded, not only to England, but also
> to both Canada and Texas; and also as being liable to arrest
> under warrants already issued, as having been arrested and
> confined in Leverett [S]treet jail, and as having committed
> suicide; and it has also been said that I have accumulated
> great wealth, have sold vast quantities of jewelry, and pos-
> sess farms and hold money at interest.

To those charges Himes replied, "I would say, that if I have
wronged or defrauded any man, I will restore him four-fold." He
then requested any who had been defrauded "to make their case
known to the public." He also told his readers that if he had
anything "not consecrated to the advent cause, the public shall be
welcome to it." He went on to present a lengthy public defense of
specific accusations.[12]

While that defense had been written for the *Advent Herald*,
Himes was quite pleased when the *Post* editors agreed to publish
it on their front page. Himes' piece in the *Post* did much to quiet
the unjust criticism, not only in Boston but also in other places
where it had received notice. Several papers referred to his *Post*
article, and some, including the *Liberator*, republished it in full.[13]

The verbal abuse of the Millerites found expression on the personal level as well as on the printed page. Thus Bates related to
J. O. Corliss that on October 23, the neighborhood boys followed

him as he went to buy groceries, yelling out: " 'I thought you were going up yesterday.' " Bates went on to tell of the almost unbearable stress he experienced in his community. "If the earth could have opened and swallowed me up, it would have been sweetness compared to the distress I felt."[14]

In a similar vein, on November 18, Miller wrote to Himes of the problem. "Some," he penned,

> are tauntingly inquiring, "Have you not gone up?" Even little children in the streets are shouting continually to passersby, "Have you a ticket to go up?" The public prints, of the most fashionable and popular kind, in the great Sodoms of our country, are caricaturing in the most shameful manner the "white robes of the saints," Rev. 6:11, the "going up," and the great day of "burning." Even the pulpits are desecrated by the repetition of scandalous and false reports concerning the "ascension robes," and priests are using their powers and pens to fill the catalogue of scoffing in the most scandalous periodicals of the day.

Miller went on to note that even London and Paris, Europe's "sinks of pollution, . . . cannot, will not, and dare not, compete with our Boston, New York, or Philadelphia, in scoffing."[15]

Some Millerites, of course, still had their wits about them. One such, upon being queried as to why he didn't go up, responded, "And if I *had* gone up, where would you have gone?"[16]

Beyond verbal abuse, the physical violence that had begun prior to October 22 continued with even more vigor and destructiveness after the passing of the time. Pent-up fears and anxieties in many places found release in mob action.

Illustrative of the problems faced by the Millerites in New York State during this period were the burning of the Millerite place of worship in Ithaca, the tearing down of their temporary tabernacle in Dansville, and the removal and burning of the benches in the Scottsville meetinghouse after the worshipers had been driven out. In Troy "the wicked . . . paraded the streets, clad in white—

blew a trumpet, and cried, 'Come, Lord Jesus, come quickly!!' "[17]

Even after the Adventists moved their meetings to private houses, sometimes the services were still broken up by mobs. In early 1845 one lecturer in Canada reported that after being driven out of public meetinghouses by an armed force, his group met in a private house, only to have "thirty heavy guns . . . fired close at the window." On another occasion a mob rushed "into" a house in which the Millerites were meeting. While some flaunted "deadly weapons: others threw stones and clubs through the windows. Most of the windows in the principal rooms were entirely smashed in. Some of the brethren were wounded in the head, and some received blows." The astounded lecturer went on to indicate that the head of the mob was a church member.[18]

Henry Bear returned to his home to find that it had been pelted with eggs and stones at the urging of some of his relatives. His wife never washed the eggs off as long as they lived there, but left them as silent witnesses of the Bears' persecution. Similar stories of oppression were reported from other parts of North America in late 1844 and early 1845.[19]

Even though most believed the Millerites to be mistaken, not everyone reacted to them with violence. Some sought to calmly reason with their Adventist acquaintances. For example, on October 24, Phoebe Palmer, the leading woman in Methodism's holiness movement, wrote to Miller that even though he had been sincere, he had been mistaken, and his trumpet had "not given a certain sound." It was therefore his "*duty* to sound a retreat." She went on to compare Miller's sincerity with that of Paul in his persecution of the early Christians. "You say you were sincere, but Paul, when he sincerely thought he was doing God's service, found he had been deceived, and do you think he would have been forgiven if he had not made acknowledgement of his error? I rest this matter with you." Palmer had been personally affected by Millerism through the loss of such close friends as Charles Fitch to the movement.[20]

On November 13, 1844, the *Advent Herald* acknowledged that a fair portion of the public press had begun to treat the Adventists civilly, especially since the publication of Himes' defense in the Boston *Post* early in the month. Along that line, the *Liberator* thought it was unfortunate "that the Millerites have attracted the attention of a portion of our population, who delight to molest them." The position of the *Liberator* was that "all sincere convictions should be treated respectfully."[21]

In a similar vein, the *Oberlin Evangelist*, after deploring the Millerite error and hoping the believers had learned their lesson not "to pry into those secret things which belong to God alone," "affectionately and fraternally" invited the Adventists "back to re-engage in the work of converting the world to Jesus Christ" and thus help bring in the temporal millennium.[22]

A Leadership in Turmoil

Bewilderment and disorientation characterized both Millerite leaders and followers between October 22, 1844, and the end of the year. For a time many continued to look daily for the immediate fulfillment of the 2300-day prophecy and the coming of Christ. Some set the coming for October 23, while others hoped for subsequent dates—but all predictions ended in frustration. One can suppose that the Millerite leaders could have wished for the problems associated with their unfulfilled predictions concerning October 22 to disappear, but such was not to be the case. As the days moved on, they realized that they would have to make public statements regarding the seventh-month movement for the benefit of both the watching public and the disappointed believers.

But from the very date itself, the leadership differed among themselves as to what had gone wrong and what should be said and done. Thus on October 24, Nathaniel Whiting advised Miller of the "duty" of "all who participated" in the October movement to make "a public acknowledgement of their error. . . . Any shuffling on this point will authorize the community to say that we are not merely . . . credulous but absolutely *dishonest*."[23]

At the other extreme, Himes and the other editors of the *Advent Herald* published a piece on October 30 that upheld October

22 as a fulfillment of prophecy. "In view of all the circumstances attending this movement," they wrote,

> the blessed effect it has produced on the minds of God's children, and the hatred and malice His enemies have displayed, we *must still regard it as the true midnight cry*. And if we have a few days in which to try our faith, it is still in accordance with the parable of the ten virgins; for when they had all arisen and trimmed their lamps, there was still to be a time when the lamps of the foolish virgins would be going out. This could not be without a passing by of the 10th day; for till that time their lamps would burn.... A little delay is therefore no cause for discouragement, but shows how exact God is in the fulfillment of [H]is word.[24]

But as more than "a few days" passed, the situation became more serious. Even the two foremost promoters of the October 22 date split over the issue. By November 7, Storrs had concluded that he had been wrong in preaching the seventh-month message with such positiveness. Time itself had proved the error. If that was so, he was forced to ask, what had inspired him to preach the date with such forcefulness and certainty? The answer, Storrs suggested, was that he had been under the hypnotic influence of "*Mesmerism*." While sorry for preaching the exact time, Storrs assured his readers that he was "looking *daily* for the coming of our Lord, and striving by grace, to be always ready for it."[25]

By early 1845, Storrs had come to the conclusion that the Bible did not teach definite time at all and that the seventh-month movement was a "delusion" based on the "monstrous perversion" of certain texts of Scripture. For those insights, S. S. Snow, the originator of the October movement, consigned Storrs to perdition as one of the three unfaithful shepherds of Zechariah 11:8 whom God cut off.[26]

In mid-November the two foremost Millerite papers finally had to admit that all the seventh-month time was really past and that "we now find ourselves occupying a time, beyond which we can extend none of the prophetic periods, according to our chronology and date of commencement." Unlike their October 30 pronouncement, the editors could no longer plead a bit more tarrying time while they waited for the lamps of the foolish to go out. They frankly admitted that they had been "twice disappointed."[27]

But the editors of the *Advent Herald* and the *Midnight Cry* still held that God had been in the movement. They now saw Jonah as a type of their experience. God had commanded Jonah to preach a definite time for the destruction of Nineveh, but factors unbeknown to Jonah influenced the outcome. "We thus have an instance on record where God has justified the preaching of *time*, although the event did not occur as predicted." Thus the editors concluded that "we should as much have sinned against God, had we refrained from giving that message, as Jonah did when he" fled from God by heading for Tarshish.[28]

While the editorial leaders of the movement wrestled through their problem, so did the individuals within the long-established leadership. Not the least to struggle in the waning days of 1844 was William Miller. Immediately after October 22, Miller supposed that "a few weeks only might elapse between that time and the appearing of Christ." On November 10 he penned a letter to Himes, explaining his feelings. "Although," he wrote,

> I have been twice disappointed, I am not yet cast down or discouraged. God has been with me in Spirit, and has comforted me. I have now much more evidence that I do believe in God's word; and although surrounded with enemies and scoffers, yet my mind is perfectly calm, and my hope in the coming of Christ is as strong as ever. I have done only what after years of sober consideration I felt to be my solemn duty to do. If I have erred, it has been on the side of charity, the love of my fellow man, and my conviction of duty to God.[29]

Far from giving up hope, Miller penned, "I have fixed my mind upon another time, and here I mean to stand until God gives me more light.—And that is *To-day*, TO-DAY, and TO-DAY, until he comes, and I see HIM for whom my soul yearns."[30]

Eight days later, Miller wrote that he felt confident "that God will justify us in fixing the year. And," he added, "I believe as firmly, that this Jewish year will not terminate before this wicked and corrupted earth's history will be all told." The event could not be far off. That November 18 letter also claimed that the door of human probation had been shut and that the Adventists' work in warning the sinful world was complete. Their only evangelistic function was to work for the confused Adventists in their ranks.[31]

On December 3, a little more than a month after the historic disappointment, Miller was so certain of the nearness of the time that he suggested that the letter he was writing might not have time to reach its destination before the end. He noted that the position they had taken on prophecy and chronology was still the best, but if the problem was in the historical data, the knowledge of the age was insufficient to correct it. Thus they had no grounds for further date setting.[32]

His letters for the next month continued more or less along the same track. But by the end of December, he was willing to grant a possible error of four or five years in their calculations due to disputes among the best chronologists of the day. Thus the date for the conclusion of the 2300 days could not be settled beyond a doubt. "Therefore," he claimed in a conference address to the advent leaders, "we must patiently wait the time in dispute, before we can honestly confess we are wrong in time."[33]

That December 28 address evidences a definite erosion of Miller's conviction concerning the accuracy of the seventh-month movement. By the late summer of 1845, Miller was still holding to the few-years-of-possible-error theory and was quite satisfied that his teachings had not been materially affected by the disappointment, since the exact time had not been based on biblical data but upon human chronology.[34]

Slowly but surely, however, the force of time was eroding his belief that anything had happened on October 22, 1844. By mid-September 1845, he had concluded that "the seventh month movement was not a fulfillment of prophecy in any sense."[35]

Another issue that troubled Miller's mind in the months after October 1844 was the call made by Fitch, Storrs, Marsh, and others to separate from the churches. On December 3 he complained that "we have . . . cried Babylon! Babylon!! Babylon!!! against *all but Adventists*. . . . May God forgive us!" He also bemoaned the fact that the Adventists had been "guilty of raising up a sect" of their own.[36]

The next summer he wrote that he had never intended to form a sect but had hoped to benefit all the denominations. He still believed the call to come out of Babylon was "a wresting of the Scriptures" and "a perversion of the word of God" that had prejudiced many against the movement.[37]

Miller must have been suffering from a great deal of internal tension and personal confusion over the Babylon issue. After all, not only had many Millerites been expelled from their churches while others were refused the right to speak their beliefs in church, but on January 29, 1845, Miller himself and his fellow advent believers in Low Hampton were disfellowshiped from their Baptist church.[38]

Charges by the church were first laid against Miller and the advent believers in Low Hampton on November 10, 1844. It is probably no coincidence that on that very day, Miller penned a letter to Himes in which he complained that the name *Babylon* had been applied to all the churches. However, he significantly added that "in *too many* instances it was not unjustly applied."[39]

Even though Miller was loathe to admit it, the Millerites had few choices regarding separation. After all, returning to their own churches was not only humiliating, it would solve nothing, since they more than ever derided the Adventists' cherished belief in the second coming. The earlier reasoning of Litch still held. When asked why they did not give up and return to the churches, he had replied: "The plain answer is, because we never can, and the Lord helping us, we never will, sit down under the lullaby song of this world's conversion, and the return of the Jews to Palestine. They are, both of them, in our estimation, snares of the devil."[40]

Whether he liked it or not, Miller's doctrine of the premillennial second coming, which he saw as nonsectarian in the sense that he believed it belonged to all denominations, had, in reality, pushed his movement down the track to the formation of its own sect, with the advent as the central doctrine. But Miller never wanted to come to that conclusion. Time was short, he held in late 1844, and he believed the sectarian decision could be avoided if they just calmly waited until the second advent. Thus, he suggested, let us "enter into our chambers, and hide ourselves for a little while until the danger is over."[41] That solution, of course, was at best temporary, but neither Miller nor his associates could have known that at the time.

Himes' counsel to the believers, as expected, was much more down to earth and realistic in late 1844 and early 1845 than Miller's. After calling for the organization of relief committees for the destitute believers and getting the presses back in operation, Himes was faced with the task of thinking things through. Like it or not, he was the leader of the discouraged Adventists. After October 22, the aging Miller considered his "own work as completed," even if time continued. What "was to be done . . . , must be done by younger brethren."[42]

One of Himes' first tasks was to explain what he believed happened on October 22. Up through the end of October he seems to have held that the seventh-month movement was "the true midnight cry," and thus a fulfillment of prophecy. On October 30 he wrote to Joseph Bates that the movement had been a great blessing. But, by November 5, Himes, in agreement with Storrs, seems to have begun to shift his position on the veracity of the October date. "We are now satisfied," he penned, "that the authorities on which we based our calculations cannot be depended upon for *definite time*." The only thing he could say with certainty was that the advent was near and that they must wait and watch.[43]

Himes' radical shift from acceptance to rejection of the October date seems to have been based on the fact that his belief in the date had not been founded so much on the facts of chronology as it was upon the seventh-month movement's practical success as it rushed in power throughout the Adventist ranks in September and early October. The October movement's "supernaturalism," Himes had believed, was attested to by the fact that "it was entirely unanticipated by ourselves, and equally uncontrolled."[44]

But the pragmatic attestation provided by the movement's fruits had reversed itself after the October 22 disillusionment. As a result, Himes' thinking followed suit. After all, his conviction had not rested upon Scripture, but on the practical aspects of the movement.

Having lost his own conviction in the fulfillment of prophecy on October 22, Himes set about leading Miller and the rest of the movement in the same direction. Thus, in the erosion of Miller's own views on the seventh-month movement, he had not only to contend with his internal tensions, but also with pressures from the vigorous Himes.

Himes' major task in early 1845 would be to hold the remaining parts of Adventism together. That was no small undertaking, since the movement was literally disintegrating. Beyond that task, Himes was anxious to get Adventists working again and to avoid all speculation and date setting. "We have counted the cost," he penned on January 10, 1845, "and shall to the extent of the means which God has, or may give us, *agitate*, AGITATE, AGITATE, until the slumbering watchmen with their churches shall see the falsity of their position, or feel the full force of the truth, that the kingdom of God *is nigh at hand*. . . . Our position as to labor is, fully to occupy until the Lord shall come."[45]

The trajectory of Litch regarding the validity of the seventh-month movement followed roughly the same course as Miller's. On October 27 he expressed full faith in the movement. But by May 1845, he had rejected the seventh-month effort and suggested that "we erred, and ran off our track about one year ago."[46]

It is of interest to note that the major old-line leaders in Millerism all eventually focused on a probable error in *time* in the interpretation of the October 22 event. But Joseph Marsh, editor of the *Voice of Truth*, began to think in another direction. "We cheerfully admit," he penned in early November 1844, "that we have been mistaken in the *nature* of the event we expected would occur on the tenth of the seventh month; but we cannot yet admit that our great High Priest did not *on that very day*, accomplish *all* that the type would justify us to expect."[47]

Thus Marsh shifted the ground from *time* to the *nature* of what took place on October 22. While not being explicit as to what might have taken place on that day, he did put confidence in the fulfillment of prophecy on October 22 and hinted that high priestly typology might hold the answer to the dilemma of the nature of the event. The ideas in Marsh's short editorial would be taken up and fleshed out by two of the three divisions of Adventism in the next couple of years. We will return to their lines of interpretation in chapters 12 and 14.

The problem of what, if anything, had happened on October 22, 1844, became increasingly problematic for the Millerites as post-disappointment time extended into early 1845. Different Adventist parties began to take shape over the issue early in that year. Adventism had entered into what some of the participants would refer to as the scattering time.

The Scattering Time

David Arthur notes that in early 1845, "the cause of Adventism was flying off in several directions."[48] It should be recalled that pre-1845 Millerism was not a denomination. Rather, it was an ecumenical movement composed of ministers and laypeople from all the evangelical denominations. Thus, under the surface of Millerism, there existed a large number of divergent religious traditions.

Even though Storrs and others had agitated for what Miller and others believed to be disruptive doctrines in 1843 and 1844, on the whole the movement focused on a single doctrine—the premillennial second advent. That doctrine had held the movement together, aided by a mutually agreed upon forbearance on those points of doctrine that had split the denominations into contending parties.[49] After all, Christ would soon return and put all doctrinal bickering to rest. The important thing was to get the message of the rapidly approaching advent out. That task kept the Millerites pulling together. The focus on the time element especially functioned to keep the movement goal oriented and unified. But after October 22, the time element itself became divisive, and the long-submerged differences began to rise to the surface as various individual Millerites searched for identity and meaning.

Thus by 1845, that which had held Adventism together was no longer as strong as those beliefs that separated its constituent parts. Fragmentation was the result. That splintering effect was intensified by the heavy impact that both restorationism and the Jacksonian aura of the common man had on Millerism. As a result, everybody, even laypeople in the tradition of Miller himself, could do theology. The resulting doctrinal war was rich, diverse, and divisive. While some of it was healthy and biblical, much of it was erratic.

By mid-1845 the various factions among the Adventists were in the midst of sect building, even though many of the participants would have denied involvement in that type of activity. But the emphasizing and hardening of doctrinal lines could have no other outcome. As a result, J. P. Cowles could write in 1855: "Now there exists some twenty-five divisions of what was once the ONE Advent body, and all this arises from withdrawing fellowship from those who differ from us in opinion."[50]

Of course, a large number of Millerites simply disappeared from the movement in late 1844 and early 1845. As James White put it, "there seemed to be a strong inclination with many to draw back, which ripened in them into a general stampede in the direction of Egypt." In November 1844, Miller's son George feared that "there will be but a remnant of those who have professed to be looking for Christ, [who] will endure until the end."[51]

Arthur suggests that it was easiest for those Millerites who had remained in their denominational churches to fade out of Adventism. It was those individuals, he surmises, who had formed separate advent congregations who were more likely to stick with their Millerite beliefs. After all, for this group it would be discouraging and humiliating to return to their churches. Beyond that, they had already established fellowship with like-minded believers. Thus it was the hard core of those who had heeded the call to "come out of Babylon" who probably made up the 54,000 Adventists of all varieties that Daniel Taylor enumerated in 1860 in the first Adventist census.[52]

While some drifted out of Millerism, other participants rejected it vigorously. One such, signing himself as "A Convalescent," shared his experience in the non-Adventist *Christian Reflector*. "Thank God for permitting his sun of reason to shine again upon my darkened mind," he penned. "Let those who would attempt to unravel the secret of their end, which he has so wisely kept to himself, take warning, lest they are smitten, as I have been, with the worst of all madness—THE MADNESS OF THE SOUL!"[53]

Among those who maintained a faith in Adventism, 1845 witnessed a proliferating array of doctrinal interests. Some, in the established tradition of Millerism, kept setting dates, even though Miller himself avoided all new time setting and discouraged his followers from such activity. But the habit was deeply ingrained, and the sense of certainty it engendered must have encouraged many in setting further dates, even though each failure proved to be more discouraging to those believers than the earlier ones had been. But hope in the midst of seeming hopelessness pushed them on in their search for certitude.

Others turned to new emphases that stressed such teachings as foot washing, charismatic gifts, holy kissing, the seventh-day Sabbath, soul sleep, the millennium as a past event, and a fair number of other topics. To say the least, Adventism was becoming a doctrinal jungle by the summer of 1845.

However, the most inflammatory divisions in Adventism in 1845 centered on the significance of October 22 as a fulfillment of the seventh-month typology. On February 15, I. E. Jones wrote to Miller that, amidst all the confusion, he was striving to keep his "head cool" and his "heart warm." But such an accomplishment was difficult to achieve in that "stormy latitude of time." "I do not wonder," Jones continued, "that the Saviour closed all his discourses on the end of time with the injunction to especially watch and pray. He foresaw that the circumstances of this time would abundantly demand it."

Jones went on to point out that

> our brethren this way are catching at every conceivable hypothesis to reconcile the movement of the Tenth—some believing it to have been a trick of the "old advent-hater";—others that it was a *part* of the midnight cry, the tenth being an error which God only permitted but graciously over-ruled —some that it was the antitype of the trumpet of the tenth of the 7th month in the 49th year, & that Christ will come next spring—some that the Saviour then came *out* of the Holie [sic] of Holies, & has since been upon a white cloud—others, that he never *entered* the Holie [sic] of Holies till then—some, that the Saviour came then or rather *went* before the Ancient of Days to receive the New Jerusalem, & that he came only as Bridegroom & not as his second coming as King of glory,—& that the door of mercy was then for-ever closed. . . . Some believe all of these!!! And every one of these opinions has been broached by most of their abettors as a test by which the wise & foolish virgins were to be made apparent!! We have therefore damned & been damed [sic] several times apiece.

In short, Jones concluded, we are in a "supremely ridiculous, painful, & dangerous . . . state of things among ourselves."[54]

It is little wonder that Miller suggested that "in *too many* in-stances," Adventism had taken on the attributes of Babylon. A few weeks later he cried out in his frustration that "we have, like them [the churches] cried Babylon! Babylon!! Babylon!!! against *all but Adventists*. We have proclaimed and discussed, 'pro et con,' many sectarian dogmas, which have nothing to do with our mes-sage. May God forgive us."[55]

Miller would have preferred to retire from all the Adventist con-troversies along with the other problems and challenges faced by Adventism after the October disappointment, but such could not be. His name and influence were still crucial if Himes was to hold the movement together. Thus Himes wrote to Miller in a sympathetic but firm tone in November 1844. "I do not wonder," he penned, "at your despairing state of mind about further labor. You have done your duty to the church and the world. And now you have put the armour of[f] in the hope of a discharge, it is very hard to think of putting it on again. Yet we must do it. God requires it—the world requires it."[56]

Thus through the urging of Himes, Miller had been forced into a recognition of some responsibility. Yet his role in 1845 seems to have been that of senior advisor to Himes as the younger man sought to guide the advent ship through stormy seas. Himes, of course, couldn't use just any counsel in those troublesome times. We will therefore find him further pressuring Miller to line up with the "proper understanding" of their experience in early 1845. In short, Himes needed behind him the authority of the man who had lent his name to the movement.

Miller, meanwhile, continued to provide Himes with independent but sagacious counsel from time to time. By early 1845, Miller was becoming quite distressed. "I must confess," he wrote, "I am pained at heart to see the battle we are now in. . . . After having silenced our common enemy, . . . that we should now turn our weapons against each other! Every [Adventist] paper which has come into my hands recently is full of fight, and that, too, against our friends."

He went on to urge the Adventist editors to realize that "an interchange of thought and opinion" was necessary, but that editors should think twice before putting anything bordering on faultfinding with other Adventists in their papers. "Unless we are harmless and wise, there are breakers ahead which will be to much damage and loss."

Miller further noted that "it would be remarkable if there were no discordant views among us." On the other hand, lest the advent believers themselves were going to act like bishops and popes, they would have to let their brethren have freedom of thought, opinion, and speech. He saw no other alternatives. "Have we not blamed the sects and churches for shutting their eyes, ears, doors, pulpits and presses against this [advent] light? And shall we become as one of them? No. God forbid. . . . We had better suffer the abuse of liberty, than to strengthen the bands of tyranny."[57]

That line of thought not only came forth from Miller but was deep in the Baptist and restorationist traditions from which so many of the Adventists had come. As a result, early 1845 saw a rather open discussion in the press on many of the issues that divided the advent believers. Not the least of the divisive issues was that of the "shut door."

The Shut Door and the Forming of the Battle Line

Adventism's shut-door belief was rooted in one of the key Bible passages that they saw as identifying their movement—the bridegroom parable of Matthew 25. After the tarrying time (v. 5) and the midnight cry (v. 6), we read in verse 10 that while the foolish virgins were out trying to buy more oil, "the bridegroom came; and they that were ready went in with him to the marriage: and *the door was shut*." But "afterward came also the other virgins, saying, Lord, Lord, open to us. But he answered and said, Verily I say unto you, I know you not" (vv. 11, 12). In the 1840s many Adventists interpreted the shut door to be the close of human probation. In other words, after the door was shut, there would be no additional salvation. The wise virgins (true believers) would be in the kingdom, while the foolish virgins and all others would be on the outside.

That point became a controversial issue in Millerite Adventism in January 1845, when Apollos Hale and Joseph Turner tied the shut-door concept to the fulfillment of prophecy on October 22, 1844. Thus they taught that the work of general salvation was over as of that date. On October 22, Christ had come spiritually as the Bridegroom, the wise virgins had gone in to the marriage with Him, and the door was shut on all others.[58]

As a result of Hale and Turner's article, a whole school of Adventist historiography grew up as early as 1851 around the idea that those two leaders had originated the shut-door doctrine. But that interpretation will not stand in the light of the historical data.[59]

It was actually Miller who fathered the shut-door teaching among Adventists. In his *Evidence From Scripture and History of the Second Coming of Christ*, he had written that the phrase " 'the door was shut,' implies the closing up of the mediatorial kingdom, and finishing the gospel period." He also directly tied the preadvent passage of Revelation 22:11 ("He that is unjust, let him be unjust still: and he which is filthy, let him be filthy still: and he that is righteous, let him be righteous still.") to the coming of the bridegroom and the shutting of the door.[60]

Following Miller's lead, the 1842 Boston general conference resolved "that the notion of a probation after Christ's coming, is a lure to destruction, entirely contradictory to the word of God, which positively teaches that when Christ comes the door is shut, and such as are not ready can never enter in."[61]

Since the Millerite leaders had been expecting Christ to return at the end of the 2300 days mentioned in Daniel 8:14, they had, in effect, been teaching the close of probation at the end of that period. As a result, for a short period after the October 1844 disappointment, Miller and many others thought that their work for the world was finished, that there was only a little additional tarrying time left until Christ would appear.

Thus it is not surprising to find Miller (who at that time still believed that prophecy had been fulfilled on October 22) writing on November 18, 1844, that

we have done [finished] our work in warning sinners, and in trying to awake a formal church. God, in his providence has shut the door; we can only stir one another up to be *patient*. . . . We are now living in the time specified by Malachi iii.18, also Daniel xii.10, Rev. xxii.10-12. In this passage we can not help but see, that a little while before Christ should come, there would be a separation between the just and the unjust, the righteous and the wicked, between those who love his appearing, and those who hate it. And never since the days of the apostles, has there been such a division line drawn, as was drawn about the 10th or 23d day of the 7th Jewish month.[62]

Certainly the nasty and even violent reactions of unbelievers and ex-Millerites seemed to provide demonstrable proof to the believers that the door of probation had been shut. Most Millerites accepted the shut door immediately after October 22 because the interpretation was built into their belief system.

But that acceptance would soon change, since the shut door was tied to the fulfillment of prophecy in October. The logic was clear. If there was no fulfillment of prophecy, there could be no shut door—and vice versa.

With that fact in view, it is of crucial importance to remember that as early as November 5, 1844, Himes, the most powerful spokesman for postdisappointment Adventism, had already come to the conclusion that nothing had happened on October 22. From that point on, Himes began to lead the Adventist majority (including Miller) away from the October date and the shut-door belief.[63]

It is in that context that Hale and Turner's January 1845 article on the bridegroom and the shut door became explosive early in the year. They argued that prophecy had indeed been fulfilled on October 22. But, they went on, the coming of the bridegroom had not been properly understood. Even though Christ had not come in the clouds of heaven as expected, *He had come spiritually* as the bridegroom to the marriage. Tying that concept to the coming of the Son of Man of Daniel 7 to the Ancient of Days, Turner and Hale argued that "*the judgment is here*" and that Christ would not come in the clouds of heaven until the judgment was complete—until He returned from the wedding. Meanwhile, the door of human probation had been shut.[64]

That interpretation, of course, flew directly in the face of everything Himes believed. After all, he was trying to get the Adventists back to their work of warning the world of the nearness of the coming. Turner's interpretation was bad enough in itself, as far as Himes and his colleagues in belief were concerned. But to make matters worse, the radical wing of Adventism, which was already deep into an increasing fanatical excitement, utilized the shut door and its related prophetic implications to justify their fanaticism. We will return to the disruption caused by the fanatical element in chapter 12.

By early February, Turner had preached his shut-door and bridegroom theories in S. S. Snow's New York church. Snow and many of his followers "drank down the truth, as the thirsty traveller in the sultry desert would drink water from the cooling fountain." Soon, Snow was preaching that Himes and others who were "clamoring for an open door" were the foolish virgins. Worse, "they arc fallen, apostate 'Adventists' " in their "knocking and crying out against that closed door." "God has rejected them."[65]

Snow, identifying himself as Elijah the prophet, who was to prepare the way of the Lord, began publishing the *Jubilee Standard* in early 1845 to set forth his shut-door views. Beyond that, in the minds of Snow and like-minded individuals, Adventists not accepting the shut door had, in effect, become Babylon. The call was now to separate from the open-door Adventists. Meanwhile, Snow had discovered that Himes, Litch, and Storrs (who had all rejected his seventh-month message) were the three shepherds of Zechariah 11:8, who were "cut off in one month" and were "loathed" and "abhorred" by God.[66]

It is little wonder that we find I. E. Jones writing in February 1845 that "Brother Turner's views . . . have done more to distract us than all the rest together."[67]

Miller, of course, was seen as a central player in the power struggle between the open-door and the shut-door Adventists; between those who had rejected the seventh-month movement as a fulfillment of prophecy and those who accepted it; between those who believed they still had a missionary work for the world and those who believed probation to be closed and gospel work completed. Two separate strands of Adventism had developed, and there was no middle ground between them. Under such circumstances, given the power of his name in the movement, the position of Miller on the shut door was of crucial importance to both sides.

While Miller had been quite convinced in late 1844 that the door had been shut and that prophecy had been fulfilled on October 22, both those positions began to shift in the first few months of 1845. In early February, Miller noted in a published letter in the *Advent Herald* that he had received many letters from all over the country, asking his opinion on the shut door and the close of probation. While noting that it was a close point and he would rather keep his opinions on the topic to himself, he went on basically to endorse both the shut-door and the seventh-month movement.[68]

The editors took the unprecedented step of adding a four-column rebuttal to Miller's article, frankly stating that they were "unable to see the correctness of the application of some of the above texts, i.e., how they prove the door of mercy will be closed before the end." The day after the article was published, Himes penned Miller a forceful letter in which he told him that the shut-door teaching was "*producing the most disastrous effects, both to believers, and to the movement.*" Things were so serious along that line, Himes informed Miller, that he was on the verge of having to close down his publishing work because of the inroads of the problem and the accusations being made against the *Herald.*[69]

Himes went on to inform Miller that Bliss had written a letter to Miller, apologizing for the note that Miller had attached to his last article. By way of justification for that breach of protocol, however, Himes pointed out that "*there never was so dangerous, and critical a time with us as now.*" There was, he noted, a growing disposition to crush him, but he would not "lay down and die."[70]

If Himes was distressed over the shut-door crisis on February 13, he must have been near collapse when the February 19 issue of the *Voice of Truth* arrived at his door. That issue contained a letter from Miller, claiming that he believed that Hale and Turner's January *Advent Mirror* article on the bridegroom and shut door was right "in the main."[71]

Himes' response to the intensified crisis was a massive, frontal assault on the shut-door and the bridegroom questions in the *Advent Herald* issues of February 26 and March 5. Nearly the whole of both numbers treated the topics, as Himes and his colleagues threw down the gauntlet. The time for play was over. The *Morning Watch* was also brought into action on the topic.[72]

Beyond the frontal attack on the shut door in his publications, Himes also worked intensely on Miller behind the scenes through a series of rapid-fire letters. On March 12 he related the fanaticism connected to the shut-door movement in Portland, Maine. "*They will lay all in ruins*," he penned, "if they have time enough to do it." Himes turned up the pressure on his mentor when he wrote: "They are using *your influence* [in supporting the shut-door theory] . . . your *name* and *letters* to sustain themselves in their new and visionary movements."[73]

Three days later, Himes penned a similar letter in reporting Snow's work and how his extremist following was also relying on Miller's advocacy of the shut-door position. At that point, Himes made his crucial pitch for Miller's support. "I think," he wrote, "it is time that you gave a letter, or word in some way that will enable us to exculpate you, from any sympathy with them in their wild movements." In order to leave nothing to chance, Himes also visited with Miller on the topic in Low Hampton for two days. In addition to his other arguments, Himes demonstrated to Miller's satisfaction that probation could not be over because souls were being converted.[74]

Himes' various lines of attack finally brought Miller over to his side. The March 26 *Advent Herald* sported a front-page, three-column letter from Miller written the day after Himes' visit. In this letter, Miller definitely came out against the shut-door position. Himes' efforts had brought him around at last. Meanwhile, Himes, ever the politician, was lining up a major advent conference to meet in April. He was determined to gain control of the splintering advent movement.[75]

By that time Miller was finished with the shut-door theory. He never wavered again. In the summer of 1845, he penned,

I have no confidence in any of the new theories that have grown out of that [seventh-month] movement, viz., that

Christ then came as the Bridegroom, that the door of mercy
was closed, . . . or that it was a fulfillment of prophecy in any
sense. The spirit of fanaticism which has resulted from it, in
some places, leading to extravagance and excess, I regard as of
the same nature as those which retarded the reformation in
Germany.[76]

Thus by late March, Himes could breathe a sigh of relief. The
titular head of the movement was in his camp, and Himes could
now prepare for the Albany conference, in which he hoped to con-
solidate his gains and keep Adventism both as sane and as unified
as possible. But for Miller there was a cost. Many of the Millerites
who had seen him as an "Angel" now saw him as a *"fallen man!"*[77]

Two years later, the charge surfaced that Himes had unduly
controlled Miller's opinions. Miller replied in a published letter.
"I would say to all, that I have never been dictated to by Bro.
Himes; nor has he, to my knowledge, ever tried to direct me."
The facts, of course, do not match up with that statement. The
statement itself is either a reflection of Miller's naiveté in his
weakened condition, an indication of Himes' ability to manipu-
late, or, as is most likely the case, both.[78]

In summary, by late March 1845, the battle line had been drawn
between the Adventists. That line formed along the shut-door
doctrine, with its related acceptance or rejection of the validity
of the seventh-month movement. April and May 1845 would
see the open-door Adventists organize at the Albany conference.
But things were not as clear for the shut-door Adventists. They
themselves would split into two major divisions, each one following a lead put forth by Hale and Turner in their January 1845 *Advent Mirror* article. One branch would emphasize the spiritual-
coming-of-Christ aspect of that article, while the other, building
upon a variation of Hale and Turner's bridegroom argument,
would focus on their pre-advent-judgment suggestion. Part 3 will
examine these and subsequent divisions in Adventism as the Millerites moved away from the year of the end of the world.

Part III

MOVING AWAY FROM THE YEAR OF THE END

Chapter 12

ADVENTISM'S RADICAL FRINGE

Disorientation and *disarray* are two words that help us capture the mood and structure of Millerite Adventism after October 22, 1844. Whereas once the movement knew exactly where it was going and had fair ideas of how to reach its goals, after the passing of the date, the Adventists had neither of those comforting convictions of certainty. The months and years after October 1844 catapulted the Adventists into a search for identity, a task they had never thought they would have to undertake, and one for which, in many ways, they were ill-equipped.

This chapter and the next two trace the development of the various strands of Adventism in the postdisappointment period. The first branch we will look at has often been called the "Spiritualizers," since they found their genesis in a spiritualization of the Millerite hope in the coming of Christ. The early vigor and success of this Millerite branch eventually forced the other strands of Millerism to define themselves by contrasting themselves with the Spiritualizers. That makes them an especially important element to understand in Adventist history.

The Rise of the Spiritualizers

As we noted in chapter 11, the central theological insight undergirding the Spiritualizers' theology was the "deliteralization" of the second coming of Christ. In an attempt to hold on to October 22 as a fulfillment of prophecy, Apollos Hale and Joseph

Turner had concluded that the seventh-month movement had indeed been a fulfillment of prophecy. They held that *both* the *date* and the *event* had been fulfilled. *Thus Christ had come on October 22, 1844.* But He had not come in the clouds of heaven. Rather, He had come as the bridegroom to the Ancient of Days in heaven to receive the kingdom.[1]

The bridegroom's coming, in the thought of Hale and Turner, would precede the coming in power and glory to earth. There would be an interval between the two comings. That fine distinction, unfortunately, was lost to many of those who followed their lead. For many, the fact that Christ had "come" was sufficient. Others specified that He had come into human hearts.

The important point to understand at this juncture is not the various possibilities of nonliteral interpretations of the coming of Christ but the fact that a major shift had taken place in the thinking of some Adventists on how they should read and interpret Scripture.

Whereas Miller had held to the literal interpretation of the Bible except in cases where it was obviously symbolic,[2] the Spiritualizers looked for spiritual meanings everywhere. Thus they had stepped off the platform of Miller's principles of interpretation. Having begun to read nonliteral interpretations into the Bible, they soon arrived at some fanciful explanations that informed both their theology and their daily lives.

Turner's theories spread rapidly through the disoriented Adventism of early 1845. Of course, he was no slouch as an evangelist. January and February found an aggressive Turner preaching his message throughout New England, New York, and elsewhere.

That preaching was not without success. On January 23, 1845, he wrote from Maine of his tour: "In every place I visited," he penned, "I found a goodly number, I think quite a majority, who were and are now believing that our work is all done for this world, and that the atonement was completed on the tenth day of the seventh month. Nearly all who heard me gladly received the message." Turner, of course, was preaching to other Adventists. After all, holding the shut-door theory, he believed that trying to awaken non-Adventists would be like "preaching in the tombs," since probation had closed. The effect of Turner's preaching was that the "wise virgins" separated themselves from the other Adventists and began to hold separate meetings.[3]

The magnitude of Turner's success is not only attested to by Turner himself but also by the panic he called forth from Joshua Himes, Sylvester Bliss, and others. They saw Turner's spiritual interpretation of the second advent as the major threat facing them in early 1845.

Turner's conversion of S. S. Snow to his position accelerated the spread of his spiritualized view of the advent. After the October disappointment, Snow concluded that "the message he had borne from God to the people, related only to *time*: the *manner* of the great events of the day of God, he did not comprehend." He had preached as he had in October because "he had been, erroneously, taught by men, that the coming of the Bridegroom to the marriage was the descent of the Lord from heaven."[4]

The month after accepting Turner's spiritual interpretation, Snow began to circulate that vision of the "good news" through the *Jubilee Standard*. The *Standard* thus joined Turner's *Advent Mirror*, Hale's *Hope of Israel*, Enoch Jacobs' *Day-Star*, Orlando Squires' *Voice of the Shepherd*, Joseph Marsh's *Voice of Truth*, and other Adventist periodicals in spreading aspects of the new interpretation and serving as a forum for new ideas in the struggle for answers to the 1844 disappointment. Everybody sought a voice for his or her opinion, and, in terms of numbers, Himes' "official" Adventist periodicals were definitely in the minority. Unfortunately, in the hands of many advocates of the new ideas, Adventism lost its traditional rationality.

Aberrant Adventism

The welter of new interpretations led to some strange conclusions in both theory and practice that made pre-October 1844 Adventist fanaticism seem mild by comparison. We noted above that at least part of the new thought in the Spiritualizer camp arose when certain advocates moved away from Miller's predominantly literal principles of interpretation. The spiritualized meaning of the second advent stemmed from that process.

On other occasions, Miller's own principles were put to strange uses to arrive at novel conclusions. One illustration of that phenomenon is that of Orlando Squires. Squires took Miller's advice to compare scripture with scripture to arrive at biblical truth to bizarre extremes. Thus we read:

One truth is clearly proved to my mind by a comparison of Scripture with Scripture, viz. that *chariots, horses, clouds, heavens, flames of fire, wings of the wind, wheels, fowls of heaven, feathered fowls, mansions, inheritance, dwelling-place, sheep, flock, spiritual house, house of God, city of God, habitation of God, temple of God, people of God, holy people, Israel, Jacob, Judah, David, saints, angels,* and many other names, are used as synonymous terms, denoting the same thing, viz. the *true body of Christ*—the *Church.*[5]

Having built an interpretive base, Squires went on with the use of his method to reach some rarified conclusions. One was that Christ had " '*entered into the holiest of all, even into* HEAVEN ITSELF,' " which we are assured over and over, is "**IN US.**" "Glory to God!" Squires exulted, we finally know where heaven is. It is "**IN US.** 'Christ **IN** you the hope of glory.' 'Jesus Christ IS COME IN THE FLESH.' 'Every SPIRIT that confesseth not' this most precious truth, 'is not of God.' " Like so many other Millerites, Squires founded a periodical—the *Voice of the Shepherd*—to sound his version of the Adventist gospel.[6]

"The views presented in this sheet are light, and not darkness," proclaimed Olive Patten in an article seconding that of Squires. "The Spirit constantly witnesses to the truth. The inward voice cries, Light, Light; and the Scriptures open to me like a stream of light, and *fire* too." For Patten the time message was but the preparation for the present work, "the spiritual part. . . . The *test* [for God's people] has come, at last" in the form of Squires' message.

"Earnest and sincere as I have been about a personal appearing of Christ," penned Patten, "I have now become perfectly satisfied that *there is no such thing as a literal body of Jesus, in the universe of God. . . . Christ in us* [is] our life now, and hope of future glory." She went on to note that Christ would make Himself manifest in them as they were progressively "fashioned like unto Christ's most glorious body."[7]

It is but a short step from the views propounded by Squires and his followers to the aberrant perfectionism espoused by a significant portion of the Adventists during early 1845. Like Calvin French and John Starkweather in the earlier Millerite movement and like countless enthusiasts down through church history, some of the Adventists in 1845 and 1846 had come to the place where they believed that they lived above sin. As one participant put it, "they declared that they were perfected, that body, soul, and spirit were holy. . . . They declared that as their flesh was purified, they were ready for translation."[8] Thus their every action was prompted by the Holy Spirit. Such a viewpoint fit nicely into the scheme set forth by Squires, Patten, and their fellow believers with their aberrant views of the incarnation.

The Spiritualizers put forth numerous beliefs during Adventism's crisis period, beginning in early 1845. One was the thesis set forth by J. D. Pickands and J. B. Cook of Cleveland, Ohio. Basing their argument on Revelation 14, Pickands and Cook held that the three angels had already progressively sounded their voices in the Millerite movement and that the world was now ready for the cry of the fourth angel of verses 14 to 16.[9]

In essence, Pickands and Cook taught that Christ was sitting on a white cloud waiting for the harvest of the earth, having on His head a golden crown and in His hand a sharp sickle. The end would not come until the fourth angel, in the person of the believers, prayed in earnest to Him "that sitteth on the cloud, 'thrust in thy sickle and reap.' " The harvest would take place when such prayer became "general, earnest, agonizing, [and] importunate." Naturally Pickands and Cook established a periodical to spread their bit of truth. Thus the going forth of the *Voice of the Fourth Angel*.

Like the other new doctrines of this period, the truth of the fourth angel became a "test," and those who rejected it were assigned to perdition.[10]

Eventually Pickands led his followers into more extreme views. Having rejected "the absurd and unscriptural theory of Father Miller" that Christ would come personally and visibly in a single event, Pickands concluded that the second coming was a series of events. The stage had already been reached where the saints were immortal, incorruptible, and *would not die*. Pickands realized that his new light would be ridiculed by many, but so what? "Never mind the barking of the 'dogs' that are without the city," he wrote to Enoch Jacobs. "We are within, and have a right to the tree of life, of which if we eat we *shall* live for ever!"[11]

The doctrine of present immortality and incorruptibility was a fairly widespread belief among those who held that Christ had come spiritually on October 22, 1844. Thus Joseph Turner had also become immortal in early 1845. "God is with us," he wrote to Snow on June 24. "He hears our cries, our sick are healed by the power of faith, and no Israelite has died among us since the seventh month, and we believe they may be preserved whole and blameless unto the coming of the Lord Jesus. Such things will be scoffed at by those who are fallen, but they are, nevertheless true."[12]

Another line of extremism among the Spiritualizers was those aspects of behavior directly affected by their belief that Christ had already come. On one level, a significant number held that it was wrong to work, since they were now in the seventh millennium and God's eternal Sabbath had begun. To work would "result in their *final destruction*." Boston had its teachers of the it-is-a-sin-to-labor doctrine. "Their principal message was, 'Sell that ye have, and give alms.' They said they were in the jubilee, the land should rest, and the poor must be supported without labor."[13]

On March 12, 1845, Himes wrote of a similar situation in which the shut-door/bridegroom movement had led many farmers to neglect planting, while others were "selling off their cattle &c— say[ing] they only want enough to last till the 23d of April. The door is shut, and the bridegroom has come[,] the marriage has taken place and now they say His cloud *must come*."[14]

The shut-door extremists were also active on the humility front. In order to demonstrate that they were spiritually in heaven, they sought to follow Christ's injunction to humble themselves and become as little children. Thus, recalled Sylvester Bliss, some sat on the floor as an act of humility, while others shaved their heads or acted like children in understanding. Even more impressive (or humbling) must have been those who crawled around their houses on all fours. Not only was such humility practiced at home and in church, but some found it necessary to witness to the world around them by crawling through the busy streets of town.[15]

While the non-Adventist community might smile at the sight of their neighbors crawling to the local store, they did not find some of the actual and supposed sexual aberrations of the Spiritualizers nearly so humorous. Topping the list of complaints in this area were beliefs regarding holy kissing and spiritual wifery. Mixed in with those two public offenses was foot washing between the sexes.

We should not be surprised to find that some Adventists, with their restorationist desire to get back to the teachings of the New Testament, initiated foot-washing services. George Peavey of New York was one of the most enthusiastic promoters of this widespread teaching. As justification for the practice, Peavey and others cited Christ: "If I then, your Lord and Master, have washed your feet; ye also ought to wash one another's feet" (John 13:14).

Although many Adventists could see the logic behind foot washing, mainline believers (along with some in the fringe groups) took strong exception to men and women washing one another's feet. Thus L. Delos Mansfield condemned Peavey for supposedly having "*selected as his victim* a YOUNG GIRL!" for this "ridiculous, revolting and indecent" ceremony. "Why," queried Mansfield, "if his heart is pure, and his desires holy, did he not cho[o]se a male, or a matron in the presence of her husband?"[16]

On another occasion, a correspondent of the *Day-Star* favorably reported that "the Lord was with us and we had a good love-feast. The brethren and sisters all got very happy and went to washing one another's feet, just as Jesus said his children should do, & saluted one another with the holy kiss."[17]

The fringe Adventists also got their teaching of holy kissing from Scripture, but many were the accusations that this religious exercise, like "promiscuous" foot washing, frequently took on less than holy aspects. In that vein, Mansfield claimed that Peavey approached a woman who had rebuffed his efforts to wash her feet and, "without giving her any declaration of his intentions, actually gave her a (holy! ah! what mockery!) kiss!" According to Joseph Turner, "Bro. Peavey contended for promiscuous feet-washing, and kissing on the principle that we are '*all one*,' and that '*in* Christ there is neither male nor female.' "[18]

Spiritual wifery, as might be expected, raised the ire of both the non-Adventist community and mainline Adventism to new heights. The *Advent Herald* not only protested "against all such abominations," but it publicly disowned the participants and claimed that it was "gratifying that they were not left to run into these excesses until they had renounced 'Millerism.' "[19]

On the other hand, the practitioners of spiritual wifery claimed they were building their belief on scriptural grounds. After all, in the kingdom of heaven, there would be no marrying or giving in marriage. Beyond that, since Christ had come and they were immortal, they were already in their spiritual state. Then again, didn't Christ say that if people really loved Him, they would forsake their families?

Following that line of thought, Pickands defended a man and a woman who had deserted their spouses and families and had lived together for several months as a "spiritual pair" as they traveled from place to place. Pickands said that such conduct "was consistent with their doctrine, which would permit a 'spiritual matrimony without sexual connexion.' " The judge, having less exalted views of the case, ordered the couple to post bail at " '$200 each, on the charge of adultery.' "[20]

Another fringe Adventist lecturer, Israel Dammon (also involved, among other activities, in multiple and repeated "holy kissing" of other men's wives), had obtained a spiritual wife by early February 1845 and "was glad of it." In Dammon's case the evidence seems to be quite clear that the union was less than spiritual.[21]

Enoch Jacobs was another leader involved in the marriage and family peculiarities of the fringe Adventists. Jacobs argued that Christ had commanded people to forsake all for His sake. As a result, Jacobs left his wife and five children and chose a life of celibacy. In parting, he and his wife wept and washed each other's feet as they became "submissive [to] the will of God." Thus Jacobs passed the test of faith and obedience as he gave his family over to God.

Jacobs, of course, had to pay the social price for his decision. But then, his type expected to be persecuted for righteousness sake. "Almost every one," Jacobs penned in his paper (the *Day-Star*), "concluded that I was either crazy, mad, or possessed with a devil—not excepting my own brethren. Though called a *Spiritualizer*, I know I was doing no more than what Christ commanded, and that I was doing it for His sake alone."

In spite of Jacobs' evident sincerity, his "faithfulness" got him into a "heated . . . furnace . . . seven times hotter than it was wont to be heated." In addition, his comforters were no more helpful than Job's as they made " 'railing accusations' " against him. The lesson from all this, said Jacobs, is that literal obedience accomplishes the same today as it did in gospel times.

Jacobs' furnace got "seven degrees" hotter when a Sister Curtis showed up from Oberlin and "advanced the idea, that in the glorified state . . . the children of God, though no longer 'male and female,' would be united in pairs, and that God had shown her that" he "was to be her companion in the eternal world."

Since Curtis lacked "scripture testimony" on that suggestion, Jacobs did his best to disclaim sympathy for her view. But still her idea "was enough to set in motion every thing in the shape of chaff, indeed a perfect tempest was created in a short time. . . . This circumstance was wrought up into capital enough to feast the children of the devil for some time." Yet in the mind of Jacobs, "it was a circumstance, absolutely necessary, for without it, how could 'all manner of evil' be spoken falsely?"

Jacobs went on to expound upon this whole sequence of events as the most precious of his "whole life," since it had taught him to no longer " 'despise the chastening of the Lord, nor faint when rebuked of him.' " This step in Jacobs' experience soon proved to be one of many esoteric developments in a circuitous spiritual journey that would land him in several strange places. We will return to Jacobs later.[22]

The fringe Adventists also supported other new doctrines. Pickands and Cook, for example, accepted the seventh-day Sabbath early in 1845, while Turner pointed to a pre-advent judgment, and Jacobs was quite friendly to new light on Christ's ministry in the Most Holy Place of the heavenly sanctuary beginning on October 22, 1844. Jacobs also published one of the early visions of a young woman by the name of Ellen Harmon.[23]

Visionary manifestations was another predominant characteristic of the shut-door groups. One such group espousing prophecy was headquartered in Springwater Valley, New York. An unmarried man by the name of Houston had taken over a family dwelling with "his *Miss*" and several other people living together out of wedlock. The family remained in their home, but Houston had taken charge. He not only ordered fine furniture smashed up for firewood and had the carpet pulled up in at least one room, but he also made "the most licentious proffers to the woman of the house, as the last *test* of her consecration to God!" Having convinced the family that he was filled with the Holy Ghost, they were afraid to put him out, since "he would take the Holy Ghost with him, and the family must consequently go to hell!"[24]

By early 1846 the Springwater commune had taken on the names of Household of Faith and Household of Judgment. In May they sent a communication to William Miller, telling him what God, "who sits here upon his throne," had revealed to Houston. "Many times every day for months past," went the epistle, "have we had communications from God by those whom he takes away in the visions of the spirit among us." In their household, the letter noted, "God's Car is moving forward with its wheels of burning fire . . . utterly consuming every vestige of our old nature."

The prophet condemned Miller for his disbelief. After noting that God would come in a few days and that He was even then perfecting the 144,000 in "the perfection of beauty," Houston proclaimed that it was up to God to "make his word a fire and William Miller wood, that the fire may consume the wood and stubble, and the Son of God in thee alone be saved in the day of Glory."[25]

S. S. Snow also joined the ranks of the prophets in 1845. In that year he came to see himself as Elijah the prophet, who would appear just before the advent of the Saviour. His followers began publishing *The True Day Star* to set forth his claims. In the first issue, fifty of the believers affixed their names to a statement certifying that "*Jesus is King, and Elijah, his messenger, is here*," in the person of Snow. "With all our souls," the attestation read,

> we believe that our brother has been raised up and conse-
> crated by the Holy Ghost, as the minister of the law and the
> prophets: that the blessed Spirit of God, guides him in the
> high and special work which is committed to him, of ex-
> pounding the sacred Scriptures, for the infallible guidance
> of the household of faith.[26]

One of Snow's followers noted that we must be careful how we relate to God's messenger. "*If we reject him, we reject him [Christ] that sent him.*" Interestingly enough, Snow tells us that by 1848, twenty of the fifty who had certified his calling three years before had rejected "the truth, and are now its enemies."[27] They were undoubtedly assigned in his *Book of Judgment Delivered to Israel by Elijah the Messenger of the Everlasting Covenant* to someplace besides heaven, along with Miller, Himes, Litch, Storrs, and all others who rejected the October 22 date.

By 1848 Snow had also glorified his role somewhat. In that year he issued "*A Proclamation to All People, Nations, Tongues, and Kings.*" In part the proclamation read:

> By the special favor of God, through Jesus Christ my Father, I have been called and commissioned to go before the face of the Lord, in the spirit and power of Elijah, to prepare the way for his descent from heaven. And as his Prime Minister, I demand of all Kings, Presidents, Magistrates, and Rulers, civil or ecclesiastical, a full surrender of all power and authority, into my hands, on behalf of King Jesus the Coming One.

If the nations failed to obey, Snow claimed, his proclamation would be enforced by "WAR, FAMINE, PESTILENCE, and DESTRUCTION." He signed the document "SAMUEL SHEFFIELD SNOW, *Premier of* KING JESUS."[28]

David Arthur claims that Snow ended his life in insanity, while Clyde E. Hewitt (both Advent Christian scholars) asserts that "Bishop" Snow served as pastor among his followers in the "Church of Mount Zion" in New York City until his death in 1889. Neither writer gives a source for his information, but a student of Snow's life might conclude that those two endings may have been equivalent.[29]

Visions were also prevalent among other groups of shut-door Adventists in early 1845. One of the more prominent centers was Maine, which had had at least five visionaries by that time—four of them women.[30]

Joshua V. Himes was especially concerned with aberrant Adventism in Portland, Maine, in the group associated with Israel Dammon. Himes put it straight to Miller on March 27, 1845: "Things are in a Bad way at Portland." He then went on to discuss Dammon and his "*spiritual wife*" and her visions. A few days before the all-important Albany convention of the moderate Adventists, Himes again went out of his way to notify Miller that "things in Maine, are *bad*—very *bad*!" Turner's "new fangled theology, if it may be called *theology*," had done its damage in Maine and other places. But Himes looked forward to the Albany conference to help stabilize the advent cause.[31]

We will return to the Albany conference in chapter 13, but before doing that, we need to examine one more shut-door aberrancy—the Shaker temptation.

The Shaker Temptation

At first glance it seems strange that Millerite Adventists, with their literal interpretation of the Bible and the second coming, could be attracted to Shakerism. After all, the Shakers believed that the second coming of Christ's spirit had taken place in their prophetess Ann Lee in 1770. But it was that very interpretation that appealed to some in the Spiritualizer wing of Adventism after the October disappointment. It was not too long a step for these disoriented Adventists to conclude that perhaps the Shakers had had the truth all along—Christ had come in spirit.[32]

Beyond that, the doctrinally agreeable Shakers opened their arms to Adventists who felt the need to escape from the sneers of a hostile world. The self-contained communal Shaker societies provided the discouraged Adventists with an acceptance they could no longer find in the larger world. As Henry Bear saw it, that acceptance appealed to some of his fellow advent believers. "Come and be gathered. . . . I know there can be no happiness in being thus scattered." In the Shaker villages, they found both acceptance and stability in a context that took their second-advent concerns seriously.[33]

Other aspects of Shakerism that appealed to shut-door Adventists were the Shakers' restorationist impulse to get back to the New Testament and their acceptance of charismatic gifts in the modern church. The first of those elements was illustrated by the Shakers' practice of holding property in common as in the book of Acts, while the second was strongly in evidence in the charismatic revival taking place in Shaker communities in the 1840s.

Timing was also conducive to Millerite conversions to Shakerism. Beginning in 1837, the Shakers "experienced a convulsive religious revival" that lasted for more than a decade. Thus the 1844 disappointment hit at the high point of Shaker revivalism, and the

Millerites probably provided the communalists with their largest influx since their early days in the late 1700s. Michael Barkun notes that "the Shakers did not have to labor in order to convince Millerites that they had unmet spiritual needs; they had merely to open themselves to the yearnings of people suddenly deprived of their sense of meaning."[34]

Perhaps the greatest test of Shakerism was its doctrine of celibacy. According to Ann Lee, lustful sexual intercourse was the original sin in Eden. Just as sin correlated with sexual intercourse, so there was a correlation between righteousness and celibacy.[35] That teaching, of course, was the great test of Shakerism; it separated the true believers from the insincere—those who were willing to give up all for Christ from those who were not. Rigorous tests, however, appealed to many shut-door Adventists, who had focused on innumerable tests that supposedly distinguished Matthew's "wise virgins" from the "foolish" ones.

The ideal of celibacy was not unknown among those waiting for the Lord to return, even though that ideal was not generally built upon the same theological foundation as it was in Shakerism. Ellen Harmon and James White, for example, "had no idea of marriage at any future time" because they believed in "the coming of Christ near, even at the doors. . . . Most of our brethren," penned White, "who believed with us that the second advent movement was the work of God, were opposed to marriage because they believed that time was very short" and that marriage was a denial of the advent faith. Because of that widespread conviction, some believers were startled by White and Harmon's announcement to marry in the late summer of 1846, fearing that it represented a breach of faith.[36]

On the other hand, by that time, other Adventist believers had concluded, in the light of Paul's counsel to the Corinthians and in the face of the shortness of time, that even married couples should practice celibacy until the crisis was over. Such found the Shaker doctrine to be anything but new and surprising.[37]

There had been some contact between Millerites and Shakers before October 1844. One Millerite preacher had lectured to the

New Lebanon Shaker community in 1842, telling them that "Christ would make his second Appearance" in 1843, "and this world would be consumed by fire." The Shaker record of the meeting notes that they would be happy "to have the world burned up" because they believed the world represented "the lust of the flesh." Another pre-disappointment contact between the two religious groups was the charismatic Shaker/Millerite who wrote to Miller that he had left his body and found himself flying through the air until he arrived in heaven to meet Christ.[38]

But despite occasional contact between the movements prior to October 1844, the most extensive and significant interaction between them took place in 1846 and 1847. By that time the Spiritualizer Adventists had about exhausted themselves in their perpetual excitement and new theories, and Shakerism looked like it could be the answer to the desperate believers.

The most important Millerite leader to convert to Shakerism was Enoch Jacobs (earlier discussed in terms of celibacy), who had headed up the Adventist work in the "far west" from Cincinnati and had edited the *Western Midnight Cry* (later renamed the *Day-Star*). In early January 1846, he had gone to Cleveland to convince J. D. Pickands that he was wrong in his views that Christ had come spiritually and that the saints were already immortal. But Jacobs failed. He returned home a Pickands convert. By February, as we saw above, he had also become a celibate.[39]

From those positions it was but a short step to Shakerism. In June 1846 we find Jacobs making the essence of his conversion to Shakerism explicit. "Have you found salvation?" he queried.

> It was that for which we all looked in 1843, and in the autumn of 1844. On the 10th day of the 7th month, of the last named year, we were all placed in a situation to receive it, if it had come in our way. George Storrs told me that he felt just as completely dead to the world, as though he had been laid in his coffin—buried under ground, and waiting for a resurrection. This was the feeling of thousands, it was mine. Earthly ties were as completely sundered, for the time being, as

though they had never been known. Thus we waited, but Salvation did not come: We thought the fault was all without:—Sad mistake!! It was all *within*.[40]

Jacobs had completely spiritualized his eschatology.

But Jacobs didn't stay with the Shakers. For him they were a way station on his spiritual journey. After about a year, he left them, even though he still seemed to be in harmony with their theology. Isaac Wellcome tells us Jacobs' problem was that "he violated their rules and was cut off" by the Shakers. Jacobs himself put it much more picturesquely, stating he would "rather go to hell with Electra his wife than to live among the Shakers without her."[41]

After leaving the Shaker village in Whitewater, Ohio, Jacobs became a spiritualist. That is not particularly strange, given the drift of his religious evolution and the fact that throughout the 1840s, Shakerism was undergoing a spiritualistic revival.[42]

We run across Enoch Jacobs again in 1891. By that time he had concluded that no organized religious system "exists on earth . . . to meet the demands of the Universe." But he went on to suggest that he was then, in essence, a Buddhist and a pantheist. He offered his prayers to the "God within" him, and his "spirit friends," who came to him "in answer to prayer; sometimes in materialized bodies."[43]

Although Jacobs left the Shakers in 1847, while with them, he must have been one of their most successful evangelists. He initially converted thirty or forty of his Cincinnati flock to Shakerism, and twenty-four had moved to the Whitewater commune by March 27, 1846. More would follow. Jacobs himself moved there for his own safety, since many in Cincinnati were upset over the families that had been destroyed by his new teaching. By August 1846, eighty of the 144 Whitewater residents were former Millerites. Altogether, he helped attract some two hundred disaffected Adventists to Shakerism in the West and Midwest.[44]

Beyond interpersonal public evangelism, Jacobs also took the

Day-Star to Whitewater with him. From there he publicized Shakerism among Adventists across the nation. The pages of the *Day-Star* in 1846 and 1847 mentioned several meetings of Shakers and Adventists in various places in the northern states. Beyond that, its pages are full of Shaker articles appealing to Adventists to leave Babylon and to accept the truth.[45]

Among other Adventist converts to Shakerism were G. W. Peavey and Henry B. Bear. Bear is of special interest because he published his memoirs of his advent experience while at Whitewater. Bear had moved to Union County, Indiana, in June 1845 and soon came under the influence of Jacobs, who "seemed at this time to take the lead in bringing forward the most advanced ideas of the advent movement" through the *Day-Star*.

Bear's move to Shakerism was a step-by-step process. First, he became convinced, for at least the second time, to sell *everything* he had and give to the poor, including such seeming necessities as beds, cookstoves, dishes, and house. That conviction, he mused, "seemed a very tight place to be in." After five or six days of agonizing, he followed his convictions. Relieved from anxiety and realizing that he would be in the kingdom, Bear experienced "laughing a week." It was the "happiest week" in his life, even though some people thought him crazy, as they previously had in 1844.

Bear's second step toward the Shakers was attending a meeting in Whitewater, but he went away quite suspicious, since they communally held houses and lands—things he had been convicted should be disposed of. In the third step, Bear claims that God providentially set his "faith-quieted tooth" to aching as a sign that he should not go on a certain trip. That led Bear to attend a meeting where Adventists were encouraged to " 'go on.' " That impressed Bear, since so many were saying, " 'Come back [to the old Adventist ways and beliefs], you are going astray, you are going crazy, etc.' The words 'go on,' " he penned, "impressed me with this idea: Here is a person that speaks as though he comprehends our whereabouts, and understands our path ahead."

After that experience, Bear joined those "Adventists that . . .

were going up to the Shakers to take possession of the kingdom."
He then had peace and could comprehend his spiritual journey.
"It was all beautiful and harmonious," he wrote.

> I could literally see the circuitous road; I came along the
> winding mountain, ascending from the plain below up to the
> top of the mountain, and entering in at the arched gate into
> the everlasting plain above—the kingdom of God. I now felt
> that the most dangerous part of my journey was over.

His wife readily responded to the sacrifices of Shakerism. To
her, " 'this is too good news.' " Thus they became "wise virgins . . . and entered in, while other foolish virgins went to buy
more oil."

But still they might have some pride. On the evening they
joined the Shaker commune, Jacobs claimed in a meeting that if
"he had the least spark of pride in him, he would get right down
on the floor and roll over." That remark stimulated the ever-
sensitive Bear to self-examination. "My feelings," he wrote,

> soon convinced me of pride within, and I received convic-
> tions that I ought to get down on the floor and roll: I took
> resolution and did so. The Shakers present followed suit im-
> mediately, and then many of the adventists. Consequently it
> began to work on Enoch Jacobs, and he got down at last,
> but his awkward, still unnatural movements, convinced me
> that he had some pride left, if they did not convince himself.

Thus Bear, writing in retrospect twenty-seven years later, could
account for Jacobs' apostasy from Shakerism in 1847. As for Bear,
he had found the security he needed. Living in a commune of
like-minded believers, he no longer had to suffer persecution for
his faith. "Here no evil spirits can come . . . to deceive." As for
Adventism, Bear claims that he often remarked: " 'Not for all the
world would I have missed going through my advent experience;
nor for all the world would I want to go through it again.[']"[46]

Though Shakerism was the most popular communal experience embraced by security-seeking Adventists, it was not the only one. Barkun has discovered at least three Adventist communes that began in the 1850s and 1860s. One of them kept the seventh day and practiced vegetarianism; another "sought to establish a mountain retreat where the 144,000 saints of the Book of Revelation would gather at the Judgment." Such experimentation was not unique in Christian history, as the drive for monasteries in the Medieval church demonstrates. Beyond that, Americans of all social strata in the first half of the nineteenth century did a great deal of experimenting with communal utopias.[47]

In addition to independent communes and Shakerism, ex-Millerites were attracted to one other communal society. At the opposite end of the sexual spectrum from Shakerism among nineteenth-century communes was John Humphrey Noyes' Oneida community, with its practice of plural marriage. In essence, at Oneida, sexual relations could be shared by all adults with the opposite sex under the planning of Noyes.[48]

In 1846 Noyes noted that the Adventists "hear the same voice we have heard, that God is coming into the world and the day of judgment is at hand; but to them the voice is not clear enough to save them from the delusions of their own imagination." To be more specific, "Miller's fatuous [stupid] doctrine of the speedy coming of Christ 'in the clouds of heaven,' is based on that old desperate delusion of Christendom,—the denial that *he has already come*" back in the time of the early church. By the late 1840s, former Millerites were beginning to join the Oneida community.[49]

"Who Is *We*?"

Miller, to say the least, was beside himself with the fanaticism that began to develop in 1845. In April he wrote to Himes that

this is a peculiar time. The greatest variety of fanciful interpretations of Scripture are now being presented by new luminaries, reflecting their rays of light and heat in every direction. Some of these are wandering stars, and some emit only twilight. I am sick of this everlasting changing; but, my dear brother, we must learn to have patience. If Christ comes this spring, we shall not need it long; and if he comes not, we shall need much more. I am prepared for the worst, and hope for the best.[50]

Unfortunately for Miller, time continued to last, and they witnessed something less than the hoped-for "best." Eighteen months later, an ailing Miller penned:

I have not done with *pain*. I have been troubled with head-ache, teeth-ache, bones-ache, and heart-ache, since you left; but much more of the *last* ache, when I think of so many of my once dearly beloved brethren, who have since our disappointment, gone into fanaticism of every kind, and left the first principles of the glorious appearing of the great God and our Saviour, Jesus Christ.[51]

Miller wasn't the only one confused and perturbed by the welter of shut-door Adventists in early 1845. Himes noted in May that "the seventh month movement [had] produced mesmerism seven feet deep."[52]

Then there was the "old woman" who was one of Miller's first converts. Miller weekly passed on his Adventist papers to her after he had read them. One week after having glanced through sixteen periodicals all purporting to be Adventist publications, but most of them setting forth contradictory positions, he passed them on to his neighbor lady.

Before long, he received an urgent message from her, requesting a visit as soon as possible. On his arrival, she began to question him:

"Have you read all these papers?"
"Why, I have looked them over."
"But are they all Advent papers?"

"They profess so to be."

"Well, then," [said she], "I am no longer an Adventist; I shall take the old Bible, and stick to that."

"But," said he, "we have no confidence in one half there is advocated in those papers."

"But," said the old lady, "who is *we?*"

"Why," [replied Miller,] "we are those who do not fellowship those things."

"Well, but I want to know who *we is.*"

"Why, all of us who stand on the old ground."

"But that an't telling who *we* is. I want to know who *we* is."

"Well," said [Miller, in relating the story], "I was confounded, and was unable to give her any information who *we* are."[53]

It was the dilemma of identity that forced Himes, Miller, and their colleagues to issue a call for a conference to define their position and to ascertain who sympathized with their views and who did not. That conference became another turning point in Adventist history. It began at Albany, New York, on April 29, 1845, and turned out to be one of the most significant Adventist meetings in the history of post-October 1844 Adventism. The Albany conference will be the subject of our next chapter.

Meanwhile, we need to take a parting glance at Adventism's radical fringe. The various movements growing out of the radical Adventism of post-1844 came to nothing by the end of the nineteenth century. Most of them had probably disappeared by the late 1860s. Given the radical fringe's propensity to grasp at every new and strange doctrine, its various strands tended toward making their "peculiar" beliefs into tests that shut out all Adventists who didn't accept that perspective. All other views became Babylons that needed to be escaped from. That schismatic tendency eventually played itself into oblivion as the various periodicals holding the splinter movements together lost their support. The majority of both leaders and followers of the various fringe groups eventually joined other "isms" of the day that sported exciting new doctrines. Thus they drifted out of Adventism or found themselves aligning with more stable Adventist bodies. As a result, in the late twentieth century, no surviving fringe Adventist sects remain that grew directly out of the radical movements of 1845 and 1846.

If that is so, some readers may be asking, why did we spend so much time examining Adventism's radical wing? Is it just a matter of historical curiosity? Definitely not! Though historical curiosity is a justification in itself, we have at least two additional reasons for understanding the radical aspect of Adventism's history. The first is that the spirit of the radicals lives on among some of the more stable descendants of Millerism. As a result, various forms of present-day Adventism not only house those who tend toward the cool, biblical rationalism of Miller, but they also contain elements exemplifying the characteristics of the radical fringe. One of the lessons of church history is that millennial movements tend to pick up their share of those on the radical edge who get carried away by the excitement and are quick to identify esoteric "new truth" and to pronounce those who do not agree with them as both apostate and Babylon. Thus an understanding of Adventism's past can help people better grasp the significance of tensions and movements in the present.

A second reason, and one of even greater importance for understanding Adventism's radical fringe of the late 1840s, is that all other Adventists were forced to define themselves in terms of the radical wing. The task was not only one of defining but also one of distancing themselves from the "fanatics."

The radicals had set the agenda. The next step in the development of Adventism would be up to the less radical elements in the movement. There would be two basic modes of distancing and defining between late 1844 and 1850. One would be the course of the Albany Adventists; the other would be that of the Sabbatarian Adventists. It is to the Albany group that we now turn.

Chapter 13

THE ALBANY REACTION

The spring of 1845 saw the advent movement growing more divided with each passing week. Differing opinions over the seventh-month movement, the shut-door, and the ever-proliferating number of doctrines arising out of the shut-door segment of Adventism were creating havoc in the movement. Coupled with the doctrinal crisis was the behavioral crisis, which, in many cases, led to fanaticism.

By March 1845 the initiative was definitely in the hands of the fringe groups. Moderate Adventism, under the leadership of Himes, was fighting desperately to hold the movement together, but the struggle seemed to be one that the moderates were losing. The forum for the contest was the large number of Adventist periodicals, with Himes' *Advent Herald* and *Morning Watch* on one side, and the growing number of shut-door journals on the other. Joseph Marsh's *Voice of Truth* seemed to be holding a middle ground, open to the shut-door teaching but speaking out regularly against the extremes of many of the fringe journals.

By March the battle had been joined, and the positions were rapidly hardening. It was at that crucial juncture that Himes moved beyond strategies related to periodicals to the second piece of ordinance in the Millerite/restorationist arsenal—the convention or conference. In March, Himes issued a public call for a conference to convene at Albany, New York, on April 29, 1845.

Up to Albany

The call for the Albany conference was first published in the *Morning Watch* of March 20. It prominently listed Miller as one of those issuing the invitation. Significantly, that invitation was not to all Adventists, but only to those "who still adhere to the *original Advent faith*." In other words, the shut-door Adventists and those who had developed new doctrines were *not* invited.

The stated purpose of the meeting was not to debate controversial doctrines or "questions of doubtful disputation" but (1) "to strengthen one another in the faith of the Advent at the door," (2) "to consult on the best mode of unitedly carrying forth our work, in comforting, and preparing the Advent congregations among us for the speedy coming of the Lord," and (3) "to unite our efforts, for the conversion and salvation of sinners." The plea was for unity of action. Each Adventist congregation was invited to send one or two representatives.

The Albany announcement's closing sentence is significant. It noted that Miller would be making presentations at Albany. To Himes it was absolutely essential to the success of the meetings for Miller to be there and for him to give the advent trumpet a certain and unmistakable sound.[1]

On March 27, Himes wrote to Miller that "all depends upon your being there [at Albany]." In order to get Miller there on time, Himes requested that he lecture at Albany the week prior to the conference. Miller was assured that he would have a "crowded house" and "do much good." For his part, Himes promised to "keep the 'Herald' and 'Watch' going till the Albany meeting." Then he ominously suggested that if something significant did not take place at Albany, he would have to stop publication.[2]

It is impossible to know whether the suggestion of the possibility of ceasing publication was based on financial reality or whether it was a technique to put all possible pressure on Miller to attend. Given the chaos in Adventism at the time and what we know of Himes' personal traits, both factors probably entered into his plea to Miller. We do know that even with the success of the Albany conference, Himes' two journals were combined into one shortly after the meetings. We also know that Miller attended.

The timing of the conference, it should be noted, was not accidental. It was significant for two reasons. First, the beginning date of April 29 was beyond the March 23 and April 23, 1845, dates on which many were still pinning their hopes for the Lord's return. Second, Himes did not call the conference until *after* he had won Miller over to coming out in public against the shut door and related doctrines. But by April, Himes could wait no more. If the advent movement were to be saved at all, something would have to be done soon.

While the conference invitation was set forth in a manner that definitely excluded those who held to the shut door and related doctrines, Himes and the organizers hoped to pull Marsh and his Rochester-based *Voice of Truth* into their sphere of influence. Marsh and several other western leaders had been invited, but Marsh had some definite reservations about the Albany conference. For one thing, he still believed that the Lord would return before April 23. For another, given the excitable state of Adventism, he doubted the wisdom of bringing a large group of Adventists together. But, most significantly, Marsh foresaw that "*a formidable division will unavoidably be the result*" of the Albany meetings.

Behind those words seems to be the apprehension that Albany was a step, however small, toward the creation of a denomination. Marsh feared any authority outside the Word of God.[3]

That apprehension seems to have been founded upon genuine insight into Himes' mentality. After all, hadn't periodicals and conference meetings formed the organizational structure of the Christian Connexion, in which Himes and Marsh had pastored? Himes was operating in the way he knew best to bring order out of chaos. The alternative to organization was to lose control of the movement to the radical fringe groups with their fanaticism. The still-aggressive Himes was a long way from that solution. Still in his fortieth year, he had another fifty yet ahead of him in which to fight the Lord's battles.

Albany

The important Albany conference opened on April 29 with singing and a prayer by Miller. In attendance were such prominent Adventist leaders as William Miller, J. V. Himes, Elon Galusha, Josiah Litch, and Sylvester Bliss. But those not there were conspicuous by their absence. Into that latter group were such leaders as George Storrs, Joseph Bates, Joseph Turner, S. S. Snow, and Joseph Marsh. Marsh's absence would prove to be especially problematic for the Albany Adventists. His was an influential voice that had the potential to pull many marginal types into the Albany sphere.

Miller's "Address to the Brethren Scattered Abroad" set the tone for the Albany meetings. After calling for patience, love, and forbearance in light of the "present state of our faith and hope," he went on to suggest that "among the thousand and one expositions of Scripture, which are every day being palmed upon us, some of them, at least, must be wrong." Beyond that, "many of them are so weak and silly, that they bring a stigma on the blessed Book, confuse the mind of the inquirer after truth, and divide the children of God."

After identifying the issues in a general way, Miller went on to give some specific advice to the believers. Among those counsels were admonitions to avoid "any man whose object is to obtain followers"; to stay by the lamp of God's Word, since some of the brothers were walking "by sparks of their own kindling"; to receive no evidence but the Bible as the ground of faith; and to avoid those who murmured against the pioneers of the message. Miller brought his presentation to a climax with two suggestions: that love for the brethren was the true "test" of one's love to Christ and that many of the brethren would do well if they spent less time writing and more time studying the Bible. Along that line, it would be best if one's theories were submitted for scrutiny "by some judicious friend" before they were set before the public. "We have arrived," he pointed out, "at a period of deep interest and peril."[4]

The Albany conference picked up on Miller's keynote address.

The delegates accomplished three main tasks. First, "in view of the many conflicting opinions, unscriptural views leading to unseemly practices, and the sad divisions which have been thereby caused by some professing to be Adventists," the conference set forth a ten-point doctrinal platform that emphasized items related to the advent and salvation. That statement of belief was not unlike its predecessors prior to October 1844, with the exception that the Albany statement had no provisions regarding the time element. As to be expected, it contained none of the controversial doctrines then dividing Adventism. Nor did it include an affirmation of the seventh-month movement.

The second major accomplishment of the Albany conference was to set forth a plan of action for preaching the message to the world as Adventism continued to seek converts to its beliefs. To achieve that purpose, the conference recommended preaching services, literature distribution, Sunday schools, and Bible classes. The provision of further evangelism was a definite rejection of the shut door.

The third accomplishment of the Albany meetings took the form of a series of resolutions. One rejected the "*anti-Scriptural*" postmillennial doctrine that the world would be converted to Christ. A second resolution denied the restoration of the natural Jews as a nation, "either *before* or *after* the second advent of Christ."

The next resolution was aimed directly at those "Adventists . . . with which we can have no sympathy or fellowship" because of their "unseemly practices." It was resolved that they have no fellowship with any who created new tests as conditions of salvation beyond the acceptance of Christ and "a looking for and loving his appearing." The resolution included a breaking off of fellowship with those involved in "promiscuous feet-washing," the salutation kiss as a "*religious*" ceremony, "sitting on the floor as an act of voluntary humility, shaving the head to humble one's self, and acting like children in understanding." Such teachings were declared to be not only unscriptural but also subversive of purity and morality if persevered in.

The last resolution suggested that selected believers be encouraged toward the gospel ministry. While that suggestion seems innocuous enough by itself, when it is combined with two other elements in the Albany report, it can be seen that Albany was, in effect, the staging ground for the formation of a church organization. The first of those elements was the examination and ordination of five ministers at the conference. The second was a statement on church order along "New Testament" lines. "We regard," reads the report,

> any congregation of believers who habitually assemble for the worship of God, and the due observance of the gospel ordinances, as a church of Christ. As such, it is an independent body, accountable only to the great Head of the Church. To all such we recommend a careful examination of the Scriptures, and the adoption of such principles of association and order, as are in accordance therewith, that they may enjoy the advantages of that church relation which Christ has instituted.[5]

The effect of that statement was to authorize a congregational form of church government much like that of the Baptists and the Connexionists, to which Miller and Himes respectively belonged. Thus Albany represents the formation, or at least authorization for the formation, of the first "Adventist" church. What Miller had sought to avoid was now taking place with his apparent blessing. The self-preservation of moderate Adventism had forced the issue.

According to David Arthur, the Albany conference had four major results. First, it identified, unified, and strengthened the moderate Adventists in their defense of the original advent faith. Second, it led several preachers to reject the new views and return to the leadership of the Albany group. Among the "converts" were Apollos Hale, W. S. Campbell, and F. G. Brown. Third, it led to the development of an elitist leadership core that tended to include the best-educated Adventist ministers. Fourth, it made the division among the Adventists more permanent. From this time forward, an Adventist belonged either to the Albany faction or to the opposition.[6]

Miller returned from Albany glad to be able to tell the "old woman" who had wondered "who *we* is" who they were. After reading the conference reports, she informed him: "I have found out who *we* is; and I shall still be an Adventist, and stand by the old ship."[7]

Miller, in narrating that story at Boston in May, thanked the leadership of moderate Adventism for telling the world "who you are." He pledged his support to those who approved of "the doings of that Conference."[8]

Immediately After Albany

In order to hold on to and extend the momentum initiated at Albany, Himes and his colleagues held conferences in New York City, Philadelphia, Boston, and Baltimore in May.[9] Each conference aimed at strengthening the hands of those who preached the "original advent faith" as defined at Albany.

Each conference also ratified the positions taken at Albany. There were, however, two points of clarification that should be noted. First, the New York City conference went on record as being against charismatic gifts. Thus it was "*Resolved*, That we have no confidence in any new messages, visions, dreams, tongues, miracles, extraordinary gifts, revelations, impressions, discerning of spirits, or teachings, &c. &c., not in accordance with the unadulterated word of God." In light of the fanaticism then taking place among the shut-door Adventists, it is not difficult to see what prompted that resolution. A similar one had been approved in the midst of the Starkweather crisis in May 1843.[10]

The second important clarification of the Albany principles was set forth in the last of the ratifying conferences at Boston in late May. By that time, Marsh and others had come out firmly against the church-building implications of Albany. As a result, the brethren at Boston deemed it necessary to downplay that aspect of the Albany meetings. It was therefore

> *Resolved*, That we do not regard the expression of senti-ment, or principles of Associated Action, adopted by the Albany Conference, as instituting a test of Christian charac-ter, or as having anything to do with church organization, but merely as a disclaiming of erroneous sentiments and practices which are ascribed to us, and a declaration of the views which we entertain in relation to the cause for the promotion of which we co-operate.[11]

That denial of Albany having "anything to do with church organization," however, did not change the fact that the delegates at Albany had opted for a congregational church structure, had examined and ordained men for the ministry, and had excluded those from their fellowship who did not agree with them on the open door and related doctrinal issues.

The Boston resolution had no intention of softening the hard line against the fringe Adventists, but it did hope to quiet the fears of Marsh and others like him whom the moderate Albany Adventists hoped to bring into their camp in the power struggle of late spring 1845.

It seems that David Rowe is correct when he states that "the Albany Conference did not so much create an Adventist sect as give shape and direction to a body that already existed." Beyond that, Rowe asserts, Albany "assured that Second Adventism would survive." Thus Albany gave evidence by its move toward organi-zation that Adventism had capitulated on its teaching of the immediacy of the second advent and was settling down for an "extended sojourn" in this world.[12]

It was those very insights that Marsh had intuited. As a result, he reacted to the Albany conference with vigor. Marsh, as we noted above, at first felt that the Lord would come before the conference and thus make it a nonevent. But when the Lord did not return in April, Marsh still made no plans to attend the Albany meetings. To the contrary, in the May 7 *Voice of Truth*, he suggested that he had been too busy to attend, thus providing us with some insight as to his priorities.

Even more insightful is an editorial blurb on the same page entitled "Give Us a King." In that short piece, Marsh set forth not only the apostasy of ancient Israel but also suggested that seceding Christians who had formed sects in the past had come from "the 'mother of harlots' " and had become like their mother. He praised the Adventists for having heeded the call " 'COME OUT OF HER.' " Then he admonished them not to "go back to her polluted temples, nor [to] build one of *our own* after any of her patterns."[13]

Thus even before Marsh had received reports from Albany, he was showing his hand. It had been no accident that he had chosen not to attend. It had been a conscious choice built upon the logic of George Storrs, who had preached that "no church can be organized by man's invention but what it becomes Babylon *the moment it is organized*."[14]

While the Albany Adventists expected to face the "harlot daughter" argument from S. S. Snow, Enoch Jacobs, Joseph Turner, Emily Clemons, and the like, they did not expect it from Marsh, who had by May backed away from some of his earlier attractions to the new doctrines related to the shut door. As a result, some of the Albany men were undoubtedly stunned when they read Marsh's critique in the May 21 issue of the *Voice of Truth*.

Marsh began his critique of the Albany report in a rather affirming manner. He praised the conference for uplifting "a certain degree" of order in "the household of faith" and suggested that both the conference and its report had the potential for much good.

After those affirming remarks, Marsh turned to his "fears." In short, he found many things at Albany out of harmony with the Bible. His extensive objections were four in number. First, he objected to the fact that they had taken the name "Adventist" to identify themselves. All names other than "CHURCH OF GOD" were "unscriptural, and antichristian, and should be rejected by every child of God." Second, Marsh saw Albany's declaration of beliefs to be the forming of a creed—one of the roots of evil in Christian history. That point hit at the heart of the concerns of the large number of anticreedal believers. Third, Marsh declared it was wrong for a religious body to vote certain things as being true or false. True faith, not resolutions, was the answer to fanaticism and heresy.

Lastly, Marsh objected "to the doings of the Albany conference because the proceedings as a whole, look like forming a new sect, under a sectarian name, instead of *coming to the order* of the New Testament under the name there given to the true church." Beyond that, Albany appeared to have laid plans for the future, "when we profess to be looking for his coming every hour."[15]

Himes was furious when he discovered the direction Marsh was taking. "*Marsh* . . . did not stay at home for nothing," the Albany organizer snorted in a letter to Miller in early May. "He is determined to have things go at loose ends—or go to support *him*, and not the *mutual*, or *general cause*." Marsh's war on creeds, Himes suggested, "was *designed* to strike against what he thought we should do at Albany. . . . He has had a good harvest [of subscribers] out of the *Herald* & Watch [sic], and now he seeks another, by raising the 'cry' of creeds, bondage[,] etc."[16]

Marsh's critique on Albany in the May 21 issue of *Voice of Truth* elicited a wave of defenses, but the most extended and significant answer to Marsh came from William Miller. On May 27, Miller replied to Marsh point by point. Miller had no problem with the name *Adventist* as long as it referred to a group of believers in the advent, but he had no desire to attach that name or any other to a church. Regarding Marsh's accusation about the forming of a creed, Miller replied that a creed is merely what a person believes. As such, there was nothing improper with writing it down.

On Marsh's charge that Albany had recommended organization, Miller noted that they had simply recommended that the subject be studied from the Bible. On that point, it seems that Miller had still not recognized the full implications of what had transpired at Albany.

By the time Miller got to Marsh's accusation that they had passed "resolutions" at Albany, he was clearly impatient. "This is a great sin, truly," he quipped. On Marsh's final point—Albany looked like "doing something for the future"—Miller refused to comment.

In conclusion, Miller claimed he was delighted that so many believers had found the Albany decisions to provide an anchor for their faith. The advent believers had been mixed up and needed direction. "It must be evident," he penned,

> that unless we come out of the BABYLON into which we have been thrust, God will not bless us. The question then comes home to each one of our hearts, Shall we continue in the anarchy in which we have been, or shall we take gospel measures to restore gospel order, that at the Master's coming we may be approved of him? It must be evident to all, that without union we can do nothing; and if there are no "important truths" in which we are united, all can see that there can be no union among us:—"how can two walk together except they be agreed?" . . . All union consists in a sacrifice of individual pre-possessions for the common good. Those who love the peace of Zion more than they do their private opinions, will be prompt thus to unite. Those who love self more than they do the general good, will contend for their own selfish ends. . . . The union that prevailed at the Albany Conference was what should ever characterize the children of God.[17]

There was no doubt about it. Miller believed Albany to be a good thing. In his desire to escape the Babylon of confusion and disorder, he had gradually backed into what Marsh and his friends saw as the Babylon of the ordered and oppressive sect.[18]

From Albany to Miller's Death

The years after Albany were not easy ones as the moderate Adventists groped along, struggling with the problem of what it meant to continue to exist as Adventists in a world that stubbornly refused to come to an end.

The Albany conference had settled at least one issue in the Adventist community. It had separated the shut-door and fanatical Adventists from the moderate Albany Adventists in a permanent way. That does not mean that the shut-door Adventists disappeared from association with the moderates overnight. Rather, it implies a gradual separation over the next few years. But by late 1846, much of the fanatical element had burned itself out, while other practitioners of extremes were opting for the Shakers and other "isms." The separation seems to have been well underway by November 1846. Miller wrote in that month of a seven-week tour of Vermont and Canada. "Fanaticism," he reported, "such as discerning of spirits, private revelations, denouncing of others, &c. &c., is nearly extinct among the Advent congregations I have visited." Note that he did not suggest that fanaticism was altogether dead, but that it was visibly lessening in the Albany-related congregations he had visited. The leaven of Albany was doing its work.[19]

But while Albany had brought about a progressive degree of separation between the more radical Adventists and the Albany moderates, it had not created nearly so large a cleavage between those moderates and Marsh and certain other proponents of antiorganization. One result of Marsh's ongoing influence would be the inability of the Albany Adventists to organize in any effective way in the late 1840s.

Another factor that needs to be taken into account between 1845 and late 1849 is the presence of Miller. Even though Miller himself continued to stand against moves that looked like too much organization, he was for good order in the work of God. One reason Miller looked askance at too much organization is that he continued until his death to believe in the immediate coming of Christ. He never quite got away from the idea that the dating scheme, being founded on human data, could have been off more than a few years.

But as time continued in the late 1840s, the younger leaders of Albany Adventism were more or less forced to deal with the reality of certain pressing issues. Two of the most important challenges facing them were mission outreach and the need for some sort of organizational structure to facilitate that outreach.

One thing emphasized by the Albany Adventists between 1845 and 1847 was the fact that they were gaining converts who had not heard the second-advent message prior to October 1844. They saw those conversions as empirical confirmation that the shut-door/close-of-probation teaching was not valid. Thus an emphasis of the moderates was the necessity "to continue in obedience to the great commission to preach the gospel." Some soon tied that imperative to Revelation 10, which they saw as portraying the experience of the advent people. They had "eaten" the little book of Daniel and found it "sweet" in the mouth as they looked forward to the advent, but "bitter" in their belly when Christ failed to return. But, noted Luther Boutelle, according to Revelation 10, these people of the sweet/ bitter experience were to " 'prophesy again before many peoples, and nations, and tongues, and kings.' "[20]

In response to their convictions, the Albany ministers not only continued their publishing ventures, but they also put the "big tent" back into action as their lecturers resumed the evangelistic trail.[21] Not only did they set to work in the United States, but they also, for the first time, actually began to send foreign missionaries to other countries. One of those nations was Great Britain. We earlier noted that Himes and Litch had wanted to visit the British Millerites in 1844, but that mission had been canceled when they accepted the seventh-month message. That deferred dream became a reality in the summer of 1846.

On June 1, Himes set sail for Britain with F. G. Brown and Robert Hutchinson. It was Himes' intention to hold conferences, "scatter publications," and establish a publishing headquarters and a periodical. The Americans preached in various parts of England, Scotland, and Ireland. Himes also initiated the *European Advent Herald*. While the Americans met with a fair degree of success, "this special mission was closed up in 1847, as there were not then men and means to effect an organization to continue the work in an efficient manner." The Adventist work in

Britain continued, but once again under local leadership.[22]

The Albany Adventists would not send another missionary to the "old world" until 1865, when they sponsored M. B. Czechowski to the continent. But his mission proved to be a major disappointment to them when they discovered he had become a Sabbatarian Adventist and thereby "cut off his usefulness" as far as they were concerned.[23]

Himes' earlier reform interests surfaced again in England. He attended both the World's Temperance Convention and the Evangelical Alliance, which hoped to build union between the Protestant bodies. It was at the Alliance meeting that Himes especially made his mark as an aggressive reformer. He took the initiative in arguing for the exclusion of slaveholders from membership on the basis that their membership would corrupt the Alliance, since nothing could touch slavery "without being corrupted." Himes' advocacy of antislavery proved to be unpopular in a meeting called for unity. Following Himes' speech, the chairman suggested that they ought to "acknowledge the goodness of God, in granting His grace" in helping the delegates remain silent in the face of the onslaught.[24]

On the other hand, the report of the meeting made William Lloyd Garrison rejoice that at least "one voice from across the water was heard" on the issue.[25] Of course, Himes' reputation as a Millerite certainly didn't help his acceptance with the Alliance delegates.

The British mission was not the only one by the Albany Adventists in 1846. L. D. Mansfield and his wife were sent to the West Indies late in the year. But by 1849, Mansfield was back in the United States due to a lack of financial backing.[26]

The sense of a need to preach the second advent both at home and abroad soon forced the Albany leaders toward further steps in organization. After all, if mission was to be successful, there must be some way to give it direction, gather funds, and send workers.[27]

That felt need led to a proposal in 1847 to form an "Advent Home Mission." That mild proposition, as might be expected, aroused opposition because it necessitated organization. The *Ad-*

vent Herald defended the proposal, since the alternative was to "consent to live in anarchy." Accordingly, "as churches of the Lord Jesus Christ, it is our duty to 'set things in order,' to appoint the Scriptural officers, to attend to the ordinances and discipline of God's house, and support a pure and faithful ministry among us." The editorial went on to speak despairingly of those who "would rather see us living in confusion and strife, till we are 'consumed one of another.' " A few months later the *Herald* reported that the home and foreign missions connected to it could "only be sustained . . . by . . . united effort."[28]

By the force of events, the Albany Adventists had begun to function like a denomination, even though many would continue to deny that reality. But not all denied it. In 1849, Litch, in a general reference work on American religion, presented the Albany Adventists as a religious body of between fifteen thousand and twenty thousand members in the United States, Canada, England, Scotland, and the West Indies. In addition to those numbers, Litch noted, there were also many sympathetic to Albany who had remained in their own churches. On the other hand, he refused to include those "fanatics and impostors" who had led off "disciples after them" to their "fanatical doctrines and practices."[29]

Unbeknown to Litch at the time, Albany Adventism would soon experience additional radical changes after the death of Miller. In the next decade, the moderate Adventists would war with each other and finally splinter into several denominations.

Miller passed his last years faithfully but feebly. Between 1846 and 1849, he went through increasingly rapid physical decline. But his mind was still alert. He continued to preach when well enough, even though he realized that his body would soon be "under the cold clods of the valley."[30]

Up to his death, Miller rued the day when the call to come out of Babylon had been issued. That had not only begun an "unholy crusade," but it had also "brought . . . men of blood instead of men of peace" into the Adventist midst. Miller never did see that the course of events had had a great deal to do with that development. In his own way, he was seeking to fix the blame for the Adventist crisis on something. As he saw it, those who spent so much time in criticizing others were "like the obscene fowls of the air who live only on carcasses and putrid flesh." Miller abhorred sectarianism and considered himself to be a Baptist to the day of his death.[31]

Miller also continued to dislike doctrinal strife. His faith had always been simple. His theology focused on two essential elements: salvation in Christ and the second advent. On September 15, 1847, he wrote to Himes, complaining of those Adventists who gravely discussed nonessentials as though "life and death depended on them." He was upset with those who argued whether we will have two wings, four, six, or more in the resurrected life. Into that same category Miller put debates over the annihilation of the wicked. "I do not wonder that the world calls us insane; for I must confess it looks like insanity to me, to see religious, candid men, spend their time and talents on questions of so little consequence to us here or hereafter."[32]

As Miller moved toward the end of his life, he had no regrets about his advent doctrine. "If I have any regret," he penned in May 1847, "it is because I have done so little, and because I have been so inefficient." A year later he was wishing he were young enough to "shake the world tremendously." But one of his sons added that "the shaking is going on pretty well, without the aid of the old gentleman."[33]

The year 1848 found Miller largely blind. That was discouraging to him, but not devastating. "It would, indeed, be a sad and melancholy time with me," he wrote to Himes, "were it not for the 'blessed hope' of soon seeing Jesus. . . . And although my natural vision is dark, yet my mind's vision is lit up with a bright and glorious prospect of the future."[34]

Miller's health failed rapidly after April 1848. His end came in December of the following year. Himes spent the last few days with his beloved mentor. Miller was feeble but happy at the younger man's presence. "Elder Himes has come," he whispered. "I love Elder Himes."

The morning of December 20, 1849, was his last. Witnesses report that in his weakened condition, he made no conversation. But from time to time he would break forth in expressions like " 'Mighty to save!' 'O, I long to be there!' 'Victory! Victory!' 'Shouting in death!' &c." He passed away a little after three o'clock in the afternoon.[35]

He was buried in the Low Hampton cemetery. The top of his tombstone has a quotation from Daniel: "At the time appointed the end shall be."

Miller's life had been more fruitful than most people's. Not only had he made an impact on the world during his life, but he had also left a legacy of believers behind in his death.

Those believers closest to him at the time of his death were the still largely unorganized Albany Adventists. Up to the end, his influence had been greater than many realized in both holding the movement together and in keeping it from forming its own denomination. "His death," however, as Advent Christian historian Clyde Hewitt points out, removed "a genuine barrier to fractionalism, strife, and the advocacy of new doctrines and structured organizations." The next two decades would witness unfortunate infighting and schism in the ranks of the Albany believers.[36]

The Albany Denominations

By the time of Miller's death, the line of battle for the Albany Adventists was no longer the shut door and whether prophecy had been fulfilled on October 22, 1844. Albany and the intervening years had progressively segregated the shut-door Adventists. Between the Albany convention and Miller's death, the major in-group struggle had been over organization. That struggle would continue into the 1850s, but it would be overshadowed by one even more divisive—the immortality question.[37]

That issue, we noted in chapter 10, had been raised by Storrs in 1843 and had become problematic in 1844. In that year Miller and Himes had spoken out against conditionalism and annihilationism. In addition, Litch had begun publishing *The Anti Annihilationist* to combat the doctrine, since the mainline Millerite journals did not want to muddy the waters by dealing with what they deemed to be a minor issue.

Himes probably expressed the sentiments of most of the main-line Millerite leadership when he wrote:

> Occupied as I was with the imminence of the Second Advent, these other views seemed to me to be a side issue, and of no special importance. Jesus was at hand, and it was in my es-timation of more importance to prepare a people for his coming, than to enlighten them on these other questions. Whether men slept or were conscious in death, and were destroyed or suffered eternally for sin, were questions of minor importance to me. God would do right; and we should soon know all about it. My business was to proclaim the glorious coming and kingdom of Christ and prepare myself and others to meet the Judge.[38]

That order of priorities continued to be that of Himes and the *Advent Herald* throughout the late 1840s and the 1850s. Editorial policy was to not make the issue a bone of contention. Thus it was virtually ignored as being unimportant. The *Herald* chose to emphasize the advent in support of publicizing "the original adventist faith" as defined at Albany.[39] As a result, the *Herald* encouraged individuals to go elsewhere to publish on the topic of human nature in death.

The problem with that policy was that a growing number of Albany Adventists denied that merely preaching the coming of the Lord was the sum total of Adventist doctrine. "The *Advent doctrine*," they held, "embraces all the items of [doc]trine that are to be realized in connection with [the] second advent of the Son of man." The rise of modern spiritualism with the Fox sis-ters in upstate New York in the late 1840s aided the condition-alist cause in that it enabled many people to better see the sig-nificance of the issue. In addition, Storrs' *Six Sermons* was being circulated by the tens of thousands. That volume was not only affecting ex-Millerite Adventists in large numbers, but it would eventually convert the founder of the Jehovah's Witnesses on the topic.[40]

Insensitivity on the part of the *Advent Herald* editors to growing conditionalist sentiment progressively set the stage for schism in the Albany ranks in the late 1840s and early 1850s. Insensitivity was bad enough, but the *Herald* leadership added insult to injury, claims David Dean, by taking on superior and patronizing airs toward the conditionalists. Worse yet for the unity of Albany Adventism, the generally gentlemanly editors of the *Herald* became vindictive and sarcastic toward the conditionalists.[41]

Being shut out of the *Advent Herald*, the conditionalists (or "life and death" Adventists) found outlets for their position in the *Bible Advocate* and the *Second Advent Watchman*. Thus the growing number of conditionalist believers began to look to those journals for guidance and direction. The conditionalist periodicals were soon supplemented by annual camp meetings at Wilbraham, Massachusetts. Thus the Albany Adventists in the early 1850s were being split into two parties over the state-of-the-dead issue, with Himes, Litch, and the *Herald* in one party and the conditionalists in the other.[42]

Things became more complicated when another party arose among the Albany Adventists in the early 1850s, proclaiming that Christ would return in 1854. These "timeists," under the leadership of Miles Grant, soon established their own periodical, the *World's Crisis*, to set forth their views. The *Crisis* not only trumpeted the 1854 date, but also conditionalism. When Christ did not come in 1854, the *Crisis* became the major organ of communication for the conditionalists. That development was particularly important, since by that time, Joseph Turner's *Second Advent Watchman* had moved toward strange new ideas.[43]

The developing impasse between the two Albany parties came to a head in May 1858, when the *Herald* Adventists formed the American Evangelical Adventist Conference to disseminate "original" Adventism as defined in 1845 at Albany. November 1858 found the Evangelical Adventists approving a constitution and electing a slate of officers. Thus they had formed a denomination.[44]

That move horrified many of the *Crisis* Adventists. In the line of Storrs and Marsh, many of them were dead set against any form of organization above the local level, while others were willing to accept minimal organization but were opposed to the choosing or "making" of a name for a church. Still others were not overly concerned with the evils of either organization or choosing a name.[45]

The organization of the Evangelical Adventists, however, forced the *Crisis* Adventists to reexamine the organizational issue. Between June 2 and September 8, the *World's Crisis* ran an eight-part series entitled "Are We a People?" as it grappled with the pros and cons of the topic. Then on October 6, 1858, the *Crisis* published the statement issued by Storrs' New York congregation as a model. To say the least, that model was nondenominational. It was hardly congregational, since its climactic emphasis was that "every man has an inalienable right to private judgment in matters of religion." Such a provision left no room for either doctrinal platforms or church discipline, except in cases of obvious violation of the law of God and the rights of fellow humans.[46]

In the meantime, the two Albany parties continued to drift farther apart. Abrasive leaders such as Miles Grant did much to widen the gap. His antagonism toward the Evangelical Adventists was highlighted in a four-day debate between him and Josiah Litch in November 1858 on the question "Do the Scriptures teach the doctrine of the eternal conscious suffering of the wicked?" Litch, of course, had done his share to antagonize the conditionalists. Over the years he had initiated two periodicals (*The Anti Annihilationist* and *The Pneumatologist*) to uplift the doctrine of the conscious state of the dead.[47]

The debate was soon published in pamphlet form, while charges and countercharges flowed back and forth between the *Herald* and the *Crisis*. All hope of union between the two groups was extinguished.[48]

Gradually, the *Crisis* Adventists drifted toward formalizing church organization. A few weeks after the founding of the Evangelical Adventists, W. S. Campbell (a pro-organization man) told the readers of the *Crisis* that

> it is almost madness—if we expect the continuance of our existence—to leave it all for the Lord to do. To raise and discipline churches, send them ministers, and his people have no responsibility upon them! He has enough to do without that! More properly, he has set us at work, in his vineyard; this seems to be appropriate to us.[49]

Then in July 1860, the leading ministers of the *Crisis* Adventists issued a call for a conference at Providence, Rhode Island, to discuss "a more efficient system of action, whereby the cause of truth may be advanced, and especially those great principles with which we as a people are more particularly identified." "While there has been no unanimity as to a plan of operations," read the call, "we have been perfectly unanimous in having none." Part of the problem they were facing was keeping ministers in the field and supporting them in their work.[50]

The July 25 Providence meeting led to the election of a slate of officers and the formation of The Christian Association. The Association's purpose was to enhance the promulgation of Bible truth and vital piety through (1) the formation of a "Christian Publication Society," (2) "the organization of churches," and (3) "the recognition and support of an efficient gospel ministry."[51]

The Association's first annual meeting was held on October 16 of that same year. That meeting led to establishment of the Christian Publication Society and changing the name of the parent association to the Advent Christian Association. Thus was born the Advent Christian denomination, although the strong antidenominational feelings among many led it to be called an association rather than a church. Needless to say, even though the Advent Christians were now organized, the administrative structure was extremely weak. The most recent historian of the Advent Christians claims that that weakness never was overcome and that it was a contributing factor to the denomination's lack of growth.[52]

Unfortunately, the Advent Christians did not experience peace in their camp for too long. In 1861 the editor of the *World's Crisis* began to advocate the doctrine that the wicked dead would not be resurrected. That view was an extension of the conditionalist teaching that sinners have "life only in Christ." Storrs also got behind that position, even though he had earlier opposed it. Then on August 30, 1863, the believers in this view established their own "quasi-denomination," the Life and Advent Union, with George Storrs as president. Before long, they had their own paper, the *Herald of Life and of the Coming Kingdom*, under the editorship of Storrs, to spread their views. The Life and Advent Union's separate existence was made permanent by an action of the Advent Christians in 1864, stating that Union members were not eligible for membership in the Advent Christian Association.[53]

A fourth sect related to Albany Adventism was the Age to Come Adventists. This group, under the early leadership of Joseph Marsh and his *Advent Harbinger and Bible Advocate* (successor to the *Voice of Truth*), taught that the Jews would return to Israel and that individuals would have a second chance to be saved during the millennium, or the "Age to Come." Such positions were closer to those of the British premillennial literalists than they were to Millerism. In fact, they had been explicitly rejected at the first Millerite general conference in 1840 and repeatedly thereafter.[54]

Storrs, Henry Grew, J. B. Cook, O. R. L. Crosier, and others joined Marsh in these beliefs, even though Storrs found it impossible to work with Marsh. During the 1850s there was a great deal of interaction between the Age to Come believers and those evolving into the Advent Christians. But after the organization of the Advent Christians, the two groups drifted apart, though both held to conditionalism and annihilationism.

Under the influence of such men as Marsh, the Age to Come Adventists found it next to impossible to organize. There were, however, several abortive attempts at organization in the 1850s. One leader toward organization concluded that "you might as well talk of organization with a herd of bisons or the union of a rope of sand." Extreme individualism was at the center of this group. They did not even want organization at the congregational level. Every person was to be his or her supreme authority.[55]

While the Age to Come Adventists experimented with several short-lived but weak organizational schemes in the 1850s, they had no national organization until 1888, when the Church of God in Christ Jesus was organized in Philadelphia. That organization, however, ceased to function the next year. Significant organization did not take place until 1921, when the Church of God of the Abrahamic Faith was organized, with headquarters in Oregon, Illinois.[56]

We will briefly return to an examination of the Albany denominations in the last chapter. But first we need to examine the closing of the careers of Himes and Litch and the rise of the Sabbatarian Adventists.

Josiah Litch, perhaps Millerism's greatest prophetic expositor, joined the Evangelical Adventists at the time of their organization in 1858. Over the years he never lost his interest in prophecy, even though he totally reversed himself on prophetic interpretation.

In 1873, Litch published *A Complete Harmony of Daniel and the Apocalypse*. In that work he rejected one of the foundation stones of Miller's interpretive system: the principle that in prophecy, a day equals one year. Litch also came to take a strong stand for a futurist interpretation of prophecy in place of Millerism's historicist position. Historicism views apocalyptic prophecy as unfolding continuously from the first century down to the second coming, while futurism sees most apocalyptic prophecy being fulfilled immediately before the second advent. As a result, Wellcome warned his readers in 1874 that his one-time colleague had come to the place where he interpreted "nearly all of Revelation, after the fifth chapter," as being of "future fulfillment."[57]

Litch's prophetic revisionism had begun as early as 1848, when he reversed his previous understanding regarding the Jews. He had come to believe that a remnant of the Jews would return to Palestine. Those changes put Litch in harmony with the dispensationalist movement that developed between the Civil War and the end of the century. The dispensationalists were not only futuristic in prophetic interpretation, but they also made the return of the Jews to Palestine a major plank in their entire scheme of end-time events. Thus it is not surprising to find Litch in attendance at one of the most important conferences in the genesis of the American dispensationalist movement. Litch, however, was not the only one of the old advent leaders present. Henry Dana Ward, chairman of the first Millerite general conference, also attended.[58]

Litch also surfaces periodically as an opposer to some of the newer doctrines of the various Adventist branches. Not only did he square off with the conditionalists, but in 1880 he debated D. T. Bourdeau, a Sabbatarian Adventist, over the proper day of worship. From the record it appears that he apparently saw it as a part of his mission to oppose the Sabbatarians from time to time.[59]

Litch made Philadelphia his home base for most of his career. The year 1884 found him as conference president of Messiah's Church of Pennsylvania. He died in Providence, Rhode Island, in 1886.[60]

Himes outlasted all of the foremost Millerite leaders of the early 1840s. After his tour of the British Isles in 1846, he continued to edit the *Advent Herald*. In the early 1850s, however, he got into a power struggle with two Adventist leaders who sought to discredit him. The case finally went to the Supreme Court of Rhode Island in 1852 before his accusers dropped their charges. Ready for a change, in 1855 Himes set out for California to rest, preach the message, and pan (recreationally) for a little gold.[61]

The year 1858 witnessed Himes siding with the Evangelical Adventists and their American Millennial Association. He soon sold the *Advent Herald* to that group. Then in 1860 several major changes transpired in his theology. For one thing, he took a renewed interest in the time question as it related to the second advent, concluding that Christ would return between 1866 and 1868. For three years he published the *Voice of the Prophets* to set forth that view, which he held until the time passed. After that failure, he gave up forever the idea that the date could be known.[62]

More important than Himes' new view on dating was his gradual transition in about 1860 from consciousness in death to conditionalism and annihilationism, a position he had fought against all his life. That, of course, led him to move from the Evangelical Adventists to a closer relationship with the Advent Christians.[63]

That switch eventuated in Himes beginning what proved to be a second career in Adventism in 1863. In that year the Advent Christians formally asked him to move west to publish a paper and encourage development of the work in that area. February 1864 saw the first issue of *The Voice of the West and Second Advent Pioneer* flow from Himes' press in Buchanan, Michigan. In 1870 the *Voice* became the *Advent Christian Times*.[64]

But once again Himes was plagued by the personal animosities of some of his colleagues, this time in the person of the assertive and aggressive Miles Grant, who had sided with Himes' opponents in the Rhode Island trial of 1852. Between 1869 and 1872, Grant obtained letters from three women who charged Himes with immorality. While the aged leader eventually admitted to certain improprieties, the more serious charges appear to be false. But Grant, through sustained effort, was able to force Himes out of his Buchanan publishing work and get him suspended from the ministry. At that point, Himes' son, William Lloyd Garrison Himes, moved the paper to Chicago, where he served as editor until the power struggle also led him to resign a year later.[65]

J. V. Himes, in an effort to defend himself, began to publish the *Himes Journal* in 1874. That defense prompted Grant to secure the publication of *A Statement of Facts Relating to Elder Joshua V. Himes* in January 1875. Grant's brutal and vulgar attack not only did much to destroy Himes' remaining influence in the Advent Christian movement, but it also led to the disciplining of Grant, who in 1876 was removed from the editorship of the *World's Crisis* after twenty years of service.[66]

By 1876 the seventy-year-old Himes was about ready to call it quits with formal Adventism. "I have made my defence," he penned in a public statement,

> and my accusers have not corrected their untruthful statements, nor done me justice. And so I leave them in the hands of God, before whose throne I will soon meet them, where *justice* will be done.
>
> If it be God's will that I should continue to suffer wrong, that my name should be cast out as evil, that my influence should be curtailed in any degree, then it is *my will also*. It shall work for good, God will be glorified, and I trust I shall be saved.
>
> I am an *Adventist*. I have ever been true and faithful to the cause. In all the burdens and reproaches connected with the advocacy of the Advent cause from the beginning, I have stood in the thickest of the fight, and still stand true and faithful. And I can say that I
>
> > "Wish Mount Zion well,
> > Whatever becomes of me."

He went on to note that he had no wish "to divide, or to embarrass the cause."[67]

Three years later Himes returned to the church of his childhood, being ordained in the Episcopal Church in 1879 at the age of seventy-four. For the next sixteen years, he served as the rector of St. Andrews Church in Elk Point, South Dakota.[68]

But he was not quite finished with Adventism. The fiftieth anniversary of the October 1844 disappointment found Himes under the care of Dr. J. H. Kellogg in the Seventh-day Adventists' Battle Creek Sanitarium. He was suffering from cancer on the left side of his face. He appreciated the work of the seventh-day people and contributed liberally to their expanding mission effort. But he was deeply concerned with their interest in building up institutions. "The way you 'build and plant,' " he penned, "looks like [you expect] a long delay [in the coming of Christ], if present plans are carried out." He repeatedly pointed to what he believed to be duplicity in a people who claimed they were expecting the advent but were "heaping up riches."[69]

Ellen White, a Seventh-day Adventist leader who had met Himes at the Battle Creek Sanitarium in the 1870s and with whom he had developed a correspondence in the 1890s, thanked him for his interest and generosity toward the Sabbatarian cause. "The spirited participation evidenced by your donation for this field [Australia]," she penned in early 1895,

> has rejoiced my heart; for it testifies that you have not lost the missionary spirit which prompted you first to give your-self to the work and then to give your means to the Lord to proclaim the first and second angels' messages in their time and order to the world. This is a great gratification for me; for it bears honorable testimony that your heart is still in the work; I see the proof of your love to the Lord Jesus Christ in your freewill offering for this "region beyond."[70]

The old man had spirit, but Kellogg had pronounced his cancer incurable. "If so," opined Himes, "I must yield, after all my efforts for help, to the inevitable!—I may live a year or more, but it will be great suffering. And so, *my last years will be very bad— but the morning will soon break and sickness, disease and death will pass away forever."*[71]

Himes died on July 27, 1895, in his ninety-first year. He is buried in Mount Pleasant Cemetery in Sioux Falls, South Dakota. That cemetery was chosen because it has a hill, and Himes had told his bishop that " 'he wanted to be on top of a hill when Gabriel blows his trumpet.' "[72]

Chapter 14

THE SABBATARIAN DISENTANGLEMENT

Modern Seventh-day Adventists prefer to ignore it, but their movement began in the midst of a segment of Adventism up to its armpits in fanaticism by early 1845.

Born in Confusion

Unfortunately, the early leaders of what was to become Sabbatarian Adventism had little choice about the quality of their companions, because, as we noted above, post-October 1844 Millerism had split over the shut-door issue. In early 1845 there were only two basic types of Adventists: the shut-door Adventists and the open-door Adventists. The first accepted October 22 as a fulfillment of prophecy; the second rejected that position and eventually came to see the seventh-month movement as a mistake.

Those Adventists who later became the originators of Sabbatarian Adventism held that they could hardly accept fellowship with the open-door/Albany Adventists since, in their rejection of the seventh-month movement, they had denied the very principles that had undergirded Miller's interpretation of prophecy. To take the open-door position was to say, in effect, that the 1844 experience was error or delusion. That conclusion was totally unacceptable to the Sabbatarian originators. Thus they were left in the company of the Spiritualizers and their fanatical outgrowths.

As a result, we find Ellen Harmon's first writings being published in the *Day-Star* at the very time that Jacobs was using the journal to steer many Adventists toward Shakerism. James White was utilizing the pages of the *Day-Star* for his letters at the same time. Meanwhile, Joseph Bates was corresponding through the pages of S. S. Snow's *Jubilee Standard* and Joseph Marsh's *Voice of Truth*. Beyond that, even a casual reading of Ellen (Harmon) White's earliest writings repeatedly indicates that both her and her husband's work took place in the midst of fanatical elements as they struggled to bring some rational order out of the chaotic situation of shut-door Adventism between 1845 through 1849. Thus it should not come as a total shock to find the public press noting that one of her early visions took place in the midst of the Israel Dammon fanaticism.[1]

Nor were the Whites and Bates the only future Sabbatarians closely related to shut-door fanaticism. But whereas they were combating it, other future Sabbatarians were actually a part of that fanaticism. For example, both Uriah Smith and J. N. Andrews married into a Paris, Maine, family deeply involved in erratic behavior. Nor was Andrews' paternal family exempt from the problem. Ron Graybill put it succinctly when he noted that Andrews' "father was a no-work fanatic" and "his future father-in-law . . . a crawler!" James and Ellen White had to confront the fanaticism in those families more than once in their struggle to bring some sort of order into their sector of Adventism. Given J. N. Andrews' background, it is little wonder that he would later declare, "I would exchange a thousand errors for one truth." He had seen plenty of fanatical error at close range.[2]

Although the individuals who would later become leaders among Sabbatarian Adventism (i.e., Joseph Bates and James and Ellen White) found themselves in the midst of the Spiritualizers with their fanatical excesses, they were almost as much out of harmony with some of their basic beliefs as they were with the ideas of the Albany Adventists. For example, Bates claimed that the Spiritualizers' interpretation of Scripture was as deceptive as sailing into Boston Harbor at night during a severe storm that could put both ship and passengers on the rocks without warning. "Good God!" he exclaimed, "help us to steer clear of these spiritual interpretations of Thy word, where it is made so clear that the second coming and kingdom of Christ will be as literal and real, as the events that transpired at the first Advent, now recorded in history." What was probably his first book, *The Opening Heavens*, was published against the Spiritualizers' use of Scripture, the very use of Scripture that had set them up for their wild ideas.[3]

Thus there was an element among the shut-door Adventists that argued for a rational and literal interpretation of the Bible. But that minority group, because of its shut-door views, was rejected by the Albany Adventists. At the same time, it was essentially out of harmony with the Spiritualizers. But it took time to discover that disharmony in the disorientation of late 1844 and early 1845.

The future Sabbatarians faced a different situation than the Albany Adventists in seeking to define themselves in relation to the Spiritualizers. The Albany group had merely to react against those Adventists with whom it was in basic theological disharmony. By way of contrast, the future Sabbatarians were in basic harmony with the Spiritualizers on the seventh-month movement and the shut door.

Thus the Sabbatarians and the open-door Adventists had quite different tasks of self-definition. The open-door Adventists had merely *to define themselves over against the Spiritualizers*, while the future Sabbatarians *had to extract themselves from the midst of the fanatical element*. The open-door Adventists, in essence, accomplished their separation task at Albany, but the Sabbatarians would struggle at self-definition for the rest of the decade. Their task was not nearly so simple.

The task of the Albany group was also simplified by the fact that it had well-defined leaders, established periodicals to publicize its message, and a system of periodic conferences to give shape and direction to its movement. The future Sabbatarians had none of those advantages. Outside of rather nebulous views that *something* had happened on October 22, 1844, and that Christ's coming would be literal and visible, they had no doctrinal platform. Nor did they have any leaders, conference system, or periodicals. The only thing that can be said is that there were some like-minded believers who were independently groping for direction in the semidarkness of post-disappointment Adventism.

Three things would have to take place before the Sabbatarians would even have discrete visibility: (1) the rise of leaders, (2) the evolution of doctrines that explained the Millerite experience and clarified wrong notions, and (3) the development of periodicals and organizational strategies that could spread those clarified doctrines. It is to those topics that we now turn.

New Personalities

The only one of the founders of Sabbatarian Adventism who had had any prominence in the Millerite movement was Joseph Bates. Bates, the senior member of the founders, had been born in 1792. Going to sea at an early age, he spent the years of the War of 1812 as a British prisoner of war. The 1820s found him as master of his own sailing ship. During that decade, he became interested in the many personal and social reforms of the day and joined the Christian Connexion. Retiring with a comfortable purse in the late 1820s, he devoted the next decade to working in various reform movements.[4]

Bates accepted Miller's teachings in 1839. That new interest subsequently swallowed up his energies, even though he remained a reformer at heart. Like other Adventists, he saw the second advent as the ultimate reform that would solve all the world's ills. Having known Himes from his youth, Bates had worked with Himes in the various reforms. Now they teamed up as Adventists.[5]

Bates was one of sixteen persons who issued the call for the first Millerite general conference, and he served with Himes, Litch, and two others on the conference's "committee of arrangements." He also served as one of the assistant chairs of the second general conference.[6]

Perhaps his most important "official" function in the Millerite movement was the chairmanship of the pivotal May 1842 general conference in Boston. That conference was the first that came out solidly for 1843 as the year of the end of the world. In addition, it was decided at that conference to hold camp meetings and to adopt the influential 1843 prophetic chart. Bates, as noted earlier, was also one of those who attempted to preach the message in the American South.[7]

Isaac Wellcome, his onetime colleague, notes that Bates was "an able speaker and writer, who was very useful in the work of Christ until he became a Seventh Day Sabbath advocate."[8] Those talents, however, were not lost in the Sabbatarian movement. Through a stream of pamphlets beginning in 1846, Bates became the Sabbatarian's first publicist and theologian. He was also instrumental in bringing the other two Sabbatarian founders into an understanding of the central doctrines that were basic to the formulation of Sabbatarian Adventism. In fact, it was Bates who united the various doctrines of the new movement with each other and with Miller's prophetic scheme. Beyond that, he extended that prophetic scheme as he integrated the new doctrines into it.

A young Millerite preacher by the name of James White would eventually join Bates in organizing the Sabbatarian believers. Born in 1821, White became a member of the Christian Connexion at age fifteen. Up until 1842 he regarded Millerism to be "wild fanaticism" and wanted no part of it. But that all changed at a camp meeting in eastern Maine, where he heard the preaching of Miller, Himes, and T. M. Preble. At the conclusion of the meetings, writes White, "I found myself happy in the faith that Christ would come about the year 1843."[9]

White's convictions, however, brought tension into his life. Up to the time of his conversion to Millerism, he reports, he had "worshipped" education. But now he was under strong conviction that he should renounce his worldly plans and give himself "to the work of warning the people to prepare for the day of God." He prayed for release but could not find it. As a result, he begrudgingly surrendered to what he believed to be God's will.[10]

White's theological education took place through a study of

Fitch's 1843 Chart, the Bible, and a few second-advent books. He studied diligently for a few weeks, gaining a "clearer view of the subject." After using his previous summer's earnings to purchase clothes, the chart, and the books noted above, he borrowed a horse from his father and was given "a saddle with both pads torn off, and several pieces of an old bridle." Thus he was ready to hit the evangelistic trail.[11]

White's meetings were a success from the beginning, as people gave their lives to God and came under the conviction that Christ was coming soon. During the winter of 1842/1843, he reports that more than one thousand people were converted through his ministry. That April he was ordained into the ministry of the Christian Connexion.[12]

Young White was dedicated, quick witted, a preacher of conviction, and an evangelist of boundless energy. While those talents were evident in the exciting months of 1843 and 1844, other gifts would come to the surface between October 1844 and 1850. Foremost among those gifts were ones related to writing, editing, and the ability to formulate a connected line of thought to explain his advent experience. Thus White would build up, extend, and clarify the theological system that Bates had set forth. But beyond those talents were White's abilities to organize and publish. By the end of the decade, he had succeeded Bates as the publisher for the Sabbatarian Adventists. The 1850s would see him lead out in their organizational development.

The third member of the trio who developed and organized the Sabbatarian Adventist movement was Ellen G. Harmon (White after August 30, 1846). Born in 1827, she was too young to do much in the 1844 movement, except testify to her friends and fellow church members.[13]

She and her family were converted to Millerism in early 1840, when they heard Miller preach in Portland, Maine. Two years later she was accepted into the Methodist Episcopal Church through baptism by immersion, even though many of her Methodist friends had tried to convince her that sprinkling was Bible baptism. But she followed her convictions. Thus from an early age, Ellen Harmon was willing to take unpopular public stands on what she believed to be Bible truth.[14]

That same characteristic can be seen in her rejection of the immortality of the soul in 1843. Before then, she had been deeply troubled by the thought of endless punishment in hell by a God who evidently "delighted in the torture of His creatures, who were formed in His image." Up to that time, she had also had difficulty reconciling the immediate reward of individuals upon their death with the need for their bodily resurrection. After all, "if at death the soul entered upon eternal happiness or misery, where was the need of a resurrection of the poor moldering body?"[15]

The willingness to take unpopular stands for what she believed to be Bible truth is also evidenced in relation to Ellen Harmon's second-advent belief. The Harmon family was caught in the general purge of Millerites from the Methodist Church in Maine that we discussed in chapter 7. Like many Millerites, the Harmon family were busy testifying about their belief to their local church. Their minister visited them in the hope of convincing them either to put their ideas aside or to quietly withdraw from the church and thus avoid a public trial. But Ellen's father answered that they preferred such a trial so that the issue could be brought into the open. In the fall of 1843, the Harmon family was disfellowshiped from the Methodist Church for advocacy of Millerite views.[16]

With great anticipation Ellen Harmon waited with her fellow believers for Christ to come in 1844. She would later declare that 1844 "was the happiest year of my life." The second advent had become the center of her existence.[17]

Like her fellow believers, however, she went through a period of disorientation after October 1844. In fact, by December she had concluded that the seventh-month movement and the midnight cry of the autumn of 1844 had been errors. She had given up the idea of a fulfillment of prophecy on October 22, 1844, and the accompanying shut-door belief. Her future husband had apparently come to the same conclusion.[18]

In the light of that conviction, what she claims to be her first vision takes on special significance. She notes that God showed her in December 1844 that God's "dear saints" still had "many trials to pass through." In Ellen's report of the vision, she noted that she had the sensation of "rising higher and higher, far above the dark world." She soon saw the advent people on a

> strait and narrow path, cast high up above the world. On this path the Advent people were traveling to the City. . . . They had a *bright light set up behind them at the first end of the path, which an angel told me was the Midnight Cry.* This light shone all along the path and gave light for their feet so they might not stumble. And if they kept their eyes fixed on *Jesus*, who was just before them, *leading them to the City*, they were safe. But soon some grew weary, and said the City was a great way off, and they expected to have entered it before. . . . *Others rashly denied the light behind them, and said that it was not God that had led them* out so far. *The light behind them went out which left their feet in perfect darkness, and they stumbled and got their eyes off the mark and lost sight of Jesus, and fell off the path down in[to] the dark and wicked world below.*

She went on to describe the experiences of those who remained faithful to God.[19]

That visionary experience was to change Ellen Harmon's life. Not only did she see herself as having the prophetic gift after that experience, but it also directed her back to the seventh-month movement as a fulfillment of prophecy. From that point to her death in 1915, she saw the October 22 date as a "bright light" to guide God's end-time people. Far from being a mistake or a delusion, the seventh-month movement with its October 22 fulfillment of prophecy became an anchor point in the advent experience. Those who rejected that anchor point, she held, were left in "perfect darkness" and "stumbled and fell." In that sentiment she seemed to be giving what she saw as the fruitless long-term future of the open-door (eventually Albany) Adventists. From her perspective in December 1844, she held that those forms of Adventism that cut loose from their prophetic roots would eventually come to nothing.

Even more important, as far as Sabbatarian Adventism was concerned, Ellen's December vision brought her and others (including possibly her future husband) back to a firm faith in the October 22 date as a fulfillment of prophecy. That conviction would provide a starting point for the development of Sabbatarian theology.

Before we turn to the development of that theology, however, it is important to note how unpopular it was to claim to have the gift of prophecy among Adventists in early 1845. From a reading of contemporary literature, it becomes evident that the advent believers had many claiming the prophetic gift in that period. There were probably scores of such individuals, with most of them being absurd in their fanatical ideas and predictions. In the wake of Starkweather, Gorgas, the Springwater Valley commune, the several Portland prophets, and many others, it was a risky time to claim the prophetic gift, unless you desired to be defined as an absolute fanatic. Most believers placed young Ellen Harmon into that category. To Wellcome, who knew her and James White, she was "a wonderful fanatic and trance medium." Of course, it did not help the cause of prophets and so-called prophets that the Mormon prophet, Joseph Smith, had been murdered by a mob in the Carthage, Illinois, jail in June 1844.[20]

Not only had the Millerites taken a strong stand against "visions, dreams, or private revelations" at the May 1843 general conference, but they would also reaffirm that position at their New York meeting in May 1845.[21] Thus Ellen Harmon, like the Sabbatarian movement of which she would be a part, would have to struggle as she sought to distance herself from both the real and purported excesses of the shut-door Adventists. Beyond that, both she and her fellow Sabbatarians would have to live in the context of the doubt, accusations, and animosity of the Albany Adventists.

Only a firm conviction that they were right in their understanding of prophecy and Scripture would carry the developing Sabbatarians through a difficult period.

New Doctrines: The Answer to Confusion

Since the central prophetic belief among the developing Sabbatarians was that Daniel 8:14 ("Unto two thousand and three hundred days; then shall the sanctuary be cleansed.") had been fulfilled on October 22, their main task would be to put forth alternate interpretations of the meaning of the sanctuary in that text and the significance of its cleansing. In other words, since they were convinced that they were correct in their understanding of the 2300 days, their next task would be to unlock the meaning of the text's two other symbols.

It will be recalled that Miller had interpreted the sanctuary to be the earth and the cleansing to be the purifying of the earth by fire at the second advent—an event that had obviously failed to transpire on October 22, 1844. Doubts as to Miller's interpretation had been expressed by Litch after the spring disappointment. "It has not been proved," he penned in April 1844, "that the cleansing of the sanctuary, which was to take place at the end of the 2300 days, was the coming of Christ or the purification of the earth." Again he noted, as he wrestled with the meaning of the recent disappointment, that they were most likely to be "in error relative to the event which marked its close."[22]

That line of thought rose again soon after the October disappointment. Thus Joseph Marsh could write in early November:

> We cheerfully admit that we have been mistaken in the *nature* of the event we expected would occur on the tenth of the seventh month; but we cannot yet admit that our great High Priest did not *on that very day*, accomplish *all* that the type would justify us to expect.[23]

Apollos Hale and Joseph Turner followed Marsh's reasoning in their controversial January 1845 article on the shut door. They equated the October coming with the coming of Christ to the Ancient of Days (God) in the judgment scene of Daniel 7. Hale and Turner concluded that "the coming of the bridegroom" indicated "some change of work or office, on the part of our Lord, in the invisible world." Christ would return to earth to gather His elect *after* His work "within the veil . . . where he has gone to pre-pare a place for us" was completed. As a result, "some time must elapse" between the coming of the Bridegroom to the Ancient of Days and the coming in glory. Hale and Turner went on to in-dicate that *"the judgment is here."*[24]

The fullest exposition of the line of thought suggested by Litch, Marsh, Hale, and Turner was developed by some hereto-fore minor actors in the advent drama. On October 23, 1844, Hiram Edson, a Methodist farmer of Port Gibson, New York, be-came convicted during a season of prayer with fellow believers "that light should be given" and "our disappointment be ex-plained."

Soon thereafter, he and a companion (probably O. R. L. Cro-sier) set out to encourage their fellow believers. As they crossed a field, Edson reported, "I was stopped about midway," and

heaven seemed open to my view. . . . I saw distinctly, and clearly, that instead of our High Priest coming out [the common expectation of many Millerites] of the Most Holy of the heavenly sanctuary to come to this earth on the tenth day of the seventh month, at the end of the 2300 days, that he for the first time entered on that day the second apartment of that sanctuary; and that he had a work to perform in the Most Holy before coming to this earth.

Soon the call of his companion, who had passed far beyond him, brought Edson back to the realities of the field. To a query as to what was wrong, Edson replied that " 'the Lord was answering our morning prayer; by giving light with regard to our disappoint-ment.' "

Edson's "vision" soon led him into extended Bible study with Crosier and Dr. F. B. Hahn. Following Miller's concordance approach to unlocking the meaning of Scripture, they concluded, in line with Edson's October 23 experience, that the sanctuary to be cleansed in Daniel 8:14 was not the earth or the church, but the sanctuary in heaven, of which the earthly sanctuary had been a type or copy.

Hahn and Edson decided that their discoveries were "just what the scattered remnant needed" to explain the disappointment and "set the brethren on the right track." As a result, they agreed to share the expense of publication between them if Crosier would " 'write out the subject of the sanctuary.' " According to Edson, Crosier began to publish the findings of their combined study in early 1845 in the *Day Dawn*.[25]

Then, on February 7, 1846, their findings were published by Enoch Jacobs in the *Day-Star* Extra under the title "The Law of Moses." By that time their position had fairly well matured. Through Bible study, Crosier and his colleagues had provided answers to the questions of What happened on October 22, 1844? and What was the sanctuary that needed to be cleansed?

Their most important conclusions, as published in "The Law of Moses," can be summarized as follows: (1) A literal sanctuary exists in heaven. (2) The Hebrew sanctuary system was a complete visual representation of the plan of salvation that was *patterned after the heavenly sanctuary*. (3) Just as the earthly priests had a two-phase ministry in the wilderness sanctuary, so Christ has a two-phase ministry in the heavenly. The first phase began in the Holy Place at His ascension; the second began on October 22, 1844, when Christ moved from the first apartment of the heavenly sanctuary to the second. Thus the antitypical or heavenly day of atonement began on that date. (4) The first phase of Christ's ministry dealt with forgiveness; the second deals with the blotting out of sins and the cleansing of both the sanctuary and individual believers. (5) The cleansing of Daniel 8:14 was a cleansing from sin and was therefore accomplished by blood rather than fire. (6) Christ would not return to earth until His second-apartment ministry was completed.[26]

Thus the combined study of Edson, Crosier, and Hahn confirmed Edson's October 23 "vision." By intensive study of such books as Hebrews and Leviticus, in connection with Daniel 7 through 9 and the book of Revelation, they had come to an explanation of both the cleansing and the sanctuary that needed to be cleansed. The new understanding of the cleansing of the sanctuary became a primary building block in the development of Sabbatarian Adventist theology.

Before moving away from the cleansing of the sanctuary, it should be noted that this teaching was soon linked to the teaching of the investigative or preadvent judgment.

Miller, of course, had tied the judgment scene of Daniel 7, the cleansing of the sanctuary of Daniel 8:14, and "the hour of his judgment is come" of Revelation 14:7 to the judgment to take place at the second advent.

However, as early as 1841, Litch had taught the necessity of a preadvent judgment. In February of that year, Litch indicated that the judgment must take place *before* the resurrection. By 1842 Litch had refined his view and pointed out that the divine act of raising some persons to life and others to death at the second coming constitutes an "executive judgment" that must of necessity be preceded by a trial judgment.[27]

That theme would later be developed by the Sabbatarians. Crosier, while not making the preadvent judgment explicit in his February 1846 article, pointed out that the high priest did wear the breastplate of judgment on the Day of Atonement and that the cleansing of the sanctuary was a cleansing from sin.

It was only a short step beyond that position for Bates, in 1847, to equate the heavenly Day of Atonement with a preadvent judgment that must, of necessity, be completed before Christ could return to execute the advent judgment, at which all would receive their just rewards. Although resisted by some (including James White) at first, that teaching became firmly entrenched by the mid-1850s.[28]

Thus in the developing Sabbatarian Adventist theology, the cleansing of the sanctuary of Daniel 8:14 came to be seen as Christ's act of investigative or preadvent judgment in the Most Holy Place of the heavenly sanctuary. As a result, when the Sabbatarians preached the first angel's message of Revelation 14 ("the hour of his judgment is come" [v. 7]), they eventually came to see this as an announcement of the beginning of the preadvent judgment on October 22, 1844.[29]

In conclusion, while the majority of the Millerite Adventists, under the leadership of Himes, looked back on the time element in their interpretation of the 2300-day prophecy of Daniel 8:14 as an error, Sabbatarians held that the Millerites had been correct on the time but wrong as to the event to take place on October 22, 1844. After all, they noted, no one had been able to refute Miller's time calculations. But further study had made it obvious to them that the Millerites had misinterpreted the symbolism of both the "cleansing" and the "sanctuary."

The Sabbatarians chose to build upon the leads of Miller and Snow in their 1844 experience rather than to abandon it. Their new sanctuary doctrine not only explained their disappointment, but it also provided a theological framework that enabled the Sabbatarians to press into the future with certainty. As they saw it, they were convinced that God had led them in the past, and that gave them confidence that He was with them in the present. That conviction eventually became the mainspring of their evangelistic and missionary thrust as they came to believe that they had a worldwide mission.[30]

The doctrine of the heavenly sanctuary was not an expendable item in Sabbatarian theology. Rather, it stood at its center. Thus James White could declare that a correct understanding "of the cleansing of the sanctuary . . . is the key to the great Advent movement, making all plain. Without it the movement is inexplicable." For White it was "the great center" that defined their present position and oriented their theology.[31]

The early Sabbatarians did not see the sanctuary and second-advent doctrines as being two separate entities. Rather, they saw them in one scheme, with the events surrounding the sanctuary explaining the sequence of events leading up to the second advent.

A third building block in their theological understanding developed concurrently with an understanding of the sanctuary. That third element was the doctrine of the sanctity of the seventh-day Sabbath, from which they eventually derived their Sabbatarian identity.

An interest in the seventh-day Sabbath among Adventists had originated before the October disappointment. It was first called to their attention in early 1841 by J. A. Begg, a student of prophecy in Scotland. But the real push for the Sabbath came from the Seventh Day Baptists. The first known attempt of that group to influence the Millerites took place in early 1842, but the *Signs of the Times* refused to publish the material.[32]

However, a felt need to spread the message of the Sabbath was building among the Seventh Day Baptists. In 1843 their general conference determined to take a more aggressive approach toward spreading their view of the Sabbath. Thus it was resolved that it was their "solemn duty" to enlighten their fellow citizens on the topic. The 1843 conference also took steps to put that resolution into practice. Their efforts had some positive results. At their 1844 meeting, the Seventh Day Baptists thanked God that "a deeper and wider-spread interest upon the subject has sprung up than has ever before been known in our country."[33]

Part of that interest had developed among the Millerites. While the extent of the interest is impossible to determine, we do know that a Seventh Day Baptist by the name of Rachel Oakes became interested in the second advent. By 1844 she had not only accepted the advent near, but she had also shared her Sabbath perspective with the Adventist congregation in Washington, New Hampshire. Several Millerite preachers learned of and accepted the Sabbath in connection with that congregation. One was T. M. Preble.[34]

By September 1844 the amount of agitation over the seventh day had become extensive enough for the *Midnight Cry* to publish an extensive two-part editorial on the topic. "Many persons," noted the *Cry*, "have their minds deeply exercised respecting a supposed obligation to observe the *seventh day*."[35]

The editorials concluded that the first day of the week was not the biblical Sabbath. They also noted that Christians were not under obligation to observe any special holy time. However, if there would have been such an obligation, "then we think *the seventh day* is the *only day* for the observance of which there is any LAW."[36]

Those pre-disappointment seventh-day Sabbath seeds would produce more fruit in early 1845. On February 28, Preble set forth his beliefs on the Sabbath in the *Hope of Israel*. Later that year he republished his views in a twelve-page pamphlet not so subtly entitled *Tract, Showing that the Seventh Day Should Be Observed as the Sabbath, Instead of the First Day; "According to the Commandment."*[37]

In March of 1845, Preble's writings fell into the hands of Joseph Bates. Bates accepted the Sabbath and soon shared it in a meeting with Crosier, Hahn, and Edson. Edson and Crosier accepted the biblical Sabbath, and Hahn was at least favorable toward it. Meanwhile, they shared their insights on the heavenly sanctuary with Bates, which he readily accepted as being founded on solid Bible study. Thus by late 1845 or early 1846, a small group of believers began to form around the united doctrines of the ministry of Christ in the heavenly sanctuary and the binding nature of the seventh-day Sabbath.[38]

Bates soon published a tract entitled *The Seventh Day Sabbath, a Perpetual Sign* in August 1846. Bates was also instrumental in introducing James White and Ellen Harmon to the seventh-day Sabbath. They began to observe the seventh day that autumn. Thus the three founders of Sabbatarian Adventism were united on the Sabbath doctrine by the end of 1846.[39]

Bates gave the seventh-day Sabbath doctrine a richness and prophetic meaning that it never could have had among the Seventh Day Baptists. For the Baptists, the seventh day was merely the correct day. But with Bates, steeped as he was in a prophetic faith informed by extensive study of the books of Daniel and the Revelation, the seventh-day Sabbath took on an eschatological richness that was beyond the realm of the Baptists' theological perspective.

Through a series of small books, Bates interpreted the Sabbath within the framework of Revelation 11 to 14. Between 1846 and

1849, Bates made at least three contributions to a prophetic under-standing of the Sabbath.

First, he began to see connections between the Sabbath and the sanctuary. As he studied the sounding of the seventh trumpet in Revelation 11:15-19 (a passage obviously having to do with the last days), Bates was particularly drawn to verse 19: "And the temple of God was opened in heaven, and there was seen in his temple the ark of his testament."

Bates noted that recently there had been an upsurge of writing on the seventh-day Sabbath. Why? When the seventh angel began to sound, he proposed, the second apartment of the temple of God was opened in heaven, the ark of the covenant was spiritually revealed, and people began to search the Scriptures. The ark of the covenant in the earthly sanctuary, of course, contained the Ten Commandments. Thus, through typological comparison, it was concluded that the Most Holy Place of the heavenly sanctuary had an ark containing the Decalogue, as did the earthly sanctuary. God's law, of course, eventually came to be seen as the basis for the preadvent judgment that had been underway since October 22, 1844. On that date the second apartment had been opened in heaven, exposing the ark of the covenant and pointing to a renewed emphasis on God's law and its neglected Sabbath com-mand.[40]

Bates' second contribution to the developing understanding of the Sabbath in prophetic history came through his study of the three angels' messages of Revelation 14. He presented these messages as sequential. The first two[41] (the hour of God's judg-ment and the fall of Babylon), he said, were preached by the Millerites. But he held that verse 12, "Here is the patience of the saints, here are they that *keep the commandments of God*," began to be fulfilled after October 22, 1844. Thus, he penned in 1847, a people "have been uniting in companies for the last two years, on the commandments of God."

Bates, of course, did not lose the prophetic forcefulness of Revelation 12:17: "And the dragon was wroth with the woman, and went to make war with the remnant of her seed, which keep

[all] the commandments of God."[42]

That "war," he held, was described in Revelation 13 as the beast powers sought to overcome God's commandment-keeping people, finally issuing the death decree of verse 15. Thus Bates' third contribution to Sabbath theology (in the framework of prophecy) was to develop the concepts of the seal of God and the mark of the beast in the context of allegiance to God or the beast. Faithfulness to the biblical Sabbath would be the outward focal point in the struggle.[43]

The seventh-day Sabbath became an interconnected part of Sabbatarian theology. Because of their conviction of its centrality in end-time events, Bates and the Whites held fast to their seventh-day teaching. By way of contrast, those Adventist preachers (such as J. B. Cook, J. D. Pickands, and T. M. Preble) who saw the Sabbath merely as the correct day gave it up within a few years. Preble later turned against the seventh-day teaching and wrote a book entitled *The First-Day Sabbath: Clearly Proved by Showing that the Old Covenant, or Ten Commandments, Have Been Changed, or Made Complete, in the Christian Dispensation.* Preble's brother-in-law doubted his sincerity in the change back to Sunday. According to him, Preble became the administrator of a large estate, and when the Sabbath interfered with his business, he gave it up. "The no law theory was his after excuse in the matter."[44]

Such disaffections, however, did not hinder those who had united the seventh-day doctrine to the sanctuary and the second advent. They preached their theology with increasing vigor and cohesion throughout the late 1840s. Bates even managed to preach it to Miller's widow in January 1853. "Sister M.," he penned, "welcomed us, and listened attentively to our explanation of the last message from the [Sabbatarian Adventist] Chart: said she did not know but the Sabbath which we taught was right."[45]

By early 1847 the Sabbatarian leaders had developed a cohesive theological package, which they would enrich and flesh out during the following months. It was an eschatological theology focusing on a firm belief in the premillennial ministry of Jesus in the Most Holy Place of the heavenly sanctuary between October 22, 1844, and the second coming, and the seventh-day Sabbath as a point of conflict in the last great struggle between the forces of good and evil foreshadowed in Revelation 11 to 14.

Coupled with those doctrines were beliefs in conditionalism, annihilationism, and adult baptism by immersion, which the Sabbatarian founders had also accepted. In addition to those beliefs was an acceptance of the continuing validity of the gift of prophecy, with progressively more of the believers seeing Ellen White's ministry as a modern manifestation of that gift.

A final point of Sabbatarian theology that should be noted is their integration of their shut-door belief into their overall theological package. As noted in chapter 12, the shut door as the close of human probation had been tied by Miller and others to the idea that the cleansing of the sanctuary was the second advent of Christ. Because of that equation, probation would obviously be over at the end of the 2300 days.

The Sabbatarians had accepted that equation, and all of their leaders taught the shut-door position in the late 1840s. However, Bible study, as noted earlier, soon led the Sabbatarians to conclude that the cleansing of the sanctuary was not the second advent, but had to do with Christ's ministry in the heavenly temple.

At that point they were holding a theology that no longer fit together. They had changed their interpretations of the cleansing and the sanctuary but had not reinterpreted the shut door. A change in one belief, however, demanded a change in the other. That point was not immediately obvious to the Sabbatarians.

It would be the early 1850s before they had worked out a harmonized position on the topic. But they *gradually* came to see the shut door in the framework of shutting the door of the Holy Place of the heavenly sanctuary, when the first phase of Christ's ministry had been completed in 1844, and the opening of the door to the second phase of His heavenly ministry that same year.[46]

The new understanding of the shut and open doors also included the opening up of a new divine imperative to preach the Sabbath and the third angel's message of Revelation 14 "to every nation, and kindred, and tongue, and people." That imperative would eventually propel the Sabbatarian Adventists to the far corners of the earth as they sought to complete Miller's mission in preparing people for Christ's return.[47]

Meanwhile, the shut-door misconception had served a utilitarian purpose. It provided the Sabbatarians with time to solidify their theological foundation. Thus little of their scarce resources was spent on evangelism until they had a message. After sorting out their own theological identity, their next step was to try to convince other Millerites of their doctrinal package and prophetic interpretation. That task took place between 1848 and 1850. Larger concepts of mission awaited the early 1850s and beyond.[48]

The Third Angel

The core of Revelation 14 is the messages of the three angels that are to be given immediately before the harvest of the earth. The first angel proclaims that the hour of God's judgment has arrived (vs. 6, 7), the second preaches the fall of Babylon (v. 8), and the third contrasts those who have the mark of the beast with those who have "the patience of the saints," "keep the commandments of God," and have "the faith of Jesus" (vs. 9-12). Then follows the second-coming harvest (vs. 14-20).

Those three messages would become a unifying chronological theme for the Sabbatarian Adventist leaders, indicating to them their place in prophetic history. The early Sabbatarians tied their key sanctuary and Sabbath doctrines to the three angels' messages. In particular, they came to see their special mission as being that of the third angel.

The idea of identifying the angels of Revelation 14 with Adventism was not new, but that identification had not played a large role in other forms of Adventism. The Sabbatarians, however, would carefully integrate previous views with Adventist history, extend those views, and eventually develop them into one of the unifying matrices of their theology.

Even though Litch had identified the Millerite preaching with the judgment-hour message of the first angel, and though Miller and others had pointed out the sequential nature of the three end-time messages, they had not tied the three messages to the development of Adventism in a point-by-point correlation. Perhaps that was due in part to Miller's outright rejection of the fall of Babylon as taught by Fitch and the ambivalence of other leading Millerites on that teaching.[49]

Fitch, of course, had preached Babylon's fall primarily from Revelation 18. The Millerites, in general, never emphasized the fall in Revelation 14, nor did they emphasize a sequential linkage between the preaching of the judgment-hour message of the first angel with the fall of Babylon presented by the second. Those connections were left for the Sabbatarians to make.

Bates writes that while he had believed that the Millerites had been preaching the first angel's message before the disappointment, it was not until "*after* the passing of the time, [that] our eyes were opened to the fact that two other messages followed, before the coming of Christ." In a similar vein, in early 1847, James White expounded upon the three messages as a "chain of events" that match the progression of Adventist history.[50]

In early 1850, White published a helpful exposition on the three angels that made a point-by-point correlation of the three messages with the development of Adventism. He began with Miller and took his argument up through what he saw as the end-time role of Sabbatarian Adventism in the flow of prophetic history. His overall goal was to win over other Adventists to the view that Sabbatarianism was the only genuine continuation of original Adventism.

White equated the first angel's message with the Millerite preaching of the second advent. For him the time element in "the *hour* of his judgment is come" was crucial. "The whole advent host," he penned, "once believed" that something special would happen about 1843. "The unbelief of those who doubt now," he continued, "does not prove that we were all mistaken then. The passing of the time, and the perpetual backsliding and unbelief of Adventists has not changed this truth of God into a lie; but it remains truth still."[51]

The second angel, White emphasized, *"followed"* the first angel. When, in reaction to the preaching of the soon return of Christ, the churches began to shut their doors to the Millerites and to disfellowship them, then—under the leadership of Charles Fitch—the second angel sounded with the message of " 'Babylon is fallen. . . . Come out of her my people.' "[52]

"This prophecy," White penned,

> was exactly fulfilled, and in the right time, and place. . . . We heard it with our ears, our voices proclaimed it, and our whole being felt its power, and with our eyes we saw its effect, as the oppressed people of God burst the bands that bound them [t]o the various sects, and made their escape from Babylon. . . .
>
> The second angel's message called us out from the fallen churches where we are now free to think, and act for ourselves in the fear of God. It is an exceedingly interesting fact, that the Sabbath question began to be agitated among second advent believers immediately after they were called out of the churches by the second angel's message. *God's work moves in order. The Sabbath truth came up in just the right time to fulfil prophecy.*[53]

White saw the message of the third angel as the climax to this prophetic sequence. It would be God's last message of mercy to the world, just prior to the great harvest of souls at the second advent (see Revelation 14:15-20).

He pointed out that in Revelation 13 and 14 and in the message of the third angel, there are but two classes of people. One persecutes the saints and receives the mark of the beast; the other continues to be patient in waiting for Christ to return (in spite of the October 22, 1844, disappointment) and is "KEEPING THE COMMANDMENTS OF GOD." Thus the importance of preaching God's Sabbath.

"Never," wrote James as he moved toward his presentation's emotional climax, did I have such feelings while holding my pen as now.—And never did I see and feel the importance of the Sabbath as I do this moment. Surely the Sabbath truth, like the rising sun ascending from the east, has increased in light, in power and in importance until it is the great sealing truth. . . .

. . . Many stopped at the first angel's message, and others at the second, and many will refuse the third; but a few will "follow the Lamb whithersoever he goeth," and go up and possess the land. Though they have to pass through fire and blood, or witness the "time of trouble such as never was," they will not yield, and "receive the mark of the beast," but they will struggle on, and press their holy warfare until they, with the harps of God, strike the note of victory on mount Zion.[54]

Thus the Sabbatarian Adventists saw themselves as a movement of prophecy, the only genuine heir of Millerism. Because of their convictions, they often referred to their movement as the "Third Angel's Message."

White saw all other forms of Adventism as betrayals of the genius that gave meaning and power to the Millerite movement in the early 1840s. Thus he penned that "those who cowardly yielded to the clamors of opponents, to confess that they had been in error on the time, occupied the unhappy position of wearing the Advent name after giving up as error the very means which had made them Adventists."[55]

Again, he penned:

The position of those who discard the great movement which made them Adventists, and yet cherish some of the leading views of William Miller, and rejoice in the Advent name, is more inconsistent, and their course far more sinful in the sight of God, than that of those who made an entire surrender of both position and name. What a position in the sight of God, angels and men! They bless the Advent faith, hope and name, and curse the very means which has made them what they profess to be![56]

It was holding onto their advent experience in the light of the three angels' messages, he argued, that presented "a connected system" that "explains the past, definitely points out present duty, and lights up the glorious future." To White, the other Adventist groups had lost their direction.[57]

As might be expected, not everyone agreed with White's Sabbatarian assessment. Wellcome, for example, compared White to "the inebriate who staggered through the street badly intoxicated and then entered the complaint that every one in the street staggered; that the posts and the trees ran against him." The Albany Adventists, of course, rejected the seventh-day Sabbath, the new sanctuary teaching, a fulfillment of prophecy on October 22, and the visions of Ellen White. As a result, Sabbatarian Adventism followed a different line of development from that of its much larger advent siblings.[58]

In the heated post-1844 battle over which group had the "original advent faith," however, it appears that the Sabbatarians were correct in their claim to be the only genuine continuation of Millerism. The two other major sectors of the movement had given up those biblical principles of interpretation that had first given birth to Miller's deep convictions and had later given convicting power to Millerite preaching. The Spiritualizers had surrendered the basic concept of the literal coming of Christ in the clouds of heaven, while the Albany groups had given up the prophetic basis that undergirded Miller's historicist interpretation of prophecy. Both those solutions would eventually erode the dynamics of the movements that had accepted them. In one way or another, the new solutions circumnavigated the essential element that provided Millerism with its forcefulness.

On the other hand, the genius of the Sabbatarian solution was that it had captured the dynamics of Millerism and had found a way to extend and prolong those dynamics through its utilization of the biblical model of the end-time three angels, who had an imperative to preach "to every nation, and kindred, and tongue, and people" (Revelation 14:6). That imperative would eventually take the Sabbatarians throughout the world. But before that mission could take place, the Sabbatarians had to overcome their shut-door/close-of-probation mentality, gain insight into the full implications of the three messages, and develop a population base and an organization to accomplish their mission. It is to that latter task that we now turn.

The Gathering Time

By 1848 the Sabbatarian leaders had agreed on a set of basic doctrines. They also believed that they had a responsibility to share their beliefs with those Adventists who were still suffering from confusion concerning what had taken place in October 1844. The Sabbatarians chose typically Millerite approaches for sharing their beliefs.

Their first tactic to spread their message was to organize a series of conferences. The first Sabbatarian conference was held in the spring of 1848 in Rocky Hill, Connecticut. At least five more were held that year, another six in 1849, and ten in 1850. Joseph Bates and the Whites attended most of those conferences.[59]

The purpose of the conferences, according to James White, was the "uniting [of] the brethren on the great truths connected with the message of the third angel."[60] By 1848 many in New England and western New York had become convinced of the truth of one or more of the Sabbatarian Adventist doctrines, but they lacked a common consensus.

James White's report of the first Sabbatarian conference illustrates both the purpose of these conferences and some of the dynamics involved. "We had a meeting that evening [Thursday, April 20, 1848] of about fifteen in all," White wrote.

> Friday morning the brethren came in until we numbered about fifty. *They were not all fully in the truth.* Our meeting that day was very interesting. *Bro. Bates presented the commandments* in a clear light, and their importance was urged home by powerful testimonies. *The word had effect to establish those already in the truth, and to awaken those who were not fully decided.*[61]

The purpose and dynamics of the conferences came out even more clearly in Ellen White's report of the second one, which took place in "Bro. Arnold's barn" in Volney, New York, in August 1848. "There were about thirty-five present," she penned,

> all that could be collected in that part of the State. *There were hardly two agreed*. Each was strenuous for his views, declaring that they were according to the Bible. *All were anxious for an opportunity to advance their sentiments*, or to preach to us. *They were told that we had not come so great a distance to hear them, but had come to teach them the truth.*

After a strenuous meeting in which many of the confused ideas of shut-door adventism were set forth, she noted that many yielded their errors and united "*upon the third angel's message*. Our meeting ended victoriously. Truth gained the victory."[62]

Note in the above recollections that Bates and the Whites took a strong leadership role early in these conferences. Forceful, goal-oriented leadership was demanded to form a body of believers within the chaotic conditions of post-disappointment Adventism.

According to James White, by November 1849 the conferences were fulfilling their primary purpose. "By the proclamation of the Sabbath truth in . . . connection with the Advent movement," he penned to a Brother Bowles,

> God is making known those that are His. In western N.Y. the number of Sabbath keepers is increasing fast. There are more than twice the number now than six months ago. So it is [also] more or less in Maine, Mass., N.H., Vermont, and Conn. . . .
>
> *The scattering time* [as a result of the October disappointment] *we have had; it is in the past, and now the time for the saints to be gathered into the unity of the faith, and be sealed by one holy, uniting truth has come*. Yes, Brother, it has come.
>
> It is true that the work moves slowly, but it moves sure, and it gathers strength at every step. . . .

Our past Advent experience, and present position and future work is marked out in Rev. 14 Chap. as plain as the prophetic pencil could write it. Thank God that we see it. . . .

. . . I believe that the Sabbath truth is yet to ring through the land, as the Advent never has. . . .

. . . I am sick of all our Advent papers, and all our Advent editors, poor creatures. Lamps gone out, still trying to light their blind brethren to the Kingdom of God.

James added that he had no desire to be like them. "I only ask the precious privilege to feed, if possible[,] my poor brethren—'the outcasts.' "[63]

Thus from their beginning, the Sabbatarians saw themselves as a mission-driven people, a people propelled by the imperative of the three angels of Revelation 14. The first step in their mission was to reach out to the confused Millerites during the late 1840s. The Sabbatarian conferences became the initial avenue to accomplish that goal.

The second step in the Sabbatarian gathering lay in the area of publications. Like the conferences, the initial publications were for the purpose of calling out, informing, and uniting a body of believers on the three angels' messages from the scattered ranks of the confused Millerite Adventists. Also, like the conferences, was the fact that publications stood at the heart of Millerite concepts of organization.

The first publications of the Sabbatarians were occasional tracts that highlighted their newfound truths in the context of Millerism as a prophetic movement. These tracts, or small books, included Bates' *The Opening Heavens* (1846), *The Seventh-day Sabbath, a Perpetual Sign* (1846 and significantly revised in 1847), *Second Advent Way Marks and High Heaps* (1847), *Vindication of the Seventh-day Sabbath, and the Commandments of God* (1848), and *A Seal of the Living God* (1849).

Beyond Bates' pamphlets was the first joint publishing venture of the Sabbatarian leadership—*A Word to the "Little Flock"* (1847). The main thrust of this twenty-four-page document was to encourage advent believers to hold on to their 1844 experience as they sought greater light for the future.

A major transition in Adventist publishing was stimulated by an Ellen White vision in Dorchester, Massachusetts, in November 1848. After coming out of vision, she told James that she had "a message" for him. "You must begin to print a little paper and send it out to the people. Let it be small at first; but as the people read, they will send you means with which to print, and it will be a success from the first. From this small beginning it was shown to me to be like streams of light that went clear round the world."[64]

Her prediction of a worldwide publishing work could not have arisen from anything particularly encouraging that existed among the scattered Sabbatarian believers at that time. Humanly speaking, it looked absurd. What could be done by a few penniless preachers backed by about one hundred believers? Certainly a more humble beginning for a publishing venture could hardly be imagined.

In spite of the daunting circumstances, the financially prostrate and homeless James White stepped out in faith to write and publish the "little paper." Looking back at the experience, he later wrote: "We sat down to prepare the matter for that little sheet, and wrote every word of it, our entire library comprising a three-shilling pocket Bible, Cruden's Condensed Concordance, and Walker's old dictionary, minus one of its covers. . . . Our hope of success was in God."[65]

Destitute of means, White sought out a non-Adventist printer, who printed an eight-page paper for a total stranger and waited for his pay until contributions filtered back from the hoped-for readers. The first issue of one thousand copies of *The Present Truth* came off the press in July 1849. "When he brought the first number from the printing office," Ellen White recalled,

we all bowed around it, asking the Lord, with humble hearts and many tears, to let His blessing rest upon the feeble efforts of His servant. He [James] then directed the papers to all he thought would read them, and carried them to the post office [eight miles distant] in a carpetbag.... Very soon letters came bringing means to publish the paper, and the good news of many souls embracing the truth.[66]

The subject matter of *The Present Truth* was the message for that time, as the Sabbatarians saw it—the Sabbath, the three angels' messages, and related doctrinal topics. The "little paper" played its part in the "gathering time" in the late 1840s.

The publication of *The Present Truth*, however, was only the first step in the development of Sabbatarian periodicals. The summer of 1850 saw James publishing the first issue of *The Advent Review*—a journal that reprinted many of the most important Millerite articles of the early 1840s. The purpose of *The Advent Review* was to impress the scattered Millerites with the forceful-ness and reasonableness of the arguments undergirding the 1844 movement.

November 1850 witnessed the combining of *The Present Truth* and *The Advent Review* into *The Second Advent Review and the Sabbath Herald*. For many years the *Review and Herald* was essen-tially "the church" for most Sabbatarians. After all, they generally had no church building or regular preacher. The periodic arrival of the *Review* provided the scattered Sabbatarians with news of their church and fellow believers, sermons, and a sense of be-longing.

The third stage in the Sabbatarian gathering time had to do with formal denominational organization. As with the other Adventist groups, organization came hard. Their experience of being cast out and silenced in the denominations, along with the anti-church teachings of Storrs, Marsh, and others, made them suspicious of formal church organization. But the Sabbatarians, like the other advent bands, eventually discovered some sort of organization to be necessary.[67]

The same problems that plagued the Albany Adventists in the 1850s also afflicted the Sabbatarians. They had to worry about traveling preachers presenting themselves as Sabbatarians to the believers, the support of faithful Sabbatarian pastors, and the ownership of their publishing house. Almost in lock step with other Adventist groups, the Sabbatarians developed safeguards for ministerial certification, systematic means of gathering funds, and more secure ways of holding community property.

Like the Albany Adventist groups, the Sabbatarians also formally organized between 1860 and 1863. The Whites were at the forefront of the struggle for Sabbatarian organization. "God," James argued,

> did not design to bring his people out of the confusion of Babylon into the greater confusion of no order nor discipline. This would only be making a bad matter worse. His object in bringing them out from the churches was to discipline and unite them for the last great battle of truth under the third message. It was not ambition to build up a denomination that suggested organization, but the sheer necessities of the case.[68]

A "general conference" of the Sabbatarians was called by the leading ministers for September 28 to October 1, 1860. At that meeting, despite impassioned airing of the "Babylon" arguments, it was decided to incorporate the publishing house. Beyond that, the name "Seventh-day Adventist" was adopted as best representing the beliefs of the evolving denomination. The next step was the incorporation of the Seventh-day Adventist Publishing Association on May 3, 1861, under the laws of the state of Michigan.[69]

Thus a major battle had been won on the organizational front. At that point, complete victory was not far off, even though in August 1861, James White complained of "a stupid uncertainty upon the subject of organization."[70]

In October, however, the Michigan Conference of Seventh-day Adventists was formed.[71] With the logjam finally broken, 1862 saw the organization of seven more local conferences. Others soon followed.

The final step in the development of church organization

among the Sabbatarians took place in a meeting of representatives of the local conferences at Battle Creek in May 1863. At that time the General Conference of Seventh-day Adventists was formed, with John Byington as its first president. James White had been the unanimous choice for the denomination's presidency, but he wisely declined the office because of his forceful role in urging organization.[72] The Seventh-day Adventists' organizational structure was the only one among the various Adventist denominations to be centralized. All the others were essentially congregational.

But not everyone in the new Seventh-day Adventist denomination appreciated its centralized organizational system. As a result, the disaffected drew off in 1866 and established their headquarters in Marion, Iowa. Among other things, the "Marion Party" resented the leadership of James and Ellen White. They eventually formed the Church of God (Seventh Day). The history of that denomination is one of splits and schisms. With an abundance of independent spirits and a lack of ecclesiastical authority, its fractured history resembles that of other Adventist denominations that made reaction against organization a priority.[73]

In spite of the Marion defection, the Seventh-day Adventist gathering time continued under the guidance of Bates and the Whites. The number of Sabbatarians had risen from about one hundred in 1850 to roughly thirty-five hundred in 1863, when the General Conference of Seventh-day Adventists was organized. That growth would continue, propelled by what the seventh-day people considered to be the divine command of the three angels of Revelation 14 to preach their unique message "to every nation, and kindred, and tongue, and people."

Chapter 15

MILLERISM AT 150

The year 1994 marks the 150th anniversary of the October 22 disappointment. That event, as we noted in chapters 12 through 14, radically changed the shape of Millerism. Between 1844 and 1866, six denominations or movements that became denominations arose. The Albany Adventists spawned four of those denominations—the American Evangelical Adventist Conference, the Advent Christians, the Church of God (Oregon, Illinois), and the Life and Advent Union. The Sabbatarian movement resulted in two denominations—the Seventh-day Adventists and the Church of God (Seventh Day). With their diversity, individuality, and lack of organization, the Spiritualizer wing of Adventism formed no permanent bodies. Various adherents gravitated to other "isms," to more stable Adventist groups, or were absorbed back into the larger culture.

The Changing Shape of Adventism

Although membership statistics are not available, it seems safe to suggest that the Evangelical Adventists and the Advent Christians were the most numerous in the early 1860s, with the Advent Christians constantly gaining over the Evangelicals. One reason for the Advent Christian's relatively greater success seems to be that they had unique doctrines, which gave them something to stand for. Those teachings—conditionalism and annihilationism—provided a needed stimulus and gradually even surpassed

their emphasis on the advent. They became their distinctive doctrines and provided the Advent Christians with a rallying point.

The Evangelicals, on the other hand, had only the premillennial
advent to separate them from the general Christian populace.
When a large share of conservative Protestantism also adopted
forms of premillennialism in the decades after the Civil War,
Evangelical Adventism had little reason to continue a separate
existence. By the early twentieth century, it had ceased to exist as
a separate religious body.[1]

Statistics among the Adventist groups were not easy to come by
in their early years. Some feared that "numbering Israel" might
bring a "curse." Others proved to be more helpful, even though
reluctant. The divisions and mutual suspicions among the Adventist groups didn't make the task any easier.[2]

The first Adventist census was published by D. T. Taylor in
1860. Taylor counted 584 ministers, with 365 believing in conditionalism and annihilationism, 67 believing in consciousness
after death, 9 undecided, and 143 not reporting. On the day of
worship, 365 held to Sunday, 57 to the seventh day, with 162 not
reporting. Taylor estimated 54,000 laymembers, but did not
attempt to break them down according to belief. However, other
sources indicate that somewhat over 3,000 were Sabbatarians.
Thus by 1860 the seventh-day keepers represented a little more
than five percent of the Adventists. The balance of them, presumably, were first-day worshipers.[3]

Taylor's census also gathered estimates regarding the subscription lists of the various Adventist journals. The Advent Christian
World's Crisis led the list with 2,900 subscribers. The *Crisis* was
followed by the Sabbatarian's *Review and Herald* (2,300) and the
Evangelical's *Advent Herald* (2,100). Taylor went out of his way
to note that the promoters of the *Review and Herald*, "though
a decided minority, are very devoted, zealous, and active in the
promulgation of their peculiar views of the Sunday and Sabbath."
The results of that zeal would show up in the decades to come.[4]

The 1890 United States government census not only provides
a more accurate picture of Adventist membership but also indi-

cates radical shifts in the relative size of the various Adventist denominations. By that time the Seventh-day Adventists had achieved predominancc, with 28,991 members in the United States. The Advent Christians were next, with 25,816. Then came the Church of God (Oregon, Illinois), with 2,872; the Evangelicals, with 1,147; the Life and Advent Union, with 1,018; and the Church of God (Seventh Day), with 647.[5]

A century later only four of the six Adventist denominations still existed. In 1990 the Seventh-day Adventists reported 717,446 members in the United States, the Advent Christians claimed 27,590, the Church of God (Oregon, Illinois) 5,688, and the Church of God (Seventh Day) 5,749.[6]

As noted above, the once-strong Evangelical Adventist denomination had been the first to go. It had disappeared in the early twentieth century. The Life and Advent Union would be the next to lose its separate identity. By 1958 the Union reported only 340 members. Six years later it merged with the Advent Christians.[7]

Thus by the early 1990s, the Seventh-day Adventists, with their more than 700,000 members in the United States and more than 7,000,000 members worldwide, dominated the ranks of the religious bodies tracing their heritage back to Millerism. As Clyde Hewitt, an Advent Christian historian, put it, "the tiniest of the Millerite offshoot groups was the one which would become by far the largest."[8]

The "Why" of Success

At this point, one is left with the question of Why? Why did the minute Sabbatarian movement with its unpopular doctrines not only survive but prosper? One can only speculate regarding the answer to that question, but there seem to be several respectable hypotheses that can be argued from the historical data.

Before exploring those hypotheses, it should be noted that closely connected to the query as to why Seventh-day Adventism succeeded is a second issue, that of why Millerism succeeded. I would like to suggest that the two movements experienced success for largely the same reasons.

Prior to moving to my analysis, we should look at the answers that others have supplied as to the why of Millerite success. Three helpful answers come from David L. Rowe, Michael Barkun, and Ruth Alden Doan.

Rowe points out that while many "prophets" predicting the end of the world have arisen in American history, none achieved a mass following like Miller's. Rowe then goes on to explain the movement's success in terms of revivalism, millennialism, and pietism. All three of those forces met at the time of the Millerite movement. Rowe argues that while Second Awakening revivalism provided the method for spreading Millerism, millennialism supplied the idea or dream of the future kingdom that gave direction to the movement, and pietism furnished the temperament of faith that enabled individuals to respond to the revival and accept the vision of the new world to come. The three working together developed a dynamic that thrust Millerism forward.[9]

Barkun calls attention to environmental factors as contributors to the success, not only of Millerism, but also of other millenarian and utopian movements of the same era. Thus natural disasters (such as changing weather patterns) and economic/social crises (such as the Panic of 1837) provided a climate in which people were looking for solutions to their individual and collective stress. In such a context, Miller's message supplied hope in a world in which human effort had failed to achieve the expected results. There seems to be a rule that the worse things get in human terms, the more feasible millennial options appear to be.[10]

In support of Barkun's point, it is an established fact that millennial groups prosper in times of crisis. Thus Seventh-day Adventist and dispensational evangelism had some of its most successful years during World War I. Likewise, Barkun notes that millenarian revivals took place, not only during the economic depression of the 1840s, but also during those of the 1890s and 1930s.[11]

Doan views one factor in the success of Millerism to be its orthodoxy—its essential harmony with the other religious forces of the day in terms of doctrine, lay leadership in understanding the Bible, and so on. Millerism's one essential heresy was its view of the premillennial advent. But the movement's very orthodoxy in most matters left the populace open to its one unorthodox message. Doan's argument, which is currently shared by most non-Adventist scholars, is a reversal from the earlier views that treated Millerism as something strange (if not weird) and out of harmony with its culture.[12]

It should be noted that the various suggestions for Millerism's success presented thus far are not mutually exclusive. Each appears to supply a portion of the explanation underlying Millerism's success (and, by extension, the success of Sabbatarian Adventism). But even collectively they supply but a part of the answer to our question.

The suggestions put forth in the next few pages should not be seen as being out of harmony with those set forth by Rowe, Barkun, Doan, and others, but as being complementary to them. But whereas their suggestions tend to focus on factors external to the Millerite movement, those developed in the following pages look more carefully at the internal factors that led to the success of pre-1845 Millerism and post-1844 Sabbatarian Adventism. Social forces and contextual factors are important (probably even essential) to the success of any religious movement, but they are not enough by themselves. The external factors are not the movement, but the soil for the successful planting and development of a movement. Both the external and internal factors must be in place for a movement such as Millerism or Sabbatarian Adventism to succeed.

We will now look at four internal factors that seem to have contributed to the success of Millerism and Seventh-day Adventism. First, it should be noted that apocalyptic movements often attract two personality types. On one side, we find the rationalism that unpacks the biblical prophecies and develops the apocalyptic scheme of events. On the other side are the emotional types who gravitate toward the excitement of the apocalyptic expectancy and often run into fanatical, irrational extremism.

Millerism had both types. Thus, although it was founded upon the cool rationalism of Miller, it also had its Starkweathers, Gorgases, and Spiritualizers. A movement disintegrates whenever the rational forces are not strong enough to stem the centrifugal forces of irrationalism or emotionalism. It was in this area that the Spiritualizer wing of Adventism came to nothing. Its irrationalism overcame its rationalism until at last there were no controls on its belief structure.

One of the strengths of Millerism was its rational development of its central doctrine. That element drew believers to its cause through its very logic. But Millerism at its best also made room for religious emotionalism, but that emotionalism ideally took place within the bounds of rationality. That combination gave both life and stability to the movement and heightened its appeal.

Seventh-day Adventism has partaken of much of that same balance, although it appears at times to wander too far toward the purely rational pole. Both Millerism and its Sabbatarian offspring, of course, have had their excitable and fanatical elements, but the stability of their success can largely be attributed to their ability to appeal to the rational element in people. Typically both have aimed at converting people to "the truth."

A second element that appears to have led to the evangelistic success of Millerism and Seventh-day Adventism is the content or doctrinal factor in their view of truth. Millerism had what it considered to be an important Bible truth to offer to individuals searching for meaning. For Millerism, that doctrinal factor was the premillennial return of Christ. Millerism was not just a part of the ecclesiastical woodwork; it stood for something distinctive from other religious groups. Thus it had a message to preach, and many responded to that message.

As noted above, one of the reasons that Evangelical Adventism died out was that it had lost its doctrinal distinctiveness once a significant portion of American Protestantism accepted premillennialism. After that, Evangelical Adventism had no further reason to exist. As a result, it blended back into generic evangelicalism. On the other hand, the Advent Christians adopted conditionalism as their new doctrinal distinctive. Thus they had at least one more reason to continue a separate existence than their Evangelical sibling.

By way of contrast, the Seventh-day Adventists developed a whole arena of unconventional beliefs that they saw as their special mission to share with the world. Just as a kite flies against the wind, so there is a dynamic in religious movements that is vitalized by differences and even opposition. Being different gives individuals and social groups meaning. And being different develops commitment to a cause, especially when it entails "bridge-burning acts" as one joins a religious subculture.[13]

In Millerism, that bridge-burning dynamic took place when people were "cast out of Babylon" for espousing premillennial beliefs. An example of that dynamic in Seventh-day Adventism takes place in family and work struggles that involve the keeping of the seventh-day Sabbath in a culture that sees Saturday as a work and/or pleasure day.

Seventh-day Adventists have established several doctrinal and lifestyle boundary markers that have had that effect. Hewitt, in seeking to explain Seventh-day Adventist growth in contrast to the lack of growth in his Advent Christian community, notes that "the distinctive beliefs and practices of the [SDA] denomination[,] while causing it to be viewed with suspicion by many traditional Christian believers[,] have seemingly given its faithful members a resoluteness of individual and group character that goes far to explain their successes." Dean Kelley sheds light on the dynamic under consideration when he notes that if people are going to join a church, they want to join a church that provides a genuine alternative to the larger culture. On the other hand, Seventh-day Adventism (like Millerism) is close enough to orthodoxy in most central doctrines to get a hearing among other Christians.[14]

A third element that led to the evangelistic success of Seventh-day Adventism was an organizational structure sufficient to carry on the mission and meet the challenges of its perceived message. At first glance it might seem that Millerism's success and that of Seventh-day Adventism might vary here. In a sense it does. But the variable appears to be time rather than organization as such.

My essential point is that Millerism, given its brief existence, had sufficient organization through its conferences and periodicals to give direction to its mission for its few intense years. But such a nebulous organizational pattern would not have been sufficient to direct the movement's mission over an extended period of time.

It was the lack of sufficient organization that spelled the demise of the Spiritualizers and the lack of growth for the two Church of God Adventist denominations. Without sufficient organization, they could not concentrate their resources for mission or maintain unity. Costly schism was the result.

It is at the point of sufficient organization that the Advent Christians and the Seventh-day Adventists also parted ways. We noted above that the Seventh-day Adventist Church was the only one of the Adventist denominations to place significant authority at any ecclesiastical level above that of the local congregation. Hewitt, in bemoaning the plight of the Advent Christians, indicates that the lack of a "strong centralized organization" is one reason that "contraction threatens to overcome expansion" in their work. What centralized organization they did get, he argues, came too late and, worse yet, represented mere structure without significant power. As a result of their congregational structure, Hewitt points out that the Advent Christians were unable to mobilize for united action. With proper organization, he suggested in 1990, the Advent Christians might be "a growing and not a dying denomination."[15]

By way of contrast, two recent studies of Seventh-day Adventist organizational structure indicate that that structure was consciously designed with mission outreach in mind.[16] Of course, that does not mean that the denomination is without significant problems in its organizational structure. To the contrary, Seventh-day Adventism, as we shall see below, is facing major organizational problems in the last decade of the twentieth century.

The fourth, and by far the most important, factor in the rapid spread of Millerism was its sense of prophetic mission and the sense of urgency generated by that prophetic understanding. Millerism was a mission-driven movement. One of the theses of the earlier chapters of this book is that it was a sense of personal responsibility to warn the world of its soon-coming end that literally *drove* Miller, Himes, and a host of others to dedicate everything they had to warn the world of coming judgment. Himes put it nicely in an editorial in the very first issue of the *Midnight Cry*. "OUR WORK," he wrote,

> is one of unutterable magnitude. It is a mission and an enterprise, unlike, in some respects, any thing that has ever awakened the energies of man. . . . It is an *alarm*, and a CRY, uttered by those who, from among all Protestant sects, as Watchmen standing upon the walls of the moral world, believe the WORLD'S CRISIS IS COME—and who, under the influence of this faith, are united in proclaiming to the world, "Behold the Bridegroom cometh, go ye out to meet him!"[17]

That sense of urgency, it must be emphasized, was built upon an interpretation of the prophecies of Daniel and the Revelation. The Millerites believed with all their hearts that they had a message people *must* hear. It was that belief and the total dedication accompanying it that pushed the Millerites into tireless mission.

I would like to suggest that the same vision, based upon the same prophecies, provided the mainspring of Seventh-day Adventist mission. From their beginning, the Sabbatarians never viewed themselves as merely another denomination. To the contrary, they understood their movement and message to be a fulfillment of prophecy. They saw themselves as a prophetic people.

Such an understanding came from the conviction that they were the only genuine continuation of Millerism, particularly as that continuation related to Miller's interpretation of prophecy. From the early Sabbatarian perspective, the other Adventist groups had lost their way and eventually their mission because of their denial of Miller's principles of prophetic interpretation.

That denial took two different directions. One was a rejection of the literal interpretation of scriptural passages that seemed to be quite literal. Thus the belief that Christ had already come sapped the missiological strength of the Spiritualizers. After all, if Christ had already come, what was the reason for mission?

Meanwhile, it can be argued, the Albany Adventists rejected the stimulus to mission that had convicted and empowered Millerism when they rejected Miller's principles of prophetic interpretation in their denial of the great time prophecies of Daniel and the Revelation. Without that certainty of the flow of prophetic history, they lost their sense of conviction and urgency. They finally had to find meaning for existence in other doctrines, such as conditionalism or the nonresurrection of the wicked. That may have been good enough for a sort of denominational existence, but the Albany groups had abandoned the mainspring that had propelled Millerism.

By way of contrast, the Sabbatarians founded their movement on that very mainspring. They not only maintained Miller's prophetic scheme of interpretation, but they also extended it in such a way as to give meaning to both their disappointment and the remaining time before Christ's advent. Central to that extended interpretation were Christ's work of pre-advent judgment in the cleansing of the heavenly sanctuary and the progressive nature of the three angels' messages of Revelation 14.

Those two prophetic extensions provided the Sabbatarians with the same sense of urgency that had inspired the Millerites in the 1840s. While the Sabbatarians saw Miller and Fitch as the initiators of the first and second angels' messages, they saw their own movement with its emphasis on the commandments of God as initiating the third. Thus, they believed, conflict over their unique Sabbath doctrine would be a focal point in the great struggle between good and evil right before the second coming.

That interpretation was reinforced by their view of the end-time struggle over the commandments of God pictured in Revelation 12:17 and the fuller exposition of that verse in Revelation 13 and 14. As a result, the Sabbatarians were convinced that they were not only the heir of Millerism, but that their movement had been predicted by God to preach the three angels' messages to all the world immediately before the great end-time harvest of Revelation 14.

That prophetic understanding did the same thing for Sabbatarian Adventism that it had done for Millerism. It eventually drove them to mission. By 1990 the conviction that their movement was a movement of prophecy had resulted in one of the most widespread mission-outreach programs in the history of Christianity. By that year they had established work in 182 of the 210 countries then recognized by the United Nations.[18]

That kind of dedication did not come by accident; it was the direct result of prophetic conviction of their responsibility. Central to that prophetic conviction was the imperative of the first angel of Revelation 14:6 to preach "to every nation, and kindred, and tongue, and people" and the command of Revelation 10:11 that the disappointed ones "must prophesy again before many peoples, and nations, and tongues, and kings."

Clyde Hewitt, in seeking to explain the success of the Seventh-day Adventists as opposed to the attrition faced by his Advent Christians, touched upon an essential element when he noted that "Seventh-day Adventists are convinced that they have been divinely ordained to carry on the prophetic work started by William Miller. They are dedicated to the task."[19]

In contrast to that conviction, Hewitt's father wrote to F. D. Nichol in 1944 that the Advent Christians had given up Miller's interpretation of Daniel 8:14 and the 2300 days and had no unanimity on the meaning of the text. Another leading Advent Christian scholar interviewed in 1984 noted that his denomination no longer even had any agreed-upon interpretation on the millennium—the very heart of Miller's contribution.[20]

In short, when the Albany Adventists stepped off Miller's prophetic platform, they began a process of deterioration in their prior understanding of the end of the world. From that perspective, the later reversals in prophetic interpretation by Josiah Litch and others become quite understandable. The seventh-day branch of the Adventist family, of course, has been quick to point out that Ellen White had predicted in December 1844 that those who rejected October 1844 as a fulfillment of prophecy would eventually be left in "perfect darkness" and would stumble in their advent experience.[21]

It should be noted that merely holding the conviction that they have the "correct doctrine" is not a sufficient explanation for the spread of Sabbatarian Adventism. After all, the Seventh Day Baptists preached the seventh-day Sabbath with conviction, but their 5,200 members in the United States in 1990 is less than their membership was in the 1840s. As one nineteenth-century Seventh Day Baptist preacher told Bates, the Baptists had been able to "convince people of the legality of the seventh-day Sabbath, but they could not get them to move as the Sabbath Adventists did."[22]

Likewise, many of the non-Sabbatarian Adventist groups preached what they believed to be the truth of the premillennial return of Christ, but without the same results as the Seventh-day Adventists. C. E. Hewitt notes that his "Advent Christian people have not been an evangelistic church" and have not made much of an impact on the world. The result, he points out, has been smallness. Not just smallness in numbers, but smallness "in dreams, in visions. Smallness breeds smallness." Hewitt also indicates that Advent Christian smallness cannot be attributed to unpopular doctrines. After all, he argues, the Seventh-day Adventist list of unpopular doctrines "includes all those of the Advent Christian faith and adds several more." In another connection, Hewitt roots Seventh-day Adventists' success in their conviction that they have a prophetic mission in the tradition of William Miller.[23]

Hewitt's conclusions go a long way toward helping us understand the spread of Sabbatarian Adventism. Its mainspring seems to have been much more than merely the fact that the Sabbatarians believed they had the "truth" on the Sabbath and the "truth" of the second advent. The driving force undergirding Seventh-day Adventism was the bedrock conviction that they were a prophetic people with a unique message concerning Christ's soon coming to a troubled world. That prophetic understanding

of their mission, integrated with their doctrines within the framework of the three angels' messages, provided the Sabbatarians
with the motive power to sacrifice in order to spread their message far and wide. That same dynamic operated in Millerism.
Unfortunately for Seventh-day Adventism, that very vision appears to be in jeopardy in the 1990s.

And What of the Fever?

The Adventist denominations growing out of Millerism are
facing possible death. That is the inference of Richard C. Nickels,
who concluded his 1973 history of the Church of God (Seventh
Day) with a section entitled "A Dying Church?" The volume's
ominous last words are from Christ's message to the Church at
Sardis: " 'It was alive, yet dead!' "[24]

Similarly, the final section of Hewitt's three-volume history
of the Advent Christians is "Should a denomination be told its
[sic] dying?" That section, published in 1990, contains a heartfelt
analysis of the denomination's situation. The final moving words
in Hewitt's trilogy are, *"I devoutly hope some are listening. Amen!"*[25]

Where is the millennial fever that brought these denominations
to birth? And what about the other post-Millerite denominations?
Are they also in danger of losing their vision? In particular, what
about the strongest of the Millerite siblings—the Sabbatarians?

At first sight it would appear that the rapidly growing Seventh-
day Adventist Church has nothing to worry about. As these words
are being written in March 1993, the denomination is approaching eight million members. Their projected membership for the
year 2000 is twelve million.

Yet all is not well. It is difficult for the older population sectors
of the denomination to maintain their Adventist identity. After
all, it is hard to keep people excited about the second coming for
150 years. The Sabbatarians face all the problems of an aging denomination that afflicted previous religious movements down
through church history. Time after time the world has witnessed
vibrant reformatory religious movements harden and lose their
vitality with age.[26]

But beyond the issue of aging, some sectors of Seventh-day Adventism in the 1990s (particularly in such places as North America, Europe, and Australia) appear to be confronted with all the threats that eroded the other Adventist bodies. Thus in their search for meaning in the face of the seemingly ever-delayed end of the world, some believers are tempted to spiritualize the nature of Christ's advent. But to lose faith in an actual historical advent is to lose Adventism itself.

Alternately, affluence has made its impact on the beliefs of some members regarding the advent hope. The Protestant ethic of hard work and frugality has led many Seventh-day Adventists into cross-generational upward mobility. Several generations of such mobility can develop a membership that locates its kingdom on this earth and has little felt need for coming kingdoms. It is easy for such members to be more at home with the larger culture than with their sectarian roots.[27] Many in such circumstances find it easy to downplay their denomination's distinctive doctrines. But such were the dynamics that spelled the end for Evangelical Adventism.

At the opposite extreme on the denominational spectrum are those who, in their reaction to their "less Adventist" Adventist neighbors, will be tempted to follow the precedent of the Adventist extremists of the post-1844 period into the fringes of the Christian community.

The challenge facing the Seventh-day Adventist Church is to maintain a healthy middle-of-the-road balance as it seeks to uplift both the doctrines that have made it unique and those doctrines that it shares with other Christians. Both acculturation to the larger community and segregation into a sectarian ghetto sound the death knell for vibrant Seventh-day Adventism.

A third tension faced by Seventh-day Adventism is in the realm of organization. On the one hand, denominational health is threatened by too much of a good thing. Nearly a century ago, Seventh-day Adventism adopted a multitiered administrative structure that, in its trim state, was well fitted for mission expansion at the time. But decades of expansion and change have created a bureaucracy that is extremely expensive to maintain and appears to be becoming progressively dysfunctional in fostering the mission of the church in the most efficient manner. Though the early 1990s have seen efforts at reform, the results have been minimal. Few in the denomination's power structure seem able to thoroughly think through the massive organizational changes necessitated by a century of internal and external change. Few seem able to catch the vision of possible new structural models for world mission in the twenty-first century.

At the other extreme are the large segments of Seventh-day Adventists who are tired of paying the cost of the administrative machinery. These members see the future of the denomination in congregational terms. That route, of course, is the one followed by all branches of Millerite Adventism except the Sabbatarians. For them, congregationalism resulted in denominations that were weak in ability to maintain their own identity and unable to efficiently focus resources on extended mission.

Thus it appears that Seventh-day Adventism is faced, on the one hand, with the increasing weight of a superstructure that could eventually crush the movement itself. On the other hand, it is faced with the quite real threat of congregationalism. Success would seem to lie in coming to grips with the compromises and structural changes that need to be made if Seventh-day Adventism is to continue to be a viable international movement, capable of operating efficiently toward accomplishing its perceived mission.

Clearly related to Sabbatarian Adventism's organizational dilemma is its inclination toward overinstitutionalism. There is a tendency for its extensive educational, publishing, conference, and medical institutions to become ends in themselves rather than means for the end of taking the denomination's peculiar message "to every nation, and kindred, and tongue, and people." Thus there is the danger of the denomination gaining its self-image from its institutions rather than from its stated mission.[28]

It was at that very point that Joshua V. Himes challenged the Seventh-day Adventists in 1895. "You have," he wrote to Ellen White, many good and great things connected with Health Reform and the churches, with the increase of wealth, and colleges as well, and to me it looks like work in all these departments that may go on for a long time to come. . . .

. . .There is a great and earnest work being done to send the message of the 3rd angel everywhere—but all classes of Adventists are prospering in worldly things, and heaping up riches, while they talk of the coming of Christ as an event very near at hand. It is a great thing to be consistent and true to the real Advent message.[29]

With those sentences, Himes put his finger on the tendency toward institutional and individual secularization in Seventh-day Adventism that was present even in his day. That tendency has not lessened in the last one hundred years.

A final temptation faced by Seventh-day Adventism will be to give up its vision of itself as a people of prophecy, to forget its prophetic heritage. It is easy to see how that could come about, but to do so would be death to the dynamic that made Seventh-day Adventism what it is today. To deny its prophetic heritage is a certain way to kill its "millennial fever."

NOTES

A Word to the Reader

1. Ernest R. Sandeen, *The Roots of Fundamentalism: British and American Millenarianism, 1800-1930* (Chicago: University of Chicago Press, 1970), 50.

2. Clara Endicott Sears, *Days of Delusion: A Strange Bit of History* (Boston: Houghton Mifflin, 1924).

3. Francis D. Nichol, *The Midnight Cry* (Washington, DC: Review and Herald, 1944).

4. Clyde E. Hewitt, *Midnight and Morning* (Charlotte, NC: Venture Books, 1983).

5. David L. Rowe, *Thunder and Trumpets: Millerites and Dissenting Religion in Upstate New York, 1800-1850* (Chico, CA: Scholars Press, 1985).

6. Michael Barkun, *Crucible of the Millennium: The Burned-over District of New York in the 1840s* (Syracuse, NY: Syracuse University Press, 1986).

7. Ruth Alden Doan, *The Miller Heresy, Millennialism, and American Culture* (Philadelphia: Temple University Press, 1987).

8. Ronald L. Numbers and Jonathan M. Butler, eds., *The Disappointed: Millerism and Millenarianism in the Nineteenth Century* (Bloomington, IN: Indiana University Press, 1987).

9. David Tallmadge Arthur, " 'Come Out of Babylon': A Study of Millerite Separatism and Denominationalism, 1840-1865" (Ph.D. dissertation, University of Rochester, 1970); David Tallmadge Arthur, "Joshua V. Himes and the Cause of Adventism, 1839-1845" (M.A. thesis, University of Chicago, 1961).

10. Everett N. Dick, "William Miller and the Advent Crisis, 1831-1844" (unpublished manuscript, 1932). This manuscript is an extension of a Ph.D. dissertation completed at the University of Wisconsin in 1930. The 1932 manuscript is scheduled for publication under the editorship of Gary Land by Andrews University Press in the autumn of 1993.

11. P. Gerard Damsteegt, *Foundations of the Seventh-day Adventist Message and Mission* (Grand Rapids, MI: Eerdmans, 1977).

12. LeRoy E. Froom, *The Prophetic Faith of Our Fathers*, 4 vols. (Washington, DC: Review and Herald, 1946-1954).

Chapter 1: **Millennial Fever**

1. William Miller, *Wm. Miller's Apology and Defence* (Boston: J. V. Himes, 1845), 11-15.

2. Sandeen, *Roots of Fundamentalism*, 42.

3. J. F. C. Harrison, *The Second Coming: Popular Millenarianism, 1780-1850* (New Brunswick, NJ: Rutgers University Press, 1979), 5, 57; Sandeen, *Roots of Fundamentalism*, 5.

4. Froom, *Prophetic Faith of Our Fathers*, 2:753-759; Sandeen, *Roots of Fundamentalism*, 6, 7.

5. Ernest R. Sandeen, "Millennialism," in *The Rise of Adventism: Religion and Society in Mid-Nineteenth-Century America*, ed. Edwin R. Gaustad (New York: Harper and Row, 1974), 108.

6. Froom, *Prophetic Faith of Our Fathers*, 4:403-406.

7. It should be noted that Miller calculated the 1843 date from several of Daniel's time prophecies. See Doan, *The Miller Heresy*, 32, 33; William Miller, *Evidence From Scripture and History of the Second Coming of Christ, About the Year 1843* (Boston: Joshua V. Himes, 1842), passim. The various calculations adding up to 1843 are graphically portrayed in the 1843 Chart developed by Fitch and Hale (see a copy of that chart in photograph section).

8. William Miller, *Letter to Joshua V. Himes, on the Cleansing of the Sanctuary* (Boston: Joshua V. Himes, 1842); W. Miller to T. Hendryx, Mar. 26, 1832.

9. William Miller to J. Atwood and Family, May 31, 1831.

10. George Bush and William Miller, *Reasons for Rejecting Mr. Miller's Views on the Advent, by Rev. George Bush; With Mr. Miller's Reply* (Boston: Joshua V. Himes, 1844), 11. Bush also wrote to Miller that "in taking a *day* as the prophetical term for a *year*, I believe you are sustained by the soundest exegesis." Ibid., 6, 7. Cf. Moses Stuart, *Hints on the Interpretation of Prophecy* (Andover, MA: Allen, Morrill, and Wardwell, 1842), 74; Sylvester Bliss, *Memoirs of William Miller* (Boston: Joshua V. Himes, 1853), 189-192.

11. Charles Finney, *Lectures on Revivals of Religion* (New York: 1835), 282, quoted in William G. McLoughlin, Jr., *Modern Revivalism: Charles Grandison Finney to Billy Graham* (New York: Ronald Press, 1959), 105; *Oberlin Evangelist*, Apr. 12, 1843, 58.

12. *Oberlin Evangelist*, Oct. 25, 1843, 173, 174; Dec. 22, 1841, 204.

13. See Conrad Cherry, *God's New Israel: Religious Interpretations of American Destiny* (Englewood Cliffs, NJ: Prentice Hall, 1971); Ernest Lee Tuveson, *Redeemer Nation: The Idea of America's Millennial Role* (Chicago: University of Chicago Press, 1968), 62.

14. See Charles I. Foster, *An Errand of Mercy: The Evangelical United Front, 1790-1837* (Chapel Hill, NC: University of North Carolina Press, 1960); Ronald G. Walters, *American Reformers, 1815-1860* (New York: Hill and Wang, 1978).

15. Timothy L. Smith, "Social Reform: Some Reflections on Causation and Consequence," in *Rise of Adventism*, 19; Doan, *The Miller Heresy*, 54. Cf. Whitney R. Cross, *The Burned-over District: The Social and Intellectual History of Enthusiastic Religion in Western New York, 1800-1850* (Ithica, NY: Cornell University Press, 1950), 291; Ruth Alden Doan, "Millerism and Evangelical Culture," in *The Disappointed*, 132.

16. Edwin S. Gaustad, "Introduction," in *Rise of Adventism*, xiii.

17. Cross, *Burned-over District*, 291.

18. David L. Rowe, "Millerites: A Shadow Portrait," in *The Disappointed*, 15, 12, 13; Doan, "Millerism and Evangelical Culture," in *The Disappointed*, 132; Rowe, *Thunder and Trumpets*, 51. For the classical treatment of Millerism as a

deviant movement, see Sears, *Days of Delusion*.

19. Keith J. Hardman, *Charles Grandison Finney, 1792-1875: Revivalist and Reformer* (Syracuse, NY: Syracuse University Press, 1987), 293-323.

20. Barkun, *Crucible of the Millennium*, 115. See pp. 103-112 for other disasters of the time.

21. Ibid., 116.

22. Dick, "William Miller," 262-265; Richard Carwardine, *Trans-Atlantic Revivalism: Popular Evangelicalism in Britain and America, 1790-1865* (Westport, CT: Greenwood Press, 1978), 52.

23. Everett N. Dick, "The Millerite Movement, 1830-1845," in *Adventism in America*, ed. Gary Land (Grand Rapids, MI: Eerdmans, 1986), 34.

24. Cross, *Burned-over District*, 320.

Chapter 2: **The Making of a Millennialist**

1. Bliss, *Memoirs of William Miller*, 28, 29.

2. Ibid., 28. See also Erik H. Erikson, *Identity: Youth and Crisis* (New York: W. W. Norton, 1968); Erik H. Erikson, *Young Man Luther: A Study in Psychoanalysis and History* (New York: W. W. Norton, 1962).

3. Bliss, *Memoirs of William Miller*, 29.

4. William Miller, diary, July 10, 1797.

5. Joshua V. Himes, *Views of the Prophecies and Prophetic Chronology, Selected From Manuscripts of William Miller, With a Memoir of His Life* (Boston: Joshua V. Himes, 1842), 9.

6. Bliss, *Memoirs of William Miller*, 29.

7. The following paragraphs dealing with Miller's education are based upon Himes, *Views of the Prophecies*, 7, 8; Bliss, *Memoirs of William Miller*, 10-16; *Midnight Cry*, Nov. 17, 1842, 1, 2.

8. Bliss, *Memoirs of William Miller*, 10.

9. Ibid., 12.

10. Ibid., 12, 13.

11. *Midnight Cry*, Nov. 17, 1842, 1; Bliss, *Memoirs of William Miller*, 16.

12. Miller, *Apology and Defence*, 3; *Advent Shield*, May 1844, 50; Bliss, *Memoirs of William Miller*, 19; Himes, *Views of the Prophecies*, 8.

13. Aleine Austin, *Matthew Lyon: "New Man" of the Democratic Revolution, 1749-1822* (University Park, PA: Pennsylvania State University Press, 1981), 81; "Alien and Sedition Acts," in *Encyclopedia of American History*, ed. Richard B. Morris (New York: Harper & Brothers, 1953), 129.

14. Miller, *Apology and Defence*, 2, 3.

15. Ibid., 3; Himes, *Views of the Prophecies*, 9.

16. Bliss, *Memoirs of William Miller*, 21-23.

17. Ibid.

18. Miller, *Apology and Defence*, 3, 4.

19. *Midnight Cry*, Nov. 17, 1842, 1.

20. Bliss, *Memoirs of William Miller*, 4.

21. Ibid., 55; cf. W. Miller to L. Miller, Nov. 11, 1814.

22. Himes, *Views of the Prophecies*, 10; cf. Bliss, *Memoirs of William Miller*, 23.

23. Himes, *Views of the Prophecies*, 10.

24. Miller, *Apology and Defence*, 4; Bliss, *Memoirs of William Miller*, 45;

"Plattsburg, Battle of," in *Concise Dictionary of American History*, ed. Wayne Andrews (New York: Charles Scribner's Sons, 1962), 739; Thomas A. Bailey, *The American Pageant: A History of the Republic* (Boston: D. C. Heath, 1961), 210, 215.

25. Miller, *Apology and Defence*, 4. (Italics supplied.) For an account of the Battle of Plattsburg from Miller's perspective, see Bliss, *Memoirs of William Miller*, 44-53.

26. Miller, *Apology and Defence*, 4; Bliss, *Memoirs of William Miller*, 63, 64.

27. Miller, *Apology and Defence*, 4, 5.

28. *Advent Shield*, May 1844, 49.

29. Bliss, *Memoirs of William Miller*, 66, 53.

30. Ibid., 65.

31. Ibid., 66.

32. *Advent Shield*, May 1844, 49.

33. Miller, *Apology and Defence*, 5. (Italics supplied.)

34. *Midnight Cry*, Nov. 17, 1842, 1.

35. On Miller's conversion following the standard model of conversions, see Doan, "Millerism and Evangelical Culture," in *The Disappointed*, 119, 120.

36. Miller, *Apology and Defence*, 4, 5; cf. *Advent Shield*, May 1844, 50.

37. Miller, *Apology and Defence*, 6.

38. Ibid.; cf. *Advent Shield*, May 1844, 50; *Midnight Cry*, Nov. 17, 1842, 1, 2.

39. Miller, *Apology and Defence*, 6, 10.

40. Ibid., 11, 12; *Advent Shield*, May 1844, 50.

41. Miller, *Apology and Defence*, 13-15.

42. For the full 1822 statement of Miller's beliefs, see Bliss, *Memoirs of William Miller*, 77-80.

43. *Midnight Cry*, Nov. 17, 1842, 4; Bliss, *Memoirs of William Miller*, 155; Himes, *Views of the Prophecies*, 11, 12.

44. See George M. Marsden, *Fundamentalism and American Culture: The Shaping of Twentieth-Century Evangelicalism, 1870-1925* (New York: Oxford University Press, 1980), passim; Theodore Dwight Bozeman, *Protestants in an Age of Science: The Baconian Ideal and Antebellum American Religious Thought* (Chapel Hill, NC: University of North Carolina Press, 1977).

45. *Advent Shield*, May 1844, 90.

46. Ibid., 88; Doan, *Miller Heresy*, 99, 100; Patricia Cline Cohen, *A Calculating People: The Spread of Numeracy in Early America* (Chicago: University of Chicago Press, 1982), 175.

47. Richard T. Hughes and C. Leonard Allen, *Illusions of Innocence: Protestant Primitivism in America, 1630-1875* (Chicago: University of Chicago Press, 1988); Richard T. Hughes, ed., *The American Quest for the Primitive Church* (Urbana, IL: University of Illinois Press, 1988); David Edwin Harrell, Jr., "Restorationism and the Stone-Campbell Tradition," in *Encyclopedia of the American Religious Experience*, ed. Charles H. Lippy and Peter W. Williams (New York: Charles Scribner's Sons, 1988), 2:845-858.

48. Cross, *Burned-over District*, 297.

49. Miller, *Apology and Defence*, 12; Nathan O. Hatch, "Millennialism and Popular Religion in the Early Republic," in *The Evangelical Tradition in America*, ed. Leonard I. Sweet (Macon, GA: Mercer University Press, 1984), 119, 120.

50. Sandeen, "Millennialism," in *Rise of Adventism*, 114.

51. Ibid.; *Midnight Cry*, Nov. 17, 1842, 4.

52. *Midnight Cry*, Nov. 17, 1842, 1.

53. Miller, *Apology and Defence*, 3; *Midnight Cry*, Oct. 26, 1843, 88; Barkun, *Crucible of the Millennium*, 36.

54. Miller, *Apology and Defence*, 6, 3; *Advent Shield*, May 1844, 50; *Midnight Cry*, Nov. 17, 1842, 4.

55. *Midnight Cry*, Oct. 26, 1843, 88.

56. Miller, *Evidence From Scripture and History*, 215. Cf. Miller, *Apology and Defence*, 11; *Advent Shield*, May 1844, 49; *Advent Herald*, Nov. 27, 1844, 127.

57. Sandeen, "Millennialism," in *Rise of Adventism*, 110; Barkun, *Crucible of the Millennium*, 36.

58. W. Miller to T. Hendryx, Mar. 26, 1832; Miller, *Apology and Defence*, 12.

59. Himes, *Views of the Prophecies*, 12; Miller, *Apology and Defence*, 13.

60. Miller, *Apology and Defense*, 14.

61. Ibid., 15.

62. Ibid.

63. Ibid., 15, 16.

64. Bliss, *Memoirs of William Miller*, 85-90. Bliss (p. 85) notes that this dream was written out in full on Jan. 17, 1828.

65. See Nichol, *Midnight Cry*, 40; Froom, *Prophetic Faith of Our Fathers*, 4:478, 479.

66. Miller, *Apology and Defence*, 16; W. Miller, "A Few Evidences of the Time of the 2nd Coming of Christ to Elder Andrus" (unpublished manuscript, Feb. 15, 1831); Bliss, *Memoirs of William Miller*, 93, 94.

67. Miller, *Apology and Defence*, 16.

68. Ibid., 16, 17; *Advent Shield*, May 1844, 52.

69. Miller, *Apology and Defence*, 17.

70. Ibid.

Chapter 3: **Miller's Mission to the World**

1. Miller, *Apology and Defence*, 17; Miller incorrectly dated this experience as 1833. For argumentation for the 1831 date, see Bliss, *Memoirs of William Miller*, 98.

2. Miller, *Apology and Defence*, 17, 18.

3. Ibid., 18.

4. Ibid.

5. Ibid., 18, 19; Himes, *Views of the Prophecies*, 12.

6. Bliss, *Memoirs of William Miller*, 135, 136; T. Cole to W. Miller, July 25, 1839. See also *Christian Herald*, Nov. 28, 1839, 3; T. Cole to W. Miller, Nov. 5, 1839.

7. *Maine Wesleyan Journal*, quoted in Himes, *Views of the Prophecies*, 15; New York *Herald* Extra, quoted in Nichol, *Midnight Cry*, 130. Cf. *Advent Shield*, May 1844, 51; Dick, "William Miller," 16.

8. Lynn *Record*, quoted in Isaac C. Wellcome, *History of the Second Advent Message and Mission, Doctrine and People* (Yarmouth, ME: Isaac C. Wellcome, 1874), 75. (Italics supplied.)

9. Sandy Hill *Herald*, quoted in Bliss, *Memoirs of William Miller*, 181, 182; Cincinnati *Commercial*, Aug. 23, 1844, quoted in Froom, *Prophetic Faith of Our Fathers*, 4:688.

10. Cincinnati *Commercial*, Aug. 23, 1844, quoted in Froom, *Prophetic Faith of Our Fathers*, 4:688; *Signs of the Times*, Apr. 15, 1840, 14.

11. *Advent Herald*, Dec. 18, 1844, 147; W. Miller to T. Hendryx, Nov. 17, 1832.

12. *Maine Wesleyan Journal*, quoted in Nichol, *Midnight Cry*, 83; *The Fountain*, quoted in Wellcome, *History of the Second Advent Message*, 248.

13. *Signs of the Times*, Apr. 15, 1840, 14.

14. Wellcome, *History of the Second Advent Message*, 248.

15. W. Miller to T. Hendryx, Feb. 8, 1833; Apr. 10, 1833; cf. W. Miller to Bro. and Sis. Atwood, Sept. 16, 1833.

16. W. Miller to T. Hendryx, Feb. 25, 1834; Apr. 10, 1833.

17. W. Miller to his son, Nov. 17, 1838; W. Miller to T. Hendryx, July 21, 1836.

18. W. Miller to his son, Nov. 17, 1838; *Signs of the Times*, Apr. 15, 1840, 14.

19. Bliss, *Memoirs of William Miller*, 210-212.

20. Himes, *Views of the Prophecies*, 57. For more helpful illustrations of Miller's humor, see Bliss, *Memoirs of William Miller*, 95-97; *Signs of the Times*, Mar. 1, 1843, 186.

21. Wayne R. Judd, "William Miller," in *The Disappointed*, 29.

22. Bliss, *Memoirs of William Miller*, 207.

23. Ibid., 170; "Friend" to W. Miller, Dec. 17, 1842.

24. The best available works that explore Miller's prophetic interpretations are Damsteegt, *Foundations of the Seventh-day Adventist Message and Mission* and Froom, *Prophetic Faith of Our Fathers*, vol. 4.

25. W. Miller to T. Hendryx, Mar. 26, 1832; cf. W. Miller to T. Hendryx, Apr. 10, 1833.

26. W. Miller to T. Hendryx, Oct. 1, 1832.

27. W. Miller to T. Hendryx, May 19, 1841.

28. Miller, *Apology and Defence*, 36; Himes, *Views of the Prophecies*, 13, 14.

29. David Arnold Dean, "Echoes of the Midnight Cry: The Millerite Heritage in the Apologetics of the Advent Christian Denomination, 1860-1960" (Th.D. dissertation, Westminster Theological Seminary, 1976), 178-181.

30. *Signs of the Times*, May 15, 1840, 29.

31. Miller, *Apology and Defence*, 36. See also articles 6-12 in Miller's 1822 statement of belief, Bliss, *Memoirs of William Miller*, 78, 79.

32. *Signs of the Times*, Apr. 15, 1840, 14.

33. Bliss, *Memoirs of William Miller*, 215, 216.

34. W. Miller to T. Hendryx, Mar. 26, 1832.

35. Bliss, *Memoirs of William Miller*, 108, 109.

36. W. Miller to Bro. and Sis. Atwood, Sept. 16, 1833; W. Miller to T. Hendryx, Mar. 22, 1834.

37. W. Miller to T. Hendryx, Mar. 22, 1834.

38. Miller, *Apology and Defence*, 20; Bliss, *Memoirs of William Miller*, 122, 123; *Advent Shield*, May 1844, 84. Miller gives 1835 for the first $1.00 expense money he received, while Bliss gives 1836. Bliss is most likely correct, since he was working from Miller's records, whereas Miller was evidently working from memory.

39. *Advent Shield*, May 1844, 84.

40. *Signs of the Times*, Feb. 15, 1843, 173; W. Miller to T. Hendryx, Mar. 22, 1834.

41. This document is reproduced in Bliss, *Memoirs of William Miller*, 121, 122.

42. W. Miller to T. Hendryx, Apr. 2, 1836.

43. W. Miller to T. Hendryx, Oct. 23, 1834. That Hendryx had become convinced of the correctness of Miller's teaching in 1831 is evident from a letter Hendryx sent to Bliss when Hendryx donated his letter collection for the writing of the *Memoirs*. See pages 93, 94. The "almost two years" since Hendryx first heard Miller's message (see Miller's Oct. 23, 1834, letter) is undoubtedly an error, since the Miller collection contains correspondence to Hendryx in mid-1831.

44. W. Miller to T. Hendryx, Nov. 28, 1834; Mar. 6, 1835.

45. Bliss, *Memoirs of William Miller*, 143.

46. H. Jones to W. Miller, Dec. 27, 1832.

47. For fuller biographical treatment of Jones, see Froom, *Prophetic Faith of Our Fathers*, 4:576-579; Nichol, *Midnight Cry*, 190-193.

48. Miller, *Apology and Defence*, 19; *Advent Shield*, May 1844, 53.

49. *Olive Branch*, quoted in *Signs of the Times*, Apr. 6, 1842, 8.

50. The *Trumpet*, quoted in Wellcome, *History of the Second Advent Message*, 206.

51. *Millennial Harbinger*, July 1843, 290, 291.

52. W. Miller to T. Hendryx, Oct. 23, 1834.

53. Lowell *Courier*, Feb. 23, 1843, quoted in Nichol, *Midnight Cry*, 140.

54. W. Miller to T. Hendryx, Feb. 8, 1833.

55. Miller, *Apology and Defence*, 19; W. Miller to T. Hendryx, Feb. 11, 1835.

56. W. Miller to his son, Nov. 17, 1838.

57. Himes, *Views of the Prophecies*, 17, 18; W. H. Mitchell, *History of the Second Advent Church in Portland, ME* (Kennebunkport, ME: W. H. Mitchell, 1886), 6. Cf. L. D. Fleming to W. Miller, Apr. 11, 1840.

58. See Doan, *Miller Heresy*, 36; Barkun, *Crucible of the Millennium*, 94; Rowe, *Thunder and Trumpets*, 29; Dick, "William Miller," 76.

59. Doan, *Miller Heresy*, 14, 18.

60. The *Trumpet*, quoted in *Signs of the Times*, May 1, 1840, 23.

61. Bliss, *Memoirs of William Miller*, 140.

Chapter 4: **Enter Joshua V. Himes: Mission Organizer**

1. *Signs of the Times*, Nov. 1, 1840, 113.

2. There is no published biography of J. V. Himes. The best treatment is Arthur, "Joshua V. Himes" (M.A. thesis). The next few paragraphs are indebted to that source and Wellcome, *History of the Second Advent Message*, 89-91. Corrections that I have made in Arthur's account are from Himes' autobiographical statement found in the *Advent Christian Times*, Feb. 6, 1872.

3. For a history of the Connexionists, see Milo True Morrill, *A History of the Christian Denomination in America, 1794-1911 A.D.* (Dayton, OH: Christian Pub. Assn., 1912). See also Nathan O. Hatch, *The Democratization of American Christianity* (New Haven, CT: Yale University Press, 1989), passim; and references above in chapter 2 on restorationism.

4. *Union County Courier*, May 24, 1895, 3, quoted in Arthur, "Joshua V. Himes and the Cause of Adventism," in *The Disappointed*, 37.

5. Wellcome, *History of the Second Advent Message*, 89, 90.

6. Morrill, *History of the Christian Denomination*, 379.

7. Ibid., 162.

8. See, for example, W. L. Garrison to G. W. Benson, Mar. 10, 1838; W. L. Garrison to S. T. Benson, Mar. 5, 1838; Lewis Perry, *Radical Abolitionism: Anarchy and the Government of God in Antislavery Thought* (Ithaca, NY: Cornell University Press, 1973), 58, 74; Arthur, "Joshua V. Himes" (M.A. thesis), 16, 17.

9. Perry, *Radical Abolitionism*, 58, 59.

10. See Doan, *Miller Heresy*, 181, 182; Arthur, "Joshua V. Himes" (M.A. thesis), 10-13, 17.

11. *Union County Courier*, May 24, 1895, 3, quoted in Arthur, "Joshua V. Himes" in *The Disappointed*, 38.

12. *The Liberator*, Feb. 10, 1843, 23.

13. W. L. Garrison to H. E. Benson, Nov. 4, 1836.

14. See Arthur, "Joshua V. Himes" (M.A. thesis), 14-16.

15. Wendell Phillips Garrison and Francis Jackson Garrison, *William Lloyd Garrison, 1805-1879* (New York: Century, 1885), 2:327, 421-438; Cross, *Burned-over District*, 292, 293.

16. *Advent Shield*, May 1844, 53.

17. Boston *Times*, Mar. 13, 1838, 2.

18. Miller, *Apology and Defence*, 20; Bliss, *Memoirs of William Miller*, 134-139.

19. Bliss, *Memoirs of William Miller*, 135-137; *Christian Herald*, Nov. 28, 1839, 3.

20. Miller, *Apology and Defence*, 20, 21.

21. Ibid., 21. On the Exeter meetings, see the several articles on the topic in the *Christian Herald*, Nov. 28, 1839, 2, 3.

22. Miller, *Apology and Defence*, 21; Bliss, *Memoirs of William Miller*, 139.

23. Bliss, *Memoirs of William Miller*, 140, 141.

24. Ibid., 139, 141.

25. J. V. Himes to W. Miller, Jan. 17, 1840. (Italics supplied.)

26. *Signs of the Times*, Aug. 3, 1842, 140.

27. Bliss, *Memoirs of William Miller*, 144.

28. Miller, *Apology and Defence*, 21.

29. Ibid., 21, 22.

30. Arthur, "Joshua V. Himes" (M.A. thesis), 57. (Italics supplied.)

31. Ibid., 35-41.

32. W. L. Garrison to G. W. Benson, Jan. 15, 1844.

33. *Liberator*, Feb. 10, 1843, 23.

34. See Rowe, *Thunder and Trumpets*, 32, 34; *Advent Christian Times*, Feb. 6, 1872.

35. Arthur, " 'Come Out of Babylon,' " 15.

36. *Advent Christian Times*, Feb. 6, 1872; Hatch, *Democratization of American Christianity*, 142, 145.

37. Froom, *Prophetic Faith of Our Fathers*, 4:430, 436, 437; J. C. Furnas, *The Americans: A Social History of the United States, 1587-1914* (New York: G. P. Putnam's Sons, 1969), 557-559.

38. *Religious Telescope*, Nov. 27, 1839, quoted in Wesley Norton, *Religious Newspapers in the Old Northwest to 1861: A History, Bibliography, and Record of Opinion* (Athens, OH: Ohio University Press, 1977), 1-8.

39. *Signs of the Times*, Apr. 6, 1842, 4.

40. Ibid.

41. Ibid., Aug. 16, 1841, 78; Jan. 15, 1841, 57.

42. Dick, "William Miller," 96, 97; Arthur, "Joshua V. Himes," in *The Disappointed*, 46.

43. *Princeton Review*, Jan. 1841, 150; *Signs of the Times*, Sept. 1, 1840, 81.

44. *Midnight Cry*, Nov. 17, 1842, 2; *Signs of the Times*, Nov. 15, 1843, 110; *Advent Shield*, May 1844, 70.

45. *Midnight Cry*, Nov. 17, 1842, 2.

46. For all thirty-six titles in the Words of Warning series, see Froom, *Prophetic Faith of Our Fathers*, 4:709, 710.

47. See Dick, "William Miller," 114.

48. Joshua V. Himes, comp., *Millennial Harp, or Second Advent Hymns: Designed for Meetings on the Second Coming of Christ* (Boston: [J. V. Himes], 1842), 7.

49. *Signs of the Times*, Sept. 15, 1841, 96.

50. Ibid., Aug. 2, 1841, 70; *Second Report of the General Conference of Christians Expecting the Advent of the Lord Jesus Christ* (Boston: Joshua V. Himes, 1841), 7, 12, 4.

51. *Advent Shield*, May 1844, 87.

52. *Midnight Cry*, May 25, 1843, 74.

53. Wellcome, *History of the Second Advent Message*, 304.

54. *Signs of the Times*, Nov. 15, 1843, 109; cf. Aug. 3, 1842, 140; Mar. 8, 1843, 4.

55. Ibid., July 19, 1843, 156. Cf. Josiah Litch, *Prophetic Expositions* (Boston: Joshua V. Himes, 1842), 1:166, 167; *Signs of the Times*, May 24, 1843, 96; Jan. 4, 1843, 128.

56. *Signs of the Times*, Nov. 15, 1843, 111; *Voice of Truth*, June 8, 1844, 71; Wellcome, *History of the Second Advent Message*, 90.

57. Miller, *Apology and Defence*, 22.

58. *Signs of the Times*, Aug. 15, 1840, 76; Sept. 1, 1840, 84.

59. Morrill, *History of the Christian Denomination in America*, 140. It should be noted that the various reform associations also held annual meetings.

60. *Signs of the Times*, Sept. 1, 1840, 84; *The First Report of the General Conference of Christians Expecting the Advent of the Lord Jesus Christ* (Boston: Joshua V. Himes, 1841), 7. (Italics supplied.)

61. *Signs of the Times*, Sept. 1, 1840, 84; J. V. Himes to W. Miller [Aug. 17, 1840]. This letter is written on the bottom of a circular letter dated Aug. 10, 1840. But the envelope carries the Aug. 17 date.

62. *First Report of the General Conference*, 7, 8, 20.

63. Ibid., 14; Bliss, *Memoirs of William Miller*, 153.

64. Bliss, *Memoirs of William Miller*, 153; *First Report of the General Conference*, 17.

65. *First Report of the General Conference*, 16-18.

66. Ibid., 18; *Signs of the Times*, Nov. 1, 1840, 117; Albert C. Johnson, *Advent Christian History* (Boston: Advent Christian Publication Society, 1918), 99.

67. *Second Report of the General Conference*, 8, 9.

68. *Signs of the Times*, Aug. 2, 1841, 70.

69. *Second Report of the General Conference*, 2, 3.

70. *Signs of the Times*, Aug. 2, 1841, 68, 72.

71. Ibid., June 1, 1842, 68, 69; Joseph Bates, *Second Advent Way Marks and High Heaps, or a Connected View of the Fulfillment of Prophecy by God's Peculiar People, From*

the Year 1840 to 1847 (New Bedford, MA: n.p., 1847), 10, 11.

72. Arthur, "Joshua V. Himes" (M.A. thesis), 62, n. 28; Hewitt, *Midnight and Morning*, 133; Froom, *Prophetic Faith of Our Fathers*, 4:557-559.

73. David Arthur, quoted in Hewitt, *Midnight and Morning*, 130; Arthur, "Joshua V. Himes," in *The Disappointed*, 42.

74. *Trumpet*, quoted in *Signs of the Times*, May 1, 1840, 23.

75. *Olive Branch*, quoted in *Midnight Cry*, Dec. 5, 1842, 1.

76. *Olive Branch*, quoted in *Signs of the Times*, May 17, 1843, 88.

77. Copy of broadside, in Numbers and Butler, eds., *The Disappointed*, 93. Cf. *Signs of the Times*, Sept. 21, 1842, 8.

78. *Signs of the Times*, Aug. 17, 1842, 164.

79. Ibid., Sept. 21, 1842, 8.

80. See, e.g., ibid., May 1, 1840, 23.

Chapter 5: **More Millennial Missionaries**

1. *Advent Shield*, May 1844, 54.

2. Ibid., 54-56. Fitch will be treated in a later section of this chapter.

3. Ibid., 56; Bliss, *Memoirs of William Miller*, 136.

4. Josiah Litch, *The Probability of the Second Coming of Christ About A.D. 1843* (Boston: David H. Ela, 1838), iii.

5. *Advent Shield*, May 1844, 54.

6. Litch, *Probability of the Second Coming*, 157; *Signs of the Times*, Aug. 1, 1840, 70. For an insightful discussion of the history of Litch's interpretation of the sixth trumpet, see Eric Anderson, "The Millerite Use of Prophecy: A Case Study of a 'Striking Fulfilment,' " in *The Disappointed*, 78-91.

7. Litch, *Probability of the Second Coming*, v. cf. *Signs of the Times*, Aug. 1, 1840, 70; Wellcome, *History of the Second Advent Message*, 128.

8. Cross, *Burned-over District*, 293; Jerry Moon, "Josiah Litch: Herald of 'The Advent Near' " (unpublished paper, Andrews University, 1973), i.

9. Litch, "Address to the Clergy," May 10, 1840, in Litch, *An Address to the Public, and Especially the Clergy* (Boston: Joshua V. Himes, 1841), 13.

10. *Advent Shield*, May 1844, 62.

11. *Signs of the Times*, Sept. 1, 1841, 85.

12. *Second Report of the General Conference*, 9-12.

13. *Signs of the Times*, Aug. 2, 1841, 72, 68.

14. Ibid., Sept. 1, 1841, 86.

15. Ibid.

16. Ibid., Aug. 2, 1841, 68; Wellcome, *History of the Second Advent Message*, 232.

17. Wellcome, *History of the Second Advent Message*, 273, 274.

18. For general treatments of the nineteenth-century camp meeting, see Charles A. Johnson, *The Frontier Camp Meeting: Religion's Harvest Time* (Dallas: Southern Methodist University Press, 1955); Dickson D. Bruce, Jr., *And They All Sang Hallelujah: Plain-Folk Camp-Meeting Religion, 1800-1845* (Knoxville, TN: University of Tennessee Press, 1974).

19. *Signs of the Times*, June 1, 1842, 69.

20. Ibid., June 15, 1842, 88.

21. *Advent Shield*, May 1844, 68.

22. *Signs of the Times*, June 15, 1842, 88.

23. *Advent Shield*, May 1844, 68.

24. *Signs of the Times*, July 13, 1842, 117.

25. Ibid.; *Advent Shield*, May 1844, 68.

26. Boston *Post*, quoted in Wellcome, *History of the Second Advent Message*, 237.

27. *Signs of the Times*, June 15, 1842, 88.

28. Ibid., July 13, 1842, 116.

29. *Midnight Cry*, Mar. 7, 1844, 260; Dick, "William Miller and the Advent Crisis," 113.

30. *Signs of the Times*, July 13, 1842, 114; Wellcome, *History of the Second Advent Message*, 243.

31. For more on the big tent, see Froom, *Prophetic Faith of Our Fathers*, 4:655-657, 740-743; Arthur, "Joshua V. Himes" (M.A. thesis), 77-82, 107, 108.

32. Dick, "William Miller and the Advent Crisis," 67, 68; *Signs of the Times*, July 13, 1842, 116; Boston *Post*, quoted in Wellcome, *History of the Second Advent Message*, 237. See also, *Signs of the Times*, July 13, 1842, 114.

33. New York *Herald*, quoted in Nichol, *Midnight Cry*, 125.

34. See Dick, "William Miller and the Advent Crisis," 62, 63.

35. Hiram Munger, *The Life and Religious Experience of Hiram Munger* (Chickopee Falls, MA: Hiram Munger, 1885), 36, 37. This volume was first published in 1861.

36. Ibid., 38, 39.

37. Ibid., 41, 42.

38. Ibid., 40, 41; cf. 43-45.

39. Ibid., 43-46.

40. See Dick, "The Millerite Movement," in *Adventism in America*, 16, 17; Everett N. Dick, "Advent Camp Meetings of the 1840s," *Adventist Heritage*, 4 (Winter 1977), 3-10.

41. C. Fitch to W. Miller, Mar. 5, 1838.

42. Charles Fitch, *Letter to Rev. J. Litch on the Second Coming of Christ* (Boston: Joshua V. Himes, 1841), 6, 7.

43. C. Fitch to W. Miller, Mar. 5, 1838. Nearly all of the content of these sermons has been reproduced in *Signs of the Times*, Apr. 13, 1842, 13, 14; Apr. 27, 1842, 31, 32; May 4, 1842, 34; May 11, 1842, 42, 43; May 18, 1842, 49, 50; May 25, 1842, 58, 59; June 1, 1842, 66, 67; June 8, 1842, 74, 75. While the 1842 articles give Feb. 27 as the date the 1838 sermons were preached, the contemporary letter gives Mar. 4.

44. Fitch, *Letter to Rev. J. Litch*, 7-9; *Advent Shield*, May 1844, 56.

45. Fitch, *Letter to Rev. J. Litch*, 12; C. Fitch to Brother and Sister Palmer, July 26, 1842.

46. *Signs of the Times*, Dec. 15, 1841, 144.

47. Ibid., Oct. 12, 1842, 32.

48. Charles Fitch, *Slaveholding Weighed in the Balance of Truth* (Boston: Isaac Knapp, 1837), 32.

49. W. L. Garrison to I. Knapp, July 5, 1836; Garrison and Garrison, *William Lloyd Garrison*, 2:136.

50. The "Appeal" was published in the *New England Spectator*, Aug. 2, 1837. The *Spectator* was published by a member of Fitch's congregation. See Garrison

and Garrison, *William Lloyd Garrison*, 2:136.

51. Louis Ruchames, ed., *A House Dividing Against Itself, 1836-1840: The Letters of William Lloyd Garrison* (Cambridge, MA: Harvard University Press, 1971), 2:275, n. 2; Garrison and Garrison, *William Lloyd Garrison*, 2:142; J. T. Woodbury to C. Fitch and J. H. Towne, Aug. 17, 1837, in *A House Dividing*, 2:297, 298; W. L. Garrison to Editor of the *Spectator*, Oct. 20, 1837; W. L. Garrison to F. Jackson, June 28, 1838; H. B. Stanton to J. G. Birney, Sept. 1, 1837; Aug. 7, 1837; W. L. Garrison to G. W. Benson, Sept. 23, 1837.

52. W. L. Garrison to G. W. Benson, Oct. 20, 1837; May 25, 1838; W. L. Garrison to L. Tappan, Sept. 13, 1837.

53. C. Fitch to W. L. Garrison, Jan. 9, 1840, in Garrison and Garrison, *William Lloyd Garrison*, 2:335-337.

54. Fitch, *Letter to Rev. J. Litch*, 9.

55. R. J. Green, "Oberlin Theology," in *Dictionary of Christianity in America*, ed. Daniel G. Reid (Downers Grove, IL: InterVarsity Press, 1990), 834; Benjamin Breckinridge Warfield, *Studies in Perfectionism* (Phillipsburg, NJ: Presbyterian and Reformed Pub. Co., 1958), 64, 65.

56. Warfield, *Studies in Perfectionism*, 64, 65; Fitch's book was reproduced in the *Oberlin Evangelist* between Jan. 15, 1840, and Mar. 25, 1840, and in the *Guide to Christian Perfection*, Feb. 1840, 169-191; A. C. Guelzo, "Woods, Leonard," in *Dictionary of Christianity in America*, 1270; Leonard Woods, *Examination of the Doctrine of Perfection as Held by Rev. Asa Mahan, . . . Rev. Charles Fitch, and Others Agreeing With Them* (Rochester, NY: William Alling, 1841); William R. Weeks, *Letter to the Rev. Charles Fitch, on His Views of Sanctification* (Newark, NJ: Aaron Guest, 1840).

57. Charles Fitch, *Letter to the Newark Presbytery* (Newark, NJ: Aaron Guest, 1840), 20; cf. *Oberlin Evangelist*, Mar. 25, 1840, 54; Apr. 1, 1840, 9-13.

58. C. Fitch to Brother and Sister Palmer, July 26, 1842; *Oberlin Evangelist*, Apr. 28, 1841, 60. See also Charles Edward White, *The Beauty of Holiness: Phoebe Palmer as Theologian, Revivalist, Feminist, and Humanitarian* (Grand Rapids, MI: Zondervan, 1986), 155.

59. *New York Evangelist*, March 19, 1836; Susan Hayes Ward, *The History of the Broadway Tabernacle Church* (New York: n.p., 1901), 28; Hardman, *Charles Grandison Finney*, 311-313.

60. See George R. Knight, "Oberlin College and Adventist Educational Reforms," *Adventist Heritage*, 8 (Spring 1983):3-9; Robert S. Fletcher, *A History of Oberlin College From Its Foundation Through the Civil War* (Oberlin, OH: Oberlin College, 1943), 2 vols.

61. *Oberlin Evangelist*, Jan. 19, 1842, 14; Feb. 16, 1842, 28.

62. Ibid., June 8, 1842, 91, 92; Sept. 28, 1842, 158, 163, 164; E. Wade to H. Cowles, Dec. 16, 1842; C. Fitch to H. Cowles, Jan. 14, 1843.

63. Charles Fitch, Henry Cowles, and Asa Mahan, *Discussion on the Second Advent Near* (Cleveland, OH: n.p., 1843), 3.

64. *Oberlin Evangelist*, Oct. 11, 1843, 167; J. Starkweather to C. Finney, Oct. 25, 1842.

65. W. G. Ballentine, ed., *The Oberlin Jubilee, 1833-1883* (Oberlin, OH: E. J. Goodrich, 1883), 198, 199; cf. James H. Fairchild, *Oberlin: The Colony and the College, 1833-1883* (Oberlin, OH: E. J. Goodrich, 1883), 86, 87.

66. Bates, *Second Advent Way Marks*, 10, 11.

67. *Christian Reflector*, Nov. 28, 1844, 28.

68. *Liberator*, Feb. 10, 1843, 23.

69. Arthur, "Joshua V. Himes," in *The Disappointed*, 46; *Christian Herald*, in *Signs of the Times*, July 13, 1842, 114; *Midnight Cry*, Mar. 21, 1844, 282.

70. Dick, "William Miller and the Advent Crisis," 267-269; *Advent Shield*, May 1844, 88.

71. *Signs of the Times*, Dec. 14, 1842, 103.

72. S. M. Marsh to W. Miller, Feb. 24, 1842; *Signs of the Times*, Dec. 21, 1842, 105.

73. See Froom, *Prophetic Faith of Our Fathers*, 4:702-704.

74. Wellcome, *History of the Second Advent Message*, 288; T. D. Weld to L. Tappan, Apr. 5, 1836; E. Wright to T. D. Weld, Nov. 5, 1835; J. G. Birney to L. Tappan, Feb. 5, 1841; W. L. Garrison to H. E. Garrison, July 23, 1840; Garrison and Garrison, *William Lloyd Garrison*, 2:356; Cross, *Burned-over District*, 301.

75. W. Miller, quoted in Rowe, *Thunder and Trumpets*, 43; Cross, *Burned-over District*, 301.

76. Wellcome, *History of the Second Advent Message*, 272.

77. W. L. Garrison to E. Pease, Apr. 4, 1843; W. L. Garrison to H. C. Wright, Mar. 1, 1843; cf. Garrison and Garrison, *William Lloyd Garrison*, 3:94.

78. *Liberator*, July 22, 1842, 116; *Oberlin Evangelist*, July 7, 1841, 110, 111.

79. *Liberator*, Feb. 14, 1840, 27; cf. Feb. 10, 1843, 23.

80. P. Barbour to W. Miller, Nov. 8, 1844.

81. For secondary treatments on this topic, see Delbert W. Baker, *The Unknown Prophet* (Washington, DC: Review and Herald, 1987), 69-77; Louis B. Reynolds, *We Have Tomorrow: The Story of American Seventh-day Adventists With an African Heritage* (Washington, DC: Review and Herald, 1984), 17-28.

82. Munger, *Life and Religious Experience*, 42; [Sojourner Truth], *Narrative of Sojourner Truth* (Battle Creek, MI: n.p., 1878), 109, 110; Page Smith, *The Nation Comes of Age* (New York: McGraw-Hill, 1981), 659-662.

83. *Signs of the Times*, June 7, 1843, 108.

84. *Midnight Cry*, Feb. 29, 1844, 249.

85. Baker, *Unknown Prophet*, 75; Reynolds, *We Have Tomorrow*, 19; and Froom, *Prophetic Faith of Our Fathers*, 4:705 list a Charles Bowles as a third black Millerite preacher. But the only reference given is John W. Lewis, *The Life, Labors, and Travels of Elder Charles Bowles* (Watertown [MA]: Ingalls & Stowell, 1852). In examining that volume, I was unable to find any reference to a connection with Adventism.

86. William E. Foy, *The Christian Experience of William E. Foy Together With the Two Visions* (Portland [ME]: J. and C. H. Pearson, 1845), 9, 23. See also Baker, *Unknown Prophet* and "Foy, William Ellis," in *Seventh-day Adventist Encyclopedia* (Washington, DC: Review and Herald, 1976, ed.), 474, 475.

87. Foy, *Christian Experience*, 15, 21-23.

88. Hatch, *Democratization of American Christianity*, 78, 79; Donald W. Dayton, *Discovering an Evangelical Heritage* (New York: Harper & Row, 1976), 85-98; White, *Beauty of Holiness*.

89. Wellcome, *History of the Second Advent Message*, 305, 306.

90. *Midnight Cry*, July 6, 1843, 149.

91. G. A. Troop to "Brother Dan," Apr. 23, 1843.

92. *Signs of the Times*, May 17, 1843, 87; *Midnight Cry*, July 6, 1843, 149.

93. O. R. Fassett, *The Biography of Mrs. L. E. Fassett* (Boston: Advent Christian Pub. Soc., 1885), 26, 27.

94. *Midnight Cry*, July 6, 1843, 149. (Italics supplied.)

Chapter 6: Entering the Year of the End

1. *Signs of the Times*, Jan. 25, 1843, 150.

2. Ibid., 147-149.

3. Ibid., Jan. 4, 1843, 121; Jan. 18, 1843, 141.

4. Miller, *Apology and Defence*, 24; W. Miller to Brother and Sister Atwood, May 31, 1831. Even the title of Miller's major book contained the words *About the Year 1843*.

5. Miller, *Apology and Defence*, 24; *Advent Shield*, May 1844, 73; Wellcome, *History of the Second Advent Message*, 282. It appears that Wellcome may be dependent upon Litch's *Shield* article in his 1839 statement, but both could have been present at the same 1839 meeting.

6. *First Report of the General Conference*, 21.

7. *Second Report of the General Conference*, 7.

8. *Advent Watchman*, Apr. 30, 1851, 59; *Zion's Watchman*, July 25, 1840, 117, quoted in Doan, *Miller Heresy*, 37; cf. *Signs of the Times*, Dec. 1, 1841, 135, 136. It has sometimes been held that N. Whiting also rejected all dates (see Froom, *Prophetic Faith of Our Fathers*, 4:641) on the basis of Whiting's letter to Miller on Oct. 24, 1844. But the *Midnight Cry*, June 1, 1843, 84, puts that thesis to rest. The most that can be proved from Whiting's letter is that he did not accept the October 1844 date.

9. Bliss, *Memoirs of William Miller*, 139; Wellcome, *History of the Second Advent Message*, 452.

10. J. V. Himes to W. Miller, June 26, 1841.

11. *Signs of the Times*, June 1, 1842, 68.

12. Ibid., 69; David T. Arthur, "Millerism," in *Rise of Adventism*, 161. (Italics supplied.)

13. Henry Jones, *American Views of Christ's Second Advent* (New York: Saxton & Miles, 1842), 6, 7, 22; *Report of the Proceedings of the Third Session of the General Conference Expecting the Advent of the Lord* (Boston: J. V. Himes, 1841), 42; *Advent Watchman*, Apr. 30, 1851, 59.

14. *Signs of the Times*, Aug. 3, 1842, 140.

15. Ibid., 141.

16. Ibid., June 7, 1843, 107; Wellcome, *History of the Second Advent Message*, 253.

17. *Signs of the Times*, Jan. 4, 1843, 121; *Advent Shield*, May 1844, 73-77.

18. *Advent Shield*, May 1844, 73, 74; *Signs of the Times*, Feb. 22, 1843, 179.

19. *Signs of the Times*, Nov. 9, 1842, 61.

20. Ibid., Mar. 22, 1843, 19. For a composite newspaper description of the comet, see Dick, "William Miller," 170, 171; for a scientific opinion regarding the comet, see Nichol, *Midnight Cry*, 145.

21. *Advent Shield*, May 1844, 71; *Second Advent of Christ*, Feb. 22, 1843, 3.

22. *Signs of the Times*, Feb. 1, 1843, 157; T. D. Weld to A. G. Weld, Jan. 22, 1843.

23. *Signs of the Times*, Aug. 3, 1842, 137.

24. Ibid., May 17, 1843, 85; Bliss, *Memoirs of William Miller*, 228, 229.

25. *Signs of the Times*, Feb. 15, 1843, 173; W. Miller to his son, Nov. 17, 1838.

26. *Oberlin Evangelist*, Sept. 14, 1842, 150.

27. *Signs of the Times*, May 17, 1843, 85; June 7, 1843, 108.

28. Ibid., Aug. 9, 1843, 181.

29. See Dick, "William Miller," 138, 139.

30. *Advent Shield*, May 1844, 72.

31. Wellcome, *History of the Second Advent Message*, 219.

32. *Advent Shield*, May 1844, 71, 72.

33. *Signs of the Times*, May 17, 1843, 85.

34. Joseph Bates, *The Autobiography of Joseph Bates* (Battle Creek, MI: Seventh-day Adventist Pub. Assn., 1868), 277.

35. Ibid., 278. This account was also reported in the Newark *Daily Advertizer*, Mar. 2, 1844, quoted in Nichol, *Midnight Cry*, 197.

36. Bates, *Autobiography*, 281.

37. *Advent Shield*, May 1844, 77, 78; *Signs of the Times*, July 19, 1843, 157; Jan. 21, 1844, 24; Bliss, *Memoirs of William Miller*, 254.

38. *Signs of the Times*, Feb. 21, 1844, 24; *Midnight Cry*, Nov. 2, 1843, 94; Robert W. Olson, "Southern Baptists' Reactions to Millerism" (Th.D. dissertation, Southwestern Baptist Theological Seminary, 1972), 75, 76.

39. See Nichol, *Midnight Cry*, 166-168; Hugh I. B. Dunton, "The Millerite Adventists and Other Millenarian Groups in Great Britain, 1830-1860" (Ph.D. dissertation, University of London, 1984); Louis Billington, "The Millerite Adventists in Great Britain, 1840-1850," in *The Disappointed*, 59-77; an earlier version of that article appeared in the *Journal of American Studies*, 1967, 191-212; Arnold Dallimore, *Forerunner of the Charismatic Movement: The Life of Edward Irving* (Chicago: Moody Press, 1983); C. Gordon Strachan, *The Pentecostal Theology of Edward Irving* (Peabody, MA: Hendrickson, 1973).

40. *Advent Shield*, May 1844, 92, 47, 48; Robert Kieran Whalen, "Millenarianism and Millennialism in America, 1790-1880" (Ph.D. dissertation, State University of New York at Stony Brook, 1972); Sandeen, *Roots of Fundamentalism*; Timothy P. Weber, *Living in the Shadow of the Second Coming*, enl. ed. (Grand Rapids, MI: Zondervan, 1983); Paul Boyer, *When Time Shall Be No More: Prophecy Belief in Modern American Culture* (Cambridge, MA: Harvard University Press, 1992).

41. Billington, "The Millerite Adventists," in *The Disappointed*, 59.

42. *Midnight Cry*, May 18, 1843, 65.

43. Ibid.

44. *Signs of the Times*, June 7, 1843, 108.

45. *Midnight Cry*, Jan. 4, 1844, 189.

46. *Signs of the Times*, Nov. 15, 1843, 109.

47. *Graham's Magazine*, March 1843, 145-149.

48. New York *Tribune* Extra, Mar. 2, 1843, 1; Ira V. Brown, "The Millerites and the Boston Press," *The New England Quarterly*, 16 (1943):592-614; Vern Carner, "Horace Greeley and the Millerites," *Adventist Heritage*, 2 (Summer 1975), 33, 34; Madeline Warner, "The Changing Image of the Millerites in the Western Massachusetts Press," ibid., 5-7.

49. See Gary Scharnhorst, "Images of the Millerites in American Literature," *American Quarterly*, 32 (Spring 1980), 19-36; John Greenleaf Whittier, "The World's End," *Adventist Heritage*, 1 (July 1974): 14-17. The Whittier piece was first published in *The Stranger in Lowell* in 1845.

50. *Liberator*, Feb. 10, 1843, 23; W. L. Garrison to H. C. Wright, Mar. 1, 1843.

51. *Millennial Harbinger*, July 1843, 291, 292; T. L. Miethe, "Campbell, Alexander (1788-1866)," in *Dictionary of Christianity in America*, 214, 215. Himes had earlier written a preface to Campbell's *Delusions: An Analysis of the Book of Mormon* (Boston: Benjamin H. Greene, 1832).

52. Garth M. Rosell and Richard A. G. Dupuis, eds., *The Memoirs of Charles G. Finney: The Complete Restored Text* (Grand Rapids, MI: Zondervan, 1989), 453, 454. The autographed copy of *Miller's Works* is housed in the rare book room of the Oberlin College library.

53. See Rowe, *Thunder and Trumpets*, 63.

54. *The Witness*, Dec. 10, 1842, 184.

55. Dick, "William Miller," 183, 184; *Signs of the Times*, Feb. 1, 1843, 156.

56. M. Stuart, *Hints on the Interpretation of Prophecy*, 2d ed. (New York: Van Nostrand & Terrett, 1851), 173.

Chapter 7: **Coming Out of Babylon**

1. Miller, *Apology and Defence*, 19, 20; Bliss, *Memoirs of William Miller*, 140, 170.

2. Doan, *The Miller Heresy*, 26, 188.

3. See ibid., 40.

4. *Signs of the Times*, Aug. 3, 1842, 140.

5. *Universalist*, quoted in Froom, *Prophetic Faith of Our Fathers*, 4:760.

6. *Olive Branch*, quoted in *Signs of the Times*, May 17, 1843, 88; cf. *Advent Shield*, May 1844, 83.

7. *Advent Shield*, May 1844, 83.

8. Bliss, *Memoirs of William Miller*, 138. Sears in *Days of Delusion* did much to spread unfounded rumors regarding Millerism in the twentieth century. Twenty years later, Nichol countered Sears' work in his *Midnight Cry*.

9. *Journal of Commerce*, quoted in *Signs of the Times*, Feb. 1, 1843, 157.

10. *Graham's Magazine*, Mar. 1843, 148; *Signs of the Times*, Mar. 29, 1843, 29; Mar. 22, 1843, 20.

11. *American Journal of Insanity*, Jan. 1845, 250, 251.

12. See Dick, "William Miller," 194, 195.

13. Providence *Journal*, quoted in *Niles National Register*, May 6, 1843, 160; Alice L. Hoag, "Millerism," a paper read before the Macedon Center Historical Society, Feb. 14, 1898.

14. Nichol, *Midnight Cry*, passim; Ronald L. Numbers and Janet S. Numbers, "Millerism and Madness: A Study of 'Religious Insanity' in Nineteenth-Century America," in *The Disappointed*, 92-117; a slightly different version of the Numbers' paper appeared in the *Bulletin of the Menninger Clinic*, 49:4 (1985): 289-320; Doan, *The Miller Heresy*, 170.

15. Rowe, *Thunder and Trumpets*, 104; Alexis de Tocqueville, *Democracy in America*, ed. J. P. Mayer, trans. George Lawrence (Garden City, NY: Double-

day, 1969), 2:534; Numbers and Numbers, "Millerism and Madness," in *The Disappointed*, 110.

16. *Oberlin Evangelist*, Jan. 18, 1843, 15.

17. *Gazette and Advertiser*, quoted in Bliss, *Memoirs of William Miller*, 227.

18. *Midnight Cry*, Nov. 17, 1842, 3.

19. Ibid., Dec. 1, 1842, 3.

20. James White, *Life Incidents in Connection With the Great Advent Movement* (Battle Creek, MI: Seventh-day Adventist Pub. Assn., 1868), 108.

21. William Miller to his son, Feb. 2, 1843; *Signs of the Times*, Aug. 3, 1842, 137.

22. Miller, *Apology and Defence*, 21; *Signs of the Times*, Aug. 3, 1842, 140; *Advent Herald*, Mar. 6, 1844, 36.

23. *Advent Herald*, Mar. 6, 1844, 37.

24. Wellcome, *History of the Second Advent Message*, 306.

25. *Midnight Cry*, Feb. 8, 1844, 229.

26. Stephen Allen and W. H. Pilsbury, *History of Methodism in Maine, 1793-1886* (Augusta, ME: Charles E. Nash, 1887), 122.

27. *Advent Herald*, Feb. 14, 1844, 13.

28. Ibid., Feb. 14, 1844, 13; Feb. 21, 1844, 17, 18.

29. Wellcome, *History of the Second Advent Message*, 297.

30. Ibid.; Allen and Pilsbury, *History of Methodism in Maine*, 481.

31. Allen and Pilsbury, *History of Methodism in Maine*, 123, 124.

32. Miller, *Apology and Defence*, 23.

33. *First Report of the General Conference*, 20-22.

34. *Signs of the Times*, Aug. 2, 1841, 70.

35. Ibid., July 6, 1842, 110.

36. Ibid.

37. Ibid., June 14, 1843, 119; *Voice of Truth*, Apr. 27, 1844, 47; see also Arthur, "Joshua V. Himes" (M.A. thesis), 95-97.

38. *Midnight Cry*, Feb. 22, 1844, 245.

39. *Signs of the Times*, Jan. 10, 1844, 175.

40. *Advent Shield*, May 1844, 91, 81.

41. *Midnight Cry*, Nov. 18, 1842, 1. (Italics supplied.)

42. Damsteegt, *Foundations of the Seventh-day Adventist Message and Mission*, 48; Charles Fitch, *"Come Out of Her, My People"* (Boston: J. V. Himes, 1843), 9-11, 16.

43. Fitch, *"Come Out of Her, My People,"* 18, 19.

44. Ibid., 24.

45. *Second Advent of Christ*, July 26, 1843, 1-3; *Midnight Cry*, Sept. 21, 1843, 33.

46. H. Jones to W. Miller, May 19, 1834; *Christian Palladium*, Aug. 1, 1839, 105.

47. Doan, *The Miller Heresy*, 122.

48. *Signs of the Times*, Jan. 31, 1844, 196.

49. W. Miller to E. Galusha, Apr. 5, 1844; Miller, *Apology and Defence*, 25, 30; *Advent Herald*, Feb. 11, 1846, 3.

50. *Advent Herald*, Feb. 14, 1844, 9; May 1, 1844, 97.

51. Ibid., Sept. 18, 1844, 53; *Advent Shield*, May 1844, 46-93.

52. *Midnight Cry*, Feb. 15, 1844, 237, 238; Mar. 14, 1844, 270.

53. *Signs of the Times*, Jan. 3, 1844, 166. See also *Voice of Truth*, Apr. 27, 1844, 46, 47.

54. Froom, *Prophetic Faith of Our Fathers*, 4:783.

Chapter 8: **The Spring Disappointment**

1. *Signs of the Times*, Nov. 15, 1843, 112. (Italics supplied.)
2. Ibid., Jan. 31, 1844, 196.
3. *Midnight Cry*, Dec. 28, 1843, 172.
4. Bliss, *Memoirs of William Miller*, 248, 249; *Midnight Cry*, Feb. 22, 1844, 242.
5. *Midnight Cry*, Feb. 22, 1844, 241.
6. Ibid., Feb. 29, 1844, 243, 249; *Advent Herald*, Mar. 6, 1844, 39.
7. Bliss, *Memoirs of William Miller*, 253; *Advent Herald*, Mar. 6, 1844, 39; *Midnight Cry*, Mar. 14, 1844, 265.
8. *Midnight Cry*, Mar. 14, 1844, 265; Feb. 29, 1844, 249; *Advent Shield*, May 1844, 79.
9. "Mr. Miller" to A. P. Weaver, Mar. 17, 1844, quoted in Rowe, *Thunder and Trumpets*, 108.
10. *Advent Herald*, Apr. 10, 1844, 77, 78; *Midnight Cry*, Apr. 18, 1844, 318. (Italics supplied.)
11. J. V. Himes to W. Miller, Apr. 3, 1844. (Italics supplied.)
12. W. Miller to E. Galusha, Apr. 5, 1844.
13. *Advent Herald*, Apr. 10, 1844, 80; *Midnight Cry*, Apr. 11, 1844, 305. (Italics supplied.)
14. Miller, *Apology and Defence*, 24; Sears, *Days of Delusion*, 144.
15. *Christian Reflector*, May 16, 1844, 77.
16. *Advent Herald*, Mar. 6, 1844, 39; *Midnight Cry*, Feb. 15, 1844, 237.
17. *Signs of the Times*, June 21, 1843, 123; *Midnight Cry*, Apr. 4, 1844, 297.
18. *Advent Herald*, Apr. 24, 1844, 92; *Advent Shield*, May 1844, 80.
19. Bliss, *Memoirs of William Miller*, 256.
20. Boston *Post*, quoted in ibid., 262, 263.
21. *Advent Herald*, June 5, 1844, 140.
22. Ibid., 140, 141.
23. Ibid., Apr. 24, 1844, 93.
24. Bates, *Second Advent Way Marks*, 10, 11; see also chapter 5 of this book under the section on Fitch.
25. *Advent Herald*, Apr. 24, 1844, 93. (Italics supplied.)

Chapter 9: **The Tarrying Time**

1. *Western Midnight Cry*, quoted in *Midnight Cry*, May 9, 1844, 342.
2. Ibid.
3. Ibid., July 18, 1844, 5.
4. *Advent Herald*, Apr. 10, 1844, 80.
5. Ibid., Oct. 30, 1844, 93.
6. Bliss, *Memoirs of William Miller*, 264; *Advent Herald*, Sept. 4, 1844, 36.
7. *Advent Herald*, Aug. 21, 1844, 20; Sept. 25, 1844, 64.
8. Ibid., Sept. 25, 1844, 64.
9. Ibid., Aug. 21, 1844, 20.
10. Wellcome, *History of the Second Advent Message*, 356. See also chapter 13 below.
11. *Midnight Cry*, Sept. 12, 1844, 80; Dec. 14, 1843, 150.

12. *Christian Reflector*, May 16, 1844, 77.

13. *Christian Watchman*, quoted in Nichol, *Midnight Cry*, 185; *Advent Herald*, Aug. 14, 1844, 14.

14. *Liberator*, Feb. 10, 1843, 23; *Signs of the Times*, Sept. 27, 1843, 44.

15. Numbers and Numbers, "Millerism and Madness," in *The Disappointed*, 105; *The Witness*, Dec. 10, 1842, 184.

16. *Signs of the Times*, Jan. 25, 1843, 150; May 10, 1843, 74, 75.

17. Ibid., June 7, 1843, 107.

18. *Advent Herald*, June 5, 1844, 141; *Signs of the Times*, Jan. 31, 1844, 196.

19. *Christian Reflector*, May 16, 1844, 77.

20. *Signs of the Times*, Apr. 19, 1843, 56; *Defence of Elder Joshua V. Himes* (Boston: n.p., 1851), 16; see also Nichol, *Midnight Cry*, 326.

21. M. Barton to W. Miller, Apr. 19, 1844, quoted in Rowe, *Thunder and Trumpets*, 63; Stephen J. Stein, *The Shaker Experience in America* (New Haven, CT: Yale University Press, 1992), 207-209; *Signs of the Times*, June 5, 1844, 141.

22. *Defence of Elder Joshua V. Himes*, 6, 7; John Starkweather, *A Narrative of Conversion to the Faith of the Pre-millennial Advent of Christ in 1843* (Boston: n.p., 1843), 3-13; J. Starkweather to C. Finney, Oct. 25, 1842.

23. *Defence of Elder Joshua V. Himes*, 7, 8; *Advent Herald*, July 17, 1844, 188.

24. *Defence of Elder Joshua V. Himes*, 8-10.

25. Ibid., 10-12; *Advent Herald*, July 17, 1844, 188.

26. *Defence of Elder Joshua V. Himes*, 12.

27. Philadelphia *Public Ledger*, Sept. 11, 1843, quoted in Dick, "William Miller," 69, 70. Cf. *Advent Herald*, July 17, 1844, 188.

28. *Midnight Cry*, Sept. 14, 1843, 29.

29. See *Signs of the Times*, Sept. 20, 1843, 36, 37; Sept. 27, 1843, 45, 46; Oct. 11, 1843, 64.

30. Ibid., Nov. 8, 1843, 97.

31. Ibid., Sept. 20, 1843, 37.

32. *Defence of Elder Joshua V. Himes*, 13-15.

33. Ibid., 16. See chapter 12 below for more on post-October 1844 fanaticism.

34. *Advent Herald*, Aug. 21, 1844, 20; J. White, *Life Incidents*, 157.

35. J. White, *Life Incidents*, 157-159.

Chapter 10: **The "True Midnight Cry"**

1. Bates, *Autobiography*, 297.

2. J. White, *Life Incidents*, 159.

3. *Review and Herald*, Aug. 16, 1923, 7; J. White, *Life Incidents*, 159, 160.

4. *True Midnight Cry*, Aug. 22, 1844, 4; *Advent Herald*, Aug. 21, 1844, 20.

5. *Midnight Cry*, Oct. 3, 1844, 97-99; cf. J. White, *Life Incidents*, 165.

6. Bates, *Autobiography*, 298; cf. Bates, *Second Advent Way Marks*, 30.

7. J. White, *Life Incidents*, 166.

8. *Midnight Cry*, June 27, 1844, 394.

9. Ibid., Feb. 22, 1844, 243, 244; *Advent Herald*, Apr. 3, 1844, 68, 69.

10. *Signs of the Times*, May 17, 1843, 85.

11. *Midnight Cry*, June 27, 1844, 397; *Advent Herald*, Oct. 30, 1844, 93.

12. [S. S. Snow], *The Sacred Symbol: A Manual of the History, Laws and Doctrines of the Church of Mount Zion* (New York: Baker & Godwin, 1868), 21.

13. Ibid., 23; *Bible Examiner*, Sept. 24, 1844, 1, 2.

14. *Oberlin Evangelist*, Oct. 23, 1844, 169, 170, 175.

15. *Midnight Cry*, Mar. 7, 1844, 260.

16. Ibid.; [Snow], *Sacred Symbol*, 9, 10.

17. *Midnight Cry*, Mar. 7, 1844, 260; *Signs of the Times*, Jan. 10, 1844, 175; [Snow], *Sacred Symbol*, 11.

18. *Bible Examiner*, Mar. 1880, 398, 399.

19. *Mob, Under Pretence of Law, or, The Arrest and Trial of Rev. George Storrs* (Concord, NH: Elbridge G. Chase, 1835), 3.

20. W. L. Garrison to I. Knapp, Feb. 3, 1836; E. Wright, Jr. to T. D. Weld, Apr. 21, 1836; cf. E. Wright, Jr. to J. G. Birney, Nov. 5, 1835; Alice Felt Tyler, *Freedom's Ferment* (New York: Harper & Brothers, 1962), 505.

21. Donald G. Matthews, *Slavery and Methodism: A Chapter in American Morality, 1780-1845* (Princeton, NJ: Princeton University Press, 1965), 121, 127, 133, 138, 139, 141, 154, 169; Cross, *Burned-over District*, 223; George Storrs, *Six Sermons on the Inquiry, Is There Immortality in Sin and Suffering?* 3d ed. (New York: Bible Examiner, 1855), 9.

22. *Midnight Cry*, Feb. 15, 1844, 238; Matthews, *Slavery and Methodism*, 230; Cross, *Burned-over District*, 266, 267; *Bible Examiner*, Mar. 1880, 400.

23. Storrs, *Six Sermons* (1855 ed.), 13; *Midnight Cry*, Oct. 12, 1843, 63, 64, 70.

24. *Bible Examiner*, Mar. 1880, 399.

25. Storrs, *Six Sermons* (1855 ed.), 10. For an analysis of Grew's work, see LeRoy Edwin Froom, *The Conditionalist Faith of Our Fathers* (Washington, DC: Review and Herald, 1965), 2:300-305.

26. *Bible Examiner*, Mar. 1880, 400.

27. Ibid., 400, 401.

28. Ibid.; Wellcome, *History of the Second Advent Message*, 515. For an analysis of Storrs' work and his *Six Sermons*, see Froom, *Conditionalist Faith of Our Fathers*, 2:305-313.

29. *Bible Examiner*, May 1843, 15, 16; George Storrs, *An Inquiry: Are the Souls of the Wicked Immortal, in Six Sermons* (Albany, NY: W. and A. White and J. Visscher, 1842), 46, 47.

30. Henry Jones, *The Bible Reader No. 1: Compend of Parallel and Explanatory Scripture References on Christ's Second Advent at Hand* (New York: Piercy and Reed, 1843), 12, 13.

31. C. Fitch to G. Storrs, Jan. 25, 1844.

32. Ibid.

33. Cleveland *Herald*, Feb. 13, 1844, quoted in Nathan Gordon Thomas, "The Millerite Movement in the State of Ohio" (M.A. thesis, Ohio University, 1957), 39. See also Cleveland *Herald*, Mar. 18, 1844, 3.

34. Bliss, *Memoirs of William Miller*, 55; Miller, *Apology and Defence*, 3.

35. I. E. Jones to W. Miller, Apr. 6, 1844.

36. *Midnight Cry*, May 23, 1844, 355.

37. *Christian Standard*, Dec. 28, 1871, quoted in *Advent Christian Times*, Feb. 6, 1872.

38. *Advent Herald*, Apr. 17, 1844, 88; *Midnight Cry*, Apr. 18, 1844, 313.

39. *Christian Reflector*, May 16, 1844, 77.

40. *Advent Herald*, June 5, 1844, 141; *Midnight Cry*, June 13, 1844, 378.

41. *Bible Examiner*, July 1850, 109, 110.

42. *Advent Herald*, Aug. 21, 1844, 20.
43. Ibid., 21; Sept. 11, 1844, 46, 47.
44. Ibid., Sept. 18, 1844, 52, 53; Sept. 25, 1844, 60-62.
45. Ibid., 64; Bliss, *Memoirs of William Miller*, 268, 269.
46. *Voice of Truth*, Sept. 25, 1844, 140; July 27, 1844, 99; *Midnight Cry*, Oct. 3, 1844, 100, 97.
47. J. V. Himes to W. Miller, Sept. 30, 1844.
48. Ibid.; *Signs of the Times*, May 17, 1843, 85.
49. S. Bliss to W. Miller, Oct. 3, 1844.
50. E. C. Clemons to W. Miller, Oct. 10, 1844.
51. *Midnight Cry*, Oct. 12, 1844, 121.
52. Ibid. (Italics supplied.)
53. S. Bliss to W. Miller, Oct. 9, 1844; E. C. Clemons to W. Miller, Oct. 10, 1844.
54. *Midnight Cry*, Oct. 12, 1844, 125. (Italics supplied.)
55. Bliss, *Memoirs of William Miller*, 270.
56. Ibid., 272.
57. *Advent Herald*, Oct. 30, 1844, 93.
58. Ibid.; E. C. Clemons to W. Miller, Oct. 10, 1844.
59. *Midnight Cry*, Oct. 12, 1844, 126.
60. *Signs of the Times*, Feb. 22, 1843, 180. See also Aug. 2, 1841, 70; Miller, *Apology and Defence*, 28, 29.
61. *Voice of Truth*, July 27, 1844, 99.
62. Ibid.; *Bible Examiner*, Sept. 24, 1844, 2. See also *Midnight Cry*, Oct. 9, 1844, 73, 74; *Advent Herald*, Oct. 3, 1844, 98, 99.
63. *Midnight Cry*, Oct. 19, 1844, 133.
64. *Advent Herald*, Oct. 30, 1844, 93. See also Luther Boutelle, *Sketch of the Life and Religious Experience of Eld. Luther Boutelle* (Advent Christian Pub. Soc., 1891), 63; Wellcome, *History of the Second Advent Message*, 359.
65. Bliss, *Memoirs of William Miller*, 275, 276; Cleveland *Herald*, Oct. 19, 1844, quoted in Thomas, "The Millerite Movement in Ohio" (M.A. thesis), 41.
66. Philadelphia *Ledger*, quoted in *Liberator*, Oct. 18, 1844, 168.
67. *Midnight Cry*, Oct. 3, 1844, 104; Jane Marsh Parker, "A Little Millerite," *Century Magazine*, 11 (Nov. 1866–Apr 1867), 315.
68. *New York Evangelist*, Oct. 31, 1844, 177.
69. Parker, "A Little Millerite," 316.
70. [Henry B. Bear], *Henry B. Bear's Advent Experience* ([Whitewater, OH]: n.p., n.d.), 3. This insightful document has been published in full in the appendix to Numbers and Butler, *The Disappointed*, 217-226.
71. *Midnight Cry*, Oct. 31, 1844, 144.
72. *Christian Reflector*, Mar. 27, 1845, 52.
73. *Advent Herald*, Nov. 6, 1844, 99.
74. Ibid.
75. *Advent Shield*, May 1844, 83.
76. *Midnight Cry*, Oct. 19, 1844, 133.
77. N. Whiting to W. Miller, Oct. 24, 1844. See also Nichol, *Midnight Cry*, 336, 337; R. W. Conable, *History of the Genesee Annual Conference of the Methodist Episcopal Church* (New York: Phillips & Hunt, 1885), 520.
78. C. R. Gorgas, "In Honor of the King of Kings," broadside printed about

Oct. 16, 1844.

79. Wellcome, *History of the Second Advent Message*, 382, 383; *Midnight Cry*, Oct. 31, 1844, 143, 144.

80. *Midnight Cry*, Oct. 31, 1844, 144.

81. Ibid., 141, 142; *New York Evangelist*, Oct. 31, 1844, 174; *Morning Watch*, Apr. 3, 1845, 112; J. Litch to W. Miller, Oct. 24, 1844.

82. Nichol, *Midnight Cry*, 339-354; *New York Evangelist*, Oct. 31, 1844, 174; Nov. 14, 1844, 182.

83. N. Whiting to W. Miller, Oct. 24, 1844; *Advent Herald*, Oct. 30, 1844, 93; *Midnight Cry*, Oct. 19, 1844, 132. Cf. Rowe, *Thunder and Trumpets*, 139; *Voice of Truth*, Nov. 7, 1844, 167.

84. Boutelle, *Sketch of the Life and Religious Experience of Eld. Luther Boutelle*, 67.

85. Froom, *Prophetic Faith of Our Fathers*, 4:686; Miller, *Apology and Defence*, 22; Cross, *Burned-over District*, 287.

86. Miller, *Apology and Defence*, 22; Dick, "The Millerite Movement," in *Adventism in America*, 34; *Midnight Cry*, Mar. 21, 1844, 282.

87. Bliss, *Memoirs of William Miller*, 275, 276.

88. Boutelle, *Sketch of the Life and Religious Experience of Eld. Luther Boutelle*, 65-67.

89. *Midnight Cry*, Oct. 31, 1844, 142; Oct. 12, 1844, 126; *Voice of Truth*, Oct. 17, 1844, 163; Mary Elizabeth Fitch supplied the information about her father repeatedly baptizing in Cleveland, OH, in 1908 (see Arthur Whitefield Spalding, *Origin and History of Seventh-day Adventists* [Washington, DC: Review and Herald, 1961], 1:113).

90. *Voice of Truth*, Oct. 10, 1844, 152.

91. *Midnight Cry*, Oct. 19, 1844, 133; *Oberlin Evangelist*, Nov. 6, 1844, 182.

92. See Froom, *Prophetic Faith of Our Fathers*, 4:543.

93. Cleveland *Herald*, Oct. 19, 1844, quoted in Thomas, "The Millerite Movement in Ohio" (M.A. thesis), 41.

94. *Midnight Cry*, Sept. 26, 1844, 91.

95. Ibid., Sept. 5, 1844, 68, 69; Sept. 12, 1844, 76, 77.

96. Boston *Post*, quoted in Cleveland *Plain Dealer*, Oct. 23, 1844, 2.

Chapter 11: **The October Disappointment**

1. Baltimore *Sun*, Oct. 25, 1844, quoted in Nichol, *Midnight Cry*, 260.

2. Cleveland *Plain Dealer*, Oct. 30, 1844, 2.

3. *Day-Star*, Oct. 25, 1845, 6.

4. J. Litch to W. Miller, Oct. 24, 1844.

5. Hiram Edson, undated manuscript of his life and experience.

6. J. White, *Life Incidents*, 182.

7. W. Miller to I. O. Orr, Dec. 13, 1844.

8. Boutelle, *Sketch of the Life and Religious Experience of Eld. Luther Boutelle*, 68, 69.

9. *Midnight Cry*, Oct. 31, 1844, 140.

10. *Liberator*, Nov. 8, 1844, quoted in Walter M. Merrill, ed., *The Letters of William Lloyd Garrison: No Union With Slave Holders* (Cambridge, MA: Harvard University Press, 1973), 3:137 n. 14; *New York Evangelist*, Nov. 7, 1844, 178; *Olive Branch*, quoted in *Advent Herald*, Dec. 18, 1844, 152; Nov. 6, 1844, 99.

11. *Olive Branch*, quoted in *Advent Herald*, Dec. 18, 1844, 152; Nov. 6, 1844, 99.

12. Boston *Post*, Nov. 2, 1844, 1.

13. *Liberator*, Nov. 15, 1844, 184.

14. *Review and Herald*, Aug. 16, 1923, 7; cf. Bates, *Autobiography*, 300.

15. James White, *Sketches of the Christian Life and Public Labors of William Miller* (Battle Creek, MI: Seventh-day Adventist Pub. Assn., 1875), 310, 311.

16. See Nichol, *Midnight Cry*, 266.

17. *Voice of Truth*, Nov. 7, 1844, 167.

18. *Morning Watch*, Jan. 23, 1845, 28.

19. Bear, *Henry B. Bear's Advent Experience*, 4; *Voice of Truth*, Nov. 7, 1844, 167; *Liberator*, Oct. 25, 1844, 172.

20. P. Palmer to W. Miller, Oct. 24, 1844; C. Fitch to Brother and Sister Palmer, July 26, 1842.

21. *Advent Herald*, Nov. 13, 1844, 105; *Liberator*, Oct. 25, 1844, 172.

22. *Oberlin Evangelist*, Nov. 6, 1844, 182.

23. N. Whiting to W. Miller, Oct. 24, 1844.

24. *Advent Herald*, Oct. 30, 1844, 93. (Italics supplied.)

25. *Midnight Cry*, Nov. 7, 1844, 150; Nov. 14, 1844, 157; *Morning Watch*, Feb. 20, 1845, 59, 60.

26. *Morning Watch*, Feb. 20, 1845, 62; Mar. 6, 1845, 78-80; [S. S. Snow], *The Book of Judgment Delivered to Israel by Elijah the Messenger of the Everlasting Covenant* (New York: G. Mitchell, 1848), 138.

27. *Advent Herald*, Nov. 13, 1844, 108-112.

28. Ibid., Oct. 30, 1844, 93; Nov. 13, 1844, 109; *Midnight Cry*, Nov. 21, 1844, 161-166.

29. Miller, *Apology and Defence*, 26; *Midnight Cry*, Dec. 5, 1844, 179.

30. *Midnight Cry*, Dec. 5, 1844, 180.

31. *Advent Herald*, Dec. 11, 1844, 142.

32. Ibid., Dec. 18, 1844, 147.

33. Bliss, *Memoirs of William Miller*, 280; W. Miller to I. O. Orr, Dec. 13, 1844; *Advent Herald*, Jan. 15, 1845, 182, 183.

34. Miller, *Apology and Defence*, 33, 34, 26.

35. W. Miller to J. B. Cook, Sept. 16, 1845.

36. *Advent Herald*, Dec. 18, 1844, 147.

37. Miller, *Apology and Defence*, 23, 25, 30.

38. Bliss, *Memoirs of William Miller*, 288-292.

39. Ibid., 290; *Midnight Cry*, Dec. 5, 1844, 180.

40. *Midnight Cry*, July 11, 1844, 415.

41. *Advent Herald*, Nov. 27, 1844, 127, 128.

42. Miller, *Apology and Defence*, 26, 35.

43. *Advent Herald*, Oct. 30, 1844, 93; Bates, *Second Advent Way Marks*, 45; *Midnight Cry*, Nov. 7, 1844, 150.

44. J. V. Himes to W. Miller, Sept. 30, 1844; *Advent Herald*, Nov. 20, 1844, 116; Oct. 30, 1844, 93.

45. *Advent Herald*, Jan. 15, 1845, 180.

46. *Midnight Cry*, Oct. 31, 1844, 143; *Advent Herald*, May 21, 1845, 120.

47. *Voice of Truth*, Nov. 7, 1844, 166.

48. Arthur, "Joshua V. Himes" (M.A. thesis), 157.

49. *Advent Shield*, May 1844, 91.

50. *Christian Reformer*, Aug. 8, 1855, 6.

51. J. White, *Life Incidents*, 199; G. Miller to S. N. Nichols, Nov. 28, 1844.

52. Arthur, " 'Come Out of Babylon,' " 88; *World's Crisis*, Jan. 25, 1860, 81.

53. *Christian Reflector*, Mar. 27, 1845, 52.

54. I. E. Jones to W. Miller, Feb. 15, 1845.

55. *Midnight Cry*, Dec. 5, 1844, 180; *Advent Herald*, Dec. 18, 1844, 147.

56. J. V. Himes to W. Miller, Nov. 19, 1844.

57. W. Miller to J. V. Himes, undated letter with internal evidence pointing to early 1845, quoted in Nichol, *Midnight Cry*, 294, 295.

58. *Advent Mirror*, Jan. 1845, 1-4.

59. *Defence of Elder Joshua V. Himes*, 18; Wellcome, *History of the Second Advent Message*, 397, 398; Raymond Joseph Bean, "The Influence of William Miller in the History of American Christianity" (Th.D. dissertation, Boston University, 1949), 135.

60. Miller, *Evidence From Scripture and History* (1842 ed.), 237; (1836 ed.), 97.

61. *Signs of the Times*, June 1, 1842, 69.

62. *Advent Herald*, Dec. 11, 1844, 142.

63. *Midnight Cry*, Nov. 7, 1844, 150.

64. *Advent Mirror*, Jan. 1845, 1-4.

65. [Snow], *The Book of Judgment*, 113; *Voice of Truth*, Apr. 16, 1845, 20; *Jubilee Standard*, June 12, 1845, 108; *Morning Watch*, Mar. 20, 1845, 94.

66. [Snow], *The Book of Judgment*, 138, 153-157, passim; *Defence of Elder Joshua V. Himes*, 19, 20.

67. I. E. Jones to W. Miller, Feb. 15, 1845.

68. *Advent Herald*, Feb. 12, 1845, 2, 3.

69. *Advent Herald*, Feb. 12, 1845, 3, 4; J. V. Himes to W. Miller, Feb. 18, 1845.

70. J. V. Himes to W. Miller, Feb. 18, 1845; S. Bliss to W. Miller, Feb. 11, 1845. (Italics supplied.)

71. *Voice of Truth*, Feb. 19, 1845, quoted in J. White, *Life Incidents*, 201.

72. *Advent Herald*, Feb. 26, 1845, 17-24; Mar. 5, 1845, 26-30.

73. J. V. Himes to W. Miller, Mar. 12, 1845.

74. J. V. Himes to W. Miller, Mar. 15, 1845; *Advent Herald*, Apr. 9, 1845, 68.

75. *Advent Herald*, Mar. 26, 1845, 49; J. V. Himes to W. Miller, Mar. 22, 1845.

76. Miller, *Apology and Defence*, 28.

77. J. V. Himes to W. Miller, Mar. 27, 1845.

78. Bliss, *Memoirs of William Miller*, 360.

Chapter 12: **Adventism's Radical Fringe**

1. *Advent Mirror*, Jan. 1845, 1-4.

2. *Midnight Cry*, Nov. 17, 1842, 4.

3. *Hope of Israel*, Jan. 24, 1845, quoted in Wellcome, *History of the Second Advent Message*, 398; see also 399.

4. [Snow], *The Sacred Symbol*, 27.

5. *Voice of the Shepherd*, Mar. 1845, 1.

6. Ibid., 2, 3.

7. Ibid., 4.

8. *The General Conference Bulletin*, April 23, 1901, 420.

9. *Voice of the Fourth Angel*, cited in *Voice of Truth*, Jan. 8, 1845, 197, 198.

10. *Voice of Truth*, Jan. 8, 1845, 199; *Voice of the Fourth Angel*, quoted in *Voice of Truth*, Jan. 15, 1845, 101; Wellcome, *History of the Second Advent Message*, 400.

11. *Day-Star*, Dec. 6, 1845, 39; cf. *Voice of Truth*, Nov. 19, 1845, 531.

12. Wellcome, *History of the Second Advent Message*, 400; cf. *Defence of Joshua V. Himes*, 23.

13. *Morning Watch*, June 12, 1845, 192; [James White and Ellen G. White], *Life Sketches: Ancestry, Early Life, Christian Experience, and Extensive Labors, of Elder James White, and His Wife, Mrs. Ellen G. White* (Battle Creek, MI: Seventh-day Adventist Pub. Assn., 1888), 231.

14. J. V. Himes to W. Miller, Mar. 12, 1845.

15. Bliss, *Memoirs of William Miller*, 309; *Morning Watch*, May 8, 1845, 151; Ellen G. White, *Life Sketches of Ellen G. White* (Mountain View, CA: Pacific Press, 1915), 85, 86.

16. *Advent Herald*, Nov. 19, 1845, 119; see also *Voice of Truth*, Nov. 19, 1845, 528, 529, 531; *Piscataquis Farmer*, Mar. 7, 1845.

17. *Day-Star*, Mar. 7, 1846, 2.

18. *Advent Herald*, Nov. 19, 1845, 119; *Voice of Truth*, Nov. 19, 1845, 528.

19. *Advent Herald*, Apr. 8, 1846, 72.

20. Ibid.

21. *Piscataquis Farmer*, Mar. 7, 1845.

22. *Day-Star*, Feb. 28, 1846, 61.

23. *Advent Testimony*, Apr. 1846, 12; Arthur, " 'Come Out of Babylon,' " 120; *Advent Mirror*, Jan. 1845, 3; *Day-Star* Extra, Feb. 7, 1846, 37-44; *Day-Star*, Jan. 24, 1846, 31, 32; Feb. 27, 1846, 7, 8.

24. *Voice of Truth*, Sept. 10, 1845, 449.

25. House of Judgment to W. Miller, May 14, 1846.

26. *True Day Star*, Dec. 29, 1845, 1, 2.

27. Ibid., 2; [Snow], *The Book of Judgment*, 264.

28. Samuel Sheffield Snow, "A Proclamation," May 12, 1848.

29. Arthur, "Joshua V. Himes" (M.A. thesis), 156, n. 79; Hewitt, *Midnight and Morning*, 282.

30. J. V. Himes to W. Miller, Mar. 27, 1845; Rennie Schoepflin, ed., "Scandal or Rite of Passage? Historians on the Dammon Trial," *Spectrum*, Aug. 1987, 37-50.

31. J. V. Himes to W. Miller, Mar. 27, 1845; Mar. 12, 1845; Apr. 22, 1845.

32. The best treatment of the Shaker influence on Millerism is Lawrence Foster, "Had Prophecy Failed? Contrasting Perspectives of the Millerites and Shakers," in *The Disappointed*, 173-188. See also Stein, *The Shaker Experience*, 208-210; Edward Deming Andrews, *The People Called Shakers* (New York: Oxford University Press, 1953), 223, 292; Lawrence Foster, *Religion and Sexuality: The Shakers, the Mormons, and the Oneida Community* (Urbana, IL: University of Illinois Press, 1984), 64, 276, 277.

33. *Day-Star*, May 9, 1846, 44.

34. Stein, *The Shaker Experience*, xvi; Cross, *Burned-over District*, 311; Barkun, *Crucible of the Millennium*, 95.

35. Foster, "Had Prophecy Failed?" in *The Disappointed*, 176.

36. [J. White and E. White], *Life Sketches* (1888), 126; Michael Pearson,

Millennial Dreams and Moral Dilemmas (New York: Cambridge University Press, 1990), 58.

37. *Day-Star*, May 9, 1846, 42.

38. *Central Ministry Journal*, 1839-1850, July 24, 1842, quoted in Stein, *The Shaker Experience*, 210; M. H. Barton to W. Miller, Apr. 19, 1844, quoted in Rowe, *Thunder and Trumpets*, 63.

39. *Day-Star*, Jan. 17, 1846, 23, 24.

40. Ibid., June 13, 1846, 9.

41. Wellcome, *History of the Second Advent Message*, 299; Mary L. Richmond, ed., *Shaker Literature: A Bibliography* (Hancock, MA: Shaker Community, 1977), 1:69.

42. Wellcome, *History of the Second Advent Message*, 299; N. Gordon Thomas, "The Millerite Movement in Ohio," *Ohio History*, Spring 1972, 101; Stein, *The Shaker Experience*, 165-184.

43. *The Manifesto*, Nov. 1891, 250, 251.

44. *Advent Herald*, Apr. 22, 1846, 87; Richmond, ed., *Shaker Literature*, 1:69.

45. Richmond, ed., *Shaker Literature*, 1:69, 223-227, 230, 232, 233, 237-241, 244-246.

46. Bear, *Henry B. Bear's Advent Experience*, 5-9.

47. Barkun, *Crucible of the Millennium*, 44, 45; Arthur Eugene Bestor, Jr., *Backwoods Utopias* (Philadelphia: University of Pennsylvania Press, 1950); Mark Holloway, *Heavens on Earth: Utopian Communities in America, 1680-1880*, 2d ed. (New York: Dover, 1966).

48. See Richard DeMaria, *Communal Love at Oneida* (New York: Edward Mellon, 1978).

49. *Spiritual Magazine*, Nov. 15, 1846, 137, quoted in Cross, *Burned-over District*, 321; *The Witness*, June 6, 1840, 152; Barkun, *Crucible of the Millennium*, 97.

50. Bliss, *Memoirs of William Miller*, 298.

51. Ibid., 355.

52. *Review and Herald*, Apr. 21, 1851, 69.

53. *Morning Watch*, June 12, 1845, 189.

Chapter 13: **The Albany Reaction**

1. *Morning Watch*, Mar. 20, 1845, 96. (Italics supplied.)

2. J. V. Himes to W. Miller, Mar. 27, 1845.

3. *Voice of Truth*, Apr. 9, 1845, 13.

4. *Morning Watch*, May 8, 1845, 152.

5. Ibid., 150, 151.

6. Arthur, " 'Come Out of Babylon,' " 137-139.

7. *Morning Watch*, June 12, 1845, 189.

8. Bliss, *Memoirs of William Miller*, 313.

9. *Morning Watch*, May 15, 1845, 157-160; May 22, 1845, 168; June 5, 1845, 183; June 12, 1845, 185-190.

10. Ibid., May 15, 1845, 158; *Signs of the Times*, June 7, 1843, 107.

11. *Morning Watch*, June 19, 1845, 197; cf. June 12, 1845, 189.

12. Rowe, *Thunder and Trumpets*, 155.

13. *Voice of Truth*, May 7, 1845, 45.

14. *Midnight Cry*, Feb. 15, 1844, 238.

15. *Voice of Truth*, May 21, 1845, 61, 62.

16. J. V. Himes to W. Miller, May 3, 1845.

17. *Morning Watch*, June 12, 1845, 190-192.

18. Miller, *Apology and Defence*, 32, 33.

19. *Advent Herald*, Nov. 25, 1846, 127.

20. Wellcome, *History of the Second Advent Message*, 522; *Morning Watch*, May 15, 1845, 157, 158; May 8, 1845, 151; Boutelle, *Sketch of the Life and Religious Experience of Eld. Luther Boutelle*, 69, 70; Hiram Edson, undated manuscript of his life and experience. Miller first tied Rev. 10 to the advent movement in *Signs of the Times*, May 1, 1841, 20.

21. Wellcome, *History of the Second Advent Message*, 572, 573.

22. Ibid., 543, 544; *Advent Herald*, June 3, 1846, 133; Billington, "The Millerite Adventists in Great Britain," in *The Disappointed*, 65-69. See also Dunton, "The Millerite Adventists and Other Millenarian Groups in Great Britain, 1830-1860."

23. Wellcome, *History of the Second Advent Message*, 554, 555; Rajmund Ladyslaw Dabrowski and B. B. Beach, eds., *Michael Belina Czechowski, 1818-1876* (Warsaw, Poland: Znaki Czasu Publishing House, 1979).

24. Evangelical Alliance, *Report of the Proceedings of the Conference, Held at Freemasons' Hall, London, From August 19th to September 2nd Inclusive, 1846* (London: Partridge and Oakey, 1847), 296, 297.

25. Garrison and Garrison, *William Lloyd Garrison*, 3:165.

26. Wellcome, *History of the Second Advent Message*, 565-567.

27. *Advent Herald*, May 22, 1847, 124, 125, 128; May 29, 1847, 132, 133; June 5, 1847, 141, 142.

28. Ibid., June 26, 1847, 164; July 24, 1847, 196; Dec. 4, 1847, 140, 141.

29. Josiah Litch, "History of the Adventists," in *History of the Religious Denominations in the United States*, 2d ed. (Harrisburg, PA: John Winebrenner, 1849), 37-41.

30. Bliss, *Memoirs of William Miller*, 349, 357.

31. *Advent Herald*, Feb. 11, 1846, 3; Bliss, *Memoirs of William Miller*, 361.

32. Bliss, *Memoirs of William Miller*, 359, 360.

33. Ibid., 358; R. Miller to J. V. Himes, July 23, 1848.

34. Bliss, *Memoirs of William Miller*, 367.

35. Ibid., 377, 378.

36. Hewitt, *Midnight and Morning*, 215.

37. An extensive treatment of the Albany denominations is found in Arthur, " 'Come Out of Babylon,' " 201-371. In this section I am indebted to Dean, "Echoes of the Midnight Cry," 110-138 for providing a pattern that treats a very complex topic in a short space.

38. *Advent Christian Quarterly*, July 1869, 6.

39. *Advent Herald*, Oct. 7, 1848, 80.

40. *Bible Advocate*, Nov. 30, 1848, quoted in *Advent Herald*, Dec. 16, 1848, 158; M. James Penton, *Apocalypse Delayed: The Story of Jehovah's Witnesses* (Toronto: University of Toronto Press, 1985), 15-17; J. White, *Life Incidents*, 154.

41. Dean, "Echoes of the Midnight Cry," 116-118.

42. Ibid., 119, 120.

43. Arthur, " 'Come Out of Babylon,' " 322-324; Dean, "Echoes of the Midnight Cry," 122.

44. Dean, "Echoes of the Midnight Cry," 126-129; *Advent Herald*, Nov. 20,

1858, 369-373; Wellcome, *History of the Second Advent Message*, 603-605. For the developments leading up to the establishment of the American Evangelical Adventist Conference, see Arthur, " 'Come Out of Babylon,' " 280-306.

45. Dean, "Echoes of the Midnight Cry," 129, 135. On the development of the Advent Christians, see Arthur, " 'Come Out of Babylon,' " 307-351.

46. *World's Crisis*, Oct. 6, 1858, 18.

47. J. Litch and Miles Grant, *The Doctrine of Everlasting Punishment: A Discussion of the Question, "Do the Scriptures Teach the Doctrine of the Eternal Conscious Suffering of the Wicked?"* (Boston: Damrell & Moore, 1859); Wellcome, *History of the Second Advent Message*, 586.

48. Dean, "Echoes of the Midnight Cry," 131.

49. *World's Crisis*, July 7, 1858, 53.

50. Ibid., July 4, 1860, 71.

51. Ibid., Aug. 1, 1860, 86.

52. Ibid., Oct. 24, 1860, 26; Clyde E. Hewitt, *Devotion and Development* (Charlotte, NC: Venture Books, 1990), 341. That book and Hewitt's *Midnight and Morning* and *Responsibility and Response* (Charlotte, NC: Venture Books, 1986) provide the most up-to-date history of the Advent Christian denomination. See also Clarence J. Kearney, *The Advent Christian Story* (n.p., 1968).

53. Dean, "Echoes of the Midnight Cry," 135-138; Arthur, " 'Come Out of Babylon,' " 349-351; *Herald of Life*, Oct. 21, 1863, 1-3; *World's Crisis*, Sept. 13, 1864, 97.

54. Helpful discussions of the Age to Come movement are found in Arthur, " 'Come Out of Babylon,' " 224-227, 352-371. See also *Historical Waymarks of the Church of God* ([Oregon, IL]: Church of God General Conference, 1976).

55. *Advent Harbinger and Bible Advocate*, Jan. 14, 1854, 234.

56. *Historical Waymarks of the Church of God*, 11-27; Arthur, " 'Come Out of Babylon,' " 352-371.

57. J. Litch, *A Complete Harmony of Daniel and the Apocalypse* (Philadelphia: Claxton, Remsen & Haffelfinger, 1873), 34, passim; Wellcome, *History of the Second Advent Message*, 678.

58. J. Litch, *The Restitution, Christ's Kingdom on Earth* (Boston: J. V. Himes, 1848), xiii, xiv; Sandeen, *Roots of Fundamentalism*, 148-157; *Premillennial Essays of the Prophetic Conference Held in the Church of the Holy Trinity, New York City* (Chicago: F. H. Revell, 1879), 13, 14.

59. D. T. Bourdeau, ed., *Investigation of the Sabbath: Eld. J. Litch Opposing the Ancient Sabbath, and Eld. D. T. Bourdeau Defending It* (Coaticook, P.Q.: S. C. Smith, 1881); E. G. White to W. C. and M. White, Sept. 3, 1883.

60. Hewitt, *Midnight and Morning*, 281.

61. See *The Trial of Elder J. V. Himes Before the Chardon Street Church* (Boston: Damrell & Moore, 1850); *Defence of Elder Joshua V. Himes*; Arthur, "Joshua V. Himes" (M.A. thesis), 162, 163.

62. *World's Crisis*, Apr. 18, 1860, 26; May 2, 1860, 34; Wellcome, *History of the Second Advent Message*, 609, 471.

63. Wellcome, *History of the Second Advent Message*, 609; *Advent Christian Times*, Feb. 6, 1872.

64. Arthur, " 'Come Out of Babylon,' " 338; Wellcome, *History of the Second Advent Message*, 609-611.

65. Arthur, "Joshua V. Himes" (M.A. thesis), 165; *A Statement of Facts Relating*

to Elder Joshua V. Himes (Boston: Advent Christian Publication Society, 1875), 1, 2, 13, 5, 14; Wellcome, *History of the Second Advent Message*, 626.

66. *Himes Journal*, Nov.-Dec., 1876, 88; Arthur, "Joshua V. Himes" (M.A. thesis), 167, n. 3.

67. *Himes Journal*, Nov.-Dec., 1876, 88.

68. Arthur, "Joshua V. Himes" (M.A. thesis), 167; J. V. Himes to E. G. White, Sept. 12, 1894.

69. J. H. Kellogg to E. G. White, Aug. 19, 1894; J. V. Himes to E. G. White, Sept. 12, 1894; Nov. 7, 1894; Mar. 13, 1895; E. G. White to J. V. Himes, Jan. 17, 1895.

70. J. V. Himes to E. G. White, Sept. 12, 1894; E. G. White to J. V. Himes, Jan. 17, 1895.

71. J. V. Himes to E. G. White, Mar. 14, 1895.

72. Sears, *Days of Delusion*, 255, 256.

Chapter 14: **The Sabbatarian Disentanglement**

1. *Day-Star*, Jan. 24, 1846, 31, 32, 25; Feb. 27, 1846, 7, 8; Extra, Feb. 7, 1846, 37-44; *Jubilee Standard*, May 29, 1845, 90; June 12, 1845, 110, 111; *Voice of Truth*, Dec. 18, 1844, 187, 188; Ellen G. White, *Selected Messages* (Washington, DC: Review and Herald, 1958), 2:34; E. White, *Life Sketches* (1915), 85-94; Ellen G. White, *Testimonies for the Church* (Mountain View, CA: Pacific Press, 1948), 8:292, 293; Ellen G. White, *Spiritual Gifts* (Battle Creek, MI: James White, 1860), 2:49-52, 69, 71, passim; J. White, *Life Incidents*, 116, 117; *Piscataquis Farmer*, Mar. 7, 1845.

2. Schoepflin, ed., "Scandal or Rite of Passage?" *Spectrum*, Aug. 1987, 46; Ron Graybill, "The Family Man," in *J. N. Andrews: The Man the and Mission*, ed. Harry Leonard (Berrien Springs, MI: Andrews University Press, 1985), 16-19, 25, 38, n. 17; E. White, *Life Sketches* (1915), 127.

3. Joseph Bates, *The Opening Heavens* (New Bedford, MA: Benjamin Lindsay, 1846), 22; cf. 16, 17.

4. The best treatments of Bates are Godfrey T. Anderson, *Outrider of the Apocalypse: Life and Times of Joseph Bates* (Mountain View, CA: Pacific Press, 1972); Bates, *Autobiography*.

5. Bates, *Autobiography*, 262, 250.

6. *Signs of the Times*, Sept. 15, 1840, 92; *First Report of the General Conference*, 14; *Second Report of the General Conference*, 2.

7. *Signs of the Times*, June 1, 1842, 68, 69; Bates, *Second Advent Way Marks*, 10, 11.

8. Wellcome, *History of the Second Advent Message*, 346.

9. J. White, *Life Incidents*, 15, 72. The best biography of James White is Virgil Robinson, *James White* (Washington, DC: Review and Herald, 1976).

10. J. White, *Life Incidents*, 15, 17-24, 72.

11. Ibid., 72, 73.

12. Ibid., 74, 95, 96, 104.

13. Helpful treatments of Ellen White are Arthur L. White, *Ellen G. White*, 6 vols. (Washington, DC: Review and Herald, 1981-1986); Roy E. Graham, *Ellen G. White, Co-Founder of the Seventh-day Adventist Church* (New York: Peter Lang, 1985).

14. E. White, *Life Sketches* (1915), 20, 25.

15. Ibid., 31, 49, 50.

16. Ibid., 50-53; A. White, *Ellen G. White*, 1:40-44.

17. E. White, *Testimonies for the Church*, 1:54.

18. James White, Ellen G. White, and Joseph Bates, *A Word to the "Little Flock"* (Brunswick, ME: James White, 1847), 22; Wellcome, *History of the Second Advent Message*, 404.

19. *Day-Star*, Jan. 24, 1846, 31, 32; Ellen G. White, *Early Writings* (Washington, DC: Review and Herald, 1945), 13. (Italics supplied.)

20. E. G. White, *Early Writings*, 22; Wellcome, *History of the Second Advent Message*, 402; Joseph I. Bentley, "Legal Trials of Joseph Smith," in *Encyclopedia of Mormonism*, Daniel H. Ludlow, ed. (New York: Macmillan, 1992), 3:1347.

21. *Signs of the Times*, June 7, 1843, 107; *Morning Watch*, May 15, 1845, 158.

22. Miller, *Letter to Joshua V. Himes, on the Cleansing of the Sanctuary*; *Advent Shield*, May 1844, 75, 80.

23. *Voice of Truth*, Nov. 7, 1844, 166.

24. *Advent Mirror*, Jan. 1845, 1-3.

25. Hiram Edson, undated manuscript of his life and experience; J. N. Loughborough, "Apostolic and Adventist Experience Compared," unpub. manuscript, 19, 20.

26. *Day-Star* Extra, Feb. 7, 1846, 37-44.

27. Litch, *An Address to the Public* (1841), 37-39; Litch, *Prophetic Expositions*, 1:49-54.

28. Bates, *Second Advent Way Marks*, 6; *Advent Review*, Sept. 1850, 49; *Review and Herald*, Jan. 29, 1857, 100, 101.

29. For more on the early development of the sanctuary and judgment doctrines, see Bates, *Opening Heavens*, 25-39; Frank B. Holbrook, ed., *Doctrine of the Sanctuary: A Historical Survey* (Silver Spring, MD: Biblical Research Institute, General Conference of Seventh-day Adventists, 1989); Arnold V. Wallenkampf and W. Richard Lesher, *The Sanctuary and the Atonement: Biblical, Historical, and Theological Studies* (Washington, DC: Review and Herald, 1981); Paul A. Gordon, *The Sanctuary, 1844, and the Pioneers* (Washington, DC: Review and Herald, 1983).

30. For an examination of the ever-widening understanding of Sabbatarian mission responsibility, see George R. Knight, "From Shut Door to Worldwide Mission: The Dynamic Context of Early German Adventism," in *Die Adventisten und Hamburg: Von der Ortsgemeinde zur internationalen Bewegung*, ed. B. Ed. Pfeiffer, Lothar Trader, and George R. Knight (Frankfurt am Main: Peter Lang, 1992), 46-69.

31. J. White, *Life Incidents*, 308, 309.

32. *Signs of the Times*, Apr. 1, 1841, 3; Apr. 6, 1842, 5.

33. James Bailey, *History of the Seventh-Day Baptist General Conference* (Toledo, OH: S. Bailey, 1866), 243, 244. See also *Seventh Day Baptists in Europe and America* (Plainfield, NJ: American Sabbath Tract Society, 1910), 1:185, 186.

34. J. N. Andrews, *History of the Sabbath and First Day of the Week*, 3d ed. (Battle Creek, MI: Review and Herald, 1887), 505, 506; J. White, *Life Incidents*, 268, 269.

35. *Midnight Cry*, Sept. 5, 1844, 68, 69.

36. Ibid., Sept. 5, 1844, 68, 69; Sept. 12, 1844, 76, 77.

37. T. M. Preble, *Tract, Showing that the Seventh Day Should Be Observed as the*

Sabbath, Instead of the First Day; "According to the Commandment" (Nashua, NH: Murray & Kimball, 1845).

38. Hiram Edson, undated manuscript of his life and experience; J. White to Bro. and Sis. Hastings, Aug. 26, 1848.

39. On Bates' contribution to the Sabbath, see C. Mervyn Maxwell, "Joseph Bates and Seventh-day Adventist Sabbath Theology," in *The Sabbath in Scripture and History*, ed. Kenneth A. Strand (Washington, DC: Review and Herald, 1982), 352-363.

40. Joseph Bates, *The Seventh Day Sabbath, A Perpetual Sign*, 2d ed. (New Bedford, MA: Benjamin Lindsey, 1847), iii, iv, 58, 59.

41. The description in this paragraph is true, as far as it goes, in describing Bates' early understanding of the three angels' messages. But in actuality he held for much of the late 1840s that all three of the messages had been preached before Oct. 22, 1844, and that the preaching of Rev. 14:12 began at that time, since it came *after* the three messages. Only later did he conclude, in line with James White, that verse 12 was a part of the third angel's message and that the entire message began to be preached after Oct. 22.

42. Bates, *Seventh Day Sabbath*, 2d. ed., 58, 59.

43. Ibid.; Joseph Bates, *A Vindication of the Seventh-day Sabbath and the Commandments of God* (New Bedford, MA: Benjamin Lindsey, 1848), 95, 96; Joseph Bates, *A Seal of the Living God* (New Bedford, MA: Benjamin Lindsey, 1849), 20, 37, 38.

44. T. M. Preble, *The First-day Sabbath: Clearly Proved by Showing that the Old Covenant, or Ten Commandments, Have Been Changed, or Made Complete, in the Christian Dispensation* (Buchanan, MI: Western Advent Christian Pub. Assn., 1867); Loughborough, "Apostolic and Adventist Experience Compared," 18.

45. *Review and Herald*, Feb. 3, 1853, 151.

46. E. White, *Early Writings*, 42; J. White, *Life Incidents*, 207, 208; "Open and Shut Door," in *Seventh-day Adventist Encyclopedia*, rev. ed., Don F. Neufeld, ed. (Washington, DC: Review and Herald, 1976), 1034-1037.

47. See Damsteegt, *Foundations of the Seventh-day Adventist Message and Mission*; Knight, "From Shut Door to Worldwide Mission," in *Die Adventisten und Hamburg*.

48. George R. Knight, *Anticipating the Advent: A Brief History of Seventh-day Adventists* (Boise, ID: Pacific Press, 1993), 37-39.

49. *Advent Shield*, May 1844, 86, 87, 89; *Signs of the Times*, July 1, 1840, 50; Miller, *Apology and Defence*, 30, 31; Bliss, *Memoirs of William Miller*, 283.

50. Bates, *Autobiography*, 301; White et al, *A Word to the "Little Flock,"* 10, 11. (Italics supplied.)

51. *Present Truth*, April 1850, 65.

52. Ibid., 66.

53. Ibid., 66, 68. (Italics supplied.)

54. Ibid., 66-68.

55. J. White, *Life Incidents*, 265.

56. Ibid., 266.

57. Ibid., 268; J. White to Bro. Bowles, Nov. 8, 1849.

58. Wellcome, *History of the Second Advent Message*, 407; Arthur, " 'Come Out of Babylon,' " 144, 145.

59. For helpful discussions of the Sabbatarian conferences, see Gordon O.

Martinborough, "The Beginnings of a Theology of the Sabbath Among American Sabbatarian Adventists, 1842-1850" (M.A. thesis, Loma Linda University, 1976), 122-151; "Sabbath Conferences," in *Seventh-day Adventist Encyclopedia* (1976 ed.), 1255, 1256.

60. *Review and Herald*, May 6, 1852, 5.
61. J. White to Bro. Howland, in E. White, *Spiritual Gifts*, 2:93. (Italics supplied.)
62. E. White, *Spiritual Gifts*, 2:97-99. (Italics supplied.)
63. J. White to Bro. Bowles, Nov. 8, 1849. (Italics supplied.)
64. E. White, *Life Sketches* (1915), 125.
65. *Review and Herald*, June 6, 1880, 393.
66. E. White, *Testimonies for the Church*, 1:88.
67. On early Seventh-day Adventist organization, see Andrew G. Mustard, *James White and SDA Organization: Historical Development, 1844-1881* (Berrien Springs, MI: Andrews University Press, 1988); R. W. Schwarz, *Light Bearers to the Remnant* (Mountain View, CA: Pacific Press, 1979), 86-98.
68. J. White, *Life Incidents*, 299.
69. *Review and Herald*, Oct. 9, 1860, 161-163; Oct. 16, 1860, 169-171; Oct. 23, 1860, 177-179; Apr. 30, 1861, 188, 189.
70. Ibid., Aug. 27, 1861, 100.
71. Ibid., Oct. 8, 1861, 148, 149.
72. Ibid., May 26, 1863, 204-206.
73. Richard C. Nickels, *A History of the Seventh Day Church of God* (n.p., 1973); Richard C. Nickels, *Six Papers on the History of the Church of God* (n.p., 1977). For the most complete catalog of offshoots from Seventh-day Adventism over time, see Lowell Tarling, *The Edges of Seventh-day Adventism* (Barragga Bay, Australia: Galilee, 1981).

Chapter 15: **Millerism at 150**

1. See Arthur, " 'Come Out of Babylon,' " 306.
2. *World's Crisis*, Jan. 11, 1860, 75.
3. Ibid., Jan. 25, 1860, 81; "SDA Church," in *Seventh-day Adventist Encyclopedia* (1976 ed.), 1326.
4. *World's Crisis*, Feb. 15, 1860, 96; Feb. 8, 1860, 89.
5. H. K. Carroll, *The Religious Forces of the United States* (New York: Christian Literature Co., 1893), 1-15.
6. Kenneth Bedell and Alice M. Jones, eds., *Yearbook of American and Canadian Churches* (Nashville, TN: Abingdon, 1992), 270-277.
7. Benson Y. Landis, ed., *Yearbook of American Churches*, edition for 1960 (New York: National Council of the Churches of Christ, 1959), 253; Hewitt, *Midnight and Morning*, 267.
8. Knight, *Anticipating the Advent*, 120; Hewitt, *Midnight and Morning*, 275.
9. Rowe, *Thunder and Trumpets*, 48, 70, 71, 93.
10. Barkun, *Crucible of the Millennium*, 103, 111, 112, 117-119, 46, 139, 143, passim.
11. Howard B. Weeks, *Adventist Evangelism in the Twentieth Century* (Washington, DC: Review and Herald, 1969), 78-85; Weber, *Living in the Shadow of the Second Coming*, 127; Barkun, *Crucible of the Millennium*, 152.

12. Doan, *The Miller Heresy*, passim; Doan, "Millerism and Evangelical Culture," in *The Disappointed*, 132. Cf. Rowe, "Millerites," in *The Disappointed*, 12, 13; Cross, *Burned-over District*, 320; Sandeen, "Millennialism," in *The Rise of Adventism*, 112.

13. Luther P. Gerlach and Virginia H. Hine, *People, Power, Change: Movements of Social Transformation* (Indianapolis, IN: Bobbs-Merrill, 1970), 183, 137.

14. Hewitt, *Midnight and Morning*, 277; Dean M. Kelley, *Why Conservative Churches Are Growing: A Study in Sociology of Religion* (New York: Harper & Row, 1972); Walter R. Martin, *The Truth About Seventh-day Adventists* (Grand Rapids, MI: Zondervan, 1960), passim.

15. Hewitt, *Devotion and Development*, 211, 341, 371.

16. Mustard, *James White and SDA Organization*; Barry David Oliver, *SDA Organizational Structure: Past, Present and Future* (Berrien Springs, MI: Andrews University Press, 1989).

17. *Midnight Cry*, Nov. 17, 1842, 2.

18. *128th Annual Statistical Report—1990* (Silver Spring, MD: General Conference of Seventh-day Adventists, 1990), 42.

19. Hewitt, *Midnight and Morning*, 277.

20. C. H. Hewitt to F. D. Nichol, May 24, 1944, in Nichol, *The Midnight Cry*, 476, 477; Interview of Moses C. Crouse by George R. Knight, Aurora College, Aurora, IL, Oct. 18, 1984.

21. *Day-Star*, Jan. 24, 1846, 31, 32.

22. Bedell and Jones, eds., *Year Book of American and Canadian Churches*, 1992, 276; O. P. Hull, quoted in Spalding, *Origin and History of Seventh-day Adventists*, 1:257.

23. Hewitt, *Devotion and Development*, 334, 362, 357, 156; Hewitt, *Midnight and Morning*, 277.

24. Nickels, *A History of the Seventh Day Church of God*, 364-366.

25. Hewitt, *Devotion and Development*, 367, 373.

26. See George R. Knight, "Adventism, Institutionalism, and the Challenge of Secularization," *Ministry*, June 1991, 6-10, 29.

27. Malcolm Bull and Keith Lockhart, *Seeking a Sanctuary: Seventh-day Adventism and the American Dream* (San Francisco: Harper & Row, 1989), 256-268.

28. See George R. Knight, "The Fat Woman and the Kingdom," *Adventist Review*, Feb. 14, 1991, 8-10.

29. J. V. Himes to E. G. White, Mar. 13, 1895; cf. Sept. 12, 1894.

INDEX